Presented to

_____

From

_____

Date

_____

Student Discovery
BIBLE

A Journey
Through God's Word

International
Children's Bible

Thomas Nelson, Inc.
Since 1798

For other products and live events, visit us at:
www.thomasnelson.com

Student Discovery Bible

Copyright © 2007 by Thomas Nelson, Inc.

Produced in cooperation with Educational Publishing Concepts, Inc.,
Wheaton, IL

Bible text selections from the International Children's Bible®
Copyright © 1986, 1988, 1999 by Thomas Nelson, Inc.
All rights reserved.

Supplemental text © 2006 by Carolyn Larsen

Design by Diane Bay Design, dianebay.com

ISBN 1-4003-1006-7

Printed in China

1 2 3 4 5 - 11 10 09 08 07

Student Discovery
BIBLE

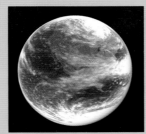

A Journey
Through God's Word

International
Children's Bible

Thomas Nelson, Inc.
Since 1798

For other products and live events, visit us at:
www.thomasnelson.com

Table of Contents

The Beginning Books. 1

The Creation of Everything *Genesis 1:1–2:3* 2

The Beginning of Sin *Genesis 3:1-24* 6

Noah Obeys God *Genesis 6:5-22* 8

The Great Flood *Genesis 7:1-24* 10

God's Promise *Genesis 8:1-22; 9:12-17* 12

The Tower of Babel *Genesis 11:1-9* 15

Abram and Sarah *Genesis 12:1-20* 16

Abraham and Lot *Genesis 13:1-18* 18

Isaac Is Born *Genesis 18:1-16; 21:1-5* 20

God Tests Abraham *Genesis 22:1-19* 22

A Wife for Isaac *Genesis 24:1-67* 24

Jacob's Lie *Genesis 27:1-44* 28

Jacob's Dream at Bethel *Genesis 28:10-22* 32

A Wife for Jacob *Genesis 29:1-30* 34

Jacob Meets Esau *Genesis 33:1-20* 36

Joseph and His Brothers *Genesis 37:1-36* 38

Joseph in Prison *Genesis 39:1-23* 42

Joseph Interprets Dreams *Genesis 40:1–41:36* 44

Joseph Is Made Ruler *Genesis 41:37-49, 53-57* 48

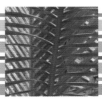

Joseph Forgives *Genesis 42:1-3, 6-13; 45:1-11* 50

Joseph's Family Comes to Egypt *Genesis 47:1-12, 27-31* 52

Trouble for the People of Israel *Exodus 1:8-22* 54

The Birth of Moses *Exodus 2:1-10* 56

Moses Goes to Midian *Exodus 2:11-25* 58

The Burning Bush *Exodus 3:1-22* 60

Proof for Moses *Exodus 4:1-23* 62

The Plagues *Exodus 7–11* 64

The People of Israel Leave Egypt *Exodus 12:31-51* 68

Crossing the Red Sea *Exodus 14:1-31* 70

Food from Heaven *Exodus 16:1-31* 74

Jethro's Advice *Exodus 18:1-27* 78

The Ten Commandments *Exodus 20:1-17* 80

The Golden Calf *Exodus 32:1-20* 82

The Meeting Tent *Exodus 40:1-38* 84

Spies in Canaan *Numbers 13:1-33* 88

Miracles in the Desert *Numbers 17:1-11; 20:1-13; 21:4-9* 90

Balaam's Donkey *Numbers 22:1-35* 92

Israel's New Leader *Numbers 27:12-23* 95

Another Beginning Book 96

Books of History 97

Spies Sent to Jericho *Joshua 2:1-24* 98

Crossing the Jordan *Joshua 3:1-17* 100

Rock Reminders *Joshua 4:1-24* 102

The Fall of Jericho *Joshua 6:1-27* 104

The Sun Stands Still *Joshua 10:1-21* 108

God's Angel Visits Gideon *Judges 6:11-24* 110

Gideon's Army *Judges 7:1-23* 112

The Birth of Samson *Judges 13:1-25* 116

Samson *Judges 16:4-30* 118

Ruth *Ruth 1:1-22* 122

Boaz Meets Ruth *Ruth 2:1-20* 124

Naomi's Plan *Ruth 3:1-18* 126

Boaz Marries Ruth *Ruth 4:1-22* 128

Samuel's Birth *1 Samuel 1:1-28* 130

God Calls Samuel *1 Samuel 3:1-21* 132

King Saul Disobeys *1 Samuel 13:1-14* 134

Jonathan Fights the Philistines *1 Samuel 14:1-23* 136

David Is Anointed *1 Samuel 16:1-13* 138

David and Goliath *1 Samuel 17:1-51* 140

David and Jonathan *1 Samuel 20:1-42* 144

David Hides from Saul *1 Samuel 23:14-18* 147

David and Nabal *1 Samuel 25:4-42* 148

David Is Made King of Israel *2 Samuel 5:1-25* 152

David and Mephibosheth *2 Samuel 9:1-13* 154

Solomon's Wisdom *1 Kings 3:1-28* 156

Solomon Builds the Temple *1 Kings 6:1-38* 158

Queen of Sheba *1 Kings 10:1-10, 13* 162

Solomon's Wealth *1 Kings 10:14-29* 163

Elijah's Work *1 Kings 17:1-24* 164

Elijah and the Prophets of Baal *1 Kings 18:1-39* 166

Elijah at Mount Sinai *1 Kings 19:1-18* 170

Elijah Is Taken to Heaven *2 Kings 2:1-18* 172

Elisha *2 Kings 4:1-37* 174

Naaman Is Healed *2 Kings 5:1-14* 178

Esther's Courage *Esther 2:17-18; 3:8-11; 7:1-7* 180

The Other Books of History 182

Books of Poetry 184

God's Works and Word *Psalm 19* 184

The Lord the Shepherd *Psalm 23* 186

The Majesty of God *Psalm 93* 187

Wisdom and Foolishness *Proverbs 15:1-33* 188

There Is a Time for Everything *Ecclesiastes 3:1-8* 192

The Other Books of Poetry 194

The Prophets 195

God's Suffering Servant *Isaiah 53:1-12* 196

Daniel Taken Captive *Daniel 1:1-21* 198

The Fiery Furnace *Daniel 3:1-30* 200

The Writing on the Wall *Daniel 5:1-8, 13-14, 17, 25-31* 203

Daniel and the Lions *Daniel 6:1-23* 204

Jonah Obeys *Jonah 1:1–3:5* 206

The Other Books of Prophets 209

The Gospels 213

The Gospels as One Story 214

Two Special Babies *Luke 1:5-38* 216

Births of John and Jesus *Luke 1:57-64; 2:1-21* 218

Presented in the Temple *Luke 2:26-38* 220

The Wise Men Come *Matthew 2:1-12* 221

Jesus Goes to Egypt *Matthew 2:13-19* 222

Jesus as a Boy *Luke 2:41-52* 223

Jesus' Temptation *Mark 1:9-11; Matthew 4:1-11* 224

Jesus Chooses Some Followers *Mark 1:14-20; 3:13-19* 225

The Wedding Miracle *John 2:1-11* 226

Jesus Cleans the Temple *John 2:12-25* 227

Jesus and Nicodemus *John 3:1-21* 228

The Woman at the Well *John 4:1-42* 230

Four Friends' Faith *Mark 2:1-12* 234

Jesus Chooses a Tax Collector *Mark 2:13-17* 235

Sermon on the Mount *Matthew 5:1-20* 236

Jesus' Works *Matthew 8:1-17* 238

Jesus' Stories *Matthew 13:1-52* 240

Jesus Stops a Storm *Mark 4:35-41* 245

Jesus Heals *Mark 5:21-43* 246

Feeding the 5,000 *Matthew 24:13-21* 247

Walking on Water *Matthew 14:22-33* 248

Jesus with Moses and Elijah *Luke 9:28-36* 249

More Stories of Jesus *Luke 10:25–11:4* 250

The Lost Things *Luke 15:1-32* 252

Jesus Brings Lazarus Back to Life *John 11:28-44* 254

A Woman with Perfume for Jesus *Mark 14:3-9* 256

Palm Sunday *Luke 19:28-40* 257

A Story About Three Servants *Matthew 25:14-29* 258

Foot Washing *John 13:1-20* 260

The Last Supper *Matthew 26:17-25; Mark 14:22-31* 262

Garden of Gethsemane *Mark 14:32-50* 264

Peter's Denial and the Trial *Mark 14:66–15:20* 266

The Crucifixion *Mark 15:21-47; Matthew 27:62-66* 268

The Resurrection *Mark 16:1-11* 272

On the Road to Emmaus *Luke 24:13-35* 274

The Ascension *Mark 16:14-20* 276

The Gospel Writers 278

The Acts of the Apostles 279

The Coming of the Holy Spirit *Acts 2:1-42* 280

Philip Teaches an Ethiopian *Acts 8:26-39* 283

Saul Is Convertred *Acts 9:1-19* 284

Saul's Early Ministry *Acts 9:19-31* 286

Peter in Joppa *Acts 9:36-42* 287

Peter and Cornelius *Acts 10:1-48* 288

Peter in Jail *Acts 12:1-18* 292

Paul and Silas in Jail *Acts 16:16-34* 294

Paul's Travels *Acts 17:1-34* 296

Shipwreck *Acts 27:1-44; 28:1-6* 300

Paul in Rome *Acts 28:16-20* 303

More Stories from Acts 304

The Epistles 305

Instructions for Living *Ephesians 5:21–6:4* 306

The Armor of God *Ephesians 6:10-20* 308

Be like Christ *Philippians 2:1-16; 4:4-9* 310

The Hall of Faith *Hebrews 11:1-40* 312

Run the Race *Hebrews 12:1-3* 315

Faith That Works *James 1:2-8, 19-27; 3:1-12* 316

Live like God's Children *1 John 3:1-24* 318

The Other Pauline Epistles 320

The Other General Epistles 323

Help from Scripture 324

The Revelation of Jesus Christ 325

Heaven *Revelation 21:1-27* 326

THE BEGINNING BOOKS

The Big Picture:

The Bible is made up of 66 separate books. Thirty-nine of those books are in the Old Testament which gives the history of the world before Jesus was born. Of course, the beginning is the . . . beginning of earth—creation. From there God tells us about Noah and Moses. After that, the main characters of the Old Testament are the families of Abraham, Isaac and Jacob and their descendants.

    The Old Testament was written between the years 1450 B.C. (that means "before Christ lived on earth") and 400 B.C.

The Pentateuch:

The first five books of the Old Testament are called the Pentateuch. "Penta" means five in Greek.

    Experts generally agree that Moses wrote all five books of the Pentateuch. That means that he had to write them while he was leading the Israelites through the wilderness of Mt. Sinai to the Promised Land. He was one busy guy!

    There are some other names you might hear these books called by:

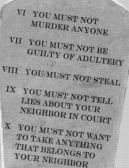

I YOU MUST NOT HAVE ANY OTHER GODS EXCEPT ME

II YOU MUST NOT MAKE FOR YOURSELVES ANY IDOLS

III YOU MUST NOT USE THE NAME OF THE LORD YOUR GOD THOUGHTLESSLY

IV REMEMBER TO KEEP THE SABBATH AS A HOLY DAY

V HONOR YOUR FATHER AND YOUR MOTHER

VI YOU MUST NOT MURDER ANYONE

VII YOU MUST NOT BE GUILTY OF ADULTERY

VIII YOU MUST NOT STEAL

IX YOU MUST NOT TELL LIES ABOUT YOUR NEIGHBOR IN COURT

X YOU MUST NOT WANT TO TAKE ANYTHING THAT BELONGS TO YOUR NEIGHBOR

Books of the Law
Law of Moses
The Law

    When you hear any of those titles mentioned, you'll know it is referring to the first five books of the Old Testament.

2

GENESIS EXODUS LEVITICUS NUMBERS DEUTERONOMY JOSHUA JUDGES RUTH 1 SAMUEL 2 SAMUEL 1 KINGS 2 KINGS 1 CHRONICLES 2 CHRONICLES EZRA NEHEMIAH ESTHER JOB PSALMS PROVERBS

GENESIS

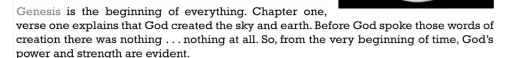

The Creation of Everything

Genesis 1:1–2:3

Words You Should Know

Genesis (JEN-eh-ses)
Beginning.

Form (FORM)
To have shape and structure. The earth had no structure. Everything was in chaos.

Sky (SKY)
Planets, stars, sun, moon, clouds—everything in the sky you can see.

Divided (dah-VY-ded)
Separated into parts. God separated the light and darkness in verse 3. In verse 6 he separated the land and the water. Then in verse 14 he put lights in the sky to separate day and night.

Grain (GRAIN)
A small, hard seed. Some plants grow grain that can be used for seeds to make more of the exact same plant.

Genesis is the beginning of everything. Chapter one, verse one explains that God created the sky and earth. Before God spoke those words of creation there was nothing . . . nothing at all. So, from the very beginning of time, God's power and strength are evident.

The Beginning of the World

1 In the beginning God created the sky and the earth. ²The earth was empty and had no form. Darkness covered the ocean, and God's Spirit was moving over the water.

³Then God said, "Let there be light!" And there was light. ⁴God saw that the light was good. So he divided the light from the darkness. ⁵God named the light "day" and the darkness "night." Evening passed, and morning came. This was the first day.

⁶Then God said, "Let there be something to divide the water in two!" ⁷So God made the air to divide the water in two. Some of the water was above the air, and some of the water was below it. ⁸God named the air "sky." Evening passed, and morning came. This was the second day.

Seeing God

There are many different terms used to refer to God in the Bible. Right here in Genesis 1 the Hebrew term referring to God is *Elohim*. It means the fullness of deity or God—very God.

3

ECCLESIASTES SONG OF SONGS ISAIAH JEREMIAH LAMENTATIONS EZEKIEL DANIEL HOSEA JOEL AMOS OBADIAH JONAH MICAH NAHUM HABAKKUK ZEPHANIAH HAGGAI ZECHARIAH MALACHI

⁹Then God said, "Let the water under the sky be gathered together so the dry land will appear." And it happened. ¹⁰God named the dry land "earth." He named the water that was gathered together "seas." God saw that this was good.

¹¹Then God said, "Let the earth produce plants. Some plants will make grain for seeds. Others will make fruit with seeds in it. Every seed will produce more of its own kind of plant." And it happened. ¹²The earth produced plants. Some plants had grain for seeds. The trees made fruit with seeds in it. Each seed grew its own kind of plant. God saw that all this was good. ¹³Evening passed, and morning came. This was the third day.

¹⁴Then God said, "Let there be lights in the sky to separate day from night. These lights will be used for signs, seasons, days and years. ¹⁵They will be in the sky to give light to the earth." And it happened.

¹⁶So God made the two large lights. He made the brighter light to rule the day. He made the smaller light to rule the night. He also made the stars. ¹⁷God put all these in the sky to shine on the earth. ¹⁸They are to rule over the day and over the night. He put them there to separate the light from the darkness. God saw that all these things were good. ¹⁹Evening passed, and morning came. This was the fourth day.

Creation Recap

Day 1 – Creation of light and dark.

Day 2 – Creation of earth and the heavens and separation of them.

Day 3 – Separation of the oceans and dry land; creation of all plants, grasses and trees.

Day 4 – Creation of the sun, moon and stars.

Day 5 – Creation of fish and all creatures that live in the oceans and seas; creation of birds and all flying creatures.

Day 6 – Creation of man; creation of all animals that are on earth. God put man in charge of the animals and ordered man and animals to reproduce.

Day 7 – God rested from all the work he had done in creating the world.

4

GENESIS EXODUS LEVITICUS NUMBERS DEUTERONOMY JOSHUA JUDGES RUTH 1 SAMUEL 2 SAMUEL 1 KINGS 2 KINGS 1 CHRONICLES 2 CHRONICLES EZRA NEHEMIAH ESTHER JOB PSALMS PROVERBS

GENESIS

Words You Should Know

Produces (pruh-DYOOS-es)
To give birth to or bear. The animals God created had babies and produced more animals.

Image (IM-ij)
A reproduction or copy of. God created man to be a copy of himself.

Rule (RULE)
Having authority or control. God gave man the authority over the animals he made.

Holy Day (HO-lee DAI)
A day set aside for special religious observances. God made the seventh day a day when mankind stops activity to worship him and recognize his work.

²⁰Then God said, "Let the water be filled with living things. And let birds fly in the air above the earth."

²¹So God created the large sea animals. He created every living thing that moves in the sea. The sea is filled with these living things. Each one produces more of its own kind. God also made every bird that flies. And each bird produces more of its own kind. God saw that this was good. ²²God blessed them and said, "Have many young ones and grow in number. Fill the water of the seas, and let the birds grow in number on the earth." ²³Evening passed, and morning came. This was the fifth day.

²⁴Then God said, "Let the earth be filled with animals. And let each produce more of its own kind. Let there be tame animals and small crawling animals and wild animals. And let each produce more of its kind." And it happened.

FAQs

Q: What does it mean that man is made in God's image?

A: God made humans able to think, make decisions, feel emotions, speak and relate to others. Humans are unique in this way from the rest of God's creation.

Q: Where was the Garden of Eden?

A: Four rivers are mentioned in Genesis 2: Pishon, Gihon, Tigris and Euphrates. Those rivers are considered to have been in Mesopotamia. Modern day Mesopotamia is Iran and Iraq.

5

ECCLESIASTES SONG OF SONGS ISAIAH JEREMIAH LAMENTATIONS EZEKIEL DANIEL HOSEA JOEL AMOS OBADIAH JONAH MICAH NAHUM HABAKKUK ZEPHANIAH HAGGAI ZECHARIAH MALACHI

²⁵So God made the wild animals, the tame animals and all the small crawling animals to produce more of their own kind. God saw that this was good.

²⁶Then God said, "Let us make human beings in our image and likeness. And let them rule over the fish in the sea and the birds in the sky. Let them rule over the tame animals, over all the earth and over all the small crawling animals on the earth."

²⁷So God created human beings in his image. In the image of God he created them. He created them male and female. ²⁸God blessed them and said, "Have many children and grow in number. Fill the earth and be its master. Rule over the fish in the sea and over the birds in the sky. Rule over every living thing that moves on the earth."

Painting by Liita Forsyth

²⁹God said, "Look, I have given you all the plants that have grain for seeds. And I have given you all the trees whose fruits have seeds in them. They will be food for you. ³⁰I have given all the green plants to all the animals to eat. They will be food for every wild animal, every bird of the air and every small crawling animal." And it happened. ³¹God looked at everything he had made, and it was very good. Evening passed, and morning came. This was the sixth day.

The Seventh Day—Rest

2 So the sky, the earth and all that filled them were finished. ²By the seventh day God finished the work he had been doing. So on the seventh day he rested from all his work. ³God blessed the seventh day and made it a holy day. He made it holy because on that day he rested. He rested from all the work he had done in creating the world.

Seeing Jesus

Read John 1:1-5, 14

John 1:1 refers to Jesus. These verses are connected to the creation story because they indicate that Jesus was with God when he created the heavens and the earth. In fact, God created everything through him. Jesus was very important to the creation process. Verse 14 then says that Jesus became human. This is called "incarnation"—God becoming human.

Think About This

Our universe is so vast that it takes a beam of light (which travels about 700 million miles per hour) over 100,000 years just to cover the length of our galaxy called the Milky Way.

The Milky Way is only one among many billions of galaxies in the universe.

Earth is spinning on its axis at 1,000 miles per hour.

Earth travels around the sun at 67,000 miles per hour.

Our solar system moves across the galaxy at a speed of 64,000 miles per hour.

Earth orbits the galaxy at 481,000 miles per hour.

Earth travels through space at 1,350,000 miles per hour.

Every twenty-four hours we cover 57,360,000 miles.

Each year we travel 20,936,400,000 miles.

All material in our universe is made up of atoms. Atoms in turn are made up of three "building blocks," protons and neutrons (which make up the center of an atom, called the nucleus) and electrons (which circle the nucleus as our earth circles the sun). *(Willmington, pages 13-14)*

6

GENESIS EXODUS LEVITICUS NUMBERS DEUTERONOMY JOSHUA JUDGES RUTH 1 SAMUEL 2 SAMUEL 1 KINGS 2 KINGS 1 CHRONICLES 2 CHRONICLES EZRA NEHEMIAH ESTHER JOB PSALMS PROVERBS

GENESIS

The Beginning of Sin

Genesis 3:1-24

God made the earth and everything in it. He was happy with his creation. He made man and woman in his image and gave them everything they needed to live a wonderful life in Eden. But things didn't go smoothly for Adam and Eve. God's enemy, Satan, came to visit.

Words You Should Know

Clever (KLEH-ver)
Mentally quick or cunning, but lacking depth and soundness.

Naked (NAI-kid)
Not covered by clothing. Having no concealment or disguise. Adam and Eve had no clothes on, and their emotions and wills were also naked before God.

Fig Leaves (FIG LEVES)
The leaves from a fig tree. Adam and Eve wove or sewed the leaves together to cover parts of their bodies.

Commanded (kah-MAND-ed)
An order given by a superior. Adam and Eve knew that God was in charge. He gave them one command, but they broke it.

Curse (KERSE)
Calling injury or harm to come on another. God called a curse to come down on Satan for tempting Adam and Eve.

Descendants
(dih-SEN-dents)
Family members born to a person and his children. Grandchild, great-grandchild and so on.

3 Now the snake was the most clever of all the wild animals the Lord God had made. One day the snake spoke to the woman. He said, "Did God really say that you must not eat fruit from any tree in the garden?"

²The woman answered the snake, "We may eat fruit from the trees in the garden. ³But God told us, 'You must not eat fruit from the tree that is in the middle of the garden. You must not even touch it, or you will die.' "

⁴But the snake said to the woman, "You will not die. ⁵God knows that if you eat the fruit from that tree, you will learn about good and evil. Then you will be like God!"

⁶The woman saw that the tree was beautiful. She saw that its fruit was good to eat and that it

would make her wise. So she took some of its fruit and ate it. She also gave some of the fruit to her husband who was with her, and he ate it.

⁷Then, it was as if the man's and the woman's eyes were opened. They realized they were naked. So they sewed fig leaves together and made something to cover themselves.

⁸Then they heard the Lord God walking in the garden. This was during the cool part of the day. And the man and his wife hid from the Lord God among the trees in the garden. ⁹But the Lord God called to the man. The Lord said, "Where are you?"

¹⁰The man answered, "I heard you walking in the garden. I was afraid because I was naked. So I hid."

¹¹God said to the man, "Who told you that you were naked? Did you eat fruit from that tree? I commanded you not to eat from that tree."

¹²The man said, "You gave this woman to me. She gave me fruit from the tree. So I ate it."

7

ECCLESIASTES SONG OF SONGS ISAIAH JEREMIAH LAMENTATIONS EZEKIEL DANIEL HOSEA JOEL AMOS OBADIAH JONAH MICAH NAHUM HABAKKUK ZEPHANIAH HAGGAI ZECHARIAH MALACHI

[13]Then the Lord God said to the woman, "What have you done?"

She answered, "The snake tricked me. So I ate the fruit."

[14]The Lord God said to the snake, "Because you did this, a curse will be put on you. You will be cursed more than any tame animal or wild animal. You will crawl on your stomach, and you will eat dust all the days of your life. [15]I will make you and the woman enemies to each other. Your descendants and her descendants will be enemies. Her child will crush your head. And you will bite his heel."

[16]Then God said to the woman, "I will cause you to have much trouble when you are pregnant. And when you give birth to children, you will have great pain. You will greatly desire your husband, but he will rule over you."

[17]Then God said to the man, "You listened to what your wife said. And you ate fruit from the tree that I commanded you not to eat from.

"So I will put a curse on the ground. You will have to work very hard for food. In pain you will eat its food all the days of your life. [18]The ground will produce thorns and weeds for you. And you will eat the plants of the field. [19]You will sweat and work hard for your food. Later you will return to the ground. This is because you were taken from the ground. You are dust. And when you die, you will return to the dust."

[20]The man named his wife Eve. This is because she is the mother of everyone who ever lived.

[21]The Lord God made clothes from animal skins for the man and his wife. And so the Lord dressed them. [22]Then the Lord God said, "Look, the man has become like one of us. He knows good and evil. And now we must keep him from eating some of the fruit from the tree of life. If he does, he will live forever." [23]So the Lord God forced the man out of the garden of Eden. He had to work the ground he was taken from. [24]God forced the man out of the garden. Then God put angels on the east side of the garden. He also put a sword of fire there. It flashed around in every direction. This kept people from getting to the tree of life.

Think About This

Was the snake just . . . a snake? No, the snake was actually Satan, either controlling the creature or in the form of a snake.

Who is Satan? Satan is God's enemy. At one time he was an angel, called Lucifer. But he rebelled against God, and he and his followers were cast out of heaven. From that time on, Satan has fought against God. His prime target to battle with is God's creation—man.

The tree in the middle of the garden that God told Adam and Eve to stay away from was the Tree of the Knowledge of Good and Evil.

This story of the first time man disobeyed God is called, "The Fall of Man."

Genesis 3:15 refers to Jesus when God says that the woman's descendant (Jesus) will crush Satan.

God made Adam and Eve leave the garden, and he put guards at the entrance of it so they could never return. Eventually, no one even knew for certain where the garden was located. God probably wanted it that way so no one could try to eat fruit from the tree of life.

8

GENESIS EXODUS LEVITICUS NUMBERS DEUTERONOMY JOSHUA JUDGES RUTH 1 SAMUEL 2 SAMUEL 1 KINGS 2 KINGS 1 CHRONICLES 2 CHRONICLES EZRA NEHEMIAH ESTHER JOB PSALMS PROVERBS

GENESIS

Words You Should Know

Wicked (WIK-id)
Morally very bad. People on earth seemed to have no consciences. They ignored God.

Destroy (di-STROI)
Completely demolish or annihilate. God wiped out his creation, except for those who were safely inside the boat.

Innocent (IN-uh-sent)
Blameless. God saw that Noah was blameless. He tried to obey God. Genesis 6:9 says that Noah walked with God. He knew God's commands and lived by them. This is why God chose to save Noah and his family.

Noah Obeys God

Genesis 6:5-22

Adam and Eve committed the first sin and were sent out into the world to make a living. They had two sons, Cain and Abel, and Cain ended up murdering Abel. From that point on, things went from bad to worse. By the time of Noah, God was sorry he had even made people. He decided to do something drastic.

The Human Race Becomes Evil

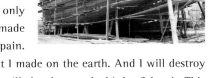

6 ⁵The Lord saw that the human beings on the earth were very wicked. He also saw that their thoughts were only about evil all the time. ⁶The Lord was sorry he had made human beings on the earth. His heart was filled with pain. ⁷So the Lord said, "I will destroy all human beings that I made on the earth. And I will destroy every animal and everything that crawls on the earth. I will also destroy the birds of the air. This is because I am sorry that I have made them." ⁸But Noah pleased the Lord.

Noah and the Great Flood

⁹This is the family history of Noah. Noah was a good man. He was the most innocent man of his time. He walked with God. ¹⁰Noah had three sons: Shem, Ham and Japheth.

¹¹People on earth did what God said was evil. Violence was everywhere. ¹²And God saw this evil. All people on the earth did only evil. ¹³So God said to Noah, "People have made the earth full of violence. So I will destroy all people from the earth. ¹⁴Build a boat of cypress wood for yourself. Make rooms in it and cover it inside and outside with tar. ¹⁵This is how big I want you to build the boat: 450 feet long, 75 feet wide and 45 feet high. ¹⁶Make an opening around the top of the boat. Make it 18 inches high from the edge of the roof down. Put a door in the side of the boat. Make an upper, middle and lower deck in it. ¹⁷I will bring a flood of water on the earth. I will destroy all living things that live under the sky. This includes everything that has the breath of life. Everything on the earth will die. ¹⁸But I will make an agreement with you. You, your sons, your wife and your sons' wives will all go into the boat. ¹⁹Also, you must bring into the boat two of every living thing, male and female. Keep them alive with you. ²⁰There will be two of every kind of bird, animal and crawling thing. They will come to you to be kept alive. ²¹Also gather some of every kind of food. Store it on the boat as food for you and the animals."

²²Noah did everything that God commanded him.

9

ECCLESIASTES SONG OF SONGS ISAIAH JEREMIAH LAMENTATIONS EZEKIEL DANIEL HOSEA JOEL AMOS OBADIAH JONAH MICAH NAHUM HABAKKUK ZEPHANIAH HAGGAI ZECHARIAH MALACHI

FAQs

Q: How did Noah have enough food for all the animals?

A: It's possible that the animals on the boat went into hibernation and simply slept for a good portion of the time. Also, since they weren't expending much energy in the confined space, they didn't need as much food as they would have normally. Noah most likely had plenty of food stored on the bottom deck of the boat.

How Many Animals?

Noah didn't have to go out and catch the animals. Genesis 6:20 says that God brought them to him. So, how many animals were in the boat? One of America's leading taxonomists lists the following numbers for animal species, according to the best estimates of modern taxonomy:

Mammals: 3,500
Birds: 8,600
Reptiles/amphibians: 5,000
Worms: 25,000

Taking this into consideration, it is likely that about 35,000 individual vertebrate animals the size of a sheep (overall average) boarded the boat. It has been estimated that a modern train hauling 150 boxcars could easily handle these animals. But the boat had a carrying capacity of 520 stock cars! In other words, there was more than enough room on the boat Noah built.

(Willmington, page 30)

FAQs

Q: How big was the boat?

A: 450 feet long: Think about a football field, goalpost to goalpost, then add another 1/2 of a field to that. That was the length of the boat.

75 feet wide and 45 feet high: That means it was as tall as a four-story building. It had about as much space inside as 20 college basketball courts. *(Willmington, page 29)*

There were three decks or floors for the animals' cages.

The boat had no motor, no sails and no oars. All it had to do was float and stay dry inside. God took care of the rest.

10

GENESIS EXODUS LEVITICUS NUMBERS DEUTERONOMY JOSHUA JUDGES RUTH 1 SAMUEL 2 SAMUEL 1 KINGS 2 KINGS 1 CHRONICLES 2 CHRONICLES EZRA NEHEMIAH ESTHER JOB PSALMS PROVERBS

GENESIS

Words You Should Know

Clean (KLENE)
Used to describe the state of a person, animal or action that was pleasing to God. Clean animals could be eaten. Disease-free people who had not touched or eaten anything unclean were called clean. They could live and serve God normally.

Unclean (UN-klene)
Used to describe the state of a person, animal or action that was not pleasing to God. Unclean animals were not to be eaten. Unclean people had to be made clean again before they could serve God.

The Great Flood

Genesis 7:1-24

Noah obeyed God and built the boat. When it was finished God sent Noah and his family inside with all the animals. The boat had one very big door. God himself closed the door behind them (7:16). After that, it started to rain.

The Flood Begins

7 Then the Lord said to Noah, "I have seen that you are the best man among the people of this time. So you and your family go into the boat. ²Take with you seven pairs, each male with its female, of every kind of clean animal. And take one pair, each male with its female, of every kind of unclean animal. ³Take seven pairs of all the birds of the sky, each male with its  female. This will allow all these animals to continue living on the earth after the flood. ⁴Seven days from now I will send rain on the earth. It will rain 40 days and 40 nights. I will destroy from the earth every living thing that I made."

⁵Noah did everything that the Lord commanded him.

⁶Noah was 600 years old when the flood came. ⁷He and his wife and his sons and their wives went into the boat. They went in to escape the waters of the flood. ⁸The clean animals, the unclean animals, the birds and everything that crawls on the ground ⁹came to Noah. They went into the boat in groups of two, male and female. This was just as God had commanded Noah. ¹⁰Seven days later the flood started.

¹¹Noah was now 600 years old. The flood started on the seventeenth day of the second month of that year. That day the underground springs split open. And the clouds in the sky poured out rain. ¹²The rain fell on the earth for 40 days and 40 nights.

¹³On that same day Noah and his wife, his sons Shem, Ham and Japheth and their wives went into the boat. ¹⁴They had every kind of wild animal and tame animal. There was every kind of

11

ECCLESIASTES SONG OF SONGS ISAIAH JEREMIAH LAMENTATIONS EZEKIEL DANIEL HOSEA JOEL AMOS OBADIAH JONAH MICAH NAHUM HABAKKUK ZEPHANIAH HAGGAI ZECHARIAH MALACHI

animal that crawls on the earth. Every kind of bird was there. [15]They all came to Noah in the boat in groups of two. There was every creature that had the breath of life. [16]One male and one female of every living thing came. It was just as God had commanded Noah. Then the Lord closed the door behind them.

[17]Water flooded the earth for 40 days. As the water rose, it lifted the boat off the ground. [18]The water continued to rise, and the boat floated on the water above the earth. [19]The water rose so much that even the highest mountains under the sky were covered by it. [20]The water continued to rise until it was more than 20 feet above the mountains.

[21]All living things that moved on the earth died. This included all the birds, tame animals, wild animals and creatures that swarm on the earth. And all human beings died. [22]So everything on dry land died. This means everything that had the breath of life in its nose. [23]So God destroyed from the earth every living thing that was on the land. This was every man, animal, crawling thing and bird of the sky. All that was left was Noah and what was with him in the boat. [24]And the waters continued to cover the earth for 150 days.

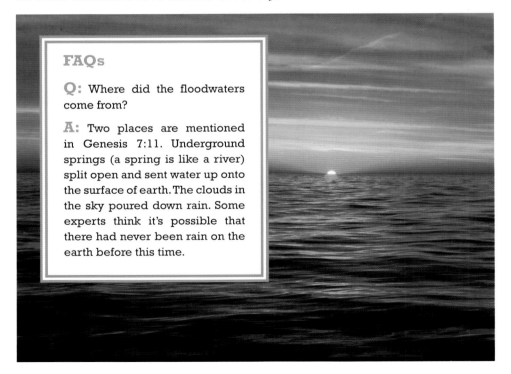

FAQs

Q: Where did the floodwaters come from?

A: Two places are mentioned in Genesis 7:11. Underground springs (a spring is like a river) split open and sent water up onto the surface of earth. The clouds in the sky poured down rain. Some experts think it's possible that there had never been rain on the earth before this time.

Time Frames

Noah was 480 years old when God told him to build the boat. Despite his old age, he apparently had no children yet. Then, strangely, 22 years after God's command to build the boat, Shem was born. Japheth came a year later, and Ham a year after that. The three sons grew up around the boat from the time they were born until they were almost 100 years old. *(Beers, page 20)*

It took 120 years to build the boat, so Noah was 600 years old when the flood began.

It rained for 40 days and 40 nights. Then Noah had to wait for the floodwaters to go away before he could come out of the boat. From the time Noah entered the boat until God said he could come out was about 370 days—over a year!

(Read Genesis 7:11; 8:4-5, 14.)

12

GENESIS EXODUS LEVITICUS NUMBERS DEUTERONOMY JOSHUA JUDGES RUTH 1 SAMUEL 2 SAMUEL 1 KINGS 2 KINGS 1 CHRONICLES 2 CHRONICLES EZRA NEHEMIAH ESTHER JOB PSALMS PROVERBS

GENESIS

God's Promise

Genesis 8:1-22; 9:12-17

Through all the chaos and destruction of the flood, God remembered Noah. God had a plan, and he instructed Noah when it was safe to leave the boat. Then God made a promise to the rest of mankind through Noah.

Mount Ararat

The Flood Ends

8 But God remembered Noah and all the wild animals and tame animals with him in the boat. God made a wind blow over the earth. And the water went down. ²The underground springs stopped flowing. And the clouds in the sky stopped pouring down rain. ³⁻⁴The water that covered the earth began to go down. After 150 days the water had gone down so much that the boat touched land again. It came to rest on one of the mountains of Ararat. This was on the seventeenth day of the seventh month. ⁵The water continued to go down. By the first day of the tenth month the tops of the mountains could be seen.

⁶Forty days later Noah opened the window he had made in the boat. ⁷He sent out a raven. It flew here and there until the water had dried up from the earth. ⁸Then Noah sent out a dove. This was to find out if the water had dried up from the ground. ⁹The dove could not find a place to land because water still covered the earth. So it came back to the boat. Noah reached out his hand and took the bird. And he brought it back into the boat.

¹⁰After seven days Noah again sent out the dove from the boat. ¹¹And that evening it came back to him with a fresh olive leaf in its mouth. Then Noah knew that the ground was almost dry. ¹²Seven days later he sent the dove out again. But this time it did not come back.

13

ECCLESIASTES SONG OF SONGS ISAIAH JEREMIAH LAMENTATIONS EZEKIEL DANIEL HOSEA JOEL AMOS OBADIAH JONAH MICAH NAHUM HABAKKUK ZEPHANIAH HAGGAI ZECHARIAH MALACHI

¹³Noah was now 601 years old. It was the first day of the first month of that year. The water was dried up from the land. Noah removed the covering of the boat and saw that the land was dry. ¹⁴By the twenty-seventh day of the second month the land was completely dry.

¹⁵Then God said to Noah, ¹⁶"You and your wife, your sons and their wives should go out of the boat. ¹⁷Bring every animal out of the boat with you—the birds, animals and everything that crawls on the earth. Let them have many young ones and let them grow in number."

¹⁸So Noah went out with his sons, his wife and his sons' wives. ¹⁹Every animal, everything that crawls on the earth and every bird went out of the boat. They left by families.

²⁰Then Noah built an altar to the Lord. Noah took some of all the clean birds and animals. And he burned them on the altar as offerings to God. ²¹The Lord was pleased with these sacrifices. He said to himself, "I will never again curse the ground because of human beings. Their thoughts are evil even when they are young. But I will never again destroy every living thing on the earth as I did this time.

²²"As long as the earth continues,
there will be planting and harvest.
Cold and hot,
summer and winter,
day and night
will not stop."

Think About This

Where is Mount Ararat? This famous mountain can be found in modern-day Turkey. There have been reports from pilots and other sources of an ark-shaped object high up on the mountain. No one knows for certain that it is actually Noah's boat.

After the flood there were 8 people on earth. How many are there now? The earth's population is estimated at 6,519,080,942 . . . and growing by the minute!

How many different kinds of plants grow on earth now? There are new species discovered all the time. But a reasonable estimate is between 230 and 270,000!

14

GENESIS EXODUS LEVITICUS NUMBERS DEUTERONOMY JOSHUA JUDGES RUTH 1 SAMUEL 2 SAMUEL 1 KINGS 2 KINGS 1 CHRONICLES 2 CHRONICLES EZRA NEHEMIAH ESTHER JOB PSALMS PROVERBS

GENESIS

Words You Should Know

Agreement (a-GREE-ment)
A contract or promise. It is sometimes called a covenant. God made agreements with his people. One agreement was the "law of Moses." God has given a new agreement to his people through Christ in the New Testament.

Think About This

There was a lot of water on earth—enough to cover mountains. Where did it all go? Genesis 8:2-3 says that the underground springs stopped flowing. Some experts think it's possible that the oceans got deeper so they could accommodate some of the water.

It's also possible that God "pushed in" some places on dry land so they could contain some of the water. Mountains rose up, continents appeared, and rivers, lakes and seas were formed. *(Concept idea from Willmington, page 31)*

Rainbow Info

The rainbow God put in the sky at the end of the flood was the first time he gave a "promise sign" to his people. When a rainbow appears, remember that God will never send a worldwide.

The New Beginning

9 ¹²And God said, "I am making an agreement between me and you and every living creature that is with you. It will continue from now on. This is the sign: ¹³I am putting my rainbow in the clouds. It is the sign of the agreement between me and the earth. ¹⁴When I bring clouds over the earth, a rainbow appears in the clouds. ¹⁵Then I will remember my agreement. It is between me and you and every living thing. Floodwaters will never again destroy all life on the earth. ¹⁶When the rainbow appears in the clouds, I will see it. Then I will remember the agreement that continues forever. It is between me and every living thing on the earth."

¹⁷So God said to Noah, "That rainbow is a sign. It is the sign of the agreement that I made with all living things on earth."

FAQs

Q: What makes a rainbow?

A: A rainbow is formed when sunlight shines through raindrops in the air. There are seven colors in a rainbow. They are red, orange, yellow, green, blue, indigo and violet. A rainbow will never be seen at high noon because the sun is too high in the sky.

Q: Can two people see the exact same rainbow at the exact same time?

A: No, a rainbow is constantly changing as the raindrops move and the sun moves. Two people can't be in exactly the same spot at exactly the same time.

15

ECCLESIASTES SONG OF SONGS ISAIAH JEREMIAH LAMENTATIONS EZEKIEL DANIEL HOSEA JOEL AMOS OBADIAH JONAH MICAH NAHUM HABAKKUK ZEPHANIAH HAGGAI ZECHARIAH MALACHI

The Tower of Babel
Genesis 11:1-9

Many years after the great flood there were once again many people on earth. Unfortunately, some of the people still did not follow God closely. One group of men made the unwise decision to try to build a tower that would reach to heaven.

The Languages Confused

11 At this time the whole world spoke one language. Everyone used the same words. ²As people moved from the East, they found a plain in the land of Babylonia. They settled there to live.

³They said to each other, "Let's make bricks and bake them to make them hard." So they used bricks instead of stones, and tar instead of mortar. ⁴Then they said to each other, "Let's build for ourselves a city and a tower. And let's make the top of the tower reach high into the sky. We will become famous. If we do this, we will not be scattered over all the earth."

⁵The Lord came down to see the city and the tower that the people had built. ⁶The Lord said, "Now, these people are united. They all speak the same language. This is only the beginning of what they will do. They will be able to do anything they want. ⁷Come, let us go down and confuse their language. Then they will not be able to understand each other."

⁸So the Lord scattered them from there over all the earth. And they stopped building the city. ⁹That is where the Lord confused the language of the whole world. So the place is called Babel. So the Lord caused them to spread out from there over all the whole world.

Tower of Babel Info

Before this time all people on earth apparently spoke the same language. At the Tower of Babel God caused many languages to be born. From this experience new nations were born, probably as people who could understand each other grouped together.

There are more than 6,000 languages spoken in our world today.

Babel actually means "the gate of God," but another word in Hebrew that looks very similar means "to confuse."

The tower that was built in Genesis 11 was probably a ziggurat. These kinds of towers were very common in the land of Babylon. They were often temples or places of worship. Most ziggurats had seven stories. Each story was a little smaller than the one below it. Stairways on the outside of the building connected the different levels. The ziggurat was always the largest building in a city. *(Beers, page 23)*

16

GENESIS EXODUS LEVITICUS NUMBERS DEUTERONOMY JOSHUA JUDGES RUTH 1 SAMUEL 2 SAMUEL 1 KINGS 2 KINGS 1 CHRONICLES 2 CHRONICLES EZRA NEHEMIAH ESTHER JOB PSALMS PROVERBS

GENESIS

Words You Should Know

Blessing (BLES-ing)
A good gift from God to
his people.

Descendants (de-SIN-dants)
Family members who are born to a
person and his children. They would
include grandchildren, great-grandchildren, great-great-grandchildren
and so on.

Worshiped (WER-shipt)
Reverence offered a divine being
or supernatural power.

Abram and Sarai

Genesis 12:1-20

Many, many years after the Tower of Babel a man named Abram lived. He was a descendant of Noah's son Shem. The rest of the book of Genesis is the story of this man and his family. Abram became the father of the Jewish nation.

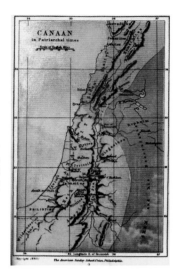

God Calls Abram

12 Then the Lord said to Abram, "Leave your country, your relatives and your father's family. Go to the land I will show you.
²I will make you a great nation, and I will bless you. I will make you famous. And you will be a blessing to others. ³I will bless those who bless you. I will place a curse on those who harm you. And all the people on earth will be blessed through you."
⁴So Abram left Haran as the Lord had told him. And Lot went with him. At this time Abram was 75 years old. ⁵Abram took his wife Sarai, his nephew Lot and everything they owned. They took all the servants they had gotten in Haran. They set out from Haran, planning to go to the land of Canaan. In time they arrived there.

⁶Abram traveled through that land. He went as far as the great tree of Moreh at Shechem. The Canaanites were living in the land at that time. ⁷The Lord appeared to Abram. The Lord said, "I will give this land to your descendants." So Abram built an altar there to the Lord, who had appeared to him. ⁸Then Abram traveled from Shechem to the mountain east of Bethel. And he set up his tent there. Bethel was to the west, and Ai was to the east. There Abram built another altar to the Lord and worshiped him. ⁹After this, he traveled on toward southern Canaan.

17

ECCLESIASTES SONG OF SONGS ISAIAH JEREMIAH LAMENTATIONS EZEKIEL DANIEL HOSEA JOEL AMOS OBADIAH JONAH MICAH NAHUM HABAKKUK ZEPHANIAH HAGGAI ZECHARIAH MALACHI

Abram Goes to Egypt

[10]At this time there was not much food in the land. So Abram went down to Egypt to live because there was so little food. [11]Just before they arrived in Egypt, Abram said to his wife Sarai, "I know you are a very beautiful woman. [12]When the Egyptians see you, they will say, 'This woman is his wife.' Then they will kill me but let you live. [13]Tell them you are my sister. Then things will go well with me. And I may be allowed to live because of you."

[14]So Abram went into Egypt. The people of Egypt saw that Sarai was very beautiful. [15]Some of the Egyptian officers saw her also. They told the king of Egypt how beautiful she was. They took her to the king's palace. [16]The king was kind to Abram because he thought Abram was Sarai's brother. He gave Abram sheep, cattle and male and female donkeys. Abram also was given male and female servants and camels.

[17]But the Lord sent terrible diseases on the king and all the people in his house. This was because of Abram's wife Sarai. [18]So the king sent for Abram. The king said, "What have you done to me? Why didn't you tell me Sarai was your wife? [19]Why did you say, 'She is my sister'? I made her my wife. But now here is your wife. Take her and leave!" [20]Then the king commanded his men to make Abram leave Egypt. So Abram and his wife left with everything they owned.

Bible Knowledge

Chapter 12 of Genesis begins a part of the Bible known as the Patriarchal Stage. The Patriarchal Stage focuses on people, specifically Abraham, Isaac, Jacob and Joseph, leaders of the nation of Israel. This period covers about 350 years.

Old Testament Covenants

God made three covenants (promises) with men in the Old Testament:

Noah. God promised Noah after the flood that he would never again send a flood that destroys all of creation (Genesis 6:18).

Abraham. God promised to make a great nation from Abraham and his descendants (Genesis 12, 15).

Moses. God promised to help His people follow him. He gave Moses the Ten Commandments to help them (Exodus 19–20).

The Abrahamic Covenant begins here in Genesis 12 with God's call and promises to Abram. There are seven parts to God's promise:

1. I will make you into a great nation (v. 2).

2. I will bless you (v. 2).

3. I will make you famous (v. 2).

4. I will make you a blessing to others (v. 2).

5. I will bless those who bless you (v. 3).

6. I will curse those who curse you (v. 3).

7. I will bless all the people of earth through you (v. 3).

18

GENESIS EXODUS LEVITICUS NUMBERS DEUTERONOMY JOSHUA JUDGES RUTH 1 SAMUEL 2 SAMUEL 1 KINGS 2 KINGS 1 CHRONICLES 2 CHRONICLES EZRA NEHEMIAH ESTHER JOB PSALMS PROVERBS

GENESIS

Total Obedience

God's command to Abram was given in Genesis 12:1 when he told Abram to leave his country, his relatives and his father's family. This was apparently a repeat of an earlier command, because in 11:31 we read that when they left Ur they planned to go to Canaan, but settled in Haran—with Terah, Abram's father. Abram had not completely obeyed God since he had taken his father with him.

In Haran, Terah died and once again God told Abram to go, leaving his relatives and father's family behind. Abram did go, but he took his nephew Lot with him. That was still not complete obedience.

In chapter 13, with their servants arguing, Abram and Lot separate. Finally, Abram was in complete obedience. Now God tells him that all the land he can see will be given to him and his descendants. The land of Canaan was the promised land.

Abram and Lot

Genesis 13:1-18

When the king of Egypt discovered that Abram had lied to him about Sarai being his sister instead of his wife, he made them leave Egypt. Abram and Sarai moved back to Canaan.

The Jordan Valley

Abram and Lot Separate

13 So Abram, his wife and Lot left Egypt. They took everything they owned and traveled to southern Canaan. ²Abram was very rich in cattle, silver and gold.

³He left southern Canaan and went back to Bethel. He went where he had camped before, between Bethel and Ai. ⁴It was the place where Abram had built an altar before. So he worshiped the Lord there.

⁵During this time Lot was traveling with Abram. Lot also had many sheep, cattle and

tents. ⁶Abram and Lot had so many animals that the land could not support both of them together. ⁷Abram's herders and Lot's herders began to argue. The Canaanites and the Perizzites were living in the land at this time.

⁸So Abram said to Lot, "There should be no arguing between you and me. Your herders and mine should not argue either. We are brothers. ⁹We should separate. The whole land is there in front of you. If you go to the left, I will go to the right. If you go to the right, I will go to the left."

¹⁰Lot looked all around and saw the whole Jordan Valley.

19

ECCLESIASTES SONG OF SONGS ISAIAH JEREMIAH LAMENTATIONS EZEKIEL DANIEL HOSEA JOEL AMOS OBADIAH JONAH MICAH NAHUM HABAKKUK ZEPHANIAH HAGGAI ZECHARIAH MALACHI

He saw that there was much water there. It was like the Lord's garden, like the land of Egypt in the direction of Zoar. (This was before the Lord destroyed Sodom and Gomorrah.) [11]So Lot

chose to move east and live in the Jordan Valley. In this way Abram and Lot separated. [12]Abram lived in the land of Canaan. But Lot lived among the cities in the Jordan Valley. He moved very near to Sodom. [13]Now the people of Sodom were very evil. They were always sinning against the Lord.

[14]After Lot left, the Lord said to Abram, "Look all around you. Look north and south and east and west. [15]All this land that you see I will give to you and your descendants forever. [16]I will make your descendants as many as the dust of the earth. If anyone could count the dust on the earth, he could count your people. [17]Get up! Walk through all this land. I am now giving it to you."

[18]So Abram moved his tents. He went to live near the great trees of Mamre. This was at the city of Hebron. There he built an altar to the Lord.

TAKING IT TO HEART

Lot's Bad Choice

Abram gave Lot the freedom to choose which land he wanted for his herds. Lot looked around at the land near the Dead Sea and saw that it had plenty of water. In fact, in Genesis 13:10 we read that it was like the Lord's garden—Eden!

Lot's choice had a downside. The cities in that area were filled with wicked, evil people. The cities of the plain were Sodom, Gomorrah, Zoar, Admah and Zeboiiim. The wickedness of the people in those cities affected Lot and his family. He and his daughters made some bad choices that showed their influence. Lot left the promised land and never again returned to it.

Sodom and Gomorrah

Archaeologists have excavated the site where Sodom is believed to have existed. They have found layers of ash indicating a great fire took place there. There is also evidence of an earthquake about the same time. Genesis 19:23-25 states that God rained down fire on Sodom and Gomorrah. God destroyed these cities because of their sinfulness. The cities were gone, and the beautiful land like the Garden of Eden was gone.

God did let Lot and his family leave Sodom because Abram asked him to. They had strict orders to run and not look back. Lot's wife disobeyed that order, and when she looked back she turned into a pillar of salt, probably covered with the sulfur raining down from the sky.

20

GENESIS EXODUS LEVITICUS NUMBERS DEUTERONOMY JOSHUA JUDGES RUTH 1 SAMUEL 2 SAMUEL 1 KINGS 2 KINGS 1 CHRONICLES 2 CHRONICLES EZRA NEHEMIAH ESTHER JOB PSALMS PROVERBS

GENESIS

Isaac Is Born

Genesis 18:1-16; 21:1-5

Words You Should Know

Circumcised

(SIR-kum-Sized)

This means to cut off the foreskin of the male sex organ. Each Jewish baby boy was circumcised on the eighth day after he was born. This act was done as a sign of the agreement God had made with his people, the Jews.

Think About This

Abraham and Sarah were getting very old—too old for Sarah to have a baby (at least that's what they thought). Sarah decided she needed to take matters into her own hands to help God keep his promise to them. She took her maid, Hagar, to Abraham and told him to have a baby with her. That way Abraham would have a son. He did, and the boy's name was Ishmael. But Ishmael wasn't the fulfillment of God's promise to make Abraham a great nation. That was still coming.

Through everything that happened, Abram and Sarai (now called Abraham and Sarah) never forgot God's promise to give them as many descendants as there were stars in the sky. However, they were very old, and they didn't have even one child. But God remembered his promise.

The Three Visitors

18 Later, the Lord again appeared to Abraham near the great trees of Mamre. At that time Abraham was sitting at the door of his tent. It was during the hottest part of the day. ²He looked up and saw three men standing near him. When Abraham saw them, he ran from his tent to meet them. He bowed face-down on the ground before them. ³Abraham said, "Sir, if you think well of me, please stay awhile with me, your servant. ⁴I will bring some water so all of you can wash your feet. You may rest under the tree. ⁵I will get some bread for you, so you can regain your strength. Then you may continue your journey."

The three men said, "That is fine. Do as you said."

⁶Abraham hurried to the tent where Sarah was. He said to her, "Hurry, prepare 20 quarts of fine flour. Make it into loaves of bread." ⁷Then Abraham ran to his cattle. He took one of his best calves and gave it to a servant. The servant hurried to kill the calf and to prepare it for

---

Seeing God

Who were the three visitors?
Genesis 18:1 says that the Lord appeared to Abraham. Two of the visitors were angels, and the third was God. All three appeared to be men, but Abraham spoke to one of them as though he knew that man was in charge. He must have realized that "man" was God.

21

ECCLESIASTES SONG OF SONGS ISAIAH JEREMIAH LAMENTATIONS EZEKIEL DANIEL HOSEA JOEL AMOS OBADIAH JONAH MICAH NAHUM HABAKKUK ZEPHANIAH HAGGAI ZECHARIAH MALACHI

food. [8]Abraham gave the three men the calf that had been cooked. He also gave them milk curds and milk. While the three men ate, he stood under the tree near them.

[9]The men asked Abraham, "Where is your wife Sarah?"

"There, in the tent," said Abraham.

[10]Then the Lord said, "I will certainly return to you about this time a year from now. At that time your wife Sarah will have a son."

Sarah was listening at the entrance of the tent which was behind him. [11]Abraham and Sarah were very old. Sarah was past the age when women normally have children. [12]So she laughed to herself, "My husband and I are too old to have a baby."

[13]Then the Lord said to Abraham, "Why did Sarah laugh? Why did she say, 'I am too old to have a baby'? [14]Is anything too hard for the Lord? No! I will return to you at the right time a year from now. And Sarah will have a son."

[15]Sarah was afraid. So she lied and said, "I didn't laugh."

But the Lord said, "No. You did laugh."

[16]Then the men got up to leave and started out toward Sodom. Abraham walked along with them a short time to send them on their way.

A Baby for Sarah

21 The Lord cared for Sarah as he had said. He did for her what he had promised. [2]Sarah became pregnant. And she gave birth to a son for Abraham in his old age. Everything happened at the time God had said it would. [3]Abraham named his son Isaac. Sarah gave birth to this son of Abraham. [4]Abraham circumcised Isaac when he was eight days old as God had commanded.

[5]Abraham was 100 years old when his son Isaac was born.

Names in the Bible

When a person's name is changed in the Bible, it is a sign of God's working in their lives.

Abram's name was changed to Abraham which means "father of a great number or nation."

Sarai's name was changed to Sarah which means "princess."

Isaac's name means "laughter."

Abraham was 100 years old and Sarah was 90 when Isaac was born.

Tent Life

Abraham and Sarah lived in a tent and moved around to find food and water for their animals. Their tent was made of one of two materials. Either it was animal skins dried and stretched over poles or it was made of fabric woven from animals' hair. The second is most likely. When the hair got wet it would shrink together and become waterproof; but when it was dry it would be looser, allowing any breezes to come through it into the tent.

22

GENESIS EXODUS LEVITICUS NUMBERS DEUTERONOMY JOSHUA JUDGES RUTH 1SAMUEL 2SAMUEL 1KINGS 2KINGS 1CHRONICLES 2CHRONICLES EZRA NEHEMIAH ESTHER JOB PSALMS PROVERBS

GENESIS

God Tests Abraham

Genesis 22:1-19

Isaac was born as the fulfillment of God's promise to Abraham and Sarah. Abraham loved Isaac very much. But God asked Abraham to do something very difficult. Abraham proved that he loved God more than anyone else.

Words You Should Know

Tested (TES-tid)
The procedure of submitting something (in this case, Abraham's faith) to conditions that lead to it's proof.

Burnt Offering
(BERNT OFF-er-ing)
An animal or food that was burned on an altar as a gift to God. This was done to ask forgiveness for sins or to praise God.

Respect (rih-SPEKT)
To consider another person worthy of high regard.

Think About This

Abraham and Isaac carried live coals up the mountain in some kind of pot. They would use these coals to start the fire to burn their sacrifice to God. Abraham also probably carried a special knife that he would use to kill the sacrifice, which he thought would be Isaac.

God Tests Abraham

22 After these things God tested Abraham's faith. God said to him, "Abraham!" And he answered, "Here I am."

²Then God said, "Take your only son, Isaac, the son you love. Go to the land of Moriah. There kill him and offer him as a whole burnt offering. Do this on one of the mountains there. I will tell you which one."

³Early in the morning Abraham got up and saddled his donkey. He took Isaac and two servants with him. He cut the wood for the sacrifice. Then they went to the place God had told them to go. ⁴On the third day Abraham looked up and saw the place in the distance. ⁵He said to his servants, "Stay here with the donkey. My son and I will go over there and worship. Then we will come back to you."

⁶Abraham took the wood for the sacrifice and gave it to his son to carry. Abraham took the knife and the fire. So Abraham and his son went on together.

⁷Isaac said to his father Abraham, "Father!"

Abraham answered, "Yes, my son."

Isaac said, "We have the fire and the wood. But where is the lamb we will burn as a sacrifice?"

⁸Abraham answered, "God will give us the lamb for the sacrifice, my son." So Abraham and his son went on together. ⁹They came to the place God had told him about. There, Abraham built an altar. He laid the wood on it. Then he tied up his son Isaac. And he laid Isaac on the wood on the altar. ¹⁰Then Abraham took his knife and was about to kill his son.

¹¹But the angel of the Lord called to him from heaven. The angel said, "Abraham! Abraham!"

Abraham answered, "Yes."

23

ECCLESIASTES SONG OF SONGS ISAIAH JEREMIAH LAMENTATIONS EZEKIEL DANIEL HOSEA JOEL AMOS OBADIAH JONAH MICAH NAHUM HABAKKUK ZEPHANIAH HAGGAI ZECHARIAH MALACHI

[12]The angel said, "Don't kill your son or hurt him in any way. Now I can see that you respect God. I see that you have not kept your son, your only son, from me."

[13]Then Abraham looked up and saw a male sheep. Its horns were caught in a bush. So Abraham went and took the sheep and killed it. He offered it as a whole burnt offering to God. Abraham's son was saved. [14]So Abraham named that place The Lord Gives. Even today people say, "On the mountain of the Lord it will be given."

[15]The angel of the Lord called to Abraham from heaven a second time. [16]The angel said, "The Lord says, 'You did not keep back your son, your only son, from me. Because you did this, I make you this promise by my own name: [17]I will surely bless you and give you many descendants. They will be as many as the stars in the sky and the sand on the seashore. And they will capture the cities of their enemies. [18]Through your descendants all the nations on the earth will be blessed. This is because you obeyed me.' "

[19]Then Abraham returned to his servants. They all traveled back to Beersheba, and Abraham stayed there.

Isaac's Brave Obedience

The biblical historian, Josephus, believes Isaac was about 25 years old when this test took place. If this is true, he could have fought his father. Isaac didn't fight however; he was an obedient son who trusted his father completely.

God's Names

The Old Testament provides many different names by which God is known. One of those names, Jehovah Jireh, appears in Genesis 22:14. This name of God literally means "The Lord Provides" or "The Lord Gives." God showed this part of his character by providing a ram for Isaac and Abraham to sacrifice.

The Mountain

God's test of Abraham's faith took place on Mt. Moriah. Many other famous events happened on this mountain that is just a little north of the city of Jerusalem:

• God stopped a terrible plague at Araunah's threshing floor on Mt. Moriah. The plague was caused by David's disobedience.

• Solomon built God's Temple on Mt. Moriah.

• The Last Supper for Jesus and his disciples happened only a short distance away from this mountain. *(Beers, page 42)*

24

GENESIS EXODUS LEVITICUS NUMBERS DEUTERONOMY JOSHUA JUDGES RUTH 1 SAMUEL 2 SAMUEL 1 KINGS 2 KINGS 1 CHRONICLES 2 CHRONICLES EZRA NEHEMIAH ESTHER JOB PSALMS PROVERBS

GENESIS

A Solemn Promise

"Put your hand under my leg." The word "hand" is one of the most used words in the Bible. When Abraham asked his servant to put his hand beneath his thigh, he was asking him to make a very serious promise. If the servant did this, he was promising to do what Abraham asked . . . no matter what.

Answered Prayer

Before the servant saw any people in the city of Nahor, he stopped and asked God to help him find the right wife for his master's son. The amazing thing about this prayer is that God answered it even before the servant had finished praying.

A Wife for Isaac

Genesis 24:1-67

Sarah died a few years after God tested Abraham. Isaac was at the age where he would be looking for a wife. Abraham was very old now, but he was concerned about his son's future wife. He came up with a plan to find the right bride for Isaac.

24 Abraham was now very old. The Lord had blessed him in every way. [2]Abraham's oldest servant was in charge of everything Abraham owned. Abraham called that servant to him and said, "Put your hand under my leg. [3]Make a promise to me before the Lord, the God of heaven and earth. Don't get a wife for my son from the Canaanite girls who live around here. [4]Instead, go back to my country, to the land of my relatives. Get a wife for my son Isaac from there."

[5]The servant said to him, "What if this woman does not want to return with me to this land? Then, should I take your son with me back to your homeland?"

[6]Abraham said to him, "No! Don't take my son back there. [7]The Lord is the God of heaven. He brought me from the home of my father and the land of my relatives. But the Lord promised me, 'I will give this land to your descendants.' The Lord will send his angel before you. The angel will help you get a wife for my son there. [8]But if the girl won't come back with you, you will be free from this promise. But you must not take my son back there." [9]So the servant put his hand under his master's leg. He made a promise to Abraham about this.

[10]The servant took ten of Abraham's camels and left. He carried with him many different kinds of beautiful gifts. He went to Northwest Mesopotamia to Nahor's city. [11]He made the camels kneel down at the well outside the city. It was in the evening when the women come out to get water.

[12]The servant said, "Lord, you are the God of my master Abraham. Allow me to find a wife for his son today. Please show this kindness to my master Abraham. [13]Here I am, standing by the spring of water. The girls from the city are coming out to get water. [14]I will say to one of the girls, 'Please put your jar down so

25

ECCLESIASTES SONG OF SONGS ISAIAH JEREMIAH LAMENTATIONS EZEKIEL DANIEL HOSEA JOEL AMOS OBADIAH JONAH MICAH NAHUM HABAKKUK ZEPHANIAH HAGGAI ZECHARIAH MALACHI

I can drink.' Then let her say, 'Drink, and I will also give water to your camels.' If that happens, I will know she is the right one for your servant Isaac. And I will know that you have shown kindness to my master."

¹⁵Before the servant had finished praying, Rebekah came out of the city. She was the daughter of Bethuel. (Bethuel was the son of Milcah and Nahor, Abraham's brother.) Rebekah was carrying her water jar on her shoulder. ¹⁶She was very pretty. She was a virgin; she had never had sexual relations with a man. She went down to the spring and filled her jar. Then she came back up. ¹⁷The servant ran to her and said, "Please give me a little water from your jar."

¹⁸Rebekah said, "Drink, sir." She quickly lowered the jar from her shoulder and gave him a

drink. ¹⁹After he finished drinking, Rebekah said, "I will also pour some water for your camels." ²⁰So she quickly poured all the water from her jar into the drinking trough for the camels. Then she kept running to the well until she had given all the camels enough to drink.

²¹The servant quietly watched her. He wanted to be sure the Lord had made his trip successful. ²²After the camels had finished drinking, he gave Rebekah a gold ring weighing one-fifth of an ounce. He also gave her two gold arm bracelets weighing about four ounces each. ²³The servant asked, "Who is your father? Is there a place in his house for me and my men to spend the night?"

²⁴Rebekah answered, "My father is Bethuel. He is the son of Milcah and Nahor." ²⁵Then she said, "And, yes, we have straw for your camels. We have a place for you to spend the night."

²⁶The servant bowed and worshiped the Lord. ²⁷He said, "Blessed is the Lord, the God of my master Abraham. The Lord has been kind and truthful to him. He has led me to my master's relatives."

²⁸Then Rebekah ran and told her mother's family about all these things. ²⁹She had a brother named Laban. He ran out to Abraham's servant, who was still at the spring.

Great Wealth

The servant brought ten of Abraham's camels with him. These were not just to carry things. Owning camels was a sign of great wealth. Ten camels with the servant would show that his master was very wealthy.

Thirsty Camels

Rebekah went above and beyond what was expected when she offered to draw water for the camels. A camel that hasn't had a drink for a few days might need as much as 25 gallons of water to quench its thirst. That meant several trips to the well for Rebekah to draw water for all ten camels. When she offered to water the camels, the servant knew for certain that God had answered his prayer.

26

GENESIS EXODUS LEVITICUS NUMBERS DEUTERONOMY JOSHUA JUDGES RUTH 1 SAMUEL 2 SAMUEL 1 KINGS 2 KINGS 1 CHRONICLES 2 CHRONICLES EZRA NEHEMIAH ESTHER JOB PSALMS PROVERBS

GENESIS

FAQs

Why couldn't Isaac marry one of the girls from where he lived?

Abraham was set against Isaac marrying a local girl. It was not because he was prejudiced or racist. He was concerned because the local people worshiped false gods. Abraham wanted his son to marry a girl who believed in the one true God and worshiped and served him.

Think About This

The servant's journey took him from Beersheba, where Abraham was living, to Haran, where he met Rebekah. It was about 450 miles. It would have taken several days.

³⁰Laban had heard what she had said. And he had seen the ring and the bracelets on his sister's arms. So he ran out to the well. And there was the man standing by the camels at the spring. ³¹Laban said, "Sir, you are welcome to come in. You don't have to stand outside. I have prepared the house for you and also a place for your camels."

³²So Abraham's servant went into the house. Laban unloaded the camels and gave them straw and food. Then Laban gave water to Abraham's servant so he and the men with him could wash their feet. ³³Then Laban gave the servant food. But the servant said, "I will not eat until I have told you why I came."

So Laban said, "Then tell us."

³⁴He said, "I am Abraham's servant. ³⁵The Lord has greatly blessed my master in everything. My master has become a rich man. The Lord has given him many flocks of sheep and herds of cattle. He has given Abraham silver and gold, male and female servants, camels and horses. ³⁶Sarah, my master's wife, gave birth to a son when she was old. My master has given everything he owns to that son. ³⁷My master had me make a promise to him. He said, 'Don't get a wife for my son from the Canaanite girls who live around here. ³⁸Instead you must go to my father's people and to my family. There you must get a wife for my son.' ³⁹I said to my master, 'What if the woman will not come back with me?' ⁴⁰But he said, 'I serve the Lord. He will send his angel with you and will help you. You will get a wife for my son from my family and my father's people. ⁴¹Then you will be free from the promise. Or if they will not give you a wife for my son, you will be free from this promise.'

⁴²"Today I came to this spring. I said, 'Lord, God of my master Abraham, please make my trip successful. ⁴³Look, I am standing by this spring of water. I will wait for a young woman to come out to get water. Then I will say, "Please give me water from your jar to drink." ⁴⁴Then let her say, "Drink this water. I will also get water for your camels." By this I will know the Lord has chosen her for my master's son.'

⁴⁵"Before I finished my silent prayer, Rebekah came out of the city. She had her water jar on her shoulder. She went down to the spring and got water. I said to her, 'Please give me a drink.' ⁴⁶She quickly lowered the jar from her shoulder. She said, 'Drink this. I will also get water for your camels.' So I drank, and she gave water to my camels also. ⁴⁷Then I asked her, 'Who is your father?' She answered, 'My father is Bethuel son of Milcah and Nahor.' Then I put the ring in

27

ECCLESIASTES SONG OF SONGS ISAIAH JEREMIAH LAMENTATIONS EZEKIEL DANIEL HOSEA JOEL AMOS OBADIAH JONAH MICAH NAHUM HABAKKUK ZEPHANIAH HAGGAI ZECHARIAH MALACHI

her nose and the bracelets on her arms. ⁴⁸At that time I bowed my head and thanked the Lord. I praised the Lord, the God of my master Abraham. I thanked him because he led me on the right road to get the granddaughter of my master's brother for his son. ⁴⁹Now, tell me, will you be kind and truthful to my master? And if not, tell me so. Then I will know what I should do."

⁵⁰Laban and Bethuel answered, "This is clearly from the Lord. We cannot change what must happen. ⁵¹Rebekah is yours. Take her and go. Let her marry your master's son as the Lord has commanded."

⁵²When Abraham's servant heard these words, he bowed facedown on the ground before the Lord. ⁵³Then the servant gave Rebekah gold and silver jewelry and clothes. He also gave expensive gifts to her brother and mother. ⁵⁴The servant and the men with him ate and drank. And they spent the night there. When they got up the next morning, the servant said, "Now let me go back to my master."

⁵⁵Rebekah's mother and her brother said, "Let Rebekah stay with us at least ten days. After that she may go."

⁵⁶But the servant said to them, "Do not make me wait. The Lord has made my trip successful. Now let me go back to my master."

⁵⁷Rebekah's brother and mother said, "We will call Rebekah and ask her what she wants to do." ⁵⁸They called her and asked her, "Do you want to go with this man now?"

She said, "Yes, I do."

⁵⁹So they allowed Rebekah and her nurse to go with Abraham's servant and his men. ⁶⁰They blessed Rebekah and said, "Our sister, may you be the mother of thousands of people. And may your descendants capture the cities of their enemies."

⁶¹Then Rebekah and her servant girls got on the camels and followed the servant and his men. So the servant took Rebekah and left.

⁶²At this time Isaac had left Beer Lahai Roi. He was living in southern Canaan. ⁶³One evening he went out to the field to think. As he looked up, he saw camels coming. ⁶⁴Rebekah looked and saw Isaac. Then she jumped down from the camel. ⁶⁵She asked the servant, "Who is that man walking in the field to meet us?"

The servant answered, "That is my master." So Rebekah covered her face with her veil.

⁶⁶The servant told Isaac everything that had happened. ⁶⁷Then Isaac brought Rebekah into the tent of Sarah, his mother. And she became his wife. Isaac loved her very much. So he was comforted after his mother's death.

Things You Should Know

Some chapters in the Bible are called "typical" chapters. This is not because they are ordinary, but because they show a comparison between things. Chapter 24 of Genesis is typical because it shows examples of things people did that can be compared to things God does:

- Abraham planned a marriage for his son; God plans the marriage of his Son, Jesus, with his church.

- Isaac is a type of Jesus because he is offered as a sacrifice, seeks his bride, and loves her very much. All of these are examples of what Jesus does.

- The servant is a type of the Holy Spirit because he searched for Isaac's bride. The Holy Spirit came at Pentecost to gather a bride for God's Son.

- Rebekah is a type of the church, Christ's bride, because she willingly came to her husband.

(Willmington, page 47)

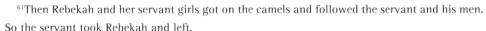

28

GENESIS EXODUS LEVITICUS NUMBERS DEUTERONOMY JOSHUA JUDGES RUTH 1 SAMUEL 2 SAMUEL 1 KINGS 2 KINGS 1 CHRONICLES 2 CHRONICLES EZRA NEHEMIAH ESTHER JOB PSALMS PROVERBS

GENESIS

Words You Should Know

Firstborn (FIRST-born)
The oldest child in a family. The son born first to a Jewish family received a double share of his father's wealth. Then he became the leader of the family when his father died. The Israelite people were called God's firstborn because he gave them special privileges. Jesus was also called God's firstborn Son. He is now ruling over all creation.

Heir (AIR)
The person who is supposed to inherit what belongs to a relative. The heir usually receives these things when the relative dies. Because we can be adopted children of God through Christ, Christians are heirs of God's riches.

Jacob's Lie

Genesis 27:1-44

Isaac and Rebekah became parents to twin boys named Esau and Jacob. The boys were very different. Isaac clearly favored Esau who was the oldest boy. This favoritism caused serious problems as the boys grew up.

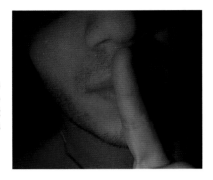

Jacob Tricks Isaac

27 When Isaac was old, his eyes were not good. He could not see clearly. One day he called his older son Esau to him. Isaac said, "Son."

Esau answered, "Here I am."

²Isaac said, "I am old. I don't know when I might die. ³So take your bow and arrows, and go hunting in the field. Kill an animal for me to eat. ⁴Prepare the tasty food that I love. Bring it to me, and I will eat. Then I will bless you before I die." ⁵So Esau went out in the field to hunt.

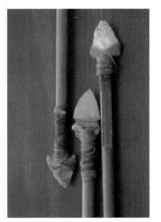

Rebekah was listening as Isaac said this to his son Esau. ⁶Rebekah said to her son Jacob, "Listen, I heard your father talking to your brother Esau. ⁷Your father said, 'Kill an animal. Prepare some tasty food for me to eat. Then I will bless you before the Lord before I die.' ⁸So obey me, my son. Do what I tell you. ⁹Go out to our goats and bring me two young ones. I will prepare them just the way your father likes them. ¹⁰Then you will take the food to your father. And he will bless you before he dies."

¹¹But Jacob said to his mother Rebekah, "My brother Esau is a hairy man. I am smooth! ¹²If my father touches me, he will know I am not Esau. Then he will not bless me. He will place a curse on me because I tried to trick him."

¹³So Rebekah said to him, "If your father puts a curse on you, I will accept the blame. Just do what I said. Go and get the goats for me."

¹⁴So Jacob went out and got two goats and brought them to his mother. Then she cooked them in the special way Isaac enjoyed. ¹⁵She took the best clothes of her older son Esau that were in the house. She put them on the younger son Jacob. ¹⁶She took the skins of the goats. And she

29

ECCLESIASTES SONG OF SONGS ISAIAH JEREMIAH LAMENTATIONS EZEKIEL DANIEL HOSEA JOEL AMOS OBADIAH JONAH MICAH NAHUM HABAKKUK ZEPHANIAH HAGGAI ZECHARIAH MALACHI

put them on Jacob's hands and neck. ¹⁷Then she gave Jacob the tasty food and the bread she had made.

¹⁸Jacob went in to his father and said, "Father."

And his father said, "Yes, my son. Who are you?"

¹⁹Jacob said to him, "I am Esau, your first son. I have done what you told me. Now sit up and eat some meat of the animal I hunted for you. Then bless me."

²⁰But Isaac asked his son, "How did you find and kill the animal so quickly?"

Jacob answered, "Because the Lord your God led me to find it."

²¹Then Isaac said to Jacob, "Come near so I can touch you, my son. If I can touch you, I will know if you are really my son Esau."

²²So Jacob came near to Isaac his father. Isaac touched him and said, "Your voice sounds like Jacob's voice. But your hands are hairy like the hands of Esau." ²³Isaac did not know it was Jacob, because his hands were hairy like Esau's hands. So Isaac blessed Jacob. ²⁴Isaac asked, "Are you really my son Esau?"

Jacob answered, "Yes, I am."

²⁵Then Isaac said, "Bring me the food. I will eat it and bless you." So Jacob gave him the food, and Isaac ate. Jacob gave him wine, and he drank. ²⁶Then Isaac said to him, "My son, come near and kiss me." ²⁷So Jacob went to his father and kissed him. Isaac smelled Esau's clothes and blessed him. Isaac said,

Think About This

Before Esau and Jacob were even born, Rebekah felt them fighting inside her. God told her that the families of each of them would become nations who would struggle with each other, and the older son would serve the younger (25:23). This was backward because the firstborn son in a Hebrew family would have received the birthright and blessing of the father. That meant that he ruled the family when the father died.

TAKING IT TO HEART

Deceit

The name "Jacob" means "Deceiver." Jacob certainly lived up to that. God meant for him to be the blessed son. God had already told that to Rebekah. But Jacob took matters into his own hands by deceiving his father. There is always a price to be paid for deceiving others. Jacob had to leave home, and he never saw his mother again.

"The smell of my son is like the smell of the field that the Lord has blessed. ²⁸May God give you plenty of rain and good soil. Then you will have plenty of grain and wine. ²⁹May nations serve you. May peoples bow down to you. May you be master over your brothers. May your mother's sons bow down to you. May everyone who curses you be cursed. And may everyone who blesses you be blessed."

30

GENESIS EXODUS LEVITICUS NUMBERS DEUTERONOMY JOSHUA JUDGES RUTH 1 SAMUEL 2 SAMUEL 1 KINGS 2 KINGS 1 CHRONICLES 2 CHRONICLES EZRA NEHEMIAH ESTHER JOB PSALMS PROVERBS

GENESIS

Birthrights

Hebrew families were patriarchal; the father ruled over everyone. When the father died, the firstborn son became the new head of the family. The firstborn son received a double share of his father's inheritance and his father's blessing. He also had responsibilities: managing the family property or business and care of his mother and any unmarried sisters.

Esau's Birthright

Esau had already shown disrespect for his birthright. He sold it to Jacob for a bowl of red soup. See Genesis 25:29-34.

[30]Isaac finished blessing Jacob. Then, just as Jacob left his father Isaac, Esau came in from hunting. [31]Esau also prepared some tasty food and brought it to his father. He said, "Father, rise and eat the food that your son killed for you. Then bless me."

[32]Isaac asked, "Who are you?"

He answered, "I am your son—your firstborn son—Esau."

[33]Then Isaac trembled greatly. He said, "Then who was it that hunted the animals and brought me food before you came? I ate it, and I blessed him. And it is too late now to take back my blessing."

[34]When Esau heard the words of his father, he let out a loud and bitter cry. He said to his father, "Bless me—me, too, my father!"

[35]But Isaac said, "Your brother came and tricked me. He has taken your blessing."

[36]Esau said, "Jacob is the right name for him. He has tricked me these two times. He took away my share of everything you own. And now he has taken away my blessing." Then Esau asked, "Haven't you saved a blessing for me?"

[37]Isaac answered, "I gave Jacob the power to be master over you. And all his brothers will be his servants. And I kept him strong with grain and wine. There is nothing left to give you, my son."

[38]But Esau continued, "Do you have only one blessing, Father? Bless me, too, Father!" Then Esau began to cry out loud.

[39]Isaac said to him,

"You will live far away from the best land, far from the rain. [40]You will live by using your sword and be a slave to your brother. But when you struggle, you will break free from him."

[41]After that Esau hated Jacob because of the blessing from Isaac. Esau thought to himself, "My father will soon die, and I will be sad for him. After that I will kill Jacob."

31

ECCLESIASTES SONG OF SONGS ISAIAH JEREMIAH LAMENTATIONS EZEKIEL DANIEL HOSEA JOEL AMOS OBADIAH JONAH MICAH NAHUM HABAKKUK ZEPHANIAH HAGGAI ZECHARIAH MALACHI

⁴²Rebekah heard about Esau's plan to kill Jacob. So she sent for Jacob. She said to him, "Listen, your brother Esau is comforting himself by planning to kill you. ⁴³So, son, do what I say. My brother Laban is living in Haran. Go to him at once! ⁴⁴ Stay with him for a while, until your brother is not so angry.

Jacob's Birthright

When Jacob became the owner of the birthright, one responsibility was to care for his mother. But he wasn't able to do this because he had to leave home to escape Esau's anger.

In his blessing, Isaac said that people would serve Jacob, and nations would bow down to him. Several generations later, one of Jacob's ancestors was Jesus. Isaac's prophecy about Jacob's family was certainly fulfilled in him. The genealogy of Jesus given in Matthew 1 lists Jacob as Jesus' ancestor (Matthew 1:2-16).

The World at the Time

Ancient Writing

One of the earliest forms of writing was cuneiform. This writing was named for the kind of instrument used to make the marks. It was a sharpened wedge-shaped reed that was pushed into the soft clay of a tablet. The word cuneiform actually means wedge-shaped. The writing was done originally in vertical columns, not across the tablet as we would do today. In the middle of the third century that changed to horizontal lines. The very earliest form of this writing was not actually letters, but small pictures that told a story. Certain pictures were understood to stand for certain things. Originally there were over 2500 signs in the "alphabet," but eventually that was reduced to around 500. If the writer wanted his tablet to be preserved, it was baked so it couldn't be erased. This writing was invented by the Babylonians and was adopted by other nations, including the Assyrians.

Cuneiform Writing

32

GENESIS EXODUS LEVITICUS NUMBERS DEUTERONOMY JOSHUA JUDGES RUTH 1 SAMUEL 2 SAMUEL 1 KINGS 2 KINGS 1 CHRONICLES 2 CHRONICLES EZRA NEHEMIAH ESTHER JOB PSALMS PROVERBS

GENESIS

Words You Should Know

Angels (AIN-gels)
A Greek word that means messengers. Angels are heavenly beings. They can sometimes look like people. God used angels to help his people and to announce important events.

One-Tenth (WON TENth)
Sometimes called a tithe. In the Old Testament the Jewish people were told to give one-tenth of what they earned to God.

Jacob's Journey

Jacob's trip from Beersheba to Bethel was about 60 miles. The rest of his journey to Haran was around 400 miles.

Jacob's Dream at Bethel

Genesis 28:10-22

Jacob tricked his father, Isaac, and stole his brother's blessing as the firstborn son. Esau was so angry that he wanted to kill his brother. Jacob had to run for his life.

28 [10]Jacob left Beersheba and set out for Haran. [11]He came to a place and spent the night there because the sun had set. He found a stone there and laid his head on it to go to sleep. [12]Jacob dreamed that there was a ladder resting on the earth and reaching up into heaven. And he saw angels of God going up and coming down the ladder. [13]And then Jacob saw the Lord standing above the ladder. The Lord said, "I am the Lord, the God of Abraham, your grandfather. And I am the God of Isaac. I will give you and your descendants the land on which you are now sleeping. [14]Your descendants will be as many as the dust of the earth. They will spread west and east, north and south. All the families of the earth will be blessed through you and your descendants. [15]I am with you, and I will protect you everywhere you go. And I will bring you back to this land. I will not leave you until I have done what I have promised you."

[16]Then Jacob woke from his sleep. He said, "Surely the Lord is in this place. But I did not know it." [17]Jacob was afraid. He said, "This place frightens me! It is surely the house of God and the gate of heaven."

[18]Jacob rose early in the morning. He took the stone he had slept on and set it up on its end. Then he poured olive oil on the top of it. [19]At first, the name of that city was Luz. But Jacob named it Bethel.

[20]Then Jacob made a promise. He said, "I want God to be with me and protect me on this journey. I want God to give me food to eat and clothes to wear. [21]Then I will be able to return in peace to my father's house. If the Lord does these things, he will be my God. [22]This stone which I have set up on its end will be the house of God. And I will give God one-tenth of all he gives me."

33

ECCLESIASTES SONG OF SONGS ISAIAH JEREMIAH LAMENTATIONS EZEKIEL DANIEL HOSEA JOEL AMOS OBADIAH JONAH MICAH NAHUM HABAKKUK ZEPHANIAH HAGGAI ZECHARIAH MALACHI

Think About This

Jacob's dream took place at Bethel. This was the same place where his grandfather, Abraham, had once set up an altar and worshiped God (Genesis 12:8).

Bethel means "house of God."

God blessed Jacob and promised to always be with him, even though Jacob had sinned and deserved nothing. He gave Jacob the same promises he had given to Abraham earlier. Later, God was called "the God of Jacob" (Exodus 3:15).

Check out Galatians 3:16 and Hebrews 6:14 to see that God's promises to Abraham passed on to Isaac, Jacob and eventually down to Jesus.

Seeing Jesus

Jacob saw angels going up and down a ladder to heaven. John 1:51 says that Jesus is the "ladder" to heaven. His death for our sins provides a ladder for us to be able to enter heaven, and his life is a ladder giving us revelations about heaven.

GENESIS

A Wife for Jacob

Genesis 29:1-30

Jacob ran away from home to get away from his brother. He had stolen Esau's birthright blessing, and Esau threatened to kill him. Jacob ended up in his mother's homeland, with his mother's relatives.

Jacob Arrives in Northwest Mesopotamia

29 Then Jacob continued his journey. He came to the land of the people of the East. [2]He looked and saw a well in the field. Three flocks of sheep were lying nearby, because they

drank water from this well. A large stone covered the mouth of the well. [3]All the flocks would gather there. The shepherds would roll the stone away from the well and water the sheep. Then they would put the stone back in its place.

[4]Jacob said to the shepherds there, "My brothers, where are you from?"

They answered, "We are from Haran."

[5]Then Jacob asked, "Do you know Laban grandson of Nahor?"

They answered, "We know him."

[6]Then Jacob asked, "How is he?"

They answered, "He is well. Look, his daughter Rachel is coming now with his sheep."

[7]Jacob said, "But look, it is still the middle part of the day. It is not time for the sheep to be gathered for the night. So give them water and let them go back into the pasture."

[8]But they said, "We cannot do that until all the flocks are gathered. Then we will roll away the stone from the mouth of the well and water the sheep."

[9]While Jacob was talking with the shepherds, Rachel came with her father's sheep. It was her job to take care of the sheep. [10]Then Jacob saw Laban's daughter Rachel and Laban's sheep. So he went to the well and rolled the stone from its mouth. Then he watered Laban's sheep. Now Laban was the brother of Rebekah, Jacob's mother. [11]Then Jacob kissed Rachel and cried. [12]He told her that he

Words You Should Know

Shepherds (SHEP-'rds)
A person who cares for and protects sheep. A shepherd loves his sheep and gives them food and water. He guides them to a quiet place to rest. He protects the sheep from wolves and other wild animals. A good shepherd will even die trying to protect his sheep.

Jesus is called the Good Shepherd because he loves and cares for his followers who are often called sheep. Jesus was willing to die for his followers to save them.

Feast (FEEST)
A special meal and celebration for a certain purpose. There were many different feasts in Bible times.

Think About This

Rachel came while Jacob was still talking, just as Rebekah (Jacob's mother) came while Abraham's servant was still praying. These two stories may have even happened at the same well.

35

ECCLESIASTES SONG OF SONGS ISAIAH JEREMIAH LAMENTATIONS EZEKIEL DANIEL HOSEA JOEL AMOS OBADIAH JONAH MICAH NAHUM HABAKKUK ZEPHANIAH HAGGAI ZECHARIAH MALACHI

was from her father's family. He said that he was the son of Rebekah. So Rachel ran home and told her father.

¹³When Laban heard the news about his sister's son Jacob, Laban ran to meet him. Laban hugged him and kissed him and brought him to his house. Jacob told Laban everything that had happened.

¹⁴Then Laban said, "You are my own flesh and blood."

Jacob Is Tricked

So Jacob stayed there a month. ¹⁵Then Laban said to Jacob, "You are my relative. But it is not right for you to keep on working for me without pay. What would you like me to pay you?"

¹⁶Now Laban had two daughters. The older was Leah, and the younger was Rachel. ¹⁷Leah had weak eyes, but Rachel was very beautiful. ¹⁸Jacob loved Rachel. So he said to Laban, "Let me marry your younger daughter Rachel. If you will, I will work seven years for you."

¹⁹Laban said, "It would be better for her to marry you than someone else. So stay here with me." ²⁰So Jacob worked for Laban seven years so he could marry Rachel. But they seemed to him like just a few days. This was because he loved Rachel very much.

²¹After seven years Jacob said to Laban, "Give me Rachel so that I may marry her. The time I promised to work for you is over."

²²So Laban gave a feast for all the people there. ²³That evening Laban brought his daughter Leah to Jacob. Jacob and Leah had sexual relations together. ²⁴(Laban gave his slave girl Zilpah to his daughter to be her servant.) ²⁵In the morning Jacob saw that he had had sexual relations with Leah! He said to Laban, "What have you done to me? I worked hard for you so that I could marry Rachel! Why did you trick me?"

²⁶Laban said, "In our country we do not allow the younger daughter to marry before the older daughter. ²⁷But complete the full week of the marriage ceremony with Leah. I will give you Rachel to marry also. But you must serve me another seven years."

²⁸So Jacob did this and completed the week with Leah. Then Laban gave him his daughter Rachel as a wife. ²⁹(Laban gave his slave girl Bilhah to his daughter Rachel to be her servant.) ³⁰So Jacob had sexual relations with Rachel also. And Jacob loved Rachel more than Leah. Jacob worked for Laban for another seven years.

Wells

Stones were often placed over the opening of wells because wind would blow dirt into the well and eventually fill it up, then no water could be drawn from it.

Usually shepherds waited until all the flocks were together to open the well.

Veils

Brides wore heavy veils, covering their faces. The groom couldn't see the bride's face, but she could see through the veil. Jacob couldn't see the face of his first bride, so he didn't know he was being tricked.

Weddings were very simple, but the wedding feast or party could last as long as two weeks!

36

GENESIS EXODUS LEVITICUS NUMBERS DEUTERONOMY JOSHUA JUDGES RUTH 1 SAMUEL 2 SAMUEL 1 KINGS 2 KINGS 1 CHRONICLES 2 CHRONICLES EZRA NEHEMIAH ESTHER JOB PSALMS PROVERBS

GENESIS

Jacob Meets Esau

Genesis 33:1-20

Jacob had a family now and hadn't been to his homeland for a long time. God told him to go home. He promised to take care of Jacob.

Behind the Story

Jacob sent a message to his brother, Esau, that he was coming home. He was afraid Esau would kill him and his wives and children.

Jacob divided his family into two camps (32:7-8) in hopes that if Esau destroyed one, part of Jacob's family could escape. He put Rachel and Joseph in the back of the crowd because they were his favorites. He wanted them to be safe.

Jacob lied to Esau once again. He told him that he couldn't travel with Esau because of the children with him. However, he said he would follow Esau. But, once Esau had gone, Jacob went in another direction.

Esau became the father of the nation of Edom. The Edomites and Jacob's ancestors, the Israelites, were never friendly.

Jacob Shows His Bravery

33 Jacob looked up and saw Esau coming. With him were 400 men. So Jacob divided his children among Leah, Rachel and the two slave girls. ²Jacob put the slave girls with their children first. Then he put Leah and her children behind them. And he put Rachel and Joseph last. ³Jacob himself went out in front of them. He bowed down flat on the ground seven times as he was walking toward his brother.

⁴But Esau ran to meet Jacob. Esau put his arms around him and hugged him. Then Esau kissed him, and they both cried. ⁵Esau looked up and saw the women and children. He asked, "Who are these people with you?"

Jacob answered, "These are the children God has given me. God has been good to me, your servant."

⁶Then the two slave girls and their children came up to Esau. They bowed down flat on the earth before him. ⁷Then Leah and her children came up to Esau. They also bowed down flat on the earth. Last of all, Joseph and Rachel came up to Esau. And they, too, bowed down flat before him.

⁸Esau said, "I saw many herds as I was coming here. Why did you bring them?"

Jacob answered, "They were to please you, my master."

⁹But Esau said, "I already have enough, my brother. Keep what you have."

¹⁰Jacob said, "No! Please! If I have pleased you, then please accept the gift I give you. I am very happy to see your face again. It is like seeing the face of God because you have accepted me. ¹¹So I beg you to accept the gift I give you. God has been very good to me. And I have more than I need." And because Jacob begged, Esau accepted the gift.

¹²Then Esau said, "Let us get going. I will travel with you."

37

ECCLESIASTES SONG OF SONGS ISAIAH JEREMIAH LAMENTATIONS EZEKIEL DANIEL HOSEA JOEL AMOS OBADIAH JONAH MICAH NAHUM HABAKKUK ZEPHANIAH HAGGAI ZECHARIAH MALACHI

[13]But Jacob said to him, "My master, you know that the children are weak. And I must be careful with my flocks and their young ones. If I force them to go too far in one day, all the animals will die. [14]So, my master, you go on ahead of me, your servant. I will follow you slowly. I will let the animals and the children set the speed at which we travel. I will meet you, my master, in Edom."

[15]So Esau said, "Then let me leave some of my men with you."

"No, thank you," said Jacob. "I only want to please you, my master." [16]So that day Esau started back to Edom. [17]But Jacob went to Succoth. There he built a house for himself. And he made shelters for his animals. That is why the place was named Succoth.

[18]Jacob left Northwest Mesopotamia. And he arrived safely at the city of Shechem in the land of Canaan. He camped east of the city. [19]He bought a part of the field where he had camped. He bought it from the sons of Hamor father of Shechem for 100 pieces of silver. [20]He built an altar there and named it after God, the God of Israel.

FAQs

Q: What was Jacob's gift for Esau?

A: 580 animals! Genesis 32:13-15 records them all:

[13]Jacob...prepared a gift for Esau from what he had with him. [14]It was 200 female goats and 20 male goats, 200 female sheep and 20 male sheep. [15]There were 30 female camels and their young, 40 cows and 10 bulls, 20 female donkeys and 10 male donkeys.

Jacob's New Name

The night before Jacob met Esau, he wrestled with God. The story is in Genesis 32:22-28.

[22]During the night Jacob rose and crossed the Jabbok River at the crossing. He took his 2 wives, his 2 slave girls and his 11 sons with him. [23]He sent his family and everything he had across the river. [24]But Jacob stayed behind alone. And a man came and wrestled with him until the sun came up. [25]The man saw that he could not defeat Jacob. So he struck Jacob's hip and put it out of joint. [26]Then the man said to Jacob, "Let me go. The sun is coming up."

But Jacob said, "I will let you go if you will bless me."

[27]The man said to him, "What is your name?"

And he answered, "Jacob."

[28]Then the man said, "Your name will no longer be Jacob. Your name will now be Israel, because you have wrestled with God and with men. And you have won."

Israel means "one who has power with God."

38

■GENESIS EXODUS LEVITICUS NUMBERS DEUTERONOMY JOSHUA JUDGES RUTH 1 SAMUEL 2 SAMUEL 1 KINGS 2 KINGS 1 CHRONICLES 2 CHRONICLES EZRA NEHEMIAH ESTHER JOB PSALMS PROVERBS

GENESIS

Words You Should Know

Jealous (JEL-us)
Having rivalry or competition with another person. Or desiring to own what belongs to another or to have another person's position.

Guilty (GIL-tee)
Feelings of responsibility for offenses done to another person.

Jacob's Family

Wives:
Leah, Bilhah, Zilpah, Rachel

Leah's sons:
Reuben, Simeon, Levi, Judah and Issachar

Bilhah's sons:
Dan and Naphtali

Zilpah's sons:
Gad and Asher

Rachel's sons:
Joseph and Benjamin

Joseph and His Brothers

Genesis 37:1-36

Jacob and his family settled in the land of Canaan. But things were not always happy in Jacob's family.

Joseph the Dreamer

37 Jacob lived in the land of Canaan, where his father had lived. ²This is the family history of Jacob.

Joseph was a young man, 17 years old. He and his brothers cared for the flocks. His brothers were the sons of Bilhah and Zilpah, his father's wives. Joseph gave his father bad reports about his brothers. ³Joseph was born when his father Israel, also called Jacob, was old. So Israel loved Joseph more than his other sons. He made Joseph a special robe with long sleeves. ⁴Joseph's brothers saw that their father loved Joseph more than he loved them. So they hated their brother and could not speak to him politely.

⁵One time Joseph had a dream. When he told his brothers about it, they hated him even more. ⁶Joseph said, "Listen to the dream I had. ⁷We were in the field tying bundles of wheat together. My bundle stood up, and your bundles of wheat gathered around mine. Your bundles bowed down to mine."

⁸His brothers said, "Do you really think you will be king over us? Do you truly think you will rule over us?" His brothers hated him even more now. They hated him because of his dreams and what he had said.

⁹Then Joseph had another dream. He told his brothers about it also. He said, "Listen, I had another dream. I saw the sun, moon and 11 stars bowing down to me."

¹⁰Joseph also told his father about this dream. But his father scolded him, saying, "What kind of dream is this? Do you really believe that your mother, your brothers and I will bow down to you?" ¹¹Joseph's brothers were jealous of him. But his father thought about what all these things could mean.

¹²One day Joseph's brothers went to Shechem to herd their father's sheep. ¹³Jacob said to Joseph, "Go to Shechem. Your brothers are there herding the sheep."

39

ECCLESIASTES SONG OF SONGS ISAIAH JEREMIAH LAMENTATIONS EZEKIEL DANIEL HOSEA JOEL AMOS OBADIAH JONAH MICAH NAHUM HABAKKUK ZEPHANIAH HAGGAI ZECHARIAH MALACHI

Joseph answered, "I will go."

¹⁴His father said, "Go and see if your brothers and the sheep are all right. Then come back and tell me." So Joseph's father sent him from the Valley of Hebron.

When Joseph came to Shechem, ¹⁵a man found him wandering in the field. He asked Joseph, "What are you looking for?"

¹⁶Joseph answered, "I am looking for my brothers. Can you tell me where they are herding the sheep?"

¹⁷The man said, "They have already gone. I heard them say they were going to Dothan." So Joseph went to look for his brothers and found them in Dothan.

Joseph Sold into Slavery

¹⁸Joseph's brothers saw him coming from far away. Before he reached them, they made a plan to kill him. ¹⁹They said to each other, "Here comes that dreamer. ²⁰Let's kill him and throw his body into one of the wells. We can tell our father that a wild animal killed him. Then we will see what will become of his dreams."

²¹But Reuben heard their plan and saved Joseph. He said, "Let's not kill him. ²²Don't spill any blood. Throw him into this well here in the desert. But don't hurt him!" Reuben planned to save Joseph later and send him back to his father. ²³So when Joseph came to his brothers, they pulled off his robe with long sleeves. ²⁴Then they threw him into the well. It was empty. There was no water in it.

²⁵While Joseph was in the well, the brothers sat down to eat. When they looked up, they saw a group of Ishmaelites. They were traveling from Gilead to Egypt. Their camels were carrying spices, balm and myrrh.

²⁶Then Judah said to his brothers, "What will we gain if we kill our brother and hide his death? ²⁷Let's sell him to these Ishmaelites. Then we will not be guilty of killing our own brother. After all, he is our brother, our own flesh and blood." And the other brothers agreed. ²⁸So when the Midianite traders came by, the brothers took

The Coat

The coat Jacob gave Joseph was different from the coats that his brothers owned. Other text states that it was brightly colored. It may have been longer and had longer sleeves. Jacob's gift may have indicated that he wished to give the birthright to Joseph rather than the oldest son.

The Dreams

Joseph's dreams showed that he was going to have the privileges reserved for the oldest son. Reuben, who was the oldest and therefore owned the birthright, was the brother who wanted to save Joseph from being killed.

The Ishmaelites

This was a group of wandering traders who traveled from town to town selling and buying things. They were descendants of Ishmael, Abraham's son by Hagar.

40

GENESIS EXODUS LEVITICUS NUMBERS DEUTERONOMY JOSHUA JUDGES RUTH 1 SAMUEL 2 SAMUEL 1 KINGS 2 KINGS 1 CHRONICLES 2 CHRONICLES EZRA NEHEMIAH ESTHER JOB PSALMS PROVERBS

GENESIS

Think About This

Joseph's brothers put him in an empty well. It probably had a small opening at the top and was wider down at the bottom. The curved shape would have made it difficult to climb out of. They may have even put a stone on the opening.

The brothers were at Dothan when they sold Joseph to the traders. That means Joseph had traveled nearly 80 miles from his home to find his brothers. Dothan was known for its rich pastureland.

The brothers sold Joseph for 20 pieces of silver. Years later, Judas was paid 30 pieces of silver to turn Jesus in to the authorities.

Joseph out of the well. They sold him to the Ishmaelites for eight ounces of silver. And the Ishmaelites took him to Egypt.

Painting by F. Overbeck

²⁹Reuben was not with his brothers when they sold Joseph to the Ishmaelites. When Reuben came back to the well, Joseph was not there. Reuben tore his clothes to show he was sad. ³⁰ Then he went back to his brothers and said, "The boy is not there! What will I do?" ³¹The brothers killed a goat and dipped Joseph's long-sleeved robe in its blood. ³²Then they brought the robe to their father. They said, "We found this robe. Look it over carefully. See if it is your son's robe."

³³Jacob looked it over and said, "It is my son's robe! Some savage animal has eaten him. My son Joseph has been torn to pieces!" ³⁴Then Jacob tore his clothes and put on rough cloth to show that he was sad. He continued to be sad about his son for a long time. ³⁵All of Jacob's sons and daughters tried to comfort him. But he could not be comforted. Jacob said, "I will be sad about my son until the day I die." So Jacob cried for his son Joseph.

³⁶Meanwhile the Midianites who had bought Joseph had taken him to Egypt. There they sold him to Potiphar. Potiphar was an officer to the king of Egypt and captain of the palace guard.

41

ECCLESIASTES SONG OF SONGS ISAIAH JEREMIAH LAMENTATIONS EZEKIEL DANIEL HOSEA JOEL AMOS OBADIAH JONAH MICAH NAHUM HABAKKUK ZEPHANIAH HAGGAI ZECHARIAH MALACHI

The World at the Time

The Near East in the Late Bronze Age

The Bronze Age was divided into three categories:

The Early Bronze Age was from 3500 – 2000 B.C.

The Middle Bronze Age was from 2000 – 1600 B.C.

The Late Bronze Age was from 1600 – 1200 B.C.

Advanced metal work was done in The Bronze Age, especially the use of copper. This metal was found in the mountains of Turkey, Cyprus, Egypt, the Negev Desert and the Persian Gulf. Powerful nations competed for dominance during this time. Four of the most powerful were Egypt, Assyria, Babylonia and the Hittite nations.

Toward the end of The Bronze Age there was a growing demand for tin, which resulted in trade routes being established out of Anatolia, modern-day Turkey, where this metal could be found. Slowly the world transitioned to the Iron Age, which was a time of political unrest.

Copper Ingot from Crete, Made About 1600 B.C.

Bronze-Age Weapons from Romania

The Life of a Slave

God was watching out for Joseph. He was purchased as a slave by Potiphar, an official in the king's court. Slaves worked hard, doing jobs that no Egyptian would choose to do. They didn't get weekends or holidays off. They had little hope of ever gaining their freedom. But Joseph quickly proved himself trustworthy and, even though he was a slave, he was given a position of authority in Potiphar's very wealthy household. Joseph managed Potiphar's household. That means he was in charge of all the other slaves and servants. He probably had a large budget to manage, too. Potiphar didn't worry about anything because he trusted Joseph.

42

GENESIS EXODUS LEVITICUS NUMBERS DEUTERONOMY JOSHUA JUDGES RUTH 1 SAMUEL 2 SAMUEL 1 KINGS 2 KINGS 1 CHRONICLES 2 CHRONICLES EZRA NEHEMIAH ESTHER JOB PSALMS PROVERBS

GENESIS

Words You Should Know

Slave (SLAVE)
A person who is bought and therefore owned by another person. The slave must do whatever jobs the owner desires. The slave serves the owner.

Warden (WAR-den)
A person who is in charge of managing a prison. He or she is also in charge of the prisoners, making sure they don't escape and that they are kept busy.

Painting by C. F. Vos

Joseph in Prison

Genesis 39:1-23

Joseph was in a position of authority in Potiphar's house, even though he was a slave. But, then he made Potiphar's wife angry and she did something very mean to Joseph.

Joseph Is Sold to Potiphar

39 Now Joseph had been taken down to Egypt. An Egyptian named Potiphar was an officer to the king of Egypt. He was the captain of the palace guard. He bought Joseph from the Ishmaelites who had brought him down there. ²The Lord was with Joseph, and he became a successful man. He lived in the house of his master, Potiphar the Egyptian.

³Potiphar saw that the Lord was with Joseph. He saw that the Lord made Joseph successful in everything he did. ⁴So Potiphar was very happy with Joseph. He allowed Joseph to be his personal servant. He put Joseph in charge of the house. Joseph was trusted with everything Potiphar owned. ⁵So Joseph was put in charge of the house. He was put in charge of everything Potiphar owned. Then the Lord blessed the people in Potiphar's house because of Joseph. And the Lord blessed everything that belonged to Potiphar, both in the house and in the field. ⁶So Potiphar put Joseph in charge of everything he owned. Potiphar was not concerned about anything, except the food he ate.

Joseph Is Put into Prison

Now Joseph was well built and handsome. ⁷After some time the wife of Joseph's master began to desire Joseph. One day she said to him, "Have sexual relations with me."

⁸But Joseph refused. He said to her, "My master trusts me with everything in his house. He has put me in charge of everything he owns. ⁹There is no one in his house greater than I. He has not

43

ECCLESIASTES SONG OF SONGS ISAIAH JEREMIAH LAMENTATIONS EZEKIEL DANIEL HOSEA JOEL AMOS OBADIAH JONAH MICAH NAHUM HABAKKUK ZEPHANIAH HAGGAI ZECHARIAH MALACHI

kept anything from me, except you. And that is because you are his wife. How can I do such an evil thing? It is a sin against God."

[10]The woman talked to Joseph every day, but he refused to have sexual relations with her or even spend time with her.

[11]One day Joseph went into the house to do his work as usual. He was the only man in the house at that time. [12]His master's wife grabbed his coat. She said to him, "Come and have sexual relations with me." But Joseph left his coat in her hand and ran out of the house.

[13]She saw what Joseph had done. He had left his coat in her hands and had run outside. [14]So she called to the servants in her house. She said, "Look! This Hebrew slave was brought here to shame us. He came in and tried to have sexual relations with me. But I screamed. [15]My scream scared him, and he ran away. But he left his coat with me." [16]She kept his coat until her husband came home. [17]And she told her husband the same story. She said, "This Hebrew slave you brought here came in to shame me! [18]When he came near me, I screamed. He ran away, but he left his coat."

[19]When Joseph's master heard what his wife said Joseph had done, he became very angry. [20]So Potiphar arrested Joseph and put him into prison. This prison was where the king's prisoners were put. And Joseph stayed there in the prison.

[21]But the Lord was with Joseph and showed him kindness. The Lord caused the prison warden to like Joseph. [22]The prison warden chose Joseph to take care of all the prisoners. He was responsible for whatever was done in the prison. [23]The warden paid no attention to anything that was in Joseph's care. This was because the Lord was with Joseph. The Lord made Joseph successful in everything he did.

Take It to Heart

Joseph was put in charge of everything Potiphar owned because Potiphar trusted him. Jesus told a story in Matthew 25 about some servants who were trusted by their master. In 25:21, the master says that a servant who has done well with a little responsibility will be given more.

Similarly, 1 Corinthians 4:2 states that, in order to be trusted, a person must show he or she is worthy of that trust.

Think About This

Prisons in Joseph's time were nothing like the prisons of today. More than likely, Joseph was in a small, dungeon-like cell. There was no toilet in the cell, and often the prisoner had no food unless his family visited and brought him food.

44

GENESIS EXODUS LEVITICUS NUMBERS DEUTERONOMY JOSHUA JUDGES RUTH 1 SAMUEL 2 SAMUEL 1 KINGS 2 KINGS 1 CHRONICLES 2 CHRONICLES EZRA NEHEMIAH ESTHER JOB PSALMS PROVERBS

GENESIS

Words You Should Know

Hebrews (HEE-brooz)
Another name for Jewish people.
The book of Hebrews is a letter
written to Jewish Christians.

Stalk (STAUK)
The part of a plant that grows up
from the ground and supports the
seeds of flowers of the plant.

Joseph Interprets Dreams

Genesis 40:1–41:36

Some of Joseph's problems had started because of dreams he had that made his brothers angry. Now Joseph is in prison, and two other prisoners have dreams that God helps Joseph interpret. God uses this to help Joseph.

Joseph Interprets Two Dreams

40 After these things happened, two of the king's officers displeased the king. These officers were the man who served wine to the king and the king's baker. ²The king became angry with his officer who served him wine and his baker. ³So he put them in the prison of the captain of the guard. This was the same prison where Joseph was kept. ⁴The captain of the guard put the two prisoners in Joseph's care. They stayed in prison for some time.

⁵One night both the king's officer who served him wine and the baker had a dream. Each had his own dream with its own meaning. ⁶When Joseph came to them the next morning, he saw they were worried. ⁷Joseph asked the king's officers who were with him, "Why do you look so unhappy today?"

⁸The two men answered, "We both had dreams last night. But no one can explain the meaning of them to us."

Joseph said to them, "God is the only One who can explain the meaning of dreams. So tell me your dreams."

⁹So the man who served wine to the king told Joseph his dream. He said, "I dreamed I saw a vine. ¹⁰On the vine there were three branches. I watched the branches bud and blossom, and then the grapes ripened. ¹¹I was holding the king's cup. So I took the grapes and squeezed the juice into the cup. Then I gave it to the king."

¹²Then Joseph said, "I will explain the dream to you. The three branches stand for three days. ¹³Before the end of three days the king will free you. He will allow you to return to your work. You will serve the king his wine just as you did before. ¹⁴But when you are free, remember me. Be kind to me. Tell the king about me so that I can get out of this prison. ¹⁵I was taken by force from the land of the Hebrews. And I have done nothing here to deserve being put in prison."

¹⁶The baker saw that Joseph's explanation of the dream was good. So he said to Joseph, "I also

45

ECCLESIASTES SONG OF SONGS ISAIAH JEREMIAH LAMENTATIONS EZEKIEL DANIEL HOSEA JOEL AMOS OBADIAH JONAH MICAH NAHUM HABAKKUK ZEPHANIAH HAGGAI ZECHARIAH MALACHI

had a dream. I dreamed there were three bread baskets on my head. [17]In the top basket there were all kinds of baked food for the king. But the birds were eating this food out of the basket on my head."

[18]Joseph answered, "I will tell you what the dream means. The three baskets stand for three days. [19]Before the end of three days, the king will cut off your head! He will hang your body on a pole. And the birds will eat your flesh."

[20]Three days later it was the king's birthday. So he gave a feast for all his officers. In front of his officers, he let the chief officer who served his wine and the chief baker out of prison. [21]The king gave his chief officer who served wine his old position. Once again he put the king's cup of wine into the king's hand. [22]But the king hanged the baker on a pole. Everything happened just as Joseph had said it would. [23]But the officer who served wine did not remember Joseph. He forgot all about him.

The King's Dreams

41 Two years later the king had a dream. He dreamed he was standing on the bank of the Nile River. [2]He saw seven fat and beautiful cows come up out of the river. They stood there, eating the grass. [3]Then seven more cows came up out of the river. But they were thin and ugly. They stood beside the seven beautiful cows on the bank of the Nile.

[4]The seven thin and ugly cows ate the seven beautiful fat cows. Then the king woke up. [5]The king slept again and dreamed a second time. In his dream he saw seven full and good heads of grain growing on one stalk. [6]After that, seven more heads of grain sprang up. But they were thin and burned by the hot east wind. [7]The thin heads of grain ate the seven full and good heads. Then the king woke up again. And he realized it was only a dream.

[8]The next morning the king was troubled about these dreams. So he sent for all the magicians and wise men of Egypt. The king told them his dreams. But no one could explain their meaning to him.

Dream Info

Dreams had great importance in Joseph's time. They were considered revelations from the gods the people worshiped. Often God spoke to people through their dreams, too. People who could interpret dreams were very important. Joseph was quick to say that only God could interpret dreams and that his explanations came from God.

The dreams of the prisoners and the king had symbols in them—vines, baskets, cows and stalks of grain. God helped Joseph explain what the symbols meant.

Other dreams recorded in the Bible:

Jacob dreamed of a ladder to heaven.

Gideon heard an enemy soldier tell of a dream where Gideon's army defeated his army.

Daniel interpreted King Nebuchadnezzar's dream.

God warned Joseph in a dream to take baby Jesus to Egypt.

46

GENESIS EXODUS LEVITICUS NUMBERS DEUTERONOMY JOSHUA JUDGES RUTH 1 SAMUEL 2 SAMUEL 1 KINGS 2 KINGS 1 CHRONICLES 2 CHRONICLES EZRA NEHEMIAH ESTHER JOB PSALMS PROVERBS

GENESIS

Joseph and the Lord

An important phrase is repeated often in the story of Joseph's life: "The Lord was with Joseph." See Genesis 39:2, 21, 23. This shows that God cared for Joseph. He protected and blessed him. He had a plan for Joseph's life.

Chief Officer Who Served Wine

He is sometimes called a cupbearer and today might be called a butler. His job was to bring food and drink to the king and serve it to him. He was partly responsible for the king's life, because he would taste the food or drink before serving it to the king in order to make sure it had no poison in it. Being a cupbearer was an important and trusted position.

⁹Then the chief officer who served wine to the king said to him, "I remember something I promised to do. But I had forgotten about it. ¹⁰There was a time when you were angry with me and the baker. You put us in prison in the house of the captain of the guard. ¹¹In prison we each had a dream on the same night. Each dream had a different meaning. ¹²A young Hebrew man was in the prison with us. He was a servant of the captain of the guard. We told him our dreams, and he explained their meanings to us. He told each man the meaning of his dream. ¹³Things happened exactly as he said they would: I was given back my old position, and the baker was hanged."

¹⁴So the king called for Joseph. The guards quickly brought him out of the prison. He shaved, put on clean clothes and went before the king.

¹⁵The king said to Joseph, "I have had a dream. But no one can explain its meaning to me. I have heard that you can explain a dream when someone tells it to you."

¹⁶Joseph answered the king, "I am not able to explain the meaning of dreams. God will do this for the king."

¹⁷Then the king said to Joseph, "In my dream I was standing on the bank of the Nile River. ¹⁸I saw seven fat and beautiful cows. They came up out of the river and ate the grass. ¹⁹Then I saw seven more cows come out of the river. They were thin and lean and ugly. They were the worst looking cows I have seen in all the land of Egypt. ²⁰And these thin and ugly cows ate the first seven fat cows. ²¹But after they had eaten the seven cows, no one could tell they had eaten them. They just looked as thin and ugly as they did in the beginning. Then I woke up.

²²"I had another dream. I saw seven full and good heads of grain growing on one stalk. ²³Then seven more heads of grain sprang up after them. But these heads were thin and ugly. They were burned by the hot east wind. ²⁴Then the thin heads ate the seven good heads. I told this dream to the magicians. But no one could explain its meaning to me."

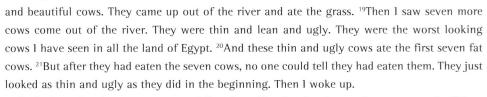

47

ECCLESIASTES SONG OF SONGS ISAIAH JEREMIAH LAMENTATIONS EZEKIEL DANIEL HOSEA JOEL AMOS OBADIAH JONAH MICAH NAHUM HABAKKUK ZEPHANIAH HAGGAI ZECHARIAH MALACHI

Joseph Tells the Dreams' Meaning

[25]Then Joseph said to the king, "Both of these dreams mean the same thing. God is telling you what he is about to do. [26]The seven good cows stand for seven years. And the seven good heads of grain stand for seven years. Both dreams mean the same thing. [27]The seven thin and ugly cows stand for seven years. And the seven thin heads of grain burned by the hot east wind stand for seven years of hunger. [28]This will happen as I told you. God is showing the king what he is about to do. [29]You will have seven years of good crops and plenty to eat in all the land of Egypt. [30]But after those seven years, there will come seven years of hunger. All the food that grew in the land of Egypt will be forgotten. The

time of hunger will eat up the land. [31]People will forget what it was like to have plenty of food. This is because the hunger that follows will be so great. [32]You had two dreams which mean the same thing. This shows that God has firmly decided that this will happen. And he will make it happen soon.

TAKING IT TO HEART

Hard Times

God does not cause bad things to happen. But he used the terrible things that happened to Joseph to do good in Joseph's life and in the lives of others.

"We know that in everything God works for the good of those who love him. They are the people God called, because that was his plan" (Romans 8:28).

[33]"So let the king choose a man who is very wise and understanding. Let the king set him over the land of Egypt. [34]And let the king also appoint officers over the land. They should take one-fifth of all the food that is grown during the seven good years. [35]They should gather all the food that is produced during the good years that are coming. Under the king's authority they should store the grain in the cities and guard it. [36]That food should be saved for later. It will be used during the seven years of hunger that will come on the land of Egypt. Then the people in Egypt will not die during the seven years of hunger."

Genesis 41:14

Joseph shaved before he went before the king. Egyptian men were typically smooth-shaven. They wore no beards or mustaches. In fact, some sources say they shaved their entire bodies. They wore wigs, and they were quite critical of the Hebrew men who usually had beards.

Famines

Natural causes such as drought, insects and plant disease cause famines. Crops are also destroyed through storm damage and because of invading armies and battles that take place in the very fields. Famines are usually temporary, but some can last several years as in this case where there were seven good years and seven years of famine. In extended times of famine people often moved to other lands in order to be able to get food for their families and their animals.

48

GENESIS EXODUS LEVITICUS NUMBERS DEUTERONOMY JOSHUA JUDGES RUTH 1 SAMUEL 2 SAMUEL 1 KINGS 2 KINGS 1 CHRONICLES 2 CHRONICLES EZRA NEHEMIAH ESTHER JOB PSALMS PROVERBS

GENESIS

Joseph Is Made Ruler

Genesis 41:37-49, 53-57

Words You Should Know

Signet Ring (SIG-nit ring)
A ring worn by a king or other important person. It had a seal on it. He would stamp things with his ring to show that he owned them. The stamp was like a signature.

Royal Seal (ROI-el SEEL)
A design or monogram that identified a document as being from or approved by a king or queen.

God helped Joseph interpret the king's dreams and warn him about a famine. Joseph had a plan to store up food for the hard times ahead. The king was so grateful that he took Joseph out of prison and made him second in command of the country.

41 ³⁷This seemed like a very good idea to the king. All his officers agreed. ³⁸And the king asked them, "Can we find a better man than Joseph to take this job? God's spirit is truly in him!"

³⁹So the king said to Joseph, "God has shown you all this. There is no one as wise and understanding as you are. ⁴⁰I will put you in charge of my palace. All the people will obey your orders. Only I will be greater than you."

⁴¹Then the king said to Joseph, "Look! I have put you in charge of all the land of Egypt." ⁴²Then the king took off from his own finger his ring with the royal seal on it. And he put it on Joseph's finger. He gave Joseph fine linen clothes to wear. And he put a gold chain around Joseph's neck. ⁴³The king had Joseph ride in the second royal chariot. Men walked ahead of his chariot calling, "Bow down!" By doing these things, the king put Joseph in charge of all of Egypt.

⁴⁴The king said to him, "I am the king. And I say that no one in all the land of Egypt may lift a hand or a foot unless you say he may." ⁴⁵The king gave Joseph the name Zaphenath-Paneah. He also gave Joseph a wife named Asenath. She was the daughter of Potiphera, priest of On. So Joseph traveled through all the land of Egypt.

⁴⁶Joseph was 30 years old when he began serving the king of Egypt. And he left the king's court and traveled through all the land of Egypt. ⁴⁷During the seven good years, the crops in the land grew well. ⁴⁸And Joseph gathered all the food

49

ECCLESIASTES SONG OF SONGS ISAIAH JEREMIAH LAMENTATIONS EZEKIEL DANIEL HOSEA JOEL AMOS OBADIAH JONAH MICAH NAHUM HABAKKUK ZEPHANIAH HAGGAI ZECHARIAH MALACHI

Seeing Jesus

Joseph is a type of Christ. Look at the similarities:

Both were dearly loved by their fathers.

Both were unjustly hated by their brothers.

Both were taken to Egypt.

Both were stripped of their robes.

Both were sold for the price of a slave.

Both were falsely accused of wrong.

Both experienced God's presence.

Both were placed with two prisoners, one who was lost and one who was saved.

Both were exalted following their suffering.

Both forgave their brothers.

produced in Egypt during those seven years of good crops. He stored the food in the cities. In every city he stored grain that had been grown in the fields around that city. ⁴⁹Joseph stored much grain, as much as the sand of the seashore. He stored so much grain that he could not measure it.

⁵³The seven years of good crops came to an end in the land of Egypt. ⁵⁴Then the seven years of hunger began, just as Joseph had said. In all the lands people had nothing to eat. But in Egypt there was food. ⁵⁵The time of hunger became terrible in all of Egypt. The people cried to the king for food. He said to all the Egyptians, "Go to Joseph. Do whatever he tells you to do."

⁵⁶The hunger was everywhere in that part of the world. And Joseph opened the storehouses and sold grain to the people of Egypt. This was because the time of hunger became terrible in Egypt. ⁵⁷And all the people in that part of the world came to Joseph in Egypt to buy grain. This was because the hunger was terrible everywhere in that part of the world.

Joseph and the King

When the king gave Joseph his signet ring everyone knew that Joseph had great power. Joseph was second in power only to the king himself.

The king gave Joseph a new name, Zaphenath-Paneah, which means "God Speaks and Lives" (Genesis 41:45).

Joseph was 30 years old when he became a ruler (v. 46). It had been 13 years since his brothers sold him to the slave traders.

The king gave Joseph a wife who was the daughter of a priest. More than likely she did not believe in God. However, Joseph raised his sons to know and honor God. When Joseph's father died, he blessed Joseph's younger son instead of the oldest son of his oldest son (48:14).

50

GENESIS EXODUS LEVITICUS NUMBERS DEUTERONOMY JOSHUA JUDGES RUTH 1 SAMUEL 2 SAMUEL 1 KINGS 2 KINGS 1 CHRONICLES 2 CHRONICLES EZRA NEHEMIAH ESTHER JOB PSALMS PROVERBS

GENESIS

Joseph Forgives

Genesis 42:1-3, 6-13; 45:1-11

Behind the Story

The brothers made two visits to Egypt to buy food. Joseph recognized them immediately, but they didn't know him. He spoke in Egyptian to them and used a translator, so they had no idea he was the brother they had sold into slavery. They couldn't understand him, but he could understand everything they said (Genesis 42:23).

Remember Joseph's dreams of the bundles of hay bowing down to his bundle and the sun, moon and 11 stars bowing down to him? They came true when his brothers bowed down to him (42:6).

People from neighboring countries came to Egypt to buy food. Joseph's own brothers, the ones who had sold him into slavery, came to Joseph for food. They didn't recognize Joseph, but he knew who they were.

The Dreams Come True

42 Jacob learned that there was grain in Egypt. So he said to his sons, "Why are you just sitting here looking at one another? ²I have heard that there is grain in Egypt. Go down there and buy grain for us to eat. Then we will live and not die."

³So ten of Joseph's brothers went down to buy grain from Egypt.

⁶Now Joseph was governor over Egypt. He was the one who sold the grain to people who came to buy it. So Joseph's brothers came to him. They bowed facedown on the ground before him. ⁷When Joseph saw his brothers, he knew who they were. But he acted as if he didn't know them. He asked unkindly, "Where do you come from?"

They answered, "We have come from the land of Canaan to buy food."

⁸Joseph knew they were his brothers. But they did not know who he was. ⁹And Joseph remembered his dreams about his brothers bowing to him. He said to them, "You are spies! You came to learn where the nation is weak!"

¹⁰But his brothers said to him, "No, my master. We come as your servants just to buy food. ¹¹We are all sons of the same father. We are honest men, not spies."

¹²Then Joseph said to them, "No! You have come to learn where this nation is weak!"

¹³And they said, "We are 10 of 12 brothers. We are sons of the same father. We live in the land of Canaan. Our youngest brother is there with our father right now. And our other brother is gone."

51

ECCLESIASTES SONG OF SONGS ISAIAH JEREMIAH LAMENTATIONS EZEKIEL DANIEL HOSEA JOEL AMOS OBADIAH JONAH MICAH NAHUM HABAKKUK ZEPHANIAH HAGGAI ZECHARIAH MALACHI

Joseph Reveals Who He Is

45 Joseph could not control himself in front of his servants any longer. He cried out, "Have everyone leave me." When only the brothers were left with Joseph, he told them who he was. ²Joseph cried so loudly that the Egyptians heard him. And the people in the king's palace heard about it. ³He said to his brothers, "I am Joseph. Is my father still alive?" But the brothers could not answer him, because they were very afraid of him.

⁴So Joseph said to them, "Come close to me." So the brothers came close to him. And he said to them, "I am your brother Joseph. You sold me as a slave to go to Egypt. ⁵Now don't be worried. Don't be angry with yourselves because you sold me here. God sent me here ahead of you to save people's lives. ⁶No food has grown on the land for two years now. And there will be five more years without planting or harvest.

⁷So God sent me here ahead of you. This was to make sure you have some descendants left on earth. And it was to keep you alive in an amazing way. ⁸So it was not you who sent me here, but God. God has made me the highest officer of the king of Egypt. I am in charge of his palace. I am the master of all the land of Egypt.

⁹"So leave quickly and go to my father. Tell him, 'Your son Joseph says: God has made me master over all Egypt. Come down to me quickly. ¹⁰Live in the land of Goshen. You will be near me. Also your children, your grandchildren, your flocks and herds and all that you have will be near me. ¹¹I will care for you during the next five years of hunger. In this way, you and your family and all that you have will not starve.'"

The Good from the Bad

The story of Joseph's life shows how God made something good from something bad.

- Jacob's family began with lies when Rebekah's father lied to Jacob and gave him Leah to marry (Genesis 29:25).

- Leah and Rachel were jealous of each other (30:1).

- Joseph's brothers were jealous of him and sold him into slavery (37:11, 28).

- Two of the brothers married women who didn't know God (38:1-3; 46:10).

But . . .

- Joseph was promoted to head of the prison where he was a prisoner (39:22).

- God helped Joseph interpret dreams (40:1–41:36).

- Joseph was made second in command of the country (41:41).

- Joseph's brothers were sorry for their actions toward him (42:21).

- Joseph and his family were reunited (47:1).

- God's promises to Abraham were passed down through Joseph's sons (48:15-16).

52

GENESIS EXODUS LEVITICUS NUMBERS DEUTERONOMY JOSHUA JUDGES RUTH 1 SAMUEL 2 SAMUEL 1 KINGS 2 KINGS 1 CHRONICLES 2 CHRONICLES EZRA NEHEMIAH ESTHER JOB PSALMS PROVERBS

GENESIS

Joseph's Family Comes to Egypt

Genesis 47:1-12, 27-31

Thirteen years after his brothers sold him into slavery, Joseph and his brothers and father were together again. His family moved to Egypt so Joseph could take care of them.

Jacob Settles in Goshen

47 Joseph went in to the king and said, "My father and my brothers have arrived from Canaan. They have their flocks and herds and everything they own with them. They are now in the land of Goshen." ²Joseph chose five of his brothers to introduce to the king.

³The king said to the brothers, "What work do you do?"

And they said to him, "We, your servants, are shepherds. Our ancestors were also shepherds." ⁴They said to the king, "We have come to live in this land. There is no grass in the land of Canaan

for our animals to eat. The hunger is very terrible there. So please allow us to live in the land of Goshen."

⁵Then the king said to Joseph, "Your father and your brothers have come to you. ⁶You may choose any place in Egypt for them to live. Give your father and your brothers the best land. Let them live in the land of Goshen. And if any of them are skilled shepherds, put them in charge of my sheep and cattle."

⁷Then Joseph brought in his father Jacob and introduced him to the king. And Jacob blessed the king.

⁸Then the king said to Jacob, "How old are you?"

⁹Jacob said to him, "My life has been spent wandering from place to place. It has been short, filled with trouble. I have lived only 130 years. My ancestors lived much longer than I." ¹⁰Then Jacob blessed the king and left.

¹¹Joseph obeyed the king. He gave his father and brothers the best land in Egypt. It was near the city of Rameses. ¹²And Joseph gave his father, his brothers and everyone who lived with them the food they needed.

Think About This

The king asked Jacob how old he was (Genesis 47: 8). This indicates that the long lives the Hebrew people lived was unusual even in that day. Perhaps the Egyptians did not enjoy such long lives.

Joseph's family settled in the land of Goshen. This was an area near the Nile River that got plenty of water. The grass grew well there, so it was a good place for shepherds and their flocks. Being in Goshen kept them away from most of the Egyptian people, so they weren't tempted to turn away from their faith in God. Goshen was sometimes called the land of Rameses.

53

ECCLESIASTES SONG OF SONGS ISAIAH JEREMIAH LAMENTATIONS EZEKIEL DANIEL HOSEA JOEL AMOS OBADIAH JONAH MICAH NAHUM HABAKKUK ZEPHANIAH HAGGAI ZECHARIAH MALACHI

The land of Goshen

Joseph's Promise

When Jacob was dying, he gave his blessing to his heir. He skipped over his two oldest sons because of their sins. He gave the blessing to Joseph. He also blessed Joseph's son, but not his older son. Jacob blessed Ephraim, not Manasseh.

"Don't Bury Me in Egypt"

²⁷The Israelites continued to live in the land of Goshen in Egypt. There they got possessions. They had many children and grew in number.

²⁸Jacob, also called Israel, lived in Egypt 17 years. So he lived to be 147 years old. ²⁹Israel knew he soon would die. So he called his son Joseph to him. He said to Joseph, "If you love me, put your hand under my leg. Promise me you will not bury me in Egypt. ³⁰When I die, carry me out of Egypt. Bury me where my ancestors are buried."

Joseph answered, "I will do as you say."

³¹Then Jacob said, "Promise me." And Joseph promised him that he would do this. Then Israel worshiped as he leaned on the top of his walking stick.

Embalming

When Jacob died, his body was prepared for burial. This was a long process that sometimes took two months. The body was washed, all the internal organs were removed. The brain was pulled out through the nose with a hook. The body was soaked in a salty liquid for a month and a half. Then it was dried out and filled with spices and other things. The body was then wrapped in cloth covered with a sticky substance. Each part of the body was wrapped individually. It might have taken 500 feet of material to wrap one body. These mummies were placed in cases and sealed. This preservation process was so good that mummies thousands of years old can still be viewed in museums today.

54

GENESIS **EXODUS** LEVITICUS NUMBERS DEUTERONOMY JOSHUA JUDGES RUTH 1 SAMUEL 2 SAMUEL 1 KINGS 2 KINGS 1 CHRONICLES 2 CHRONICLES EZRA NEHEMIAH ESTHER JOB PSALMS PROVERBS

EXODUS

Words You Should Know

Mortar (MORE-tar)
Two meanings:
A stone bowl where grain is ground into flour by pounding. Manna was ground up this way (see Numbers 11:8; Proverbs 27:22).

Mortar is also the sticky material that holds bricks together. It was often made of mud or clay (see Genesis 11:3; Exodus 1:14; Isaiah 41:25).

Things You Should Know

Moses wrote Exodus while he was leading the Israelites out of Egypt. The book focuses on how God led and protected his people who had been in Egypt for about 400 years.

This book shows that God keeps his promises. He is Lord over nations and nature. He cares about how his people worship him.

Trouble for the People of Israel

Exodus 1:8-22

The Israelites stayed in Egypt after Joseph died. Years passed and the new king didn't remember Joseph or all the good he did for Egypt. The king just got nervous that there were so many Israelites in his country. He was afraid they might help Egypt's enemies.

1 [8]Then a new king began to rule Egypt. He did not know who Joseph was. [9]This king said to his people, "Look! The people of Israel are too many! And they are too strong for us to handle! [10]We must make plans against them. If we don't, the number of their people will grow even more. Then if there is a war, they might join our enemies. Then they could fight us and escape from the country!"

[11]So the Egyptians made life hard for the people of Israel. They put slave masters over the Israelites. The slave masters forced the Israelites to build the cities Pithom and Rameses for the king. These cities were supply centers in which the Egyptians stored things. [12]The Egyptians forced the Israelites to work even harder. But this made the Israelites grow in number and spread more. So the Egyptians became more afraid of them. [13]They forced the Israelites to work even harder. [14]The Egyptians made life hard for the Israelites. They forced the Israelites to work very hard making bricks and mortar. They also forced them to do all kinds of hard work in the fields. The Egyptians were not merciful to them in all their hard work.

The Obelisk of Thutmosis 1

Slave Masters

Slave masters were the men in charge of supervising the Israelite slaves. Their job was to keep the Israelites working hard and as fast as possible. They often killed a slave or two in an effort to keep the number of Israelites from growing.

55

ECCLESIASTES SONG OF SONGS ISAIAH JEREMIAH LAMENTATIONS EZEKIEL DANIEL HOSEA JOEL AMOS OBADIAH JONAH MICAH NAHUM HABAKKUK ZEPHANIAH HAGGAI ZECHARIAH MALACHI

The World of the Israelites

Egypt was a large and powerful nation. This was due, in part, to all that Joseph had done. The Israelites lived there for about 400 years. For most of that time no one bothered them. But the new king became nervous that their nation had become so large. He decided to make them his slaves. They were forced to work very hard to build two cities where the king stored grain and food. The cities were called Pithom and Rameses. They used bricks to build the cities. But they had to collect the materials to make the bricks and make them before they could even start building.

[15]There were two Hebrew nurses named Shiphrah and Puah. These nurses helped the Israelite women give birth to their babies. The king of Egypt said to the nurses, [16]"When you are helping the Hebrew women give birth to their babies, watch! If the baby is a girl, let the baby live. But if it is a boy, kill it!" [17]But the nurses feared God. So they did not do as the king told them. They let all the boy babies live. [18]Then the king of Egypt sent for the nurses. He said, "Why did you do this? Why did you let the boys live?"

[19]The nurses said to him, "The Hebrew women are much stronger than the Egyptian women. They give birth to their babies before we can get there." [20]God was good to the nurses. And the Hebrew people continued to grow in number. So they became even stronger. [21]Because the nurses feared God, he gave them families of their own.

[22]So the king commanded all his people: "Every time a boy is born to the Hebrews, you must throw him into the Nile River. But let all the girl babies live."

Think About This

The two nurses who helped when babies were born were called midwives. They assisted the women as they gave birth.

God was kind to the nurses who refused to kill the Israelite boy babies. Their names are given, Shiphrah and Puah, but the king's name is not.

The Israelites lived in the part of Egypt known as Goshen. This was just inside the border and the place where any invading army would enter the country. The king was afraid the large Israelite nation would join an invading army and overrun his country.

God blessed the Israelites. The harder the Egyptians made them work, the larger the Israelite nation grew (Exodus 1:12).

56

GENESIS **EXODUS** LEVITICUS NUMBERS DEUTERONOMY JOSHUA JUDGES RUTH 1 SAMUEL 2 SAMUEL 1 KINGS 2 KINGS 1 CHRONICLES 2 CHRONICLES EZRA NEHEMIAH ESTHER JOB PSALMS PROVERBS

EXODUS

The Birth of Moses

Exodus 2:1-10

The king ordered that all Hebrew baby boys be drowned, because he was afraid of how many Hebrews there were. He was afraid they would join Egypt's enemies and make a very large army. But one mother refused to let her son be killed.

Baby Moses

Words You Should Know

Reeds (reedz)
Tall thick grasses which grow at the edge of lakes or ponds.

Tar (tar)
Thick heavy paste that is spread on items to make them waterproof.

FAQs

Why didn't anyone see Moses' floating basket before the princess came?

The edge of the river was lined with reeds that grow 10 to 15 feet tall. Each reed is about 3 inches thick. These reeds are also what Moses' mother used to make the basket he was floating in.

2 There was a man from the family of Levi. He married a woman who was also from the family of Levi. ²She became pregnant and gave birth to a son. She saw how wonderful the baby was, and she hid him for three months. ³But after three months, she was not able to hide the baby any longer. So she got a basket made of reeds and covered it with tar so that it would float. She put the baby in the basket. Then she put the basket among the tall grass at the edge of the Nile River. ⁴The baby's sister stood a short distance away. She wanted to see what would happen to him.

⁵Then the daughter of the king of Egypt came to the river. She was going to take a bath. Her servant girls were walking beside the river. She saw the basket in the tall grass. So she sent her slave girl to get it. ⁶The king's daughter opened the basket and saw the baby boy. He was crying, and she felt sorry for him. She said, "This is one of the Hebrew babies."

⁷Then the baby's sister asked the king's daughter, "Would you like me to find a Hebrew woman to nurse the baby for you?"

The Nile River

57

ECCLESIASTES SONG OF SONGS ISAIAH JEREMIAH LAMENTATIONS EZEKIEL DANIEL HOSEA JOEL AMOS OBADIAH JONAH MICAH NAHUM HABAKKUK ZEPHANIAH HAGGAI ZECHARIAH MALACHI

[8]The king's daughter said, "Yes, please." So the girl went and got the baby's own mother.

[9]The king's daughter said to the woman, "Take this baby and nurse him for me. I will pay you." So the woman took her baby and nursed him. [10]After the child had grown older, the woman took him to the king's daughter. She adopted the baby as her own son. The king's daughter named him Moses, because she had pulled him out of the water.

A Prince of Egypt

Moses was born about 300 years after Joseph died. His parents were named Amram and Jochebed. His father was a priest, a descendant of Aaron. No one really knows who the princess was that rescued Moses. One idea is that she was Hatshepsut. This princess was married to Thutmose II. After her husband died, she ruled Egypt, but she had no children to take over the throne after her death. She would have raised Moses to become the future ruler of the Egyptian nation. (See Acts 7:21-22.)

Column from Queen Hatshepsut's Temple

Think About This

God protected Moses (Exodus 2:9). He promises to protect his children. See 1 Samuel 2:9; Psalm 9:9; 121:8 and 2 Thessalonians 3:3.

Moses' name means "the one who was pulled from the water."

Not only did God protect Moses from being killed, he also provided money for Moses' parents. The princess paid his own mother to take care of him. Of course, she didn't know that the woman was the baby's mother.

Moses was floating in the Nile River. The Egyptians worshiped this river because they depended on it to supply food and water.

58

GENESIS **EXODUS** LEVITICUS NUMBERS DEUTERONOMY JOSHUA JUDGES RUTH 1 SAMUEL 2 SAMUEL 1 KINGS 2 KINGS 1 CHRONICLES 2 CHRONICLES EZRA NEHEMIAH ESTHER JOB PSALMS PROVERBS

EXODUS

Things You Should Know

Moses may have been taught to look down on the Hebrew slaves as lowly, uneducated people. He could read and write because he was raised as an Egyptian prince. He may have thought that the job of being a shepherd was degrading. But when he had to run away from his royal life in Egypt, he became a shepherd.

God has a plan and is in control of all situations. Because Moses was raised as a prince and learned to read and write, he was able to record God's words in the first five books of the Bible.

Moses ran to Midian, which was about 200 miles southeast of Egypt. It was named for one of Abraham's sons.

Moses Goes to Midian

Exodus 2:11-25

Moses was a Hebrew baby boy, who should have been killed at birth. But God protected him, and he grew up in the Egyptian palace as a prince. His own mother was paid to be his babysitter.

Moses Helps His People

2 ¹¹Moses grew and became a man. One day he visited his people, the Hebrews. He saw that they were forced to work very hard. He saw an Egyptian beating a Hebrew man, one of Moses' own people. ¹²Moses looked all around and saw that no one was watching. So he killed the Egyptian and hid his body in the sand.

¹³The next day Moses returned and saw two Hebrew men fighting each other. He saw that one man was in the wrong. Moses said to that man, "Why are you hitting one of your own people?"

¹⁴The man answered, "Who made you our ruler and judge? Are you going to kill me as you killed the Egyptian?"

Then Moses was afraid. He thought, "Now everyone knows what I did."

¹⁵When the king heard about what Moses had done, he tried to kill Moses. But Moses ran away from the king and went to live in the land of Midian. There he sat down near a well.

59

ECCLESIASTES SONG OF SONGS ISAIAH JEREMIAH LAMENTATIONS EZEKIEL DANIEL HOSEA JOEL AMOS OBADIAH JONAH MICAH NAHUM HABAKKUK ZEPHANIAH HAGGAI ZECHARIAH MALACHI

Moses in Midian

[16]There was a priest in Midian who had seven daughters. His daughters went to that well to get water for their father's sheep. They were trying to fill the water troughs for their father's sheep. [17]But some shepherds came and chased the girls away. Then Moses defended the girls and watered their sheep.

[18]Then they went back to their father, Reuel, also called Jethro. He asked them, "Why have you come home early today?"

[19]The girls answered, "The shepherds chased us away. But an Egyptian defended us. He got water for us and watered our sheep."

[20]He asked his daughters, "Where is this man? Why did you leave him? Invite him to eat with us."

[21]Moses agreed to stay with Jethro. And he gave his daughter Zipporah to Moses to be his wife. [22]Zipporah gave birth to a son, and Moses named him Gershom. Moses named him this because Moses was a stranger in a land that was not his own.

[23]After a long time, the king of Egypt died. The people of Israel groaned because they were forced to work very hard. They cried for help. And God heard them. [24]God heard their cries, and he remembered the agreement he had made with Abraham, Isaac and Jacob. [25]God saw the troubles of the people of Israel, and he was concerned about them.

Think About This

Moses' life can be divided into 40-year sections:

1st 40 years: From his birth to his escape to Midian. During this time, he lived as a prince in Egypt. He was trained in language, the arts and military strategy as he prepared to become king.

2nd 40 years: He was a shepherd in Midian. He married Zipporah and had two sons. While in Midian, Moses reconnected with the true God, instead of the many gods of the Egyptians.

3rd 40 years: He led the people out of Egypt and through the desert to the Promised Land. He was God's spokesman to the people.

Seeing God

God heard the prayers of his people and cared about them (Exodus 2:24-25).

He hears your prayers and cares about your problems, too. See 1 Peter 3:12 and 1 John 5:14-15.

60

GENESIS **EXODUS** LEVITICUS NUMBERS DEUTERONOMY JOSHUA JUDGES RUTH 1 SAMUEL 2 SAMUEL 1 KINGS 2 KINGS 1 CHRONICLES 2 CHRONICLES EZRA NEHEMIAH ESTHER JOB PSALMS PROVERBS

EXODUS

Things You Should Know

The first mention of "the angel of the Lord" is in Exodus 3, where he appeared to Moses in "flames of fire coming out of a bush." God was often present among his people during their experiences in Exodus.

Moses' encounter with the burning bush most likely took place on Mt. Sinai. The Old Testament records many important events that happened there. Some people believe it is the mountain called Jebel Musa today—a very rugged, steep mountain just north of the Red Sea.

Other events at Mt. Sinai:

- The Hebrews camped there after leaving Egypt.

- God gave the Ten Commandments to Moses.

- God spoke to the prophet Elijah.

The Burning Bush

Exodus 3:1-22

Moses was now a shepherd who wandered around the desert searching for food and water for his sheep. But God had saved him from death when he was born, and he had a job for Moses to do.

3 One day Moses was taking care of Jethro's sheep. Jethro was the priest of Midian and also Moses' father-in-law. Moses led the sheep to the west side of the desert. He came to Sinai, the mountain of God. ²There the angel of the Lord appeared to Moses in flames of fire coming out of a bush. Moses saw that the bush was on fire, but it was not burning up. ³So Moses said, "I will go closer to this strange thing. How can a bush continue burning without burning up?"

⁴The Lord saw Moses was coming to look at the bush. So God called to him from the bush, "Moses, Moses!"

And Moses said, "Here I am."

⁵Then God said, "Do not come any closer. Take off your sandals. You are standing on holy ground. ⁶I am the God of your ancestors. I am the God of Abraham, the God of Isaac and the God of Jacob." Moses covered his face because he was afraid to look at God.

⁷The Lord said, "I have seen the troubles my people have suffered in Egypt. And I have heard their cries when the Egyptian slave masters hurt them. I am concerned about their pain. ⁸I have come down to save them from the Egyptians. I will bring them out of that land. I will lead them to a good land with lots of room. This is a land where much food grows. This is the land of these people: the Canaanites, Hittites, Amorites, Perizzites, Hivites and Jebusites. ⁹I have heard the cries of the people of Israel. I have seen the way the Egyptians have made life hard for them. ¹⁰So now I am sending you to the king of Egypt. Go! Bring my people, the Israelites, out of Egypt!"

¹¹But Moses said to God, "I am not a great man! Why should I be the one to go to the king and

61

ECCLESIASTES SONG OF SONGS ISAIAH JEREMIAH LAMENTATIONS EZEKIEL DANIEL HOSEA JOEL AMOS OBADIAH JONAH MICAH NAHUM HABAKKUK ZEPHANIAH HAGGAI ZECHARIAH MALACHI

lead the Israelites out of Egypt?"

[12]God said, "I will be with you. This will be the proof that I am sending you: You will lead the people out of Egypt. Then all of you will worship me on this mountain."

[13]Moses said to God, "When I go to the Israelites, I will say to them, 'The God of your ancestors sent me to you.' What if the people say, 'What is his name?' What should I tell them?"

[14]Then God said to Moses, "I AM WHO I AM. When you go to the people of Israel, tell them, 'I AM sent me to you.' "

> ### YHWH: the Name of God
>
> There are many names of God given in the  Bible. But this name, YHWH, is the one God called himself. In Exodus 3:14 God says, "I AM WHO I AM." That is the translation of YHWH. Today we refer to this name as Yahweh. This name is always connected to God's covenant with Israel.

[15]God also said to Moses, "This is what you should tell the people: 'The Lord is the God of your ancestors. He is the God of Abraham, the God of Isaac and the God of Jacob. And he sent me to you.' This will always be my name. That is how people from now on will know me.

[16]"Go and gather the elders and tell them this: 'The Lord, the God of your ancestors, has appeared to me. The God of Abraham, Isaac and Jacob spoke to me. He says: I care about you, and I have seen what has happened to you in Egypt. [17]I have decided that I will take you away from the troubles you are suffering in Egypt. I will lead you to the land of the Canaanites, Hittites, Amorites, Perizzites, Hivites and Jebusites. This land grows much food.'

[18]"The elders will listen to you. And then you and the elders of Israel will go to the king of Egypt. You will tell him, 'The Lord, the God of the Hebrews, appeared to us. Let us travel three days into the desert. There we must offer sacrifices to the Lord our God.'

[19]"But I know that the king of Egypt will not let you go. Only a great power will force him to let you go. [20]So I will use my great power against Egypt. I will make miracles happen in that land. After I do this, he will let you go. [21]And I will cause the Egyptian people to think well of the people of Israel. So when you leave, they will give gifts to your people. [22]Each Hebrew woman will ask her Egyptian neighbor and any Egyptian woman living in her house for gifts. Ask for silver, gold and clothing. You will put those gifts on your children when you leave Egypt. In this way you will take with you the riches of the Egyptians."

Think About This

God told Moses to take his sandals off before approaching the burning bush. In ancient times not many people could afford shoes. However, when traveling a long distance or over rough ground, sandals were worn. In Old Testament times shoes were removed before entering a house or place of worship. It was a sign of respect to do so. By telling Moses to remove his shoes, God was indicating his presence and commanding respect.

God had "come down" to save his people (Exodus 3:8). He had heard their prayers, and he cared about their problems. However, he wanted to use Moses to lead the people to freedom.

Moses would lead the people to the Promised Land (3:8). God had promised this land to Abraham (Genesis 12:7). It was called "a land flowing with milk and honey," which meant there would be plenty of food and water there for the whole nation.

62

GENESIS **EXODUS** LEVITICUS NUMBERS DEUTERONOMY JOSHUA JUDGES RUTH 1 SAMUEL 2 SAMUEL 1 KINGS 2 KINGS 1 CHRONICLES 2 CHRONICLES EZRA NEHEMIAH ESTHER JOB PSALMS PROVERBS

EXODUS

Proof for Moses

Exodus 4:1-23

God wants to free his people from slavery. He speaks to Moses from a burning bush and tells him to lead the people out of Egypt. Moses says he can't do it. God proves to Moses that he's the man for the job.

4 Then Moses answered, "What if the people of Israel do not believe me or listen to me? What if they say, 'The Lord did not appear to you'?"

²The Lord said to him, "What is that in your hand?"

Moses answered, "It is my walking stick."

³The Lord said, "Throw it on the ground."

So Moses threw it on the ground. And it became a snake. Moses ran from the snake. ⁴But the Lord said to him, "Reach out and grab the snake by its tail." So Moses reached out and took hold of the snake. When he did this, it again became a stick in his hand. ⁵The Lord said, "When this happens, the Israelites will believe that the Lord appeared to you. I am the God of their ancestors. I am the God of Abraham, the God of Isaac and the God of Jacob."

⁶Then the Lord said to Moses, "Put your hand inside your coat." So Moses put his hand inside his coat. When he took his hand out, it was white with a harmful skin disease.

⁷Then the Lord said, "Now put your hand inside your coat again." So Moses put his hand inside his coat again. When he took it out, his hand was healthy again. It was like the rest of his skin.

⁸Then the Lord said, "The people may not believe you or be convinced by the first miracle. They may believe you when you show them this second miracle. ⁹After these two miracles they still may not believe or listen to you. Then take some water from the Nile River. Pour it on the dry ground. The water will become blood when it touches the ground."

¹⁰But Moses said to the Lord, "But Lord, I am not a skilled speaker. I have never been able to speak well. And now, even after talking to you, I am not a good speaker. I speak slowly and can't find the best words."

Think About This

Moses gave God five excuses why he couldn't lead the people out of Egypt:

1. No ability (Exodus 3:11)

2. Nothing to say (3:13)

3. No authority (4:1)

4. Couldn't speak well (4:10)

5. Wanted someone else to do it (4:13)

God answered each excuse with a miracle that showed Moses God's presence and power.

When God calls you to do a job, he will help you do it. See:

Philippians 4:13 (Christ gives strength for any job).

Galatians 1:12 (Jesus instructs in what to say).

Matthew 28:18-20 (Jesus gives his followers authority).

1 Corinthians 12:27 (Each person has a job to do and is necessary to God's work).

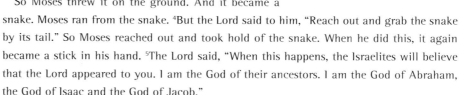

63

ECCLESIASTES SONG OF SONGS ISAIAH JEREMIAH LAMENTATIONS EZEKIEL DANIEL HOSEA JOEL AMOS OBADIAH JONAH MICAH NAHUM HABAKKUK ZEPHANIAH HAGGAI ZECHARIAH MALACHI

[11]Then the Lord said to him, "Who made man's mouth? And who makes him deaf or not able to speak? Or who gives a man sight or makes him blind? It is I, the Lord. [12]Now go! I will help you speak. I will tell you what to say."

[13]But Moses said, "Please, Lord, send someone else."

[14]The Lord became angry with Moses. He said, "Your brother Aaron, from the family of Levi, is a skilled speaker. He is already coming to meet you. And he will be happy when he sees you. [15]I will tell you what to say. Then you will tell Aaron. I will help both of you know what to say and do. [16]And Aaron will speak to the people for you. You will tell him what God says. And he will speak for you. [17]Take your walking stick with you. Use it to do the miracles."

Moses Returns to Egypt

[18]Then Moses went back to Jethro, his father-in-law. Moses said to him, "Let me go back to my people in Egypt. I want to see if they are still alive."

Jethro said to Moses, "You may go. Have a safe trip."

[19]While Moses was still in Midian, the Lord said to him, "Go back to Egypt. The men who wanted to kill you are dead now."

[20]So Moses took his wife and his sons and put them on a donkey. Then he started back to Egypt. He took with him the walking stick of God.

[21]The Lord said to Moses, "When you get back to Egypt, do all the miracles. I have given you the power to do them. Show them to the king of Egypt. But I will make the king very stubborn. He will not let the people go. [22]Then say to the king: 'This is what the Lord says: Israel is my firstborn son. [23]And I told you to let my son go. Let him go so he may worship me. But you refused to let Israel go. So I will kill your firstborn son.' "

Exodus 4:21

Many times in history God has shown that he has power over all earthly rulers. Moses needed to believe in this power. God showed that he would perform miracles to help Moses and that he would harden the king's heart in order to show his power to all the Egyptians.

God's name "YHWH" means the one who is always present.

Exodus 4:22-23

If the king refused to let the Israelites leave—even after seeing God's awesome power—the firstborn sons of all the Egyptians would die. However, God would save the firstborn sons of the Israelites. Later, God would send his firstborn Son, Jesus, to save people from their sins.

64

GENESIS **EXODUS** LEVITICUS NUMBERS DEUTERONOMY JOSHUA JUDGES RUTH 1 SAMUEL 2 SAMUEL 1 KINGS 2 KINGS 1 CHRONICLES 2 CHRONICLES EZRA NEHEMIAH ESTHER JOB PSALMS PROVERBS

EXODUS

The Plagues

Exodus 7:20-21; 8:5-6, 16-17, 20-21; 9:3-4, 8-9, 22-25; 10:12-14, 21-23; 11:4-7

Think About This

The order of the first nine plagues was a natural progression of nature. For example, the water in the river went bad, so fish died and frogs came on land. The frogs died, and gnats and flies came to feed on their bodies. The flies became carriers of diseases and bit the farm animals and made them sick. They also bit people, giving them boils and sores. The hailstorm killed part of the crops; the locusts (not unusual, especially after heavy rains) came to feed on the rest of them. The darkness could have been from thick dust clouds due to the empty fields and flooding from the rains. However, God controlled when all these things happened. Moses told the king to tell him when to pray for the frogs to go away. Then Moses said, "What you want will happen. By this you will know that there is no one like the Lord our God" (Exodus 8:9-10).

God called Moses to lead the Israelite people out of Egypt and away from slavery. But the king wouldn't let them leave. However, God is in control, even of kings. He showed his power and might to the Egyptian king through nine plagues, but still the king would not let the people go. The tenth plague—the last one—was more terrible than the king could have ever imagined.

The Water Becomes Blood

7 ²⁰So Moses and Aaron did just as the Lord had commanded. Aaron raised his walking stick and struck the water in the Nile River. He did this in front of the king and his officers. So all the water in the Nile changed into blood. ²¹The fish in the Nile died, and the river began

to stink. So the Egyptians could not drink water from it. Blood was everywhere in the land of Egypt.

The Frogs

8 ⁵Then the Lord said to Moses, "Tell Aaron to hold his walking stick in his hand over the rivers, canals and ponds. Make frogs come up out of the water onto the land of Egypt."

⁶So Aaron held his hand over all the waters of Egypt. The frogs came up out of the water and covered the land of Egypt. ⁷The magicians used their tricks to do the same thing. So even more frogs came up onto the land of Egypt.

65

ECCLESIASTES SONG OF SONGS ISAIAH JEREMIAH LAMENTATIONS EZEKIEL DANIEL HOSEA JOEL AMOS OBADIAH JONAH MICAH NAHUM HABAKKUK ZEPHANIAH HAGGAI ZECHARIAH MALACHI

The Gnats

[16]Then the Lord said to Moses, "Tell Aaron to raise his walking stick and strike the dust on the ground. Then everywhere in Egypt the dust will change into gnats." [17]They did this. Aaron raised the walking stick that was in his hand and struck the dust on the ground. Then everywhere in Egypt the dust changed into gnats. The gnats got on the people and animals.

The Flies

[20]The Lord told Moses, "Get up early in the morning. Meet the king of Egypt as he goes out to the river. Tell him, 'This is what the Lord says: Let my people go so they can worship me. [21]If you don't let them go, I will send swarms of flies. I will send them into your houses. The flies will be on you, your officers and your people. The houses of Egypt will be full of flies. And they will be all over the ground, too.'"

The Disease on the Farm Animals

9 "Then the Lord will punish you. He will send a terrible disease on all your farm animals. He will cause all of your horses, donkeys, camels, cattle and sheep to become sick. [4]But the Lord will treat Israel's animals differently from the animals of Egypt. None of the animals that belong to the Israelites will die.'"

FAQs

Q: Why did God send plagues on Egypt?

A: God had two reasons for the plagues. One was to show his own people, the Israelites, the strength and power of their God. The second was to show the Egyptians the weaknesses and ineffectiveness of their many gods.

The Boils

[8]The Lord said to Moses and Aaron, "Fill your hands with the ashes from a furnace. Moses, throw the ashes into the air in front of the king of Egypt. [9]The ashes will spread like dust through all the land of Egypt. The dust will cause boils to break out and become sores on the skin. These sores will be on people and animals everywhere in the land."

Behind the Story

The King of Egypt with whom Moses was dealing was probably Amenhotep II.

Moses was 80 years old and Aaron was 83 when they began asking the king to let the Israelites leave Egypt.

The king offered compromises to Moses four times.

1. In Exodus 8:25 he said, "Offer sacrifices to your God here in this country."

2. In 8:28 he said, "You may offer sacrifices to the Lord your God in the desert."

3. In 10:11 he said, "Only the men may go and worship the Lord."

4. In 10:24 he said, "All of you may go and worship the Lord. . . . But you must leave your sheep and cattle here.

Moses refused every compromise.

66

GENESIS **EXODUS** LEVITICUS NUMBERS DEUTERONOMY JOSHUA JUDGES RUTH 1 SAMUEL 2 SAMUEL 1 KINGS 2 KINGS 1 CHRONICLES 2 CHRONICLES EZRA NEHEMIAH ESTHER JOB PSALMS PROVERBS

EXODUS

Plague Info

The Egyptians worshiped the Nile River. They depended on it for water to drink; to water their crops; and they did ritual bathing in it to honor their gods. The first plague, against the river, showed that only God must be worshiped.

The plagues fulfilled God's promise to his people given in Exodus 3:19-20: The King of Egypt "will let you go."

The Israelites were protected from at least some of the plagues. Beginning with the fourth plague, the flies, God specifically said that his people would be spared (8:22). He also promised this with many of the following plagues. The Egyptians definitely would have noticed that the Israelites were spared.

Moses announced some of the plagues to the king before they happened. Some just came without announcement. The pattern was that two were predicted, and the third came with no warning.

The Hail

²²The Lord told Moses, "Raise your hand toward the sky. Then the hail will start falling over all the land of Egypt. It will fall on people, animals and on everything that grows in the fields of Egypt." ²³So Moses raised his walking stick toward the sky. And the Lord sent thunder and hail. And lightning flashed down to the earth. So he caused hail to fall upon the land of Egypt. ²⁴There was hail, and there was lightning flashing as it hailed. This was the worst hailstorm in Egypt since it had become a nation. ²⁵The hail destroyed everything that was in the fields in all the land of Egypt. The hail destroyed both people and animals. It also destroyed everything that grew in the fields. It broke all the trees in the fields.

LOCUST FACTS

A locust can eat enough food to match its own weight every day. One square mile of a swarm of locusts contains 200 million insects. A swarm large enough to fill Egypt could have been over 75 billion locusts!

The Locusts

10 ¹²The Lord told Moses, "Raise your hand over the land of Egypt, and the locusts will come. They will spread all over the land of Egypt. They will eat all the plants that the hail did not destroy."

¹³So Moses raised his walking stick over the land of Egypt. And the Lord caused a strong wind to blow from the east. It blew across the land all that day and night. When morning came, the east wind had brought the locusts. ¹⁴Swarms of locusts covered all the land of Egypt and settled everywhere. There were more locusts than ever before or after.

67

ECCLESIASTES SONG OF SONGS ISAIAH JEREMIAH LAMENTATIONS EZEKIEL DANIEL HOSEA JOEL AMOS OBADIAH JONAH MICAH NAHUM HABAKKUK ZEPHANIAH HAGGAI ZECHARIAH MALACHI

The Darkness

[21]Then the Lord told Moses, "Raise your hand toward the sky, and darkness will cover the land of Egypt. It will be so dark you will be able to feel it." [22]So Moses raised his hand toward the sky. Then total darkness was everywhere in Egypt for three days. [23]No one could see anyone else. And no one could go anywhere for three days. But the Israelites had light where they lived.

The Death of the Firstborn

11 [4]So Moses said to the king, "This is what the Lord says: 'About midnight tonight I will go through all Egypt. [5]Every firstborn son in the land of Egypt will die. The firstborn son of the king, who sits on his throne, will die. Even the firstborn of the slave girl grinding grain will die. Also the firstborn farm animals will die. [6]There will be loud crying everywhere in Egypt. It will be worse than any time before or after this. [7]But not even a dog will bark at the Israelites or their animals.' Then you will know that the Lord treats Israel differently from Egypt."

Painting by C.F. Vos

The Passover

God gave specific plans for his people to follow in order to be protected from the last plague. Each family was to sacrifice a healthy year-old male lamb. They were to take blood from it and smear it on the wood around their doorways. Then they were to cook the meat and eat it along with herbs and unleavened bread (bread that has no yeast in it). When the death angel passed through Egypt, he would see the blood on the doors and pass by the homes of the Israelites, therefore sparing their firstborn sons.

The Passover lamb was a "type" of Jesus who is called the Lamb of God who takes away the sins of the world (John 1:29). Just as the blood of the Passover lamb protected the Israelites from death, Jesus' blood, shed on the cross, protects believers from eternal death.

The Pride of the King

Following each of the first five plagues, the king hardened his heart. He became more and more stubborn about obeying and honoring God. After that, God hardened the king's heart.

After the seventh plague, the king admitted that he had sinned (Exodus 9:27). He repeated that confession after the eighth plague, but never softened his heart toward God.

God does not want his people to be proud of their own abilities and not submit to him. See Psalms 18:27; 147:6.

God was very specific that the Israelites would not experience the last plague—the death of their firstborn. Moses told the king that even his servants would beg Moses to take his people out of Egypt.

68

GENESIS **EXODUS** LEVITICUS NUMBERS DEUTERONOMY JOSHUA JUDGES RUTH 1 SAMUEL 2 SAMUEL 1 KINGS 2 KINGS 1 CHRONICLES 2 CHRONICLES EZRA NEHEMIAH ESTHER JOB PSALMS PROVERBS

EXODUS

When Did the People of Israel Leave Egypt?

There are a few theories as to the date. The "early date" is 1445 B.C. This is based upon the date that construction began on the Temple, which was 480 years after the people of Israel left Egypt (1 Kings 6:1).

The "late date" theory puts the Israelites leaving at 1260 B.C. The difference is due to the interpretation of the 480 years actually meaning 12 generations. Allowing 25 years per generation brings the number of years down to 300.

Think About This

Exodus 12:31 states that 600,000 Israelite men marched out of Egypt. Add in the women and children, and the number of Israelites would have been close to 2 million!

Other people who were not Israelites went with them. Perhaps they had seen the way God protected his people, and they wanted to follow him, too (12:38).

The People of Israel Leave Egypt

Exodus 12:31-51

God sent ten terrible plagues on the Egyptian people to convince the king to let the Israelites leave Egypt. Finally after the last plague, the death of all firstborn children, the king let them leave.

Israel Leaves Egypt

12 [31]During the night the king called for Moses and Aaron. He said to them, "Get up and leave my people. You and your people may do as you have asked. Go and worship the Lord. [32]Take all of your sheep and cattle as you have asked. Go. And also bless me." [33]The Egyptians also asked the Israelites to hurry and leave. They said, "If you don't leave, we will all die!"

[34]The people of Israel took their dough before the yeast was added. They wrapped the bowls for making dough in clothing and carried them on their shoulders. [35]The people of Israel did what Moses told them to do. They asked their Egyptian neighbors for things made of silver

and gold and for clothing. [36]The Lord caused the Egyptians to think well of the Israelites. So the Israelites took rich gifts from the Egyptians.

[37]The Israelites traveled from Rameses to Succoth. There were about 600,000 men walking. This does not include the women and children. [38]Many other people who were not Israelites went with them. A large number of sheep, goats and cattle went with them. [39]The Israelites used the dough they had brought out of Egypt. They baked loaves of bread without yeast. The dough had no yeast in it because they had been rushed out of Egypt. So they had no time to get food ready for their trip.

69

ECCLESIASTES SONG OF SONGS ISAIAH JEREMIAH LAMENTATIONS EZEKIEL DANIEL HOSEA JOEL AMOS OBADIAH JONAH MICAH NAHUM HABAKKUK ZEPHANIAH HAGGAI ZECHARIAH MALACHI

[40]The people of Israel had lived in Egypt for 430 years. [41]On the day the 430 years ended, the Lord's divisions of people left Egypt. [42]That night the Lord kept watch to bring them out of Egypt. So on this same night the Israelites are to keep watch. They are to do this to honor the Lord from now on.

[43]The Lord told Moses and Aaron, "Here are the rules for Passover: No foreigner is to eat the Passover. [44]Suppose a person buys a slave and circumcises him. Then the slave may eat the Passover. [45]But no one who lives for a short time in your country may eat it. No hired worker may eat it.

[46]"The meal must be eaten inside the house. None of the meat is to be taken outside the house. Don't break any of the bones. [47]The whole community of Israel must take part in this feast. [48]A foreigner who lives with you may share in the Lord's Passover. But first all the males in his house must be circumcised. Then, since he will be like a citizen of Israel, he may share in the meal. But a man who is not circumcised may not eat the Passover meal. [49]The same rules apply to an Israelite born in the country. And they apply to a foreigner living there."

[50]So all the Israelites did just as the Lord had commanded Moses and Aaron. [51]Then on that same day, the Lord led the Israelites out of Egypt. The people left by divisions.

Passover Info

God instructed the Israelites to always remember the Passover. It is associated with the Feast of Unleavened Bread (Exodus 12:17). The people took unleavened bread when they left Egypt in a hurry. When leaven is added to bread, it sometimes takes hours for the bread to rise. Unleavened bread is flat, more like a cracker.

Exodus 12:46

The Passover lamb was to have no broken bones. This lamb was a "type" or reminder of what Jesus would be. Even through the cruel punishment he suffered before his death, Jesus had no broken bones. See John 19:33-36.

The Israelites remembered (and still celebrate today) the many ways God took care of them. Read Psalm 105 to celebrate God's faithfulness.

The Seder

The Passover Feast is called the Seder. It begins with the lighting of candles to signify the start of the holiday.

Six foods are part of the Seder feast, and they each have a special meaning:

- The first two are a mixture of bitter herbs, symbolizing the difficult time of slavery in Egypt.
- Third is a chopped mixture of nuts, cinnamon and apples, symbolizing the mortar used to make bricks in Egypt.
- Fourth is a different herb or vegetable dipped in salt water. This reminds the people of the simple life and food the Israelites had in Egypt.
- Fifth is roasted meat, either lamb or chicken, remembering the Passover lamb.
- Sixth is a roasted egg, recalling the sacrifice offered in the Temple.

70

GENESIS **EXODUS** LEVITICUS NUMBERS DEUTERONOMY JOSHUA JUDGES RUTH 1 SAMUEL 2 SAMUEL 1 KINGS 2 KINGS 1 CHRONICLES 2 CHRONICLES EZRA NEHEMIAH ESTHER JOB PSALMS PROVERBS

EXODUS

Crossing the Red Sea

Exodus 14:1-31

The Egyptian king finally allowed the Israelites to leave Egypt. God led them through the desert. They camped next to the Red Sea.

Behind the Story

From the time the Israelites left Egypt, they had a visible sign of God's presence. Exodus 13:21-22 states that a pillar of cloud went before them in the daytime, and a pillar of fire led them at night and gave them light. All they had to do to be assured of God's presence was look up. This is known as God's shekinah glory and is seen several times throughout Scripture.

God had one more plan to show his power and authority to the king of Egypt. He instructed Moses to lead the people in a way that made the king think they were lost. Then the Egyptian army would come to bring the people back, and God would defeat them once and for all (14:3-4).

The story of God parting the Red Sea is told twice, in consecutive chapters. Exodus 14 is the story form. Exodus 15 is the story told in Moses' song of praise to God.

14 Then the Lord said to Moses, [2]"Tell the Israelites to turn back to Pi Hahiroth. Tell them to camp for the night between Migdol and the Red Sea. This is near Baal Zephon. [3]The king will think, 'The Israelites are lost, trapped by the desert.' [4]I will make the king stubborn again so he will chase after them. But I will defeat the king and his army. This will bring honor to me. Then the people of Egypt will know that I am the Lord." The people of Israel did just as they were told.

The King Chases the Israelites

[5]The king of Egypt was told that the people of Israel had already left. Then he and his officers changed their minds about them. They said, "What have we done? We have let the people of Israel leave. We have lost our slaves!" [6]So the king prepared his war chariot and took his army with him. [7]He took 600 of his best chariots. He also took all the other chariots of Egypt.

71

ECCLESIASTES SONG OF SONGS ISAIAH JEREMIAH LAMENTATIONS EZEKIEL DANIEL HOSEA JOEL AMOS OBADIAH JONAH MICAH NAHUM HABAKKUK ZEPHANIAH HAGGAI ZECHARIAH MALACHI

Each chariot had an officer in it. [8]The Lord made the king of Egypt stubborn. So he chased the Israelites, who were leaving victoriously. [9]The king of Egypt came with his horses, chariot drivers and army. And they chased the Israelites. They caught up with the Israelites while they were camped by the Red Sea. This was near Pi Hahiroth and Baal Zephon.

[10]The Israelites saw the king and his army coming after them. They were very frightened and cried to the Lord for help. [11]They said to Moses, "What have you done to us? Why did you bring us out of Egypt to die in the desert? There were plenty of graves for us in Egypt. [12]We told you in Egypt, 'Let us alone! Let us stay and serve the Egyptians.' Now we will die in the desert."

God's Shekinah Glory

Shekinah means "dwelling place of God" in Hebrew. It refers to the visible presence of God. The word "shekinah" is never used in Scripture, but God's presence is referred to in many ways.

Other places where his presence is recorded include:

- At Mt. Sinai when God spoke to Moses (Exodus 24:15-18)

- In the Most Holy Place within the Meeting Tent (Leviticus 16:2)

- At the angel's announcement of Jesus' birth (Luke 2:9)

- On a mountain where Moses and Elijah appeared and talked with Jesus (Mark 9:2-7)

- On clouds in the sky when Jesus returns (Matthew 24:30)

Think About This

The Israelites had spent over 400 years in Egypt where various parts of nature were worshiped as gods. Their leaving Egypt became a marking point for the people to worship God, based on an event or situation where they obviously saw his care for them.

The Israelites had the visible sign of God's presence with them; but they still let fear take over, and they complained to Moses (Exodus 14:11-12). This was the first of many times they would show lack of faith by their complaining.

What Sea?

The Red Sea itself is a huge body of water that stretches nearly 1,200 miles from north to south. There are several other bodies of water associated with this region. Some experts say that "Red Sea" has been mistranslated through the years, and the ancient text actually says "Sea of Reeds."

Most theologians believe the Israelites crossed one of the smaller seas of this region, which also would have been called the Red Sea.

72

GENESIS **EXODUS** LEVITICUS NUMBERS DEUTERONOMY JOSHUA JUDGES RUTH 1 SAMUEL 2 SAMUEL 1 KINGS 2 KINGS 1 CHRONICLES 2 CHRONICLES EZRA NEHEMIAH ESTHER JOB PSALMS PROVERBS

EXODUS

God's Salvation

In Exodus 14:13 Moses told the people that God would save them. The Hebrew word for "salvation" gives the idea of space or freedom.

God could have done a miracle and just wiped out the Egyptian army to protect the people. But he asked the people to play a part in their own salvation. All they had to do was obey him . . . and walk (14:15-16).

Behind the Story

Moses raised his walking stick over the sea (14:16). This is the same stick that God turned into a snake and was used in the miracles of the plagues.

God protected his people, front and back. The pillar of his presence brought confusion to the Egyptians, but protection and comfort to the Israelites (14:19-20).

¹³But Moses answered, "Don't be afraid! Stand still and see the Lord save you today. You will never see these Egyptians again after today. ¹⁴You will only need to remain calm. The Lord will fight for you."

¹⁵Then the Lord said to Moses, "Why are you crying out to me? Command the people of Israel to start moving. ¹⁶Raise your walking stick and hold it over the sea. The sea will split. Then the people can cross the sea on dry land. ¹⁷I have made the Egyptians stubborn so they will chase the Israelites. But I will be honored when I defeat the king and all of his chariot drivers and chariots. ¹⁸I will defeat the king, his chariot drivers and chariots. Then Egypt will know that I am the Lord."

¹⁹The angel of God usually traveled in front of Israel's army. Now the angel of God moved behind them. Also, the pillar of cloud moved from in front of the people and stood behind them. ²⁰So the cloud came between the Egyptians and the people of Israel. The cloud made it dark for the Egyptians. But it gave light to the Israelites. So the cloud kept the two armies apart all night.

²¹Moses held his hand over the sea. All that night the Lord drove back the sea with a strong east wind. And so he made the sea become dry ground. The water was split. ²²And the Israelites went through the sea on dry land. A wall of water was on both sides.

²³Then all the king's horses, chariots and chariot drivers followed them into the sea. ²⁴Between two

73

ECCLESIASTES SONG OF SONGS ISAIAH JEREMIAH LAMENTATIONS EZEKIEL DANIEL HOSEA JOEL AMOS OBADIAH JONAH MICAH NAHUM HABAKKUK ZEPHANIAH HAGGAI ZECHARIAH MALACHI

and six o'clock in the morning, the Lord looked down from the pillar of cloud and fire at the Egyptian army. He made them panic. ²⁵He kept the wheels of the chariots from turning. This made it hard to drive the chariots. The Egyptians shouted, "Let's get away from the Israelites! The Lord is fighting for them and against us Egyptians."

²⁶Then the Lord told Moses, "Hold your hand over the sea. Then the water will come back over the Egyptians, their chariots and chariot drivers." ²⁷So Moses raised his hand over the sea. And at dawn the water became deep again. The Egyptians were trying to run from it. But the Lord swept them away into the sea. ²⁸The water became deep again. It covered the chariots and chariot drivers. So all the king's army that had followed the Israelites into the sea was covered. Not one of them survived.

²⁹But the people of Israel crossed the sea on dry land. There was a wall of water on their right and on their left. ³⁰So that day the Lord saved the Israelites from the Egyptians. And the Israelites saw the Egyptians lying dead on the seashore. ³¹When the people of Israel saw the great power that the Lord had used against the Egyptians, they feared the Lord. And they trusted the Lord and his servant Moses.

Miracles

The Old Testament is filled with stories of God's miracles. Here are some of them:

Creation (Genesis 1–2)

The great flood (Genesis 6–8)

The burning bush (Exodus 3:1-2)

Moses' walking stick (Exodus 4:1-5)

Balaam's donkey (Numbers 22:20-35)

Food for Elijah (1 Kings 17:2-6)

Elijah going to heaven (2 Kings 2:9-11)

The blazing furnace (Daniel 3:21-27)

Handwriting on the wall (Daniel 5:5)

Protection in the lions' den (Daniel 6:16-22)

Jonah and the big fish (Jonah 1:17)

Think About This

God's protection of the Israelites was so obvious that even the Egyptian soldiers acknowledged his power (Exodus 14:25).

The miracle of the crossing of the Red Sea was very important to the Israelite people. They remembered God's protection. Read about it in Psalm 78:52-53; 106:8-11 and Hebrews 11:29.

It may have taken days for the 2 million Israelites to cross the sea with all their animals, tents, and wagons. Meanwhile the Egyptian army, in the king's best chariots pulled by strong horses, would have been coming toward them very quickly.

Consider what God did: He moved his presence between the army and his people. His cloud of presence gave light to the Israelites and covered the army like fog so they couldn't see. He divided the water with a strong wind. When his people were safely on the other side, Moses rasied his hand over the sea, and God made the water come together again.

74

GENESIS **EXODUS** LEVITICUS NUMBERS DEUTERONOMY JOSHUA JUDGES RUTH 1 SAMUEL 2 SAMUEL 1 KINGS 2 KINGS 1 CHRONICLES 2 CHRONICLES EZRA NEHEMIAH ESTHER JOB PSALMS PROVERBS

EXODUS

Food from Heaven

Exodus 16:1-31

God had done amazing miracles to free the Israelites from slavery in Egypt. But now the people complained to Moses that they didn't have enough food. They even said it would have been better if they had stayed in Egypt. Moses went to God with the problem, and he took care of the people again.

Behind the Story

The Israelites had already forgotten that, after the miracle at the Red Sea, they feared God and trusted his servant, Moses (Exodus 14:31).

Even after all God had done to free the people from slavery, their faith was still not very strong. They didn't even trust him to know they were hungry (16:2-3). Each time the people complained, God answered.

God provided food for the people. He did it in a miraculous way so they would know it was from him (16:4). Just as he did at the Red Sea, God provided the miracle; all the people had to do was obey. They were to gather only the food they needed for each day, not to try to save any for the future.

The People Demand Food

16 Then the whole Israelite community left Elim. They came to the Desert of Sin. This place was between Elim and Sinai. They came to this place on the fifteenth day of the second month after they had left Egypt. ²Then the whole Israelite community grumbled to Moses and Aaron in the desert. ³The Israelites said to them, "It would have been better if the Lord had killed us in the land of Egypt. There we had meat to eat. We had all the food we wanted. But you have brought us into this desert. You will starve us to death here."

⁴Then the Lord said to Moses, "I will cause food to fall like rain from the sky. This food will be for all of you. Every day the people must go out and gather what they need for that day. I will do this to see if the people will do what I teach them. ⁵On the sixth day of each week, they are to gather twice as much as they gather on other days. Then they are to prepare it."

⁶So Moses and Aaron said to all the Israelites: "This evening you will know that the Lord is the one who brought you out of Egypt. ⁷Tomorrow morning you will see the greatness of the Lord. He has heard you grumble against him. We are nothing. You are not grumbling against us, but against the Lord." ⁸And Moses said, "Each evening the Lord will give you meat to eat. And every morning he will give you all the bread you want. He will do this because he has heard you grumble against him. You are

75

ECCLESIASTES SONG OF SONGS ISAIAH JEREMIAH LAMENTATIONS EZEKIEL DANIEL HOSEA JOEL AMOS OBADIAH JONAH MICAH NAHUM HABAKKUK ZEPHANIAH HAGGAI ZECHARIAH MALACHI

not grumbling against Aaron and me. You are grumbling against the Lord."

⁹Then Moses said to Aaron, "Speak to the whole community of the Israelites. Say to them, 'Meet together in front of the Lord because he has heard your grumblings.' "

¹⁰So Aaron spoke to the whole community of the Israelites. While he was speaking, they looked toward the desert. There the greatness of the Lord appeared in a cloud.

¹¹The Lord said to Moses, ¹²"I have heard the grumblings of the people of Israel. So tell them, 'At twilight you will eat meat. And every morning you will eat all the bread you want. Then you will know I am the Lord, your God.' "

¹³That evening, quail came and covered the camp. And in the morning dew lay around the camp. ¹⁴When the dew was gone, thin flakes like frost were on the desert ground. ¹⁵When the Israelites saw it, they asked each other, "What is that?" They asked this question because they did not know what it was.

So Moses told them, "This is the bread the Lord has given you to eat. ¹⁶The Lord has commanded, 'Each one of you must gather what he needs. Gather about two quarts for every person in your family.' "

¹⁷So the people of Israel did this. Some people gathered much, and some gathered little. ¹⁸Then they measured it. The person who gathered more did not have too much. The person who gathered less did not have too little. Each person gathered just as much as he needed.

¹⁹Moses said to them, "Don't keep any of it to eat the next day." ²⁰But some of the people did not listen to Moses. They kept part of it to eat the next morning. But it became full of worms and began to stink. So Moses was angry with these people.

Think About This

God's "shekinah glory" appeared to the people once again, assuring them of his presence (Exodus 16:10). Read Psalm 97:2-6 for more about this glory.

The bread God sent from heaven was called manna, which means, "What is it?" It was something the Israelites had never seen before. It couldn't have been a natural occurrence because it appeared every day except on the Sabbath.

Again, even after the people had seen God's power and protection, some of them deliberately disobeyed by gathering more manna than they needed (Exodus 16:20).

God sent manna for the people every day (except Sabbath days) for 40 years (16:35).

76

GENESIS **EXODUS** LEVITICUS NUMBERS DEUTERONOMY JOSHUA JUDGES RUTH 1 SAMUEL 2 SAMUEL 1 KINGS 2 KINGS 1 CHRONICLES 2 CHRONICLES EZRA NEHEMIAH ESTHER JOB PSALMS PROVERBS

EXODUS

God's Day

The people readily complained and forgot God's care for them. God instructed them to set aside a day just to worship him and remember his care. The Sabbath is a day when no work is to be done. God himself set the example for this when he rested on the seventh day after creation.

What Is Worship?

It is a recognition of who God is. A time to see his power and protection. A time of thankfulness for his care. God demands our worship. For help in understanding see:

- Exodus 20:3
- 1 Chronicles 16:34
- Psalm 92:2
- Psalm 96:4
- Psalm 147:7

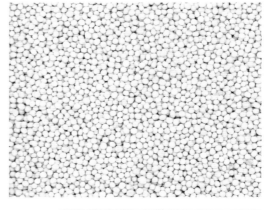

²¹Every morning each person gathered as much food as he needed. But when the sun became hot, it melted away.

²²On the sixth day the people gathered twice as much food. They gathered four quarts for every person. So all the leaders of the community came and told this to Moses. ²³Moses said to them, "This is what the Lord commanded. Tomorrow is the Sabbath, the Lord's holy day of rest. Bake what you want to bake, and boil what you want to boil today. But save the rest of the food until tomorrow morning."

²⁴So the people saved it until the next morning, as Moses had commanded. And none of it began to stink or have worms in it. ²⁵Moses told the people, "Eat the food you gathered yesterday. Today is a Sabbath, the Lord's day of rest. So you will not find any out in the field today. ²⁶You should gather the food for six days. But the seventh day is a Sabbath day. On that day there will not be any food on the ground."

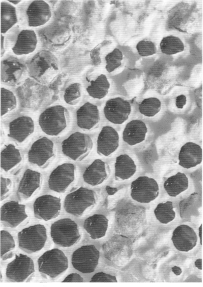

²⁷On the seventh day some of the people went out to gather food, but they couldn't find any. ²⁸Then the Lord said to Moses, "How long will all you people refuse to obey my commands and teachings? ²⁹Look, the Lord has made the Sabbath a day of rest for all of you. So on the sixth day he will give you enough food for two days. But on the Sabbath each of you must stay where you are. Do not leave your house." ³⁰So the people rested on the Sabbath.

³¹The people of Israel called the food manna. The manna was like small white seeds. It tasted like wafers made with honey.

77

ECCLESIASTES SONG OF SONGS ISAIAH JEREMIAH LAMENTATIONS EZEKIEL DANIEL HOSEA JOEL AMOS OBADIAH JONAH MICAH NAHUM HABAKKUK ZEPHANIAH HAGGAI ZECHARIAH MALACHI

The Sabbath

"The Lord has made the Sabbath a day of rest for all of you" (Exodus 16:29).

This is the first time God uses the word "Sabbath." The literal meaning of the word is "rest." Later, in the Ten Commandments, God would tell the people, "Remember to keep the Sabbath as a holy day" (Exodus 20:8). So he was actually saying, "Remember the rest day and keep it holy."

The Sabbath began at sundown on Friday and ended at sundown on Saturday of each week. It was to be a day of complete rest—no cooking, no cleaning, no playing, no work of any kind. It was to be filled with worship for God.

The people's worship of God was also commanded in the Feast of Unleavened Bread, the Feast of Harvest and the Feast of Tents. The Day of Cleansing became an important day for confessing sin and repenting.

For about the first 2,700 years of history, God was the only one who observed the Sabbath (from the week of creation). Now he instructed the people to also set aside a day to rest and worship him.

So why do most people now observe Sunday as their day of worship? Because Christ rose from the dead on Sunday (see Matthew 28:1-6; Mark 16:2-6; Luke 24:1-6; and John 20:1-9).

Worship

Worship is not something to be taken lightly. God is a jealous God and will not share our worship with anything else (Exodus 20:5).

An important part of worship is praising God. Read these verses to focus on his power and love:

- Psalm 65:5-13
- Psalm 103
- Psalm 105
- Psalm 145
- Isaiah 40:29
- John 3:16
- Acts 1:8
- Romans 3:24
- Romans 8:31-39
- Romans 10:13
- 1 John 4:7-12

78

GENESIS **EXODUS** LEVITICUS NUMBERS DEUTERONOMY JOSHUA JUDGES RUTH 1 SAMUEL 2 SAMUEL 1 KINGS 2 KINGS 1 CHRONICLES 2 CHRONICLES EZRA NEHEMIAH ESTHER JOB PSALMS PROVERBS

EXODUS

Jethro's Advice

Exodus 18:1-27

Behind the Story

The Israelites were camped at a place called Rephidim. It was probably in the southern part of the Sinai Peninsula. After God sent manna, he supplied water for the people by having Moses hit a rock.

The bow and kiss that Moses gave Jethro was a sign of respect that one person gave to another.

Moses repeated all that God had done for the people. He told Jethro of God's protection and the salvation of the Israelites (Exodus 18:8-10).

Jethro was the priest of Midian, but he did not necessarily worship only God. The Midianites had several gods; the true God may have been one of them. However, when Jethro heard all that God had done for the people, he believed that God is greater than any of the other gods he may have worshiped (18:11).

The people depended on Moses to solve every problem they had. After he talked to God about their hunger, God sent food. He told God they were thirsty, so God sent water. Moses was spending nearly every moment solving the problems of the people.

Jethro Visits Moses

18 Jethro, Moses' father-in-law, was the priest of Midian. He heard about everything that God had done for Moses and his people, the Israelites. Jethro heard how the Lord had led the Israelites out of Egypt. ²Moses had sent his wife Zipporah to Jethro, his father-in-law. ³Moses had also sent his two sons. The first son was named Gershom. When he was born, Moses said, "I am a stranger in a foreign country." ⁴The other son was named Eliezer. When he was born, Moses said, "The God of my father is my help. He saved me from the king of Egypt."

⁵So Jethro, Moses' father-in-law, went to Moses. Moses was camped in the desert near Sinai, the mountain of God. Moses' wife and his two sons came with Jethro. ⁶Jethro had sent a message ahead to Moses. He said, "I am Jethro, your father-in-law. I am coming to you with your wife and her two sons."

⁷So Moses went out to meet his father-in-law. Moses bowed down and then kissed him. The two men asked about each other's health. Then they went into Moses' tent. ⁸Moses told his father-in-law everything the Lord had done to the king and the Egyptians. The Lord had done these things to help Israel. Moses told about all the problems they had faced along the way. And Moses told him how the Lord had saved them.

⁹Jethro was very happy when he heard all the good things the Lord had done for Israel. He was happy because the Lord had saved them from the Egyptians. ¹⁰Jethro said, "Praise the Lord. He has saved all of you from the Egyptians and their king. He has saved the people from the power of the Egyptians. ¹¹Now I know the Lord is greater than all gods. He did this to those who looked down on Israel." ¹²Then Jethro, Moses' father-in-law, gave a whole burnt offering and other sacrifices to God. Aaron and all the elders of Israel came to Moses' father-in-law. They ate the holy meal together before God.

79

ECCLESIASTES SONG OF SONGS ISAIAH JEREMIAH LAMENTATIONS EZEKIEL DANIEL HOSEA JOEL AMOS OBADIAH JONAH MICAH NAHUM HABAKKUK ZEPHANIAH HAGGAI ZECHARIAH MALACHI

[13]The next day Moses solved disagreements among the people. So the people stood around Moses from morning until night. [14]Moses' father-in-law saw all that Moses was doing for the people. He asked, "What is all this you are doing for the people? Why are you the only one to solve disagreements? All the people are standing around you from morning until night!"

[15]Then Moses said to his father-in-law, "It is because the people come to me for God's help in solving their disagreements. [16]When people have a disagreement, they come to me. I decide who is right. And I tell them God's laws and teachings."

[17]Moses' father-in-law said to him, "You are not doing this right. [18]You and the people who come to you will get too tired. This is too much work for you. You can't do it by yourself. [19]Now listen to me. I will give you some advice. I want God to be with you. You must talk to God for the people. You must tell him about their disagreements. [20]You should tell them the laws

Michaelangelo's Moses

and teachings. Tell them the right way to live and what they should do. [21]But choose some capable men from among the people. Choose men who respect God and who can be trusted. They will not change their decisions for money. Make these men officers over groups of 1,000, 100, 50 and 10 people. [22]Let these officers solve the disagreements among the people all the time. They can bring the hard cases to you. But they can decide the simple cases themselves. That will make it easier for you. These men will share the work with you. [23]Do this if it is what God commands. Then you will be able to do your job. And all the people will go home with their disagreements solved."

[24]So Moses listened to his father-in-law and did everything he said. [25]He chose capable men from all the Israelites. He made them leaders over the people. They were officers over groups of 1,000, 100, 50 and 10 people. [26]These officers solved disagreements among the people all the time. They brought the hard cases to Moses. But they decided the simple cases themselves.

[27]Then Moses let his father-in-law leave. And Jethro went back to his own home.

TAKING IT TO HEART

Father's Wisdom

Moses learned an important lesson from Jethro. He needed to let other people learn to use their gifts and talents. Jethro's encouragement taught him to disciple (train) other men to be leaders (Exodus 18:13-14). The people needed to learn what they could do themselves.

Think About This

Apparently the people didn't go directly to God with their requests and complaints. Moses was their go-between to God. He told the people what God's laws and teachings were. This may have been the beginning of all the laws that are written down in Exodus (Exodus 18:16).

Leadership Qualities

Jethro advised Moses to choose a group of men to help him solve disagreements and govern the people. These men were to have five qualifications:

1. Have some abilities

2. Respect God

3. Be trustworthy

4. Be unable to be bribed

5. Be ranked, so that each one answered to another. That gave them accountability.

Compare this list to 1 Timothy 3:1-13, the qualifications given for leaders in the New Testament church.

80

GENESIS **EXODUS** LEVITICUS NUMBERS DEUTERONOMY JOSHUA JUDGES RUTH 1 SAMUEL 2 SAMUEL 1 KINGS 2 KINGS 1 CHRONICLES 2 CHRONICLES EZRA NEHEMIAH ESTHER JOB PSALMS PROVERBS

EXODUS

Words You Should Know

Covet (Ka-vet)
To want something that belongs to someone else with so much energy that you can't think about anything else. (Exodus 20:17 relates to coveting what other people have.)

Idols (Eye-d'ls)
A false god. The non-Jewish people often worshiped statues they made from wood, stone or metal. They worshiped these idols instead of the true God of heaven (see Leviticus 19:4; 2 Kings 17:12-17; Acts 7:40-43; 17:16-23; 1 Thessalonians 1:9).

Sabbath (SAB-uth)
means "rest." It was the seventh day of the Jewish week, their day of worship to God. The Jews were not allowed to work on this day. Some Jews became angry with Jesus because he healed people on the Sabbath. They thought this was breaking the Old Testament law of the Sabbath (see Exodus 16:23-30; 20:8-11; Matthew 12:9-14; Luke 6:1-11; Acts 18:4; Colossians 2:16-17).

The Ten Commandments

Exodus 20:1-17

Moses led the people from Rephidim through the desert to the foot of Mt. Sinai. They camped there and God called Moses to come up on the mountain. God's presence came with thunder and lightning and a thick cloud (his shekinah glory).

I YOU MUST NOT HAVE ANY OTHER GODS EXCEPT ME

II YOU MUST NOT MAKE FOR YOURSELVES ANY IDOLS

III YOU MUST NOT USE THE NAME OF THE LORD YOUR GOD THOUGHTLESSLY

IV REMEMBER TO KEEP THE SABBATH AS A HOLY DAY

V HONOR YOUR FATHER AND YOUR MOTHER

VI YOU MUST NOT MURDER ANYONE

VII YOU MUST NOT BE GUILTY OF ADULTERY

VIII YOU MUST NOT STEAL

IX YOU MUST NOT TELL LIES ABOUT YOUR NEIGHBOR IN COURT

X YOU MUST NOT WANT TO TAKE ANYTHING THAT BELONGS TO YOUR NEIGHBOR

20 Then God spoke all these words: ²"I am the Lord your God. I brought you out of the land of Egypt where you were slaves.

³**"You must not have any other gods except me.**

⁴**"You must not make for yourselves any idols.**
Don't make something that looks like anything in the sky above or on the earth below or in the water below the land. ⁵You must not worship or serve any idol. This is because I, the Lord your God, am a jealous God. A person may sin against me and hate me. I will punish his children, even his grandchildren and great-grandchildren. ⁶But I will be very kind to thousands who love me and obey my commands.

⁷**"You must not use the name of the Lord your God thoughtlessly.**
The Lord will punish anyone who is guilty and misuses his name.

81

ECCLESIASTES SONG OF SONGS ISAIAH JEREMIAH LAMENTATIONS EZEKIEL DANIEL HOSEA JOEL AMOS OBADIAH JONAH MICAH NAHUM HABAKKUK ZEPHANIAH HAGGAI ZECHARIAH MALACHI

8"Remember to keep the Sabbath as a holy day.
⁹You may work and get everything done during six days each week. ¹⁰But the seventh day is a day of rest to honor the Lord your God. On that day no one may do any work: not you, your son or daughter, or your men or women slaves. Neither your animals nor the foreigners living in your cities may work. ¹¹The reason is that in six days the Lord made everything. He made the sky, earth, sea and everything in them. And on the seventh day, he rested. So the Lord blessed the Sabbath day and made it holy.

¹²"Honor your father and your mother.
Then you will live a long time in the land. The Lord your God is going to give you this land.

¹³"You must not murder anyone.

¹⁴"You must not be guilty of adultery.

¹⁵"You must not steal.

¹⁶"You must not tell lies about your neighbor in court.

¹⁷"You must not want to take your neighbor's house.
You must not want his wife or his men or women slaves. You must not want his ox or his donkey. You must not want to take anything that belongs to your neighbor."

The Law

God made a covenant, or a promise, with the Israelites at Mt. Sinai. It was called the Mosaic Covenant. This covenant had three parts: moral, spiritual and social. The moral part of the covenant instructed them on how to live. That is the Ten Commandments.

The commandments were also known as the Law of God which instructed the people on how God wanted them to live. Christ came to live in the way the Law taught and to give it more meaning (Matthew 5:17).

The first four commandments are regarding the people's relationship with God. The last six are about relationships with other people.

The second commandment (to have no idols) set the Israelites apart from nations around them which did worship idols. The fourth commandment regarding the Sabbath also made them different from other nations.

EXODUS

Behind the Story

Moses had been up on the mountain 40 days. Apparently his brother, Aaron, along with the people, had also given up hope that he was coming back.

The people had become used to the stone or metal idols which the Egyptians worshiped. They wanted a god they could see. They still did not have faith in God, even after all he had done for them.

The Israelites were trying to combine worship of the true God with worship of false idols. The people broke the first and second commandments, even before Moses came down the mountain.

The gold jewelry the people gave to make the calf should have been saved to be put in the tabernacle that would be built for God (see Exodus 35:22).

The Golden Calf

Exodus 32:1-20

God called Moses to come up on Mt. Sinai so he could talk with him. The people stayed below and waited for Moses to come back. But he was gone a long time, and the people became impatient. They began to wonder if he was ever coming back, in which case, they felt they needed a new god to lead them.

Painting by Rembrandt

The People Make a Gold Calf

32 The people saw that a long time had passed. And Moses had not come down from the mountain. So they gathered around Aaron. They said to him, "Moses led us out of Egypt. But we don't know what has happened to him. So make us gods who will lead us."

²Aaron said to the people, "Take off the gold earrings that your wives, sons and daughters are wearing. Bring them to me." ³So all the people took their gold earrings and brought them to Aaron. ⁴Aaron took the gold from the people. Then he melted it and made a statue of a calf. He

finished it with a tool. Then the people said, "Israel! These are your gods who brought you out of the land of Egypt!"

⁵Aaron saw all this, and he built an altar before the calf. Then he made an announcement. He said, "Tomorrow there will be a special feast to honor the Lord." ⁶The people got up early the next morning. They offered whole burnt offerings and fellowship offerings. First the people sat down to eat and drink. Then they got up and sinned sexually.

⁷And the Lord said to Moses, "Go down from this mountain. Your people, the people you brought out of the land of Egypt, have done a terrible sin. ⁸They have quickly turned away from the things I commanded them to do. They have made for themselves a calf of melted gold. They have worshiped that calf and offered sacrifices to it. The people have said, 'Israel, these are your gods who brought you out of Egypt.' "

83

ECCLESIASTES SONG OF SONGS ISAIAH JEREMIAH LAMENTATIONS EZEKIEL DANIEL HOSEA JOEL AMOS OBADIAH JONAH MICAH NAHUM HABAKKUK ZEPHANIAH HAGGAI ZECHARIAH MALACHI

[9]The Lord said to Moses, "I have seen these people. I know that they are very stubborn people. [10]So now do not stop me. I am so angry with them that I am going to destroy them. Then I will make you and your descendants a great nation."

[11]But Moses begged the Lord his God. Moses said, "Lord, don't let your anger destroy your people. You brought these people out of Egypt with your great power and strength. [12]Don't let the people of Egypt say, 'The Lord brought the Israelites out of Egypt. But he planned to kill them in the mountains and destroy them from the earth.' So stop being angry. Don't destroy your people. [13]Remember the men who served you—Abraham, Isaac and Israel. You promised with an oath to them. You said, 'I will make your descendants as many as the stars in the sky. I will give your descendants all this land that I have promised them. It will be theirs forever.' " [14]So the Lord changed his mind. He did not destroy the people as he had said he might.

[15]Then Moses went down the mountain. In his hands he had the two stone tablets with the agreement on them. The commands were written on both sides of each stone, front and back. [16]God himself had made the stones. And God himself had written the commands on the stones.

[17]Then Joshua heard the noise of the people shouting. He said to Moses, "It sounds like war down in the camp."

[18]Moses answered:

"It is not an army's shout of victory.

It is not an army's cry of defeat.

It is the sound of singing that I hear."

[19]When Moses came close to the camp, he saw the gold calf and the dancing. He became very angry. He threw down the stone tablets which he was carrying. He broke them at the bottom of the mountain. [20]Then he took the calf that the people had made. He melted it in the fire. And he ground the gold until it became powder. He threw the powder into the water. And he forced the Israelites to drink that water.

TAKING IT TO HEART

TRUST

Trusting God means believing he is in control, even when things aren't going smoothly or you can't see what's ahead. It gets easier with practice. Being able to look back and see what he has done for you in the past, or reading his Word and seeing what he did for the people there gives confidence to trust him more.

Read Proverbs 3:5-6 for trust instructions.

Prayer

Moses asked God to give the people another chance (Exodus 32:11-14). His prayer had three points:

1. A reminder that God had brought the people out of Egypt.

2. A reminder that the Egyptians would think they had won if God destroyed the people.

3. A reminder of God's covenant with Abraham, Isaac and Jacob.

The prayers of God's people can make a difference. See James 5:16.

Gone Forever

Moses threw down the tablets with the Ten Commandments written on them and broke them before the people had a chance to see them. God had written the commands with his own hand (Exodus 31:18).

84

GENESIS **EXODUS** LEVITICUS NUMBERS DEUTERONOMY JOSHUA JUDGES RUTH 1 SAMUEL 2 SAMUEL 1 KINGS 2 KINGS 1 CHRONICLES 2 CHRONICLES EZRA NEHEMIAH ESTHER JOB PSALMS PROVERBS

EXODUS

The Meeting Tent

Exodus 40:1-38

Moses melted the golden calf; ground up the gold and sprinkled it on water. Then he made the people drink it. God gave the people a second chance. He even wrote the Ten Commandments again for them. He instructed them how to set up a place to worship him.

Words You Should Know

Meeting Tent (MEET-ing TEN-t)
Also called the Tabernacle or Holy Tent. This was the special tent where the Israelites worshiped God. It was used from the time they left Egypt until Solomon built the Temple in Jerusalem. This tent was kept in the middle of their camp to remind them that God was always with them (see Exodus 26; 39:32–40:38; Numbers 7; 2 Chronicles 1:3-13; 5:5).

Box of the Agreement
Often called the Ark of the Covenant. It was a special box made of acacia wood and gold. Gold creatures with wings covered the top. Inside were the stone tablets on which the Ten Commandments were written. Later, a pot of manna and Aaron's walking stick were also put into the box. The Box of the Agreement was to remind the people of Israel of God's promise to be with them. It is also called the Holy Box or the Holy Box of God (see Exodus 25:10-22; 26:34; Joshua 3:1-17; 2 Chronicles 35:3; Hebrews 9:4).

Setting Up the Holy Tent

40 Then the Lord said this to Moses: [2]"On the first day of the first month, set up the Holy Tent, which is the Meeting Tent. [3]Put the Box of the Agreement in the Meeting Tent. Hang the curtain in front of the Holy Box. [4]Then bring in the table. Arrange everything on the table that should be there. Then bring in the lampstand and set up its lamps. [5]Put the gold altar for burning incense in front of the Box of the Agreement. Then put the curtain at the entrance to the Holy Tent.

[6]"Put the altar of burnt offerings in front of the entrance of the Holy Tent, the Meeting Tent. [7]Put the bowl between the Meeting Tent and the altar. Put water in the bowl. [8]Set up the courtyard around the Holy Tent. Then put the curtain at the entry to the courtyard.

[9]"Use the special olive oil and pour it on the Holy Tent and everything in it. Give the Tent and all that is in it for service to the Lord. They will be holy. [10]Pour the special oil on the altar for burning offerings. Pour it on all its tools. Give the altar for service to God. It will be very holy. [11]Then pour the special olive oil on the bowl and the base under it. When you do this, they will be given for service to God.

[12]"Bring Aaron and his sons to the entrance of the

The Box of the Agreement

The Lampstand

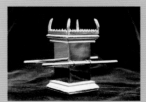

The Incense Altar

85

ECCLESIASTES SONG OF SONGS ISAIAH JEREMIAH LAMENTATIONS EZEKIEL DANIEL HOSEA JOEL AMOS OBADIAH JONAH MICAH NAHUM HABAKKUK ZEPHANIAH HAGGAI ZECHARIAH MALACHI

Meeting Tent. Wash them with water. [13]Then put the holy clothes on Aaron. Pour the special oil on him, and give him for service to God. Then he may serve me as a priest. [14]Bring Aaron's sons and put the inner robes on them. [15]Pour the special oil on them to make them priests. Do this the same way that you appointed their father as priest. Then they may also serve me as priests. Pouring oil on them will make them a family of priests. They and their descendants will be priests from now on." [16]Moses did everything that the Lord commanded him.

[17]So the Holy Tent was set up. It was the first day of the first month during the second year after they left Egypt. [18]When Moses set up the Holy Tent, he put the bases in place. Then he put the frames on the bases. Next he put the crossbars through the rings of the frames and set up the posts. [19]After that, Moses spread the cloth over the Holy Tent. Then he put the covering over the Tent. He did these things just as the Lord commanded.

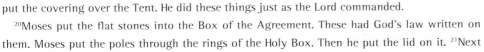

[20]Moses put the flat stones into the Box of the Agreement. These had God's law written on them. Moses put the poles through the rings of the Holy Box. Then he put the lid on it. [21]Next Moses brought the Holy Box into the Tent. He hung the curtain to cover the Holy Box. Moses did these things just as the Lord commanded him.

The Altar of Burnt Offerings

[22]Moses put the table in the Meeting Tent. He put it on the north side of the Holy Tent in front of the curtain. [23]Then he put the bread on the table before the Lord. He did this just as the Lord commanded him. [24]Moses put the lampstand in the Meeting Tent. He put it on the south side of the Holy Tent across from the table. [25]Then he put the lamps on the lampstand before the Lord. He did this just as the Lord commanded him.

[26]Moses put the gold altar for burning incense in the Meeting Tent. He put it in front of the curtain. [27]Then he burned sweet-smelling incense on it, just as the Lord commanded him. [28]Then he hung the curtain at the entrance to the Holy Tent.

[29]He put the altar for burning sacrifices at the entrance to the Holy Tent, the Meeting Tent. Then Moses offered a whole burnt offering and grain offerings on that altar. He did these things

Things You Should Know

The Meeting Tent was completed nine months after the Israelites arrived at Mt. Sinai.

When Moses poured the oil on everything in the Holy Tent, he was anointing those things. That means they were set apart to be holy for service to God (Exodus 40:9-11).

Only Aaron and members of his family could be priests (40:12-15). They were from the tribe of Levi. This shows God's forgiveness of Aaron for the golden calf sin.

The Holy Tent could only be entered by the priest. The Most Holy Place in the center of the Meeting Tent was only entered by the priest once a year.

The Holy Tent was portable because the Israelites were still on the move. They had to be able to take the tent down and take it with them as they traveled toward the Promised Land.

86

GENESIS **EXODUS** LEVITICUS NUMBERS DEUTERONOMY JOSHUA JUDGES RUTH 1 SAMUEL 2 SAMUEL 1 KINGS 2 KINGS 1 CHRONICLES 2 CHRONICLES EZRA NEHEMIAH ESTHER JOB PSALMS PROVERBS

EXODUS

Think About This

The Meeting Tent was not just an old green camping tent. Exodus 35:5-7 tells some of the materials used in building and furnishing the Holy Tent: gold, silver, bronze, blue, purple and red thread, fine linen, goat hair, male sheep skins dyed red, fine leather and acacia wood.

When everything in the Meeting Tent was prepared, God's presence filled the tent. This is another experience of God's shekinah glory. The people stayed where they were as long as God's glory filled the tent. When the cloud moved, the people knew it was time to move again.

The miracle of God coming down to be with the people was a foretaste of Jesus coming to live among people. Read John 1:14.

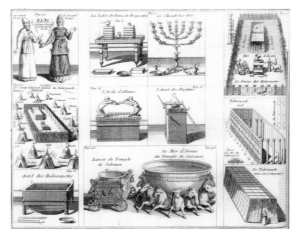

just as the Lord commanded him. ³⁰Moses put the bowl between the Meeting Tent and the altar for burning sacrifices. Moses put water in the bowl for washing. ³¹Moses, Aaron and Aaron's sons used this water to wash their hands and feet. ³²They washed themselves every time they entered the Meeting Tent. They also washed themselves every time they went near the altar for burning sacrifices. They did these things just as the Lord commanded Moses.

³³Then Moses set up the courtyard around the Holy Tent. He put the altar for burning sacrifices in the courtyard. Then he put up the curtain at the entry to the courtyard. So Moses finished the work.

The Cloud over the Holy Tent

³⁴Then the cloud covered the Meeting Tent. The greatness of the Lord filled the Holy Tent. ³⁵Moses could not enter the Meeting Tent. This was because the cloud had settled on it. And this was because the greatness of the Lord filled the Holy Tent.

³⁶When the cloud rose from the Holy Tent, the Israelites would begin to travel. ³⁷But as long as the cloud stayed on the Holy Tent, the people did not travel. They stayed in that place until the cloud rose. ³⁸So the cloud of the Lord was over the Holy Tent during the day. And there was a fire in the cloud at night. So all the Israelites could see the cloud while they traveled.

87

ECCLESIASTES SONG OF SONGS ISAIAH JEREMIAH LAMENTATIONS EZEKIEL DANIEL HOSEA JOEL AMOS OBADIAH JONAH MICAH NAHUM HABAKKUK ZEPHANIAH HAGGAI ZECHARIAH MALACHI

LEVITICUS

The third book of Moses is called Leviticus. It is named for the tribe of Levi, which was the tribe of priests. Much of this book involves the activities guiding the work and lives of the priests.

However, God wanted his people to have a relationship with him directly. They didn't have to go through the priests to talk with him. So Leviticus also outlines the five offerings the people could bring to approach God:

- **Burnt Offering** (Leviticus 1; 6:8-13) showed their commitment to God.
- **Grain Offering** (Leviticus 2; 6:14-23) showed their devotion to God.
- **Fellowship Offering** (Leviticus 3; 7:11-36) showed their thankfulness to God.
- **Sin Offering** (Leviticus 4:1–5:13; 6:24-30) cleansed them from their sins.
- **Penalty Offering** (Leviticus 5:14–6:7; 7:1-10) cleansed sins against other people.

Leviticus Info

Moses met with God in the Meeting Tent where God literally dictated the rules, regulations and guidelines of this book to Moses.

Leviticus reminds us of our sinfulness, God's forgiveness and the sacrifice needed to come before him. Jesus took care of that sacrifice once and forever by his death for us on the cross (John 3:16).

TAKING IT TO HEART

WHAT CAN YOU LEARN?

God loves you so much that he sacrificed his Son, in order for you to be able to know him and be with him in heaven one day. He is holy, and he demands that his people live holy lives. That means obeying him and living lives filled with love. Read Mark 12:30-31.

You can have a personal relationship with him, which means you can pray directly to him and learn to know him by reading his Word.

88

GENESIS EXODUS LEVITICUS **NUMBERS** DEUTERONOMY JOSHUA JUDGES RUTH 1 SAMUEL 2 SAMUEL 1 KINGS 2 KINGS 1 CHRONICLES 2 CHRONICLES EZRA NEHEMIAH ESTHER JOB PSALMS PROVERBS

NUMBERS

Spies in Canaan

Numbers 13:1-33

God had promised his people a land of their
own. Of course they would have to take the land
from the people who lived in it. That's where
the Israelites' faith once again was shown to be
weak.

The Spies Explore Canaan

13 The Lord said to Moses, "Send men to explore the land of Canaan. I will give that land to
the Israelites. Send one leader from each tribe."

³So Moses obeyed the Lord's command. He sent the Israelite leaders out from the Desert of
Paran. ⁴These are their names: from the tribe of Reuben, Shammua son of Zaccur; ⁵from the tribe
of Simeon, Shaphat son of Hori; ⁶from the tribe of Judah, Caleb son of Jephunneh; ⁷from the tribe
of Issachar, Igal son of Joseph; ⁸from the tribe of Ephraim, Hoshea [Joshua] son of Nun; ⁹from the
tribe of Benjamin, Palti son of Raphu; ¹⁰from the tribe of Zebulun, Gaddiel son of Sodi; ¹¹from
the tribe of Manasseh (a tribe of Joseph), Gaddi son of Susi; ¹²from the tribe of Dan, Ammiel son
of Gamalli; ¹³from the tribe of Asher, Sethur son of Michael; ¹⁴from the tribe of Naphtali, Nahbi
son of Vophsi; ¹⁵from the tribe of Gad, Geuel son of Maki.

¹⁶These are the names of the men
Moses sent to explore the land. (Moses
gave Hoshea son of Nun the new name
Joshua.)

¹⁷Moses sent them to explore
Canaan. He said, "Go through southern
Canaan and then into the mountains.
¹⁸See what the land looks like. Are the
people who live there strong or weak?
Are there a few or many? ¹⁹What kind
of land do they live in? Is it good or
bad? What about the towns they live

Olive Trees in Israel

89

ECCLESIASTES SONG OF SONGS ISAIAH JEREMIAH LAMENTATIONS EZEKIEL DANIEL HOSEA JOEL AMOS OBADIAH JONAH MICAH NAHUM HABAKKUK ZEPHANIAH HAGGAI ZECHARIAH MALACHI

in—do they have walls, or are they open like camps? ²⁰What about the soil? Is it fertile or poor? Are there trees there? Try to bring back some of the fruit from that land." (It was the season for the first grapes.)

²¹So they went up and explored the land. They went from the Desert of Zin all the way to Rehob by Lebo Hamath. ²²They went through the southern area to Hebron. That is where Ahiman, Sheshai and Talmai lived. They were the descendants of Anak. (The city of Hebron had been built seven years before Zoan in Egypt.) ²³In the Valley of Eshcol, they cut off a branch of a grapevine. It had one bunch of grapes on it. They carried that branch on a pole between two of them. They also got some pomegranates and figs. ²⁴They call that place the Valley of Eshcol. That is because the Israelites cut off the bunch of grapes there. ²⁵After 40 days of exploring the land, the men returned to the camp.

²⁶They came back to Moses and Aaron and all the Israelites at Kadesh. This was in the Desert of Paran. The men reported to them and showed everybody the fruit from the land. ²⁷They told Moses, "We went to the land where you sent us. It is a land where much food grows! Here is some of its fruit. ²⁸But the people who live there are strong. Their cities are walled and large. We even saw some Anakites there. ²⁹The Amalekites live in the southern area. The Hittites, Jebusites and Amorites live in the mountains. The Canaanites live near the sea and along the Jordan River."

³⁰Then Caleb told the people near Moses to be quiet. Caleb said, "We should go up and take the land for ourselves. We can do it."

³¹But the men who had gone with him said, "We can't attack those people. They are stronger than we are." ³²And those men gave the Israelites a bad report about the land they explored. They said, "The land would eat us up. All the people we saw are very tall. ³³We saw the Nephilim people there. (The Anakites come from the Nephilim people.) We felt like grasshoppers. And we looked like grasshoppers to them."

The Results
Numbers 14:30-31

14 ³⁰Not one of you will enter and live in the land I promised to you. Only Caleb son of Jephunneh and Joshua son of Nun will go in. ³¹You said that your children would be taken away. But I will bring them into the land. They will enjoy what you refused.

Numbers 13:31

The 10 spies were afraid because of their lack of trust in God—even after all he had done for them. God told them he was giving them this land (13:1), but they didn't believe him. Remember the pillars of cloud and fire, which represented God's presence, were still with the Israelites.

The people believed the 10 spies instead of Caleb and Joshua who trusted God to give them the land.

Numbers 14:1 tells the people's response—they cried because they believed their dream of a land of their own was lost.

The punishment for their unbelief was having to wander in the desert for 40 years. That was one year for each day that the spies were in the land of Canaan.

90

GENESIS EXODUS LEVITICUS **NUMBERS** DEUTERONOMY JOSHUA JUDGES RUTH 1 SAMUEL 2 SAMUEL 1 KINGS 2 KINGS 1 CHRONICLES 2 CHRONICLES EZRA NEHEMIAH ESTHER JOB PSALMS PROVERBS

NUMBERS

Miracles in the Desert
Numbers 17:1-11; 20:1-13; 21:4-9

The Walking Stick

The people had a problem with authority. They constantly complained to Moses about the rules they had to obey and who was in charge. God showed once and for all that he was giving Aaron authority and, in fact, that authority was given to his family (Numbers 17:10).

Moses' Sin

Moses disobeyed God by striking the rock. God had instructed him to speak to the rock, and the water would come as it did in Exodus 17. Moses committed a double sin of disbelief and dishonoring God in front of the people. Leaders have a greater responsibility to obey God as an example to those they lead (see James 3:1). Moses' punishment was very serious (Numbers 20:12).

Moses never got to enter the Promised Land, but God did let him see it before he died (see Deuteronomy 34:4).

Aaron's Walking Stick Buds

17 The Lord said to Moses, ²"Speak to the people of Israel. Get 12 walking sticks from them. Get 1 from the leader of each tribe. Write the name of each man on his stick. ³On the stick from Levi, write Aaron's name. There must be 1 stick for the head of each tribe. ⁴Put them in the Meeting Tent. Place them in front of the Box of the Agreement, where I meet with you. ⁵I will choose one man. His stick will begin to grow leaves. And I will stop the Israelites from always complaining against you."

⁶So Moses spoke to the Israelites. Each of the 12 leaders gave him a walking stick. And Aaron's walking stick was among them. ⁷Moses put them before the Lord in the Tent of the Agreement.

⁸The next day Moses entered the Tent. He saw that Aaron's stick had grown leaves. (It stood for the family of Levi.) It had even budded, blossomed and produced almonds. ⁹So Moses brought out to the Israelites all the walking sticks from the Lord's presence. They all looked, and each man took back his stick.

¹⁰Then the Lord said to Moses, "Put Aaron's walking stick back. Put it in front of the Box of the Agreement. It will be a sign to these people who are always turning against me. This will stop their complaining against me. Now they won't die." ¹¹So Moses obeyed what the Lord commanded him.

Water from the Rock

20 In the first month all the people of Israel arrived at the Desert of Zin. They stayed at Kadesh. There Miriam died and was buried. ²There was no water for the people. So they came together against Moses and Aaron. ³They argued with Moses. They said, "We should have died in front of the Lord as our brothers did. ⁴Why did you bring the Lord's people into this desert? Are we and our animals to die here? ⁵Why did you bring us from Egypt to this terrible place? It has no grain, figs or pomegranates. And there's no water to drink!"

91

ECCLESIASTES SONG OF SONGS ISAIAH JEREMIAH LAMENTATIONS EZEKIEL DANIEL HOSEA JOEL AMOS OBADIAH JONAH MICAH NAHUM HABAKKUK ZEPHANIAH HAGGAI ZECHARIAH MALACHI

[6]So Moses and Aaron left the people. Then they went to the entrance of the Meeting Tent. They bowed facedown. And the glory of the Lord appeared to them. [7]The Lord said to Moses, [8]"You and your brother Aaron should gather the people. Also take your walking stick. Speak to that rock in front of them. Then water will flow from it. Give that water to the people and their animals."

[9]So Moses took the stick from in front of the Lord. He did as the Lord had said. [10]He and Aaron gathered the people in front of the rock. Then Moses said, "Now listen to me, you complainers! Do you want us to bring water out of this rock?" [11]Then Moses lifted his hand and hit the rock twice with his stick. Water began pouring out. And the people and their animals drank it.

[12]But the Lord said to Moses and Aaron, "You did not believe me. You did not honor me as holy before the people. So you will not lead them into the land I will give them."

[13]These are the waters of Meribah. Here the Israelites argued with the Lord. And the Lord showed them he was holy.

The Bronze Snake

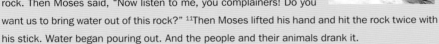

21 [4]The Israelites left Mount Hor and went on the road toward the Gulf of Aqaba. They did this to go around the country of Edom. But the people became impatient on the way. [5]They grumbled at God and Moses. They said, "Why did you bring us out of Egypt? We will die in this desert! There is no bread! There is no water! And we hate this terrible food!"

[6]So the Lord sent them poisonous snakes. They bit the people, and many of the Israelites died. [7]The people came to Moses and said, "We sinned when we grumbled at you and the Lord. Pray that the Lord will take away these snakes." So Moses prayed for the people.

[8]The Lord said to Moses, "Make a bronze snake. And put it on a pole. If anyone is bitten, he should look at it. Then he will live." [9]So Moses made a bronze snake. And he put it on a pole. Then when a snake bit anyone, he looked at the bronze snake and lived.

Behind the Story

They had to go around the land of Edom because the king would not grant them permission to cross through his land. Some kings were afraid of the Israelites because they knew that God fought for them, and they had heard what happened to the Egyptians.

The people kept complaining, even though God had miraculously met all their needs, including protection, food and water.

The Snake

Poisonous snakes were a problem in the desert. People usually tried to work some kind of magic to heal a person who was bitten.

The people were taught that deliverance (salvation) comes from God by looking at the bronze snake to be healed.

Jesus told this story when he was talking with an important Jewish leader named Nicodemus (see John 3:14-15).

92

GENESIS EXODUS LEVITICUS **NUMBERS** DEUTERONOMY JOSHUA JUDGES RUTH 1 SAMUEL 2 SAMUEL 1 KINGS 2 KINGS 1 CHRONICLES 2 CHRONICLES EZRA NEHEMIAH ESTHER JOB PSALMS PROVERBS

NUMBERS

Balaam's Donkey

Numbers 22:1-35

Behind the Story

Balak and the people of Moab were afraid of the Israelites, but God had ordered them not to attack the Moabites (Deuteronomy 2:1-9). Either Balak did not know that or did not believe it.

Balaam was not an Israelite. He didn't believe in God. He was a prophet who specialized in watching animals. The animals' behavior helped him understand what the gods were saying.

Actually, Balaam believed in many "gods." He tried to add the true God into his belief system, but that does not work.

God uses whomever he chooses to give his messages or do his work. It didn't matter that Balaam didn't believe in him.

Balak requested Balaam's help twice. The second time he sent more money and gold. God had warned Balaam against cursing the Israelites, but the offer of money convinced him to try it.

The time of wandering in the desert, which was a punishment for unbelief, was coming to an end. The people were near the Promised Land as they crossed through the land of Moab. Balak, the king, and the people of that land were afraid of the Israelites. Balak thought that if he could get a curse put on them, then his army could defeat them.

Balaam and Balak

22 Then the people of Israel went to the plains of Moab. They camped near the Jordan River across from Jericho.

²Balak son of Zippor saw everything the Israelites had done to the Amorites. ³And Moab was scared of so many Israelites. Truly, Moab was terrified by them.

⁴The Moabites said to the elders of Midian, "This mob will take everything around us. It will be like an ox eating grass."

Balak son of Zippor was the king of Moab at this time. ⁵He sent messengers to Balaam son of Beor at Pethor. It was near the Euphrates River in the land of Amaw. Balak said, "A nation has come out of Egypt. They cover the land. They have camped next to me. ⁶They are too powerful for me. So come and put a curse on them. Maybe then I can defeat them and make them leave the area. I know that if you bless someone, the blessings happen. And if you put a curse on someone, it happens."

⁷The elders of Moab and Midian went with payment in their hands. They found Balaam. Then they told him what Balak had said.

⁸Balaam said to them, "Stay here for the night. I will tell you what the Lord tells me." So the Moabite leaders stayed with him.

⁹God came to Balaam and asked, "Who are these men with you?"

¹⁰Balaam said to God, "The king of Moab, Balak son of Zippor, sent them. He sent me this message: ¹¹'A nation has come out of Egypt. They cover the land. So come and put a curse on them. Then maybe I can fight them and force them out of my land.' "

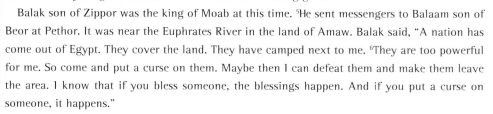

93

ECCLESIASTES SONG OF SONGS ISAIAH JEREMIAH LAMENTATIONS EZEKIEL DANIEL HOSEA JOEL AMOS OBADIAH JONAH MICAH NAHUM HABAKKUK ZEPHANIAH HAGGAI ZECHARIAH MALACHI

[12]But God said to Balaam, "Do not go with them. Don't put a curse on those people. I have blessed them."

[13]The next morning Balaam awoke and said to Balak's leaders, "Go back to your own country. The Lord will not let me go with you."

[14]So the Moabite leaders went back to Balak. They said, "Balaam refused to come with us."

[15]So Balak sent other leaders. He sent more leaders this time. And they were more important. [16]They went to Balaam and said, "Balak son of Zippor says this: Please don't let anything stop you from coming to me. [17]I will pay you well. I will do what you say. Come and put a curse on these people for me."

[18]But Balaam answered Balak's servants, "King Balak could give me his palace full of silver and gold. But I cannot disobey the Lord my God in anything, great or small. [19]You stay here tonight as the other men did. I will find out what more the Lord tells me."

[20]That night God came to Balaam. He said, "These men have come to ask you to go with them. Go. But only do what I tell you."

The World at the Time
Around 1450 B.C.

- About this time the city of Nineveh was settled. It was an important city in the book of Jonah.
- The Chinese developed an alphabet that had over 25,000 characters. They also created the Magic Squares which were used in math.

Things You Should Know

In Numbers 22:20, God tells Balaam that it is okay for him to go with the king's men—however he is only to do what God tells him. But then God got angry at Balaam for going. God could see what was in Balaam's heart and what his intentions were. He was not going to obey God and speak only the words God gave him.

Donkeys were very important in Old Testament times. They were a means of transportation, carrying heavy items, plowing and doing other farm work.

People believed in the power of curses. When an enemy could not be overcome by power, a curse was placed on them. If a person cheated another, a curse was placed on him. The people believed that one of their gods would carry out the curse.

Balaam and His Donkey

[21]Balaam got up the next morning. He put a saddle on his donkey. Then he went with the Moabite leaders. [22]But God became angry because Balaam went. So the angel of the Lord stood in the road to stop Balaam. Balaam was riding his donkey. And he had two servants with him. [23]The donkey saw the angel of the Lord standing in the road. The angel had a sword in his hand. So the donkey left the road and went into the field. Balaam hit the donkey to force her back on the road.

[24]Later, the angel of the Lord stood on a narrow path between two vineyards. There were walls

94

GENESIS EXODUS LEVITICUS **NUMBERS** DEUTERONOMY JOSHUA JUDGES RUTH 1 SAMUEL 2 SAMUEL 1 KINGS 2 KINGS 1 CHRONICLES 2 CHRONICLES EZRA NEHEMIAH ESTHER JOB PSALMS PROVERBS

NUMBERS

Balaam Info

Balaam is mentioned three times in the New Testament, always as an evil or sinful man who disobeyed God.

2 Peter 2:15—Balaam loved being paid to do the wrong thing.

Jude 11—Balaam followed the wrong way to make money.

Revelation 2:14—Balaam taught people to sin.

Balaam was famous for watching animals, in order to figure out what the gods were saying. God spoke through an animal, in order to get Balaam's attention.

Balaam came to understand that God's people could not be cursed (Numbers 23:8-10). God would always turn bad into good for his people.

on both sides. ²⁵Again the donkey saw the angel of the Lord. So the donkey walked close to one wall. This crushed Balaam's foot against the wall. So he hit her again.

²⁶The angel of the Lord went ahead again. The angel stood at a narrow place. It was too narrow to turn left or right. ²⁷The donkey saw the angel of the Lord. So she lay down under Balaam. Balaam was very angry and hit her with his stick. ²⁸Then the Lord made the donkey talk. She said to Balaam, "What have I done to make you hit me three times?"

²⁹Balaam answered the donkey, "You have made me look foolish! I wish I had a sword in my hand! I would kill you right now!"

³⁰But the donkey said to Balaam, "I am your very own donkey. You have ridden me for years. Have I ever done this to you before?"

"No," Balaam said.

³¹Then the Lord let Balaam see the angel. The angel of the Lord was standing in the road with his sword drawn. Then Balaam bowed facedown on the ground.

³²The angel of the Lord asked Balaam, "Why have you hit your donkey three times? I have stood here to stop you. What you are doing is wrong. ³³The donkey saw me. She turned away from me three times. If she had not turned away, I would have killed you by now. But I would let her live."

³⁴Then Balaam said to the angel of the Lord, "I have sinned. I did not know you were standing in the road to stop me. If I am wrong, I will go back."

³⁵The angel of the Lord said to Balaam, "Go with these men. But say only what I tell you." So Balaam went with Balak's leaders.

95

ECCLESIASTES SONG OF SONGS ISAIAH JEREMIAH LAMENTATIONS EZEKIEL DANIEL HOSEA JOEL AMOS OBADIAH JONAH MICAH NAHUM HABAKKUK ZEPHANIAH HAGGAI ZECHARIAH MALACHI

Israel's New Leader

Numbers 27:12-23

Joshua Is the New Leader

27 ¹²Then the Lord said to Moses, "Climb this mountain in the Abarim Mountains. Look at the land I have given to the Israelites. ¹³After you have seen it, you will die as your brother Aaron did. ¹⁴You both acted against my command in the Desert of Zin. You did not honor me as holy before the people at the waters of Meribah." (This was at Meribah in Kadesh in the Desert of Zin.)

¹⁵Moses said to the Lord, ¹⁶"The Lord is the God of the spirits of all people. May he choose a good leader for these people. ¹⁷He must go in and out before them. He must lead them out like sheep and bring them in. The Lord's people must not be like sheep without a shepherd."

¹⁸So the Lord said to Moses, "Take Joshua son of Nun. My Spirit is in him. Put your hand on him. ¹⁹Have him stand before Eleazar the priest and all the people. Then give him his orders as they watch. ²⁰Let him share your honor. Then all the Israelites will obey him. ²¹He must stand before Eleazar the priest. And Eleazar will get advice from the Lord by using the Urim. At his command all the Israelites will go out. At his command they will all come in."

²²Moses did what the Lord told him. Moses had Joshua stand before Eleazar the priest and all the people. ²³Then Moses put his hands on him and gave him orders. This was just as the Lord had told him.

Behind the Story

Moses was not allowed to enter the Promised Land, but God did let him see it (Numbers 27:12-13).

Moses climbed Mt. Nebo to see the land, then he died. God himself buried Moses. No one ever found his grave (see Deuteronomy 34:1-6).

Even after all their grumbling and complaining, Moses' last wish was for the well-being of the people. He knew they needed a leader (Numbers 27:16-17).

Before he died, Moses passed the leadership of the people on to Joshua. That way the people could learn to obey Joshua while Moses was still around (Numbers 27:18-19).

In Deuteronomy

Moses' challenge in 30:19-20:

Today I ask heaven and earth to be witnesses. I am offering you life or death, blessings or curses. Now, choose life! Then you and your children may live. Love the Lord your God. Obey him. Stay close to him. He is your life. And he will let you live many years in the land. This is the land he promised to give your ancestors Abraham, Isaac and Jacob.

One way of the challenge led to life and one way to death. People today still need to make this choice. Jesus gives the same challenge. Read Matthew 7:13-14 and John 14:6.

DEUTERONOMY

This is the last book written by Moses. It can be viewed as Moses' farewell speech to the people. He reviewed much of what they had been through together. He also reviewed the laws and instructions God had given them. Moses wanted the people to remember God's law and live in obedience to him.

- **In Chapters 1–4** Moses reminds the people of God's glory and of their own terrible sins. He also reminds them of his own sin which will keep him from entering the Promised Land. He encourages the people to follow Joshua because he is God's choice to lead them.
- **In Chapters 5–26** Moses reviews all the laws God has given. He does not want the people to forget. He longs for them to obey God.
- **Moses' challenge** to the people can be read in Deuteronomy 30:15-20.
- **Read Moses' Song** of praise to God in Deuteronomy 32.
- **Read Moses' farewell blessing** in Deuteronomy 33. Just before Moses died, he gave a blessing to the people he had spent the last 40 years leading.

BOOKS OF HISTORY

| 1500 BC | 1400 BC | 1300 BC | 1200 BC | 1100 BC | 1000 BC | 900 BC | 800 BC | 700 BC |

The Books of History are:

Joshua, Judges, Ruth, 1 and 2 Samuel, 1 and 2 Kings, 1 and 2 Chronicles, Ezra, Nehemiah and Esther.

As the last book of the previous section ended, the Israelites stood at the edge of the land God had promised them. Because of their lack of faith in him, it had taken them forty years to arrive in this land—forty years to make a journey that should have taken only a few days. Moses, who had led them for those forty years, was dead, and Joshua was their new leader.

The books of history begin the story of the Israelite nation as they settle in the Promised Land. It begins with the conquest of the land, told in the book of Joshua, and continues with the exile of the Israelite nation to Babylon and then, finally, their return to the land God gave them.

98

GENESIS EXODUS LEVITICUS NUMBERS DEUTERONOMY **JOSHUA** JUDGES RUTH 1 SAMUEL 2 SAMUEL 1 KINGS 2 KINGS 1 CHRONICLES 2 CHRONICLES EZRA NEHEMIAH ESTHER JOB PSALMS PROVERBS

JOSHUA

Spies Sent to Jericho

Joshua 2:1-24

Forty years had passed since the Israelites left Egypt. A whole generation had died. It was finally time for the people to enter the Promised Land. Joshua sent two spies into the land before the people went to capture it. They found an unlikely woman to help them.

2 Joshua son of Nun secretly sent out two spies from Acacia. Joshua said to them, "Go and look at the land. Look closely at the city of Jericho."

So the men went to Jericho. They went to the house of a prostitute and stayed there. This woman's name was Rahab.

²Someone told the king of Jericho, "Some men from Israel have come here tonight. They are spying out the land."

³So the king of Jericho sent this message to Rahab: "Bring out the men who came to you and entered your house. They have come to spy out our whole land."

⁴Now the woman had hidden the two men. She said, "They did come here. But I didn't know where they came from. ⁵In the evening, when it was time to close the city gate, they left. I don't know where they went. Go quickly. Maybe you can catch them." ⁶(But the woman had taken the men up to the roof. She had hidden them there under stalks of flax. She had spread the flax out there to dry.) ⁷So the king's men went out looking for the spies from Israel. They went to the places where people cross the Jordan River. The city gate was closed just after the king's men left the city.

⁸The spies were ready to sleep for the night. So Rahab went to the roof and talked to them. ⁹She said, "I know the Lord has given this land to your people. You frighten us very much. Everyone living in this land is terribly afraid of you. ¹⁰We are afraid because we have heard how the Lord helped you. We heard how he dried up the Red Sea when you came out of Egypt. We heard how you destroyed Sihon and Og. They were the two Amorite kings who lived east of the

Words You Should Know

Prostitute (PRAH-sti-toot)
A person who sells his or her body for sexual relations with someone to whom he or she is not married. This is a sin. In the Old Testament God's people often worshiped other gods. God said this was acting like a prostitute (see Genesis 38:15; Exodus 34:15-16; Proverbs 23:27; Jeremiah 3:1-6; Hosea 3:3; 1 Corinthians 6:15).

Flax (FLAKS)
A plant used to make clothing and ropes. The inside of the plant was combed and spun into thread. Then it was woven into cloth (see Exodus 9:31; Joshua 2:6; Proverbs 31:13; Isaiah 19:9).

FAQs

Why are there so many battles when Israel captures the land?

The battles were not just war for the sake of war. God was establishing his nation. He was showing the world his power and holiness. That couldn't happen without battles.

Seeing Jesus

Rahab became the great-grandmother of King David, which means she was an ancestor of Jesus. See her name in Matthew 1:5.

99

ECCLESIASTES SONG OF SONGS ISAIAH JEREMIAH LAMENTATIONS EZEKIEL DANIEL HOSEA JOEL AMOS OBADIAH JONAH MICAH NAHUM HABAKKUK ZEPHANIAH HAGGAI ZECHARIAH MALACHI

Jordan. [11]When we heard this, we became very frightened. Now our men are afraid to fight you. This is because the Lord your God rules the heavens above and the earth below! [12]So now, make me a promise before the Lord. Promise that you will show kindness to my family just as I showed you kindness. Give me some proof that you will do this. [13]Promise me you will allow my family to live. Save my father, mother, brothers, sisters and all of their families from death."

[14]The men agreed. They said, "We will trade our lives for your lives. Don't tell anyone what we are doing. When the Lord gives us our land, we will be kind to you. You may trust us."

[15]The house Rahab lived in was built on the city wall. So she used a rope to let the men down through a window. [16]She said to them, "Go into the hills. The king's men will not find you there. Hide there for three days. After the king's men return, you may go on your way."

[17]The men said to her, "You must do as we say. If not, we cannot be responsible for keeping our promise. [18]You are using a red rope to help us escape. When we return to this land, you must tie it in the window through which you let us down. Bring your father, mother, brothers and all your family into your house. [19]We can keep everyone safe who stays in this house. If anyone in your house is hurt, we will be responsible. If anyone goes out of your house and is killed, it is his own fault. We cannot be responsible for him. [20]But you must not tell anyone about this agreement. If you do, we are free from it."

[21]Rahab answered, "I agree to this." So she sent them away, and they left. Then she tied the red rope in the window.

[22]The men left and went into the hills. There they stayed for three days. The king's men looked for them all along the road. But after three days, the king's men returned to the city without finding them. [23]Then the two men started back to Joshua. They left the hills and crossed the river. They went to Joshua son of Nun and told him everything that had happened to them. [24]They said to Joshua, "The Lord surely has given us all of the land. All the people in that land are terribly afraid of us."

Behind the Story

Joshua sent the spies out "secretly" (Joshua 2:1). He didn't want a repeat of what happened when the 12 spies came back and 10 of them discouraged the people from entering the land.

Large walls surrounded cities in biblical times for protection of invading enemies. Some cities had double walls, and the poorer people lived in rooms built between the walls. Rahab's home was in or on the walls so that the windows looked over the outside of the walls.

Rahab was a Canaanite prostitute who had come to faith in God. She used God's personal name, Yahweh, when she spoke of him. Her story is so amazing that she is mentioned in the Hall of Faith in Hebrews (11:31) and also in James 2:25.

100

GENESIS EXODUS LEVITICUS NUMBERS DEUTERONOMY **JOSHUA** JUDGES RUTH 1 SAMUEL 2 SAMUEL 1 KINGS 2 KINGS 1 CHRONICLES 2 CHRONICLES EZRA NEHEMIAH ESTHER JOB PSALMS PROVERBS

JOSHUA

Crossing the Jordan

Joshua 3:1-17

Behind the Story

Joshua 3 emphasizes the importance of the Box of the Agreement. It is mentioned at least ten times. The Holy Box held the stones containing the Ten Commandments, a jar of manna and Aaron's rod that had budded. It showed God's presence with the people.

The Box of the Agreement was made of very hard wood that would resist insects and rot. It was covered with gold, and each corner had a ring for poles to slide through for carrying it (see Exodus 25:10-22).

There were special rules about the Holy Box: Only the priests could carry it (v. 3); it must be carried by poles and not be touched; the people had to stay a good distance away from it.

Up until this point, the Box of the Agreement had been carried in the middle of the crowd of people. Now God wanted it moved to the front to be a reminder that it was God who was leading the people into battle.

Rahab protected the two spies Joshua sent into Jericho. They, in turn, promised to protect her family when the Israelites came to capture the city. The spies reported back to Joshua, and he prepared to lead his men to capture the city. God was about to do another miracle to show the people he was still with them and to confirm his power was with Joshua.

The Jordan River

3 Early the next morning Joshua and all the people of Israel left Acacia. They traveled to the Jordan River and camped there before crossing it. ²After three days the officers went through the camp. ³They gave orders to the people. They said, "You will see the priests and Levites carrying the Box of the Agreement with the Lord your God. Then you should leave where you are and follow it. ⁴That way you will know which way to go. You have never traveled this way before. But do not follow too closely. Stay about a thousand yards behind the Box of the Agreement."

⁵Then Joshua told the people, "Make yourselves holy for the Lord. Tomorrow the Lord will do amazing things among you."

⁶Joshua said to the priests, "Take the Box of the Agreement. Cross over the river ahead of the people." So the priests lifted the Holy Box and carried it ahead of the people.

⁷Then the Lord said to Joshua, "Today I will begin to make you a great man to all the Israelites. So the people will know I am with you just as I was with Moses. ⁸The priests will carry the Box of the Agreement. Tell them this: 'Go to the edge of the Jordan River and stand in the water.' "

A Model of the Box of Agreement

⁹Then Joshua said to the people of Israel, "Come here. Listen to the words of the Lord your God. ¹⁰Here is proof that the living God is with you. Here is proof that he will drive out the Canaanites, Hittites, Hivites, Perizzites, Girgashites, Amorites and the Jebusites. ¹¹This is the

101

ECCLESIASTES SONG OF SONGS ISAIAH JEREMIAH LAMENTATIONS EZEKIEL DANIEL HOSEA JOEL AMOS OBADIAH JONAH MICAH NAHUM HABAKKUK ZEPHANIAH HAGGAI ZECHARIAH MALACHI

proof: The Box of the Agreement will go ahead of you into the Jordan River. It is the Agreement with the Lord of the whole world. ¹²Now choose 12 men from among you. Choose 1 from each of the 12 tribes of Israel. ¹³The priests will carry the Holy Box of the Lord, the Master of the whole world. They will carry it into the Jordan ahead of you. When they enter the water, the river will stop flowing. The water will be stopped. It will stand up in a heap as if a dam were there."

¹⁴So the priests carried the Box of the Agreement. And the people left the place where they had camped. Then they started across the Jordan River. ¹⁵During harvest the Jordan is flooded. So the river was at its fullest. The priests who were carrying the Holy Box came to the edge of the river. And they stepped into the water.

¹⁶Just at that moment, the water stopped flowing. It stood up in a heap a great distance away at Adam. This is a town near Zarethan. The water flowing down to the Sea of Arabah (the Dead Sea) was completely cut off. So the people crossed the river near Jericho. ¹⁷The ground there became dry. The priests carried the Box of the Agreement with the Lord to the middle of the river and stopped. They waited there while all the people of Israel walked across. They crossed the Jordan River on dry land.

Parting the Water

God is living and active, unlike the idols worshiped by the nations around the Israelites. His presence makes a difference. When the Holy Box—his presence— was carried into the Jordan, the waters parted. That caused the Israelites to remember the similar way he saved them at the Red Sea.

Painting by C.F. Vos

Think About This

The people had to cleanse themselves before following the Holy Box. That's because what was about to happen was an act of God. The people were to be holy, which means set apart and clean.

Joshya 3:15 states that this happened during the harvest season. That means that the spring thaw in the mountains had sent water flowing into the Jordan River. It was full, even at flood stage.

When God parted the Red Sea, the people entered the sea bed on dry ground. However, in crossing the Jordan River on this occasion, the priests had to get their feet wet (Joshua 3:13). This was a walk of faith . . . a chance for the people to show they believed God.

The people were to stay about a thousand yards behind the Holy Box. That was over half a mile.

102

GENESIS EXODUS LEVITICUS NUMBERS DEUTERONOMY **JOSHUA** JUDGES RUTH 1 SAMUEL 2 SAMUEL 1 KINGS 2 KINGS 1 CHRONICLES 2 CHRONICLES EZRA NEHEMIAH ESTHER JOB PSALMS PROVERBS

JOSHUA

Behind the Story

Joshua was instructed to choose 1 man from each of the 12 tribes of Israel. Those tribes were named for 11 of Jacob's sons: Reuben, Simeon, Levi, Judah, Issachar, Zebulun, Dan, Asher, Gad, Naphtali, Benjamin and Joseph's two sons, Manasseh and Ephraim (these 2 were half-tribes).

The stones were set in place to be a reminder to the people of what God had done for them. This is the same idea as when they were instructed to put blood on their doorposts at the time of the final plague in Egypt (see Exodus 12:13-14).

God knew that each time the people saw the pile of stones they would remember his active, loving care for them.

God also knew the stones would be a conversation starter with children and give parents a chance to pass along all that God had done for his people.

Rock Reminders

Joshua 4:1-24

God had promised to give his people their own land and had done many miracles to help that happen. He wanted to be sure that generations to come would remember his work.

Rocks to Remind the People

4 All the people finished crossing the Jordan. Then the Lord said to Joshua, ²"Choose 12 men from among the people. Choose 1 from each tribe. ³Tell the men to get 12 large rocks from the middle of the river. Take them from where the priests stood. Carry the rocks and put them down where you stay tonight."

⁴So Joshua chose 1 man from each tribe. Then he called the 12 men together. ⁵He said to them, "Go out into the river where the Holy Box of the Lord your God is. Each of you should find 1 large rock. There will be 1 rock for each tribe of Israel. Carry the rock on your shoulder. ⁶They will be a sign among you. In the future your children will ask you, 'What do these rocks mean?' ⁷Tell them the Lord stopped the water from flowing in the Jordan. When the Holy Box of the Agreement with the Lord crossed the river, the water was stopped. These rocks will help the Israelites remember this forever."

⁸So the Israelites obeyed Joshua. They carried 12 rocks from the middle of the Jordan River. There was 1 rock for each of the 12 tribes of Israel. They did this the way the Lord had commanded Joshua. They carried the rocks with them. And they put them down where they made their camp. ⁹Joshua also put 12 rocks in the middle of the Jordan River. He put them where the priests had stood while carrying the Holy Box of the Lord. These rocks are still there today.

¹⁰The Lord had commanded Joshua to tell the people what to do. It was what Moses had said Joshua must do. So the priests carrying the Holy Box continued standing in the middle of the river until everything was done. And the people hurried across the river. ¹¹The people finished

103

ECCLESIASTES SONG OF SONGS ISAIAH JEREMIAH LAMENTATIONS EZEKIEL DANIEL HOSEA JOEL AMOS OBADIAH JONAH MICAH NAHUM HABAKKUK ZEPHANIAH HAGGAI ZECHARIAH MALACHI

crossing the river. Then the priests carried the Holy Box of the Lord to the other side. As they carried it, the people watched. [12]The men from the tribes of Reuben, Gad and the eastern half-tribe of Manasseh obeyed what Moses had told them. They were prepared for war. So they crossed the river ahead of the other people. [13]About 40,000 soldiers were prepared for war. They passed before the Lord as they marched across the river. Then they went toward the plains of Jericho to go to war.

[14]That day the Lord made Joshua a great man to all the Israelites. They respected Joshua all his life, just as they had respected Moses.

[15]Then the Lord spoke to Joshua. [16]He said, "Command the priests to bring the Box of the Agreement out of the river."

[17]So Joshua commanded the priests, "Come up out of the Jordan."

[18]So the priests carried the Box of the Agreement with the Lord out of the river. As soon as their feet touched dry land, the water began flowing again. The river again overflowed its banks. It was just as it had been before they crossed.

[19]The people crossed the Jordan on the tenth day of the first month. They camped at Gilgal, east of Jericho. [20]They carried with them the 12 rocks taken from the Jordan. And Joshua set them up at Gilgal. [21]Then he spoke to the Israelites. He said, "In the future your children will ask you, 'What do these rocks mean?' [22]Tell them, 'Israel crossed the Jordan River on dry land. [23]The Lord your God caused the water to stop flowing. The river was dry until the people finished crossing it. The Lord did the same thing for us at the Jordan that he did for the people at the Red Sea. Remember that he stopped the water at the Red Sea so we could cross. [24]The Lord did this so all people would know he has great power. Then they will always respect the Lord your God.'"

The Importance of Remembrances

TAKING IT TO HEART

There are several instances in the Old Testament when people set up stones for all to see as a reminder of God's care. (See Genesis 28:18-22; 31:45 and 1 Samuel 7:12 for examples.) It was important to remember all God had done. Here in Joshua the people were instructed to tell their children of God's work. God wanted his work and his laws passed on to future generations. Moses instructed the people in Deuteronomy 6:7-9 to remember his commands and teach them to their children.

Things You Should Know

The people camped at Gilgal after crossing the Jordan River (Joshua 4:19). Gilgal became the headquarters of their invasion of the land. It took 6 years to take possession of the land.

The people crossed the Jordan on the tenth day of the first month. This was a reminder of the Passover (when God spared their firstborn children from the plague when the Egyptians' firstborn children died). The Passover lamb was chosen on the tenth day of the first month (see Exodus 12:3). It was killed four days later.

Reminding Us All

God did not do this miracle just so the Israelites would know his power. He wanted all people—people everywhere and people throughout history—to recognize his power and his care for his people (Joshua 4:24).

104

GENESIS EXODUS LEVITICUS NUMBERS DEUTERONOMY **JOSHUA** JUDGES RUTH 1 SAMUEL 2 SAMUEL 1 KINGS 2 KINGS 1 CHRONICLES 2 CHRONICLES EZRA NEHEMIAH ESTHER JOB PSALMS PROVERBS

JOSHUA

The Fall of Jericho

Joshua 6:1-27

Behind the Story

Read Joshua 5:11-12. The food from heaven that God had been sending for 40 years stopped because the people were ready to enter their own land.

Jericho was a walled city that blocked the Israelites' access to the Promised Land. It was only about half a mile around the perimeter of Jericho. It would not have taken long to march around the city.

Jericho is known to be one of the oldest cities in the world. Archaeologists have uncovered some cities in that part of the world which had walls more than 20 feet thick and 25 feet high.

The people of Jericho were afraid. They guarded the gates. They probably had guards at the top of the massive walls around the city. Those guards watched every day as the Israelites marched silently around the city. The only sound was the blowing of the priests' trumpets and the tramping of the soldiers' feet.

The Israelites stood at the edge of the land God had promised to give them—the land they had been waiting 40 years to enter. God instructed Joshua as to how the people should take the land. All the people had to do was obey.

6 Now the people of Jericho were afraid because the Israelites were near. So they closed the city gates and guarded them. No one went into the city. And no one came out.

²Then the Lord spoke to Joshua. He said, "Look, I have given you Jericho, its king and all its fighting men. ³March around the city with your army one time every day. Do this for six days. ⁴Have seven priests carry trumpets made from horns of male sheep. Tell them to march in front of the Holy Box. On the seventh day march around the city seven times. On that day tell the priests to blow the trumpets as they march. ⁵They will make one long blast on the trumpets. When you hear that sound, have all the people give a loud shout. Then the walls of the city will fall. And the people will go straight into the city."

⁶So Joshua son of Nun called the priests together. He said to them, "Carry the Box of the Agreement with the Lord. Tell seven priests to carry trumpets and march in front of it." ⁷Then Joshua ordered the people, "Now go! March around the city. The soldiers with weapons should march in front of the Box of the Agreement with the Lord."

Jewish Man Sounding a Shofar

⁸So Joshua finished speaking to the people. Then the seven priests began marching before the Lord. They carried the seven trumpets and blew them as they marched. The priests carrying the Box of the Agreement with the Lord followed them. ⁹The soldiers with weapons marched in front of the priests. And armed men walked behind the Holy Box. They were blowing their trumpets. ¹⁰But Joshua had told the people not to give a war cry. He said, "Don't

105

ECCLESIASTES SONG OF SONGS ISAIAH JEREMIAH LAMENTATIONS EZEKIEL DANIEL HOSEA JOEL AMOS OBADIAH JONAH MICAH NAHUM HABAKKUK ZEPHANIAH HAGGAI ZECHARIAH MALACHI

shout. Don't say a word until the day I tell you. Then shout!" ¹¹So Joshua had the Holy Box of the Lord carried around the city one time. Then they went back to camp for the night.

¹²Early the next morning Joshua got up. And the priests carried the Holy Box of the Lord again. ¹³The seven priests carried the seven trumpets. They marched in front of the Holy Box of the Lord, blowing their trumpets. The soldiers with weapons marched in front of them. Other soldiers walked behind the Holy Box of the Lord. All this time the priests were blowing their trumpets. ¹⁴So on the second day they marched around the city one time. Then they went back to camp. They did this every day for six days.

¹⁵On the seventh day they got up at dawn. They marched around the city seven times. They marched just as they had on the days before. But on that day they marched around the city seven times. ¹⁶The seventh time around the priests blew their trumpets. Then Joshua gave the command: "Now, shout! The Lord has given you this city! ¹⁷The city and everything in it are to be destroyed as

an offering to the Lord. Only Rahab the prostitute and everyone in her house should remain alive. They must not be killed. This is because Rahab hid the two spies we sent out. ¹⁸Don't take any of the things that are to be destroyed as an offering to the Lord. If you take them and bring them into our camp, then you yourselves will be destroyed. You will also bring trouble to all of Israel. ¹⁹All the silver and gold and things made from bronze and iron belong to the Lord. They must be saved for him."

Seeing God

Jericho and all its residents were put under a special ban from God. There could be no contact between these people and the Israelites. This was due to God's judgment on the sin of Jericho and protection of his people.

²⁰When the priests blew the trumpets, the people shouted. At the sound of the trumpets and the people's shout, the walls fell. And everyone ran straight into the city. So the Israelites defeated that city. ²¹They completely destroyed every living thing in the city. They killed men and women, young and old. They killed cattle, sheep and donkeys.

²²Joshua spoke to the two men who had spied out the land. Joshua said, "Go into the prostitute's house. Bring her out. And bring out all the people who are with her. Do this because of the

Think About This

Note the position of the Holy Box as the Israelites marched around Jericho. It was in the center, with the priests and soldiers in front of it and armed men behind it. God was in the midst of his people as they obeyed him and prepared to enter the land he had promised them.

The ram's horn, or trumpet, referred to in this passage was not really a musical instrument. It played only a few notes and was used mainly to blow as a signal, such as a battle cry. It is the most commonly mentioned instrument in the Old Testament.

The number seven is important. There were seven priests, seven trumpets, seven days, seven times around the city on the seventh day. The number seven in Scripture indicates perfection and completion—a job well done.

106

GENESIS EXODUS LEVITICUS NUMBERS DEUTERONOMY JOSHUA JUDGES RUTH 1 SAMUEL 2 SAMUEL 1 KINGS 2 KINGS 1 CHRONICLES 2 CHRONICLES EZRA NEHEMIAH ESTHER JOB PSALMS PROVERBS

JOSHUA

Rahab Info

Rahab and her family were saved, just as the spies had promised her. Rahab believed in the God of the Israelites, the true God. She survived the destruction of Jericho and became part of the family line of Jesus. She is one of only three women mentioned by name in his ancestral family (see Matthew 1:5).

Jericho Info

The story of Joshua and the Israelites' obedience is a story of the faith of God's people to trust him, even when what he's told them seems impossible. Hebrews 11 lists many acts of obedience and the faith of God's people. The capture of Jericho is mentioned in Hebrews 11:30.

Archaeologists have uncovered the ruins of the city they believe to be the ancient city of Jericho. There is evidence that the city was completely burned—just as God commanded.

promise you made to her." [23]So the two men went into the house and brought out Rahab. They also brought out her father, mother, brothers and all those with her. They put all of her family in a safe place outside the camp of Israel.

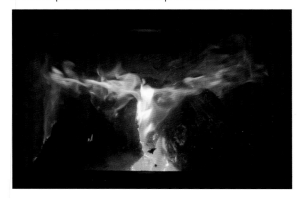

[24]Then Israel burned the whole city and everything in it. But they did not burn the things made from silver, gold, bronze and iron. These were saved for the Lord. [25]Joshua saved Rahab the prostitute, her family and all who were with her. He let them live. This was because Rahab had helped the men he had sent to spy out Jericho. Rahab still lives among the Israelites today.

[26]Then Joshua made this important promise. He said:

"Anyone who tries to rebuild this city of Jericho will be punished by a curse from the Lord. The man who lays the foundation of this city will lose his oldest son. The man who sets up the gates will lose his youngest son."

[27]So the Lord was with Joshua. And Joshua became famous through all the land.

PROPHECY FULFILLED

A man named Hiel rebuilt Jericho more than 500 years after it was destroyed by Joshua's army. In accordance with Joshua's words (Joshua 6:26), Hiel's oldest and youngest sons died as he built the city and the city gates (1 Kings 16:34).

107

ECCLESIASTES SONG OF SONGS ISAIAH JEREMIAH LAMENTATIONS EZEKIEL DANIEL HOSEA JOEL AMOS OBADIAH JONAH MICAH NAHUM HABAKKUK ZEPHANIAH HAGGAI ZECHARIAH MALACHI

The World at the Time
What was happening in the world at the time that Jericho fell?
Around 1400 B.C.

- Polaris (the Pole Star) began being used for navigation by the Phoenicians.
- Nebuchadnezzar became king of Babylon.
- An alphabet was developed by the Phoenicians which became the basis of all modern European alphabets.
- The Chinese began using chopsticks during the Shang Dynasty.

- Indians first developed the caste system.
- Topographic maps were invented by the Egyptians.
- The Chinese developed a dictionary, and also first began flying kites.
- Iron was used to make weapons and tools.
- Magnetic compasses were first developed.
- The Trojan War took place.
- Egypt split into the Northern and Southern sections.
- Gold, silverwork and literacy disappeared from Greece for three centuries—no one knows why for certain.

108

GENESIS EXODUS LEVITICUS NUMBERS DEUTERONOMY JOSHUA JUDGES RUTH 1 SAMUEL 2 SAMUEL 1 KINGS 2 KINGS 1 CHRONICLES 2 CHRONICLES EZRA NEHEMIAH ESTHER JOB PSALMS PROVERBS

JOSHUA

The Sun Stands Still

Joshua 10:1-21

God helped Joshua and his army capture the city of Jericho. Word quickly spread to other nations of how God helped his people.

Behind the Story

The Gibeonites had tricked Joshua into making a treaty with them (Joshua 9:3-15). Gibeon was a strong and powerful city. Kings of surrounding cities were terrified that the Gibeonites felt they had to resort to tricks to be safe from the Israelites.

The five kings felt they had no option but to band together to defeat the Israelites. They knew that they didn't stand a chance alone.

Joshua's men had to march all night from Gilgal. It was about 20 miles, uphill, and they were carrying their weapons. They must have been in very good physical condition.

Joshua 10:10 shows that it was God who gave the victory. He was fighting for the Israelites.

10 At this time Adoni-Zedek was the king of Jerusalem. He heard that Joshua had defeated Ai and completely destroyed it. He learned that Joshua had done the same thing to Jericho and its king. The king also learned that the Gibeonites had made a peace agreement with Israel. And they lived very near Jerusalem. ²So Adoni-Zedek and his people were very afraid because of this. Gibeon was not a little town like Ai. It was a large city. It was as big as a city that had a king. All its men were good fighters. ³So Adoni-Zedek king of Jerusalem sent a message to Hoham king of Hebron. He also sent it to Piram king of Jarmuth, Japhia king of Lachish, and Debir king of Eglon. The king of Jerusalem begged these men, ⁴"Come with me and help me attack Gibeon. Gibeon has made a peace agreement with Joshua and the Israelites."

FAQs

Q: How could the sun stand still?

A: Experts have come up with several theories to explain the miracle that God did for Joshua. One idea is that he actually stopped the earth from rotating so that the sun shined longer than normal, giving the Israelites time to win the battle. Another idea says that he lengthened the time of darkness by bringing the strong hailstorm with clouds that would have blotted out the sun. However it happened, God did a miracle for his people.

⁵Then these five Amorite kings joined their armies. They were the kings of Jerusalem, Hebron, Jarmuth, Lachish and Eglon. These armies went to Gibeon, surrounded it and attacked it.

⁶The Gibeonites sent a message to Joshua in his camp at Gilgal. The message said: "We are your servants. Don't let us be destroyed. Come quickly and help us! Save us! All the Amorite kings from the mountains have joined their armies. They are fighting against us."

⁷So Joshua marched out of Gilgal with his whole army. His best fighting men were with him. ⁸The Lord said to Joshua,

109

ECCLESIASTES SONG OF SONGS ISAIAH JEREMIAH LAMENTATIONS EZEKIEL DANIEL HOSEA JOEL AMOS OBADIAH JONAH MICAH NAHUM HABAKKUK ZEPHANIAH HAGGAI ZECHARIAH MALACHI

"Don't be afraid of those armies. I will allow you to defeat them. None of them will be able to defeat you."

[9]Joshua and his army marched all night to Gibeon. So Joshua surprised them when he attacked. [10]The Lord confused those armies when Israel attacked. So Israel defeated them in a great victory. They chased them from Gibeon on the road going to Beth Horon. The army of Israel killed men all the way to Azekah and Makkedah. [11]They chased the enemy down the road from Beth Horon to Azekah. While they were chasing them, the Lord threw large hailstones on them from the sky. Many of the enemy were killed by the hailstones. More men were killed by the hailstones than the Israelites killed with their swords.

[12]That day the Lord allowed the Israelites to defeat the Amorites. And that day Joshua stood before all the people of Israel and said to the Lord:

"Sun, stand still over Gibeon. Moon, stand still over the Valley of Aijalon." [13]So the sun stood still. And the moon stopped until the people defeated their enemies. These words are written in the Book of Jashar.

The sun stopped in the middle of the sky. It waited to go down for a full day. [14]That has never happened at any time before that day or since. That was the day the Lord listened to a man. Truly the Lord was fighting for Israel!

[15]After this, Joshua and his army went back to the camp at Gilgal.

[16]During the fight the five kings ran away. They hid in a cave near Makkedah. [17]But someone found them hiding in the cave and told Joshua. [18]So he said, "Cover the opening to the cave with large rocks. Put some men there to guard it. [19]But don't stay there yourselves. Continue chasing the enemy. Continue attacking them from behind. Don't let them get to their cities safely. The Lord your God has given you the victory over them."

[20]So Joshua and the Israelites killed the enemy. But a few were able to get back to their strong, walled cities. [21]After the fighting, Joshua's men came back safely to him at Makkedah. No one was brave enough to say a word against the Israelites.

Prayer Power

Joshua 10:12-13 reinforces the power of prayer. God listened to one man, Joshua, and answered his prayer. Read these verses about prayer:

- Philippians 4:6-7
- 1 Thessalonians 5:7
- James 1:5
- James 5:16
- 1 John 5:14

Joshua 10:21 shows just how terrified Israel's enemies were. They recognized that as long as God was fighting for his people, they had better not even speak a word against them.

Book of Jashar

The Book of Jashar, mentioned in Joshua 10:13, is also mentioned in 2 Samuel 1:18. No part of that book has been preserved.

110

GENESIS EXODUS LEVITICUS NUMBERS DEUTERONOMY JOSHUA JUDGES RUTH 1 SAMUEL 2 SAMUEL 1 KINGS 2 KINGS 1 CHRONICLES 2 CHRONICLES EZRA NEHEMIAH ESTHER JOB PSALMS PROVERBS

JUDGES

God's Angel Visits Gideon

Judges 6:11-24

The Israelites moved through the Promised Land, capturing cities and defeating enemies. But the conquest of the land was not complete. The people who lived in the land, the Canaanites, influenced God's people to turn away from him. God raised up judges to lead the people and draw them back to himself.

The Angel of the Lord Visits Gideon

6 [11]The angel of the Lord came and sat down under an oak tree at Ophrah. The oak tree belonged to Joash, who was one of the Abiezrite people. Joash was the father of Gideon. Gideon was separating some wheat from the chaff in a winepress. Gideon did this to keep the wheat from the Midianites. [12]The angel of the Lord appeared to Gideon and said, "The Lord is with you, mighty warrior!"

[13]Then Gideon said, "Pardon me, sir. If the Lord is with us, why are we having so many troubles? Our ancestors told us he did miracles. They told us the Lord brought them out of Egypt. But now he has left us. He has allowed the Midianites to defeat us."

[14]The Lord turned to Gideon and said, "You have the strength to save the people of Israel. Go and save them from the Midianites. I am the one who is sending you."

[15]But Gideon answered, "Pardon me, Lord. How can I save Israel? My family group is the weakest in Manasseh. And I am the least important member of my family."

[16]The Lord answered him, "I will be with you. It will seem as if you are fighting only one man."

[17]Then Gideon said to the Lord, "If you are pleased with me, give me proof. Show me that it is really you talking with me. [18]Please wait here. Do not go away until I come back to you. Let me bring my offering and set it in front of you."

And the Lord said, "I will wait until you come back."

Words You Should Know

Chaff (CHAF)
The husk of a head of grain. Farmers must separate it from the good part of the grain. In Bible times, they tossed the grain and chaff together into the air. Since the chaff is lighter, the wind blew it away, and the good grain fell back to the threshing floor (see Job 21:18; Psalms 1:4; 35:5; Isaiah 29:5; 41:2).

Winepress (WINE-press)
A pit where grapes were mashed to get the juice out. People stepped on the grapes. The juice ran out into another container. The winepress is sometimes used to describe how God will punish people. When they sinned terribly, God would allow the enemy armies to defeat them, as if they were grapes crushed in a winepress (see Deuteronomy 15:14; Lamentations 1:15).

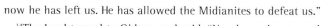

111

ECCLESIASTES SONG OF SONGS ISAIAH JEREMIAH LAMENTATIONS EZEKIEL DANIEL HOSEA JOEL AMOS OBADIAH JONAH MICAH NAHUM HABAKKUK ZEPHANIAH HAGGAI ZECHARIAH MALACHI

¹⁹So Gideon went in and cooked a young goat. He also took about 20 quarts of flour and made bread without yeast. Then he put the meat into a basket. And he put the broth from the boiled meat into a pot. He brought out the meat, the broth and the bread without yeast. He brought the food to the angel of the Lord. Gideon gave it to him under the oak tree.

²⁰The angel of God said to Gideon, "Put the meat and the bread without yeast on that rock over there. Then pour the broth on them." And Gideon did as he was told. ²¹The angel of the Lord had a stick in his hand. He touched the meat and the bread with the end of the stick. Then

fire jumped up from the rock! The meat and the bread were completely burned up! And the angel of the Lord disappeared! ²²Then Gideon understood he had been talking to the angel of the Lord. So Gideon cried, "Lord God! I have seen the angel of the Lord face to face!"

²³But the Lord said to Gideon, "Calm down! Don't be afraid! You will not die!"

²⁴So Gideon built an altar there to worship the Lord. Gideon named the altar The Lord Is Peace. It still stands at Ophrah, where the Abiezrites live.

ANGELS

God often communicates his messages to people through his messengers, angels. There are many stories of angel appearances in the Bible. Read these passages for some of them:

- Genesis 18:1-15
- Genesis 19:1-25
- Exodus 13:21-22; 14:19
- Numbers 22:21-35
- Daniel 6:1-23
- 1 Kings 19:5-11
- Luke 1:26-38
- Luke 2:8-20
- Matthew 2:13, 19-21
- Acts 23:12-15; 27:13-44

The Big Picture

The book of Judges covers about 300 years of Israel's rebellion and disobedience.

The people had been captured by the Midianites, who took everything from the Israelites. That's why Gideon was beating out wheat in a winepress—to hide it from any Midianites who happened to pass by. They would have taken it if they had seen it.

Much like Moses, Gideon didn't believe he could do the job God was calling him to (see Exodus 3:11). Just as God convinced Moses, he also showed Gideon that he could do the job and God would be with him all the way.

Gideon thought God would do a miracle to free his people from the Midianites. God chose to use Gideon. He often accomplishes his will by working through people.

Gideon built an altar and named it "The Lord is Peace" which is translated Jehovah Shalom.

112

GENESIS EXODUS LEVITICUS NUMBERS DEUTERONOMY JOSHUA JUDGES RUTH 1 SAMUEL 2 SAMUEL 1 KINGS 2 KINGS 1 CHRONICLES 2 CHRONICLES EZRA NEHEMIAH ESTHER JOB PSALMS PROVERBS

JUDGES

Gideon's Army

Judges 7:1-23

Behind the Story

God wanted the people to know, without a doubt, that this victory over the Midianites was going to be because of his power. The law of Moses gave several reasons a man could be exempt from battle (see Deuteronomy 20:5-8). However, God now adds a new way to choose soldiers—by how they drink from a stream.

God cut Gideon's army from 32,000 to 300 men by first letting those who were afraid go home. Then he cut it from 10,000 to 300 based on how they got a drink from the stream.

Judges 7:11 indicates that Gideon himself may have been afraid. Even so, he didn't leave with the first group of fearful soldiers. God allowed him to take his servant along, perhaps to bolster his courage.

God's people had conquered the Promised Land. But, in the process, they had turned away from him and began worshiping the gods of the Canaanite people. God raised up judges to lead the people back to him. One of those judges was a man named Gideon.

7 Early in the morning Jerub-Baal and all his men set up their camp at the spring of Harod. (Jerub-Baal is also called Gideon.) The Midianites were camped north of them. The Midianites were camped in the valley at the bottom of the hill called Moreh. ²Then the Lord said to Gideon, "You have too many men to defeat the Midianites. I don't want the Israelites to brag that they saved themselves. ³So now, announce to the people, 'Anyone who is afraid may leave Mount Gilead. He may go back home.' " And 22,000 men went back home. But 10,000 remained.

⁴Then the Lord said to Gideon, "There are still too many men. Take the men down to the water, and I will test them for you there. If I say, 'This man will go with you,' he will go. But if I say, 'That one will not go with you,' he will not go."

⁵So Gideon led the men down to the water. There the Lord said to him, "Separate them. Those who drink water by lapping it up like a dog will be in one group. Those who bend down to drink will be in the other group." ⁶There were 300 men who used their hands to bring water to their mouths. They lapped it as a dog does. All the rest got down on their knees to drink.

⁷Then the Lord said to Gideon, "I will save you, using the 300 men who lapped the water. And I will allow you to defeat Midian. Let all the other men go to their homes." ⁸So Gideon sent the rest of Israel to their homes. But he kept 300 men. He took the jars and the trumpets of those who went home.

Now the camp of Midian was in the valley below Gideon. ⁹That night the Lord spoke to Gideon. He said, "Get up. Go down and attack the camp of the Midianites. I will allow you to defeat them. ¹⁰But if you are afraid to go down, take your servant Purah with you. ¹¹When you come to the camp of Midian, you will hear what they are saying. Then you will not be afraid to attack the camp."

113

ECCLESIASTES SONG OF SONGS ISAIAH JEREMIAH LAMENTATIONS EZEKIEL DANIEL HOSEA JOEL AMOS OBADIAH JONAH MICAH NAHUM HABAKKUK ZEPHANIAH HAGGAI ZECHARIAH MALACHI

Gideon Is Encouraged

So Gideon and his servant Purah went down to the edge of the enemy camp. [12]The Midianites, the Amalekites and all the peoples from the east were camped in that valley. There were so many of them they seemed like locusts. They had so many camels no one could count them. There were as many as there are grains of sand on the seashore!

[13]When Gideon came to the enemy camp, he heard a man talking. That man was telling his friend about a dream. He was saying, "Listen, I dreamed that a loaf of barley bread rolled into the camp of Midian. It hit the tent so hard that the tent turned over and fell flat!"

[14]The man's friend said, "Your dream is about the sword of Gideon son of Joash, a man of Israel. God will let Gideon defeat Midian and the whole army!"

[15]When Gideon heard about the dream and what it meant, he worshiped God. Then Gideon went back to the camp of Israel. He called out to them, "Get up! The Lord has defeated the army of Midian for you!" [16]Then Gideon divided the 300 men into three groups. He gave each man a trumpet and an empty jar. A burning torch was inside each jar.

[17]Gideon told the men, "Watch me and do what I do. When I get to the edge of the camp, do what I do. [18]Surround the enemy camp. I and everyone with me will blow our trumpets. When we blow our trumpets, you blow your trumpets, too. Then shout, 'For the Lord and for Gideon!'

Soldiers

Judges 7:12 emphasizes the large number of enemy soldiers. That must have seemed even more intimidating to Gideon as he saw his army cut down to 300 soldiers.

Dreams

Judges 7:13-14 tells of a dream. Dreams were treated with great importance in the Old Testament. They always needed an interpretation of the message. In this case, God reassured Gideon once again that he would be with him. Gideon now knew that he was God's choice to lead the battle.

Horns

Gideon's men blew horns at his signal. These horns were called shofars. They were made from animal horns which were curved in shape. Shofars only blew a couple of notes and were usually blown to signal the beginning of a battle or the start of some important feast or festival. See page 104 for a picture of a shofar.

114

GENESIS EXODUS LEVITICUS NUMBERS DEUTERONOMY JOSHUA **JUDGES** RUTH 1 SAMUEL 2 SAMUEL 1 KINGS 2 KINGS 1 CHRONICLES 2 CHRONICLES EZRA NEHEMIAH ESTHER JOB PSALMS PROVERBS

JUDGES

Tactics

Gideon used military tactics to defeat the enemy.

He led the attack in the middle of the night when the enemy solders would have been sleeping—certainly not expecting an attack.

He divided his small army into three troops to give the enemy the idea that their camp was surrounded.

He depended on the elements of surprise and fear by approaching the camp quietly in the dark, then shouting and breaking the pitchers so the 300 torches could be seen.

No battle was actually fought. In fact, the Midianites were so terrified that they attacked each other before they took off running. God himself had won for Gideon's small army, without them fighting any battle at all.

Midian Is Defeated

[19]So Gideon and the 100 men with him came to the edge of the enemy camp. They came just after the enemy had changed guards. It was during the middle watch of the night. Then Gideon and his men blew their trumpets and smashed their jars. [20]All three groups of Gideon's men blew their trumpets and smashed their jars. They held the torches in their left hands and the trumpets in their right hands. Then they shouted, "A sword for the Lord and for Gideon!" [21]Each of Gideon's men stayed in his place around the camp. But inside the camp, the men of Midian began shouting and running away.

[22]When Gideon's 300 men blew their trumpets, the Lord caused all the men of Midian to fight each other with their swords! The enemy army ran away to the city of Beth Shittah. It is toward Zererah. They ran as far as the border of the city of Abel Meholah. It is near the city of Tabbath. [23]Then men of Israel from Naphtali, Asher and all of Manasseh were called out to chase the Midianites.

The Judges of Israel

Judge	Enemy	Yrs of Oppression	Yrs of Peace
Othniel	Mesopotamia	40	40
Ehud	Moab	18	80
Deborah and Barak	Canaan	20	40
Gideon	Midian	7	40
Tola	Unknown	Unknown	23
Jair	Unknown	Unknown	22
Jephtah	Ammon	18	6
Ibzan	Unknown	Unknown	7
Elon	Unknown	Unknown	10
Abdon	Unknown	Unknown	8
Samson	Philistia	40	20

115

ECCLESIASTES SONG OF SONGS ISAIAH JEREMIAH LAMENTATIONS EZEKIEL DANIEL HOSEA JOEL AMOS OBADIAH JONAH MICAH NAHUM HABAKKUK ZEPHANIAH HAGGAI ZECHARIAH MALACHI

The Judges of Israel

The book of Judges lists a total of twelve judges who served in a variety of roles during a three-century era. While some of them are major figures about whom much is known, others are only minor figures, mentioned briefly without a geographical or tribal affiliation. The significance of the judges is that no one tribe or region seems to dominate in producing these leaders. God called and equipped the necessary persons from throughout the land to lead Israel during this turbulent period.

116

GENESIS EXODUS LEVITICUS NUMBERS DEUTERONOMY JOSHUA **JUDGES** RUTH 1 SAMUEL 2 SAMUEL 1 KINGS 2 KINGS 1 CHRONICLES 2 CHRONICLES EZRA NEHEMIAH ESTHER JOB PSALMS PROVERBS

JUDGES

Words You Should Know

Judges (JUHG-es)
The leaders of Israel before
Israel had kings. A judge decided
who was guilty in court, led
the army in battle and was in
charge of the government, like a
governor. Israel had 15 judges in
all (see Judges 2:16-19; 1 Samuel
7:15-17).

Heaven (HEV-'n)
The home of God. In the New
Testament it is said to be a
place where there is no pain,
no crying, no sadness, no night
and no death. Jesus showed us
his love by leaving heaven and
coming to earth to die on a cross.
God's people will live in heaven
with him forever (see John 3:13;
6:38-40; Acts 7:56; 2 Corinthians
5:1-10; 1 Peter 1:4; Revelation
21:1-4).

Nazirite (NAZ-e-rite)
A Jewish person who made a
special promise to God. He was
to serve God by following special
rules. Samson and Samuel were
Nazirites (see Numbers 6:1-21;
Judges 16:17).

The Birth of Samson

Judges 13:1-25

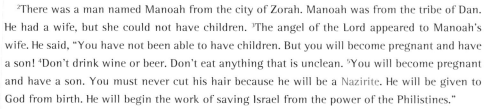

The Israelites turned their backs on God. They
disobeyed him. God sent judges to lead the people back to him. One of the judges was set apart
for God even before he was born.

13 Again the people of Israel did what the Lord
said was wrong. So he let the Philistines rule over them for 40 years.

²There was a man named Manoah from the city of Zorah. Manoah was from the tribe of Dan. He had a wife, but she could not have children. ³The angel of the Lord appeared to Manoah's wife. He said, "You have not been able to have children. But you will become pregnant and have a son! ⁴Don't drink wine or beer. Don't eat anything that is unclean. ⁵You will become pregnant and have a son. You must never cut his hair because he will be a Nazirite. He will be given to God from birth. He will begin the work of saving Israel from the power of the Philistines."

⁶Then Manoah's wife went to him and told him what had happened. She said, "A man from God came to me. He looked like an angel from God. His appearance was frightening. I didn't ask him where he was from. And he didn't tell me his name. ⁷But he said to me, 'You will be pregnant and will have a son. Don't drink wine or beer. Don't eat anything that is unclean. The reason is that the boy will be a Nazirite to God. He will be that from his birth until the day of his death.' "

⁸Then Manoah said a prayer to the Lord: "Lord, I beg you to let the man of God come to us again. Let him teach us what we should do for the boy who will be born to us."

⁹God heard Manoah's prayer. The angel of God came to Manoah's wife again. This was while she was sitting in a field. But her husband Manoah was not with her. ¹⁰So she ran to tell him, "He is here! The man who appeared to me the other day is here!"

¹¹Manoah got up and followed his wife. When he came to the man, he said, "Are you the man who spoke to my wife?"

The man said, "I am."

¹²So Manoah asked, "When what you say happens, what kind of life should the boy live? What should he do?"

117

ECCLESIASTES SONG OF SONGS ISAIAH JEREMIAH LAMENTATIONS EZEKIEL DANIEL HOSEA JOEL AMOS OBADIAH JONAH MICAH NAHUM HABAKKUK ZEPHANIAH HAGGAI ZECHARIAH MALACHI

¹³The angel of the Lord said, "Your wife must do everything I told her to do. ¹⁴She must not eat anything that grows on a grapevine. She must not drink any wine or beer. She must not eat anything that is unclean. She must do everything I have commanded her to do."

¹⁵Manoah said to the angel of the Lord, "We would like you to stay awhile. We want to cook a young goat for you."

¹⁶The angel of the Lord answered, "Even if I stay awhile, I would not eat your food. But if you want to prepare something, offer a burnt offering to the Lord." (Manoah did not understand that the man was really the angel of the Lord.)

¹⁷Then Manoah asked the angel of the Lord, "What is your name? We want to know. Then we may honor you when what you have said really happens."

¹⁸The angel of the Lord said, "Why do you ask my name? It is too wonderful for you to understand." ¹⁹Then Manoah sacrificed a young goat on a rock. He also offered some grain as a gift to the Lord. The Lord did an amazing thing. Manoah and his wife watched what happened. ²⁰The flames went up to the sky from the altar. As the fire burned, the angel of the Lord went up to heaven in the fire! When Manoah and his wife saw that, they bowed facedown on the ground. ²¹The angel of the Lord did not appear to them again. Then Manoah understood that the man was really the angel of the Lord. ²²Manoah said, "We have seen God! Surely we will die because of this!"

²³But his wife said to him, "The Lord does not want to kill us. If he wanted to kill us, he would not have accepted our burnt offering or grain offering. He would not have shown us all these things. And he would not have told us all this."

²⁴So the woman gave birth to a boy. She named him Samson. Samson grew, and the Lord blessed him. ²⁵The Spirit of the Lord began to work in Samson. This was while he was in the city of Mahaneh Dan. It is between the cities of Zorah and Eshtaol.

The Nazirite Vow

The Nazirite vow was taken by those who desired to be set apart for God's work in a special way. The rules of the vow were:

- Do not taste fruit of the vine in any way.
- Do not cut your hair.
- Do not touch a dead body.

Think About This

Samson's birth was one of four in Scripture that was announced before the mother conceived the child. The other three were Sarah with Isaac (Genesis 18:1-16), Elizabeth with John the Baptist (Luke 1:13) and Mary with Jesus (Luke 1:30-33).

Note that Samson's mother also had to observe the rules of the Nazirite vow (Judges 13:4, 7, 14). Also, the vow was placed on Samson before he was born. He did not choose to be a Nazirite.

Manoah recognized the power and holiness of God. That's why he was afraid that they would die after the angel's visit (13:22).

The Lord blessed Samson (13:24) Even so, as he grew up, Samson did not keep the rules of the Nazirite vow.

118

GENESIS EXODUS LEVITICUS NUMBERS DEUTERONOMY JOSHUA **JUDGES** RUTH 1 SAMUEL 2 SAMUEL 1 KINGS 2 KINGS 1 CHRONICLES 2 CHRONICLES EZRA NEHEMIAH ESTHER JOB PSALMS PROVERBS

JUDGES

Samson

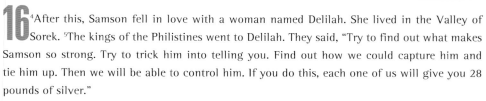

Judges 16:4-30

Samson was the strongest man who ever lived. God blessed him with great strength. But Samson did not honor and serve God. His choices got him into serious trouble.

Samson and Delilah

Words You Should Know

Bowstrings (BO-strengs)
The dried or waxed string, usually made of animal cartilage, that is used to join the two ends of a bow together.

Loom (LOOM)
A machine for weaving or braiding thread together to make fabric (see Isaiah 38:12).

Weave (WEEVE)
Threads being braided together on a loom in order to make cloth or fabric (see Exodus 28:39).

The Last Straw

Samson's weakness for beautiful women got him into trouble. He had already broken most of the rules of the Nazirite vow. When his hair was cut, God's Spirit left him, and so did his strength. That's why he was captured.

16 ⁴After this, Samson fell in love with a woman named Delilah. She lived in the Valley of Sorek. ⁵The kings of the Philistines went to Delilah. They said, "Try to find out what makes Samson so strong. Try to trick him into telling you. Find out how we could capture him and tie him up. Then we will be able to control him. If you do this, each one of us will give you 28 pounds of silver."

⁶So Delilah said to Samson, "Tell me why you are so strong. How could someone tie you up and take control of you?"

⁷Samson answered, "Someone would have to tie me up. He would have to use seven new bowstrings that have not been dried. If he did that, I would be as weak as any other man."

⁸Then the kings of the Philistines brought seven new bowstrings to Delilah. They had not been dried. She tied Samson with them. ⁹Some men were hiding in another room. Delilah said to Samson, "Samson, the Philistines are about to capture you!" But Samson easily broke the bowstrings. They broke like pieces of string burned in a fire. So the Philistines did not find out the secret of Samson's strength.

¹⁰Then Delilah said to Samson, "You've made me look foolish. You lied to me. Please tell me. How could someone tie you up?"

¹¹Samson said, "They would have to tie me with new ropes that have not been used before. Then I would become as weak as any other man."

¹²So Delilah took new ropes and tied Samson. Some men were hiding in another room. Then she called out to him, "Samson, the Philistines are about to capture you!" But he broke the ropes as easily as if they were threads.

119

ECCLESIASTES SONG OF SONGS ISAIAH JEREMIAH LAMENTATIONS EZEKIEL DANIEL HOSEA JOEL AMOS OBADIAH JONAH MICAH NAHUM HABAKKUK ZEPHANIAH HAGGAI ZECHARIAH MALACHI

¹³Then Delilah said to Samson, "Until now, you have made me look foolish. You have lied to me. Tell me how someone could tie you up."

He said, "Use the loom. Weave the seven braids of my hair into the cloth. Tighten it with a pin.

Samson and Delilah by Van Dyck

Then I will become as weak as any other man."

Then Samson went to sleep. So Delilah wove the seven braids of his hair into the cloth. ¹⁴Then she fastened it with a pin.

Again she called out to him, "Samson, the Philistines are about to capture you!" Samson woke up and pulled up the pin and the loom with the cloth.

¹⁵Then Delilah said to him, "How can you say, 'I love you,' when you don't even trust me? This is the third time you have made me look foolish. You haven't told me the secret of your great strength." ¹⁶She kept bothering Samson about his secret day after day. He became so tired of it he felt he was going to die!

¹⁷So he told her everything. He said, "I have never had my hair cut. I have been set apart to God as a Nazirite since I was born. If someone shaved my head, then I would lose my strength. I would become as weak as any other man."

¹⁸Delilah saw that he had told her everything sincerely. So she sent a message to the kings of the Philistines. She said, "Come back one more time. He has told me every-thing." So the kings of the Philistines came back to Deli-lah. They brought the silver they had promised to give her. ¹⁹Delilah got Samson to go to sleep. He was lying in her lap. Then she called in a man to shave off the seven braids of Samson's hair. In this way she began to make him weak. And Samson's strength left him.

²⁰Then she called out to him, "Samson, the Philistines are about to capture you!"

He woke up and thought, "I'll get loose as I did before and shake myself free." But he did not know that the Lord had left him. ²¹Then the Philistines captured Samson. They tore out his eyes. And they took him down to Gaza. They put bronze chains on him. They put him in prison and made him grind grain. ²²But his hair began to grow again.

Behind the Story

Samson's second lie to Delilah was that new ropes would hold him. He specified new ropes because they would be stronger than old ones.

Samson's third lie showed that Delilah was wearing him down. He began to mention his hair, even though he didn't tell her that it could not be cut. Her constant questions were weakening his resolve.

Samson's downfall came because he compromised his obedience to God. He never should have gotten involved with Delilah in the first place because she was a Philistine and did not worship, honor or obey God.

The Philistine kings promised to pay Delilah 28 pounds of silver. Samson was their number one enemy. They wanted to capture him very badly.

120

GENESIS EXODUS LEVITICUS NUMBERS DEUTERONOMY JOSHUA **JUDGES** RUTH 1 SAMUEL 2 SAMUEL 1 KINGS 2 KINGS 1 CHRONICLES 2 CHRONICLES EZRA NEHEMIAH ESTHER JOB PSALMS PROVERBS

JUDGES

The Temple

Dagon was an important god to the Philistines. Most major cities had temples dedicated to this god. These buildings had roofs made of mud bricks or large stones. Large pillars supported the roofs. Crowds of people gathered on the roofs to watch sporting events or, in this case, the humiliation of a prisoner in the courtyard below. When Samson pushed the pillars apart and the roof came crashing down, he killed more than 3,000 Philistines. Samson's strength returned because he prayed, asking God to help him (Judges 16:28-30).

Samson Dies

²³The kings of the Philistines gathered to celebrate. They were going to offer a great sacrifice to their god Dagon. They said, "Our god has given us Samson our enemy."

²⁴When they saw him, they praised their god. They said, "This man destroyed our country. He killed many of us! But our god helped us capture our enemy."

²⁵The people were having a good time at the celebration. They said, "Bring Samson out to perform for us." So they brought Samson from the prison. He performed for them. They made him stand between the pillars of the temple of Dagon. ²⁶A servant was holding his hand. Samson said to him, "Let me feel the pillars

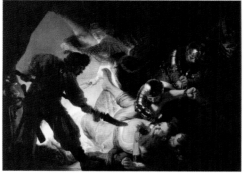

The Blinding of Samson by Rembrandt

that hold up the temple. I want to lean against them." ²⁷Now the temple was full of men and women. All the kings of the Philistines were there. There were about 3,000 men and women on the roof. They watched Samson perform. ²⁸Then Samson prayed to the Lord. He said, "Lord God, remember me. God, please give me strength one more time. Let me pay these Philistines back

for putting out my two eyes!" ²⁹Then Samson held the two center pillars of the temple. These two pillars supported the whole temple. He braced himself between the two pillars. His right hand was on one, and his left hand was on the other. ³⁰Samson said,

"Let me die with these Philistines!" Then he pushed as hard as he could. And the temple fell on the kings and all the people in it. So Samson killed more of the Philistines when he died than when he was alive.

121

ECCLESIASTES SONG OF SONGS ISAIAH JEREMIAH LAMENTATIONS EZEKIEL DANIEL HOSEA JOEL AMOS OBADIAH JONAH MICAH NAHUM HABAKKUK ZEPHANIAH HAGGAI ZECHARIAH MALACHI

The World at the Time

The experiences in the book of Judges took place around 1100 B.C. What else was happening in the world at that time?

- The powerful nation of Babylon was conquered by Assyria under the leadership of Tiglath-Pileser.
- The Phoenicians, known as the Sea People founded the cities of Tyre and Sidon, famous for their dyes, glassware and metal goods.
- Stonehenge, the stone circle which may have been a religious site in England, was completed.
- The Chinese began harvesting and storing ice.

THE IRON AGE

The time period of Judges was near the beginning of the Iron Age. The Iron Age was the last of the three periods of time in history which have been divided by archaeologists into:

The Stone Age

The Bronze Age

The Iron Age

The Iron Age simply signifies the use of metal becoming more and more common throughout the world. This happened in different countries at different times because of nations being captured or people traveling to different countries. Iron replaced bronze as the material used to make weapons or basic tools. When iron was used for pots or dishes, it sometimes led to terrible problems such as lead poisoning.

FAQs

Why didn't the Philistines kill Samson when they captured him?

They took more pleasure in humiliating him. So they gouged out his eyes and made him do work that was usually done by animals or slaves. This is the same way kings who were captured in battle were treated. Often kings or great soldiers would kill themselves rather than be captured and treated this way.

122

GENESIS EXODUS LEVITICUS NUMBERS DEUTERONOMY JOSHUA JUDGES RUTH 1 SAMUEL 2 SAMUEL 1 KINGS 2 KINGS 1 CHRONICLES 2 CHRONICLES EZRA NEHEMIAH ESTHER JOB PSALMS PROVERBS

RUTH

Loyalty

Bethlehem was on the opposite side of the Dead Sea from Moab.

When Naomi decided to return to Bethlehem, both of her daughters-in-law wanted to come along at first. She tried her best to convince them to stay in Moab and, hopefully, find new husbands. Orpah did stay, but Ruth wanted to come with Naomi. Ruth's beautiful speech declaring her loyalty to Naomi is often used today in weddings to show the unity and loyalty of the couple being married (Ruth 1:16-17).

Widows

When a man died all his possessions and wealth went to the man who owned the family birthright. The widow depended on family members to care for her and provide for her. This responsibility fell to the closest relative of the husband. This may have been one reason Naomi wished to return to Bethlehem.

Ruth

Ruth 1:1-22

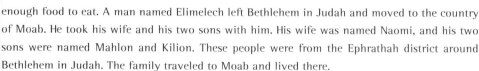

During the time of the judges, a famine settled on the land. One man took his family and moved to the land of Moab so they could survive.

The Story of a Girl from Moab

1 ¹⁻²Long ago the judges ruled Israel. During their rule, there was a time in the land when there was not enough food to eat. A man named Elimelech left Bethlehem in Judah and moved to the country of Moab. He took his wife and his two sons with him. His wife was named Naomi, and his two sons were named Mahlon and Kilion. These people were from the Ephrathah district around Bethlehem in Judah. The family traveled to Moab and lived there.

³Later, Naomi's husband, Elimelech, died. So only Naomi and her two sons were left. ⁴These sons married women from Moab. The name of one wife was Orpah. The name of the other wife was Ruth. Naomi and her sons lived in Moab about ten years. ⁵Then Mahlon and Kilion also died. So Naomi was left alone without her husband or her two sons.

⁶While Naomi was in Moab, she heard that the Lord had taken care of his people. He had given food to them in Judah. So Naomi got ready to leave Moab and go back home. The wives of Naomi's sons also got ready to go with her. ⁷So they left the place where they had lived. And they started back on the way to the land of Judah. ⁸But Naomi said to her two daughters-in-law, "Go back home. Each of you go to your own mother's house. You have been very kind to me and to my sons who are now dead. I hope the Lord will also be kind to you in the same way. ⁹I hope the Lord will give you another home and a new husband."

Then Naomi kissed the women. And they began to cry out loud. ¹⁰Her daughters-in-law said to her, "No. We will go with you to your people."

¹¹But Naomi said, "My daughters, go back to your own homes. Why do you want to go with me? I cannot give birth to more sons to give you new husbands. ¹²So go back to your own

Ruth and Naomi by C. F. Vos

123

ECCLESIASTES SONG OF SONGS ISAIAH JEREMIAH LAMENTATIONS EZEKIEL DANIEL HOSEA JOEL AMOS OBADIAH JONAH MICAH NAHUM HABAKKUK ZEPHANIAH HAGGAI ZECHARIAH MALACHI

homes. I am too old to have another husband. But even if I had another husband tonight and if I had more sons, it wouldn't help! [13]Would you wait until the babies were grown into men? Would you live for so many years without husbands? Don't do this thing. My life is much too sad for you to share. This is because the Lord is against me!"

[14]The women cried together again. Then Orpah kissed Naomi good-bye, but Ruth held on to her.

[15]Naomi said, "Look, your sister-in-law is going back to her own people and her own gods. Go back with her."

Ruth Stays with Naomi

[16]But Ruth said, "Don't ask me to leave you! Don't beg me not to follow you! Every place you go, I will go. Every place you live, I will live. Your people will be my people. Your God will be my God. [17]And where you die, I will die. And there I will be buried. I ask the Lord to punish me terribly if I do not keep this promise: Only death will separate us."

[18]Naomi saw that Ruth had made up her mind to go with her. So Naomi stopped arguing with her. [19]Naomi and Ruth went on until they came to the town of Bethlehem. When the two women entered Bethlehem, all the people became very excited. The women of the town said, "Is this Naomi?"

[20]But Naomi told the people, "Don't call me Naomi. Call me Mara, because God All-Powerful has made my life very sad. [21]When I left, I had all I wanted. But now, the Lord has brought me home with nothing. So why should you call me Naomi when the Lord has spoken against me? God All-Powerful has given me much trouble."

[22]So Naomi and her daughter-in-law Ruth, the woman from Moab, came back from Moab. They came to Bethlehem at the beginning of the barley harvest.

Names

Names in the Bible are often reflective of the personalities of people or the situations they are experiencing.

Elimelech means "God is King." Naomi means "Sweet," and Mara means "Bitter."

Behind the Story

Ruth grew up in Moab and, therefore, would not have known the true God. Naomi and her family must have been good teachers and good examples of God's love in order for Ruth to long to know and serve him rather than her Moabite gods.

Ruth had a dual reason for staying with Naomi: She was choosing to serve God, which would have been more difficult had she stayed in Moab, and she wanted to take care of Naomi.

Ruth and Naomi arrived in Bethlehem as the harvest was beginning. That means it was sometime around April or May.

It's clear from Ruth 1:20 that Naomi's heart was broken. Even though Ruth returned with her, Naomi was still grieving the loss of her husband and sons.

124

GENESIS EXODUS LEVITICUS NUMBERS DEUTERONOMY JOSHUA JUDGES RUTH 1 SAMUEL 2 SAMUEL 1 KINGS 2 KINGS 1 CHRONICLES 2 CHRONICLES EZRA NEHEMIAH ESTHER JOB PSALMS PROVERBS

RUTH

Ruth Meets Boaz

Ruth 2:1-20

Behind the Story

Since Boaz was a relative of Naomi's husband, Naomi knew that he could be the one to help her and Ruth. He was wealthy and of good character. God had ordered the Israelites to take care of widows back when he gave Moses the Law (see Deuteronomy 24:19-22). Boaz would have known that.

Ruth's action of following behind the field workers and picking up any grain they dropped or left behind was a common practice. As outlined in Deuteronomy 24, God encouraged the people to provide for widows and orphans in this way.

Naomi probably did not forget that she had relatives in Bethlehem. That may have been why she wanted to return there. She knew that her husband's closest relative was obligated to help her. Boaz was a relative, but not the closest relative.

2 Now there was a rich man living in Bethlehem whose name was Boaz. Boaz was one of Naomi's close relatives from Elimelech's family.

²One day Ruth, the woman from Moab, said to Naomi, "Let me go to the fields. Maybe someone will be kind and let me gather the grain he leaves in his field."

Naomi said, "Go, my daughter."

³So Ruth went to the fields. She followed the workers who were cutting the grain. And she gathered the grain that they had left. It just so happened that the field belonged to Boaz. He was a close relative from Elimelech's family.

⁴When Boaz came from Bethlehem, he spoke to his workers: "The Lord be with you!"

And the workers answered, "May the Lord bless you!"

⁵Then Boaz spoke to his servant who was in charge of the workers. He asked, "Whose girl is that?"

⁶The servant answered, "She is the Moabite woman who came with Naomi from the country of Moab. ⁷She said, 'Please let me follow the workers and gather the grain that they leave on the ground.' She came and has remained here. From morning until just now, she has stopped only a few moments to rest in the shelter."

Ruth and Boaz by N. Poussin

⁸Then Boaz said to Ruth, "Listen, my daughter. Stay here in my field to gather grain for yourself. Do not go to any other person's field. Continue following behind my women workers. ⁹Watch to see which fields they go to and follow them. I

have warned the young men not to bother you. When you are thirsty, you may go and drink. Take water from the water jugs that the servants have filled."

125

ECCLESIASTES SONG OF SONGS ISAIAH JEREMIAH LAMENTATIONS EZEKIEL DANIEL HOSEA JOEL AMOS OBADIAH JONAH MICAH NAHUM HABAKKUK ZEPHANIAH HAGGAI ZECHARIAH MALACHI

[10]Then Ruth bowed low with her face to the ground. She said to Boaz, "I am a stranger. Why have you been so kind to notice me?"

[11]Boaz answered her, "I know about all the help you have given to Naomi, your mother-in-law. You helped her even after your husband died. You left your father and mother and your own country. You came to this nation where you did not know anyone. [12]The Lord will reward you for all you have done. You will be paid in full by the Lord, the God of Israel. You have come to him as a little bird finds shelter under the wings of its mother."

[13]Then Ruth said, "You are very kind to me, sir. You have said kind words to me, your servant. You have given me hope. And I am not even good enough to be one of your servants."

[14]At mealtime Boaz told Ruth, "Come here! Eat some of our bread. Here, dip your bread in our vinegar."

So Ruth sat down with the workers. Boaz gave her some roasted grain. Ruth ate until she was full, and there was some food left over. [15]Ruth rose and went back to work. Then Boaz told his servants, "Let her gather even around the bundles of grain. Don't tell her to go away. [16]Drop some full heads of grain for her. Let her gather that grain, and don't tell her to stop."

[17]So Ruth gathered grain in the field until evening. Then she separated the grain from the chaff. There was about one-half bushel of barley. [18]Ruth carried the grain into town. And her mother-in-law saw what she had gathered. Ruth also gave her the food that was left over from lunch.

[19]Naomi asked her, "Where did you gather all this grain today? Where did you work? Blessed be the man who noticed you!"

Ruth told her about whose field she had worked in. She said, "The man I worked with today is named Boaz."

[20]Naomi told her daughter-in-law, "The Lord bless him! The Lord still continues to be kind to all people—the living and the dead!" Then Naomi told Ruth, "Boaz is one of our close relatives, one who will take care of us."

God Cares for His Own

Ruth didn't plan to go to Boaz's field (Ruth 2:3). God directed her to the field of this kind man who was also a relative of Naomi.

Love and Kindness

Apparently Boaz experienced "love at first sight." He may have known of Ruth's loyalty and care of Naomi even before he saw her in the field.

Ruth had gathered one-half bushel of grain. That was quite a large amount for one woman to gather. Boaz's order for his workers to leave extra grain for her was very kind.

Boaz knew that a pretty young woman such as Ruth might be in danger from some of the male field workers. He ordered them to leave her alone. The workers knew they would have to answer to Boaz if they bothered or hurt Ruth in any way.

Notice the difference in Ruth's attitude. In Ruth 2:10 she calls herself a stranger. In verse 13, she refers to herself as Boaz's servant. His kindness to her made all the difference.

126

GENESIS EXODUS LEVITICUS NUMBERS DEUTERONOMY JOSHUA JUDGES RUTH 1 SAMUEL 2 SAMUEL 1 KINGS 2 KINGS 1 CHRONICLES 2 CHRONICLES EZRA NEHEMIAH ESTHER JOB PSALMS PROVERBS

RUTH

Naomi's Plan

Ruth 3:1-18

Tool Used for Threshing

Words You Should Know

Threshing floor

(THRESH-ing flór)
A place where farmers separated grain from chaff. This was done by beating the stalks on the hard ground. Then they would throw it in the air and let the wind blow the chaff away (see Genesis 50:10; Judges 6:11; 2 Samuel 24:16-24). See "chaff" on page 110.

Behind the Story

There have been many questions about Ruth's actions at the threshing floor. More than likely, when she lay down at Boaz's feet (showing submission to him) and asked him to spread his robe over her, she was simply telling him that she knew he was a relative and she needed his help.

Boaz already cared about her. Now she showed that she cared about him, too. The fact that he was quite a bit older than Ruth was unimportant.

3 Then Naomi, Ruth's mother-in-law, said to her, "My daughter, I must find a suitable home for you. That would be good for you. ²Now Boaz is our close relative. You worked with his women servants. Tonight he will be working at the threshing floor. ³Go wash yourself and put on perfume. Change your clothes, and go down to the threshing floor. But don't let him see you until he has finished eating and drinking. ⁴Then he will lie down. Watch him so you will know the place where he lies down. Go there and lift the cover off his feet and lie down. He will tell you what you should do."

⁵Then Ruth answered, "I will do everything you say."

⁶So Ruth went down to the threshing floor. She did all her mother-in-law told her to do. ⁷After eating and drinking, Boaz was feeling good. He went to lie down beside the pile of grain. Then Ruth went to him quietly. She lifted the cover from his feet and lay down.

Kinsman Redeemer

Boaz was Ruth's kinsman redeemer. He was a relative of Naomi's husband who could "buy back" her life by marrying her and providing for her financially. In this case, Boaz married Ruth, and they both cared for Naomi.

A kinsman redeemer is a "type" of Christ. He is our "relative" who bought back our lives by giving his.

⁸About midnight Boaz woke up suddenly and rolled over. He was startled! There was a woman lying near his feet! ⁹Boaz asked, "Who are you?"

She said, "I am Ruth, your servant girl. Spread your cover over me because you are the one who is to take care of me."

¹⁰Then Boaz said, "The Lord bless you, my daughter. Your kindness to me is greater than the kindness you showed to Naomi in the beginning. You didn't look for a young man to marry, either rich or poor. ¹¹Now, my daughter, don't be afraid. I will do everything you ask. All the people in our town know you are a very good woman. ¹²And it is true, I am a relative who is to take care of you. But there is a man who is a closer relative to you

127

ECCLESIASTES SONG OF SONGS ISAIAH JEREMIAH LAMENTATIONS EZEKIEL DANIEL HOSEA JOEL AMOS OBADIAH JONAH MICAH NAHUM HABAKKUK ZEPHANIAH HAGGAI ZECHARIAH MALACHI

than I. [13]But stay here tonight. In the morning we will see if he will take care of you. If he decides to take care of you, that is fine. If he refuses to take care of you, I myself will marry you. Then I will buy back Elimelech's land for you. As surely as the Lord lives, I promise to do this. So lie here until morning."

[14]So Ruth lay near his feet until the morning. She rose while it was still too dark to be recognized. Boaz said to his servants, "Don't tell anyone that the woman came here to the threshing floor." [15]Then Boaz said to Ruth, "Bring me your shawl. Now, hold it open."

So Ruth held her shawl open, and Boaz poured six portions of barley into it. Boaz then put it on her back, and she went to the city.

[16]Ruth went to the home of her mother-in-law. And Naomi asked, "How did you do, my daughter?"

So Ruth told Naomi everything that Boaz did for her. [17]She said, "Boaz gave me these six portions of barley. He said, 'You must not go home without a gift for your mother-in-law.' "

[18]Naomi answered, "Ruth, my daughter, wait until you hear what happens. Boaz will not rest until he has finished doing what he should do this day."

Farming in Canaan

Farmers plowed the land and planted seeds in early autumn—October or November. They waited until after the rains had come at the end of summer.

Harvest time was in the spring. Harvesters cut the grain (wheat or barley) using big curved knives called sickles. Then they tied the grain into big bundles called sheaves. From there it went to the threshing floor where the chaff (hulls or husks) was separated from the good part of the grain that could be used for cooking and eating.

FAQs

Why did a rich man such as Boaz sleep on the threshing floor?

The threshing floor was in a public place. Anyone could come in and steal the grain. Apparently he trusted no one else enough to guard his grain, so he stayed there himself to guard it.

Think About This

In essence, Ruth was asking Boaz to marry her by acknowledging that he was a close relative who was the one to take care of her.

Boaz was an honorable man. He pointed out that there was a closer relative than he who actually had first choice of marrying Ruth (Ruth 3:12). He could not continue the discussion with her until after he had talked to that man.

Ruth came to Boaz and left him quietly, almost secretly. Perhaps that was to keep from embarrassing him if it became known that he had refused to marry her.

128

GENESIS EXODUS LEVITICUS NUMBERS DEUTERONOMY JOSHUA JUDGES RUTH 1 SAMUEL 2 SAMUEL 1 KINGS 2 KINGS 1 CHRONICLES 2 CHRONICLES EZRA NEHEMIAH ESTHER JOB PSALMS PROVERBS

RUTH

Boaz Marries Ruth

Ruth 4:1-22

Behind the Story

Boaz spoke to the other relative in front of other people (Ruth 4:3). This gave them witnesses to their decision. Most business took place at the city gate. That was a very public place where people passed through each day.

The responsibility of the close relative of a widow involved buying the land which had belonged to her husband and marrying her. Then any children she had would carry on her dead husband's name.

The man did not want to make this deal because he already had sons. He would have preferred them to inherit Naomi's land—rather than any sons he and Ruth might have had.

The close relative took off his sandal and gave it to Boaz to "close the deal." That symbol was the same as when a contract is signed today. It meant the deal was sealed. Now Boaz was free to buy Naomi's land and marry Ruth.

4 Boaz went to the city gate. He sat there until the close relative he had mentioned passed by. Boaz called to him, "Come here, friend! Sit down here!" So the man came over and sat down. ²Boaz gathered ten of the old men who were leaders of the city. He told them, "Sit down here!" So they sat down.

³Then Boaz spoke to the close relative. He said, "Naomi has come back from the country of Moab. She wants to sell the piece of land that belonged to our relative Elimelech. ⁴So I decided to say this to you: If you want to buy back the land, then buy it! Buy it in front of the people who live here and in front of the elders of my people. If you don't want to buy it, tell me. I am the only person after you who can buy back the land. If you don't buy it back, I will."

And the close relative said, "I will buy back the land."

⁵Then Boaz said, "When you buy the land from Naomi, you must marry Ruth, the dead man's wife. She is the woman from Moab. That way, the land will stay in her dead husband's family."

⁶The close relative answered, "Then I can't buy back the land. If I did, I might lose what I can pass on to my own sons. I cannot buy the land back. So you buy it yourself."

⁷Long ago in Israel when people traded or bought back something, one person took off his sandal and gave it to the other person. This was their proof of purchase.

⁸So the close relative said, "Buy the land yourself." And then he took off his sandal.

⁹Then Boaz spoke to the elders and to all the people. He said, "You are witnesses today of what I am buying from Naomi. I am buying everything that belonged to Elimelech and Kilion and Mahlon. ¹⁰I am also taking Ruth as my wife. She is the Moabite who was the wife of Mahlon. I am doing this so her dead husband's property will stay with his family. This way, his name will not be separated from his family and his land. You are witnesses this day."

¹¹So all the people and elders who were at the city gate said, "We are witnesses. This woman will be coming into your home. We hope the Lord will make her like Rachel and Leah. They had many children. So the people of Israel grew in number. May you become powerful in the district

129

ECCLESIASTES SONG OF SONGS ISAIAH JEREMIAH LAMENTATIONS EZEKIEL DANIEL HOSEA JOEL AMOS OBADIAH JONAH MICAH NAHUM HABAKKUK ZEPHANIAH HAGGAI ZECHARIAH MALACHI

of Ephrathah. May you become famous in Bethlehem! [12]Tamar gave birth to Judah's son Perez. In the same way, may the Lord give you many children through Ruth. And may your family be great like his."

[13]So Boaz took Ruth and married her. The Lord let her become pregnant, and she gave birth to a son. [14]The women told Naomi, "Praise the Lord who gave you this grandson. And may he become famous in Israel. [15]He will give you new life. And he will take care of you in your old age. This happened because of your daughter-in-law. She loves you. And she is better for you than seven sons. She has given birth to your grandson."

[16]Naomi took the boy, held him in her arms and cared for him. [17]The neighbors gave the boy his name. These women said, "This boy was born for Naomi." The neighbors named him Obed. Obed was Jesse's father. And Jesse was the father of David.

[18]This is the family history of Perez. Perez was the father of Hezron. [19]Hezron was the father of Ram. Ram was the father of Amminadab. [20]Amminadab was the father of Nahshon. Nahshon was the father of Salmon. [21]Salmon was the father of Boaz. Boaz was the father of Obed. [22]Obed was the father of Jesse, and Jesse was the father of David.

Lineage of Jesus

Abraham to David

Ruth ends with a description of the family from Perez up to King David. See Matthew 1 to see how that family led to Jesus.

- **Abraham** (and Sarah)
- Isaac (and Rebekah)
- Jacob (and Leah)
- Judah (and Tamar)
- Perez
- Hezron
- Ram
- Amminadab
- Nahshon
- Salmon (and Rahab)
- **Boaz (and Ruth)**
- Obed
- Jesse
- **David**

Think About This

Boaz and Ruth were married. Naomi apparently lived with them, and they cared for her. Ruth, who at the beginning of this story lived in Moab and did not know the true God, gave birth to a son named Obed, which means, "The one who serves." By marrying Boaz, Ruth came into the ancestry or lineage of Jesus. (See Matthew 1:5.)

Ruth was the great-grandmother of King David, one of the most famous people in the Old Testament and a man who was described as a man after God's own heart.

Once before, a Gentile woman had come to know God and also had come into the lineage of Jesus. Her name was Rahab, the mother of Boaz. She was the prostitute who saved the spies in Jericho and then was spared when the city was destroyed (see Joshua 6:25).

130

GENESIS EXODUS LEVITICUS NUMBERS DEUTERONOMY JOSHUA JUDGES RUTH 1 SAMUEL 2 SAMUEL 1 KINGS 2 KINGS 1 CHRONICLES 2 CHRONICLES EZRA NEHEMIAH ESTHER JOB PSALMS PROVERBS

1 SAMUEL

Think About This

The books of 1 and 2 Samuel were originally one book.

Samuel grew up to be the last of the judges. He actually anointed the first and second kings of Israel.

Ramathaim was a small village about 4 miles north of Jerusalem. It would have been a 15-mile walk to Shiloh, the religious center where the Meeting Tent was located.

Samuel was a Nazirite. This was chosen for him by his parents before he was even born.

Samuel means "Name of God."

Samuel's Birth

1 Samuel 1:1-28

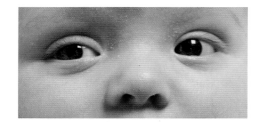

Israel was at a low point—far away from God. Then a baby was born who would grow up to love God and lead the people of Israel back to him.

1 There was a man named Elkanah son of Jeroham. He was from Ramathaim in the mountains of Ephraim. Elkanah was from the family of Zuph. (Jeroham was Elihu's son. Elihu was Tohu's son. And Tohu was the son of Zuph from the family group of Ephraim.) ²Elkanah had two wives. One was named Hannah, and the other was named Peninnah. Peninnah had children, but Hannah had none.

³Every year Elkanah left his town Ramah and went up to Shiloh. There he worshiped the Lord of heaven's armies and offered sacrifices to him. Shiloh was where Hophni and Phinehas served as priests of the Lord. They were the sons of Eli. ⁴When Elkanah offered sacrifices, he always gave a share of the meat to his wife Peninnah. He also gave shares of the meat to her sons and daughters. ⁵But Elkanah always gave a special share of the meat to Hannah. He did this because he loved Hannah and because the Lord had made Hannah unable to have children. ⁶Peninnah would upset Hannah and make her feel bad. She did this because the Lord had made Hannah unable to have children. ⁷This happened every year when they went up to the Tent of the Lord at Shiloh. Peninnah would upset Hannah until Hannah would cry and not eat anything. ⁸Her

husband Elkanah would say to her, "Hannah, why are you crying? Why won't you eat? Why are you sad? Don't I mean more to you than ten sons?"

⁹Once, after they had eaten their meal in Shiloh, Hannah got up. Now Eli the priest was sitting on a chair near the entrance to the Lord's Holy Tent. ¹⁰Hannah was very sad. She cried much and prayed to the Lord. ¹¹She made a promise. She said, "Lord of heaven's armies, see how bad I feel. Remember me! Don't forget me. If you will give me a son, I will give him back to you all his life. And no one will ever use a razor to cut his hair."

131

ECCLESIASTES SONG OF SONGS ISAIAH JEREMIAH LAMENTATIONS EZEKIEL DANIEL HOSEA JOEL AMOS OBADIAH JONAH MICAH NAHUM HABAKKUK ZEPHANIAH HAGGAI ZECHARIAH MALACHI

[12]While Hannah kept praying, Eli watched her mouth. [13]She was praying in her heart. Her lips moved, but her voice was not heard. So Eli thought she was drunk. [14]He said to her, "Stop getting drunk! Throw away your wine!"

[15]Hannah answered, "No, master, I have not drunk any wine or beer. I am a woman who is deeply troubled. I was telling the Lord about all my problems. [16]Don't think of me as an evil woman. I have been praying because of my many troubles and much sadness."

[17]Eli answered, "Go in peace. May the God of Israel give you what you asked of him."

[18]Hannah said, "I want to be pleasing to you always." Then she left and ate something. She was not sad anymore.

[19]Early the next morning Elkanah's family got up and worshiped the Lord. Then they went back home to Ramah. Elkanah had sexual relations with his wife Hannah. And the Lord remembered her. [20]So Hannah became pregnant, and in time she gave birth to a son. She named him Samuel. She said, "His name is Samuel because I asked the Lord for him."

Hannah Gives Samuel to God

[21]Every year Elkanah went to Shiloh to offer sacrifices. He went to keep the promise he had made to God. He brought his whole family with him. So once again he went up to Shiloh. [22]But Hannah did not go with him. She told him, "When the boy is old enough to eat solid food, I will take him to Shiloh. Then I will give him to the Lord. He will become a Nazirite. He will always live there at Shiloh."

[23]Elkanah, Hannah's husband, said to her, "Do what you think is best. You may stay home until the boy is old enough to eat. May the Lord do what you have said." So Hannah stayed at home to nurse her son until he was old enough to eat.

[24]When Samuel was old enough to eat, Hannah took him to the Tent of the Lord at Shiloh. She also took a three-year-old bull, one-half bushel of flour and a leather bag filled with wine. [25]They killed the bull for the sacrifice. Then Hannah brought Samuel to Eli. [26]She said to Eli, "As surely as you live, my master, I am the same woman who stood near you praying to the Lord. [27]I prayed for this child. The Lord answered my prayer and gave him to me. [28]Now I give him back to the Lord. He will belong to the Lord all his life." And he worshiped the Lord there.

Behind the Story

Hannah was very sad. She wanted children because, at that time, it was a disgrace for a wife not to give children to her husband. Some considered it a shame caused by God because of his unhappiness with the woman.

Hannah's pain was deepened by the fact that Peninnah, Elkanah's other wife, made fun of her and criticized her for not having children.

After Hannah spoke with Eli, she was not sad anymore (1 Samuel 1:18). Even though she did not yet have a baby, she knew God was working. She trusted Eli's words because he was a priest.

Hannah took Samuel back to the Tent of the Lord to live there and serve God. He was probably about 3 years old when he went to live there with Eli.

Hannah also took the things that were required to be given as offerings to the Tent of the Lord (1:24).

132

GENESIS EXODUS LEVITICUS NUMBERS DEUTERONOMY JOSHUA JUDGES RUTH **1 SAMUEL** 2 SAMUEL 1 KINGS 2 KINGS 1 CHRONICLES 2 CHRONICLES EZRA NEHEMIAH ESTHER JOB PSALMS PROVERBS

1 SAMUEL

Words You Should Know

Visions (VIZ-shuns)
Similar to a dream. A vision may come to a person when he is awake or asleep. God used visions to tell people what he wanted them to do, to teach them something or to let them know something that was going to happen (see Genesis 15:1; Daniel 2:19; Acts 9:10-12; 10:3-19; 11:5; 16:9-10; 18:9).

Holy Tent
Often called the Meeting Tent or Tabernacle. This was the special tent where the Israelites worshiped God. It was used from the time they left Egypt until Solomon built the Temple in Jerusalem. This tent was kept in the middle of their camp to remind them that God was always with them (see Exodus 25–27; 39:32–40:38; Numbers 7:1–8:4; 2 Chronicles 1:3-13; 5:5).

God Calls Samuel

1 Samuel 3:1-21

Samuel's mother prayed for a child. When God gave her Samuel, she gave him back to God to serve him. Samuel lived at the Tent of the Lord with Eli the priest, where he learned how to serve God.

3 The boy Samuel served the Lord under Eli. In those days the Lord did not speak directly to people very often. There were very few visions.

²Eli's eyes were so weak he was almost blind. One night he was lying in bed. ³Samuel was also in bed in the Lord's Holy Tent. The Box of the Agreement was in the Holy Tent. God's lamp was still burning.

⁴Then the Lord called Samuel. Samuel answered, "I am here!" ⁵He ran to Eli and said, "I am here. You called me."

But Eli said, "I didn't call you. Go back to bed." So Samuel went back to bed.

⁶The Lord called again, "Samuel!"

Samuel again went to Eli and said, "I am here. You called me."

Again Eli said, "I didn't call you. Go back to bed."

⁷Samuel did not yet know the Lord. The Lord had not spoken directly to him yet.

⁸The Lord called Samuel for the third time. Samuel got up and went to Eli. He said, "I am here. You called me."

Then Eli realized the Lord was calling the boy. ⁹So he told Samuel, "Go to bed. If he calls you again, say, 'Speak, Lord. I am your servant, and I am listening.' " So Samuel went and lay down in bed.

¹⁰The Lord came and stood there. He called as he had before. He said, "Samuel, Samuel!"

Samuel said, "Speak, Lord. I am your servant, and I am listening."

¹¹The Lord said to Samuel, "See, I am going to do something in Israel. It will shock those

God Speaks

It's not uncommon to read stories in the Bible of God speaking to people. Here are a few examples of people God spoke to:

- Adam (Genesis 1:28)
- Noah (Genesis 6:13)
- Moses (Exodus 3:4)
- Joshua (Joshua 1:1)

Now young Samuel hears God's voice, too.

133

ECCLESIASTES SONG OF SONGS ISAIAH JEREMIAH LAMENTATIONS EZEKIEL DANIEL HOSEA JOEL AMOS OBADIAH JONAH MICAH NAHUM HABAKKUK ZEPHANIAH HAGGAI ZECHARIAH MALACHI

who hear about it. [12]At that time I will do to Eli and his family everything I promised. I will not stop until I have finished. [13]I told Eli I would punish his family forever. I will do it because Eli knew his sons were evil. They spoke against me, but he did not control them. [14]So here is what I promised Eli's family: 'Your guilt will never be removed by sacrifice or offering.' "

[15]Samuel lay down until morning. Then he opened the doors of the Tent of the Lord. He was afraid to tell Eli about the vision. [16]But Eli said to him, "Samuel, my son!"

Samuel answered, "I am here."

[17]Eli asked, "What did the Lord say to you? Don't hide it from me. May God punish you terribly if you hide from me anything he said to you." [18]So Samuel told Eli everything. He did not hide anything from him. Then Eli said, "He is the Lord. Let him do what he thinks is best."

[19]The Lord was with Samuel as he grew up. He did not let any of Samuel's messages fail to come true. [20]Then all Israel, from Dan to Beersheba, knew Samuel was a prophet of the Lord. [21]And the Lord continued to show himself to Samuel at Shiloh. He also showed himself to Samuel through his word.

The Jewish Menorah

The menorah was the lampstand of the Holy Tent. It was made of a single piece of acacia wood which was overlaid with gold. Six branches curved out from the center, three on each side of the center straight one. A small cup on the tip of each branch held oil which the priest poured in each morning, then he lit a wick so that the menorah burned all day and into the evening.

Responsibility of Parents

Eli had a responsibility to teach his sons to serve God. God told the people in Deuteronomy 6:4-9 to teach their children. Proverbs 22:6 also encourages parents to teach their children about God.

FAQs

Q: Does God speak to people today?

A: Yes, though not usually in an actual voice. He speaks through his Word (the Bible), and he speaks in our hearts.

Think About This

The message God gave Samuel would not be a surprise to Eli. God had already told him these things would happen if his sons did not honor God (1 Samuel 2:27-36).

What did Eli's sons do to anger God?

- They didn't care about God (2:12).

- They didn't respect offerings given to the Lord (2:17).

- They had improper relationships with women (2:22).

When Samuel told Eli what God had told him, Eli immediately submitted to God's will (3:18).

First Samuel 3:19 is a key to Samuel's whole life—the Lord was with him. All of Israel began to hear about Samuel and understand that he was a prophet of God (3:20).

God would tell the prophets what he planned to do, and the prophets gave the messages to the people.

134

GENESIS EXODUS LEVITICUS NUMBERS DEUTERONOMY JOSHUA JUDGES RUTH **1 SAMUEL** 2 SAMUEL 1 KINGS 2 KINGS 1 CHRONICLES 2 CHRONICLES EZRA NEHEMIAH ESTHER JOB PSALMS PROVERBS

1 SAMUEL

King Saul Disobeys

1 Samuel 13:1-14

The people had stopped obeying God. Samuel began leading them back to God. But the people kept insisting they wanted a king like the nations around them. God had Samuel anoint Saul to be king. Saul started out serving God, but then he changed.

Behind the Story

Samuel warned the people against having a king, but they insisted. They wanted a king to lead their armies. Also, Samuel was leading them at this time, but he was getting older and his sons were evil and wicked, just as Eli's sons had been. So the people wanted to know who was going to lead them. They thought it should be a king.

God chose Saul to be king (1 Samuel 8–10). At first he was humble and obedient to God. Then Saul began to show his arrogant, rebellious heart.

Saul tried to justify his disobedience:
The people were running away (1 Samuel 13:11); Samuel hadn't come (13:11); and the Philistines were gathering to attack (13:11-12). But the bottom line was that he disobeyed the order God had given through Samuel (10:8).

Saul Anointed by Samuel by Guy Rowe

13 Saul was 30 years old when he became king. He was king over Israel 42 years. ²Saul chose 3,000 men from Israel. There were 2,000 men who stayed with him at Micmash in the mountains of Bethel. And 1,000 men stayed with Jonathan at Gibeah in Benjamin. Saul sent the other men in the army back home.

³Jonathan attacked the Philistine camp in Geba. And the other Phlistines heard about it. Saul said, "Let the Hebrew people hear what happened." So he told the men to blow trumpets through all the land of Israel. ⁴All the Israelites heard the news. The men said, "Saul has defeated the Philistine camp. Now the Philistines really hate us!" Then the Israelites were called to join Saul at Gilgal.

⁵The Philistines gathered to fight Israel. They had 3,000 chariots and 6,000 men to ride in the chariots. Their soldiers were many in number, like the grains of sand on the seashore. The Philistines went and camped at Micmash which is east of Beth Aven. ⁶The Israelites saw that they were in trouble. So they went to hide in caves and bushes. They also hid among the rocks and in pits and wells. ⁷Some Hebrews even went across the Jordan River to the land of Gad and Gilead.

But Saul stayed at Gilgal. All the men in his army were shaking with fear. ⁸Saul waited seven days, because Samuel had said he would meet him then. But Samuel did not come to Gilgal. And the soldiers began to leave.

FAQs

Q: Why was God's punishment so harsh?

A: Saul deliberately disobeyed God. He had been told to wait for Samuel. He took himself out from under God's authority. He had been anointed as king, not as a prophet.

135

ECCLESIASTES SONG OF SOLOMON ISAIAH JEREMIAH LAMENTATIONS EZEKIEL DANIEL HOSEA JOEL AMOS OBADIAH JONAH MICAH NAHUM HABAKKUK ZEPHANIAH HAGGAI ZECHARIAH MALACHI

[9]So Saul said, "Bring me the whole burnt offering and the fellowship offerings." Then Saul offered the whole burnt offering. [10]Just as he finished, Samuel arrived. Saul went to meet him.

[11]Samuel asked, "What have you done?"

Saul answered, "I saw the soldiers leaving me, and you were not here. The Philistines were gathering at Micmash. [12]Then I thought, 'The Philistines will come against me at Gilgal. And I haven't asked for the Lord's approval.' So I forced myself to offer the whole burnt offering."

[13]Samuel said, "You acted foolishly! You haven't obeyed God's command. If you had obeyed him, God would make your kingdom continue in Israel forever. [14]But now your kingdom will not continue. The Lord has looked for the kind of man he wants. The Lord has appointed him to become ruler of his people. He is doing this because you haven't obeyed his command."

Saul Denounced by Samuel by Guy Rowe

TIMELINE: The Prophets and Kings of Israel, 1100–800 B.C.

PROPHETS			KINGS			
Samuel	(1105)	**1100 BC**	Saul	(1050)		
			David	(1010)		
		1000 BC	Solomon	(970)		
			Kingdom is Divided (930)			
			Israel (Northern Kingdom)		**Judah** (Southern Kingdom)	
			Jeroboam I	(930)	Rehoboam	(930)
					Abijah	(913)
			Nadab	(909)	Asa	(910)
			Baasha	(908)		
		900 BC	Omri	(885)		
Elijah	(875)		Ahab	(874)	Jehoshaphat	(872)
			Ahaziah	(853)	Jehoram	(853)
			Joram	(852)		
Elisha	(848)		Jehu	(841)	Ahaziah	(841)
					Athaliah (queen)	(841)
		800 BC	Jehoahaz	(814)	Joash	(835)

Obeying

Leaders have a great responsibility to serve God because people follow them and copy what they do. Saul was in a position of great authority.

But obeying is not just for kings. Regular people should obey God in every area of their lives. Check out these verses about obedience:

- Deuteronomy 7:9
- 1 Samuel 15:22
- Jeremiah 7:23
- Ephesians 5:6
- 1 John 2:3-5

If you're going to obey, you need to know what God wants you to do. How do you live that out?

- Read God's Word.
- Listen to messages about God's Word at church or in Sunday school.
- Seek the advice of older Christians whom you respect a lot.

136

GENESIS EXODUS LEVITICUS NUMBERS DEUTERONOMY JOSHUA JUDGES RUTH 1 SAMUEL 2 SAMUEL 1 KINGS 2 KINGS 1 CHRONICLES 2 CHRONICLES EZRA NEHEMIAH ESTHER JOB PSALMS PROVERBS

1 SAMUEL

Jonathan Fights the Philistines

1 Samuel 14:1-23

Words You Should Know

Philistines (FIL-ih-steens) Israel's enemies for many years. They had five strong cities near the Mediterranean Sea: Ashdod, Ashkelon, Edron, Gath and Gaza. They worshiped several false gods. They were finally defeated by the Egyptians (see Judges 15–16; 1 Samuel 4:1-10; 6–7; 17–18; 1 Chronicles 18:1).

Battle Info

The officer traveling with Jonathan was his armor bearer. The person in this position was trusted with the life of the one he served. He was a courageous and skillful soldier. He carried his commander's weapons and protected him in battle.

Sometimes when a commander was seriously wounded in battle, he asked his armor bearer to kill him rather than let him be captured by the enemy.

Saul was king of Israel which was actually a weak nation. Saul formed an army to fight their enemies, the Philistines. But his army was poorly armed and outnumbered. However, Saul's son Jonathan trusted God and believed he would help them defeat the enemy.

14 One day Jonathan, Saul's son, spoke to the officer who carried his armor. Jonathan said, "Come, let's go over to the Philistine camp on the other side." But Jonathan did not tell his father.

²Saul was sitting under a pomegranate tree at the threshing floor near Gibeah. He had about 600 men with him. ³One man was Ahijah, who was a son of Ichabod's brother Ahitub. Ichabod was the son of Phinehas, Eli's son. Eli was the Lord's priest in Shiloh. He wore the holy vest. No one knew Jonathan had left.

⁴There was a steep slope on each side of the pass. Jonathan planned to go through the pass to the Philistine camp. The cliff on one side was named Bozez. The other cliff was named Seneh. ⁵One cliff faced north toward Micmash. The other faced south toward Geba.

⁶Jonathan said to his officer who carried his armor, "Come. Let's go to the camp of those men who are not circumcised. Maybe the Lord will help us. It doesn't matter if we have many people, or just a few. Nothing can keep the Lord from giving us victory."

⁷The officer who carried Jonathan's armor said to him, "Do whatever you think is best. Go ahead. I'm with you."

⁸Jonathan said, "Then come. We will cross over to the Philistines. We will let them see us. ⁹They may say to us, 'Stay there until we come to you.' If they do, we will stay where we are. We won't go up to them. ¹⁰But they may say, 'Come up to us.' If so, we will climb up. And the Lord will allow us to defeat them. This will be the sign for us."

¹¹Both Jonathan and his officer let the Philistines see them. The Philistines said, "Look! The Hebrews are crawling out of the holes they were hiding in!" ¹²The Philistines in the camp shouted to Jonathan and his officer, "Come up to us. We'll teach you a lesson!"

Jonathan said to his officer, "Climb up behind me. The Lord has given the Philistines to

137

ECCLESIASTES SONG OF SONGS ISAIAH JEREMIAH LAMENTATIONS EZEKIEL DANIEL HOSEA JOEL AMOS OBADIAH JONAH MICAH NAHUM HABAKKUK ZEPHANIAH HAGGAI ZECHARIAH MALACHI

Think About This

Jonathan sought direction from God. He looked for a certain sign that God was directing him to attack the Philistines. When he got that sign, he obeyed.

Jonathan and his officer threw the Philistines into a state of panic. God may have even caused an earthquake (1 Samuel 14:15).

Saul didn't even realize that his son was gone until he did a roll call and found Jonathan missing.

Saul called for the Holy Box of God to be brought. It signified God's presence with them as they went into battle. But then he was too impatient to wait for it. He ordered his soldiers into battle before the Holy Box could be brought.

Israel!" ¹³So Jonathan climbed up, using his hands and feet. His officer climbed just behind him. Jonathan cut down the Philistines as he went. And his officer killed them as he followed behind Jonathan. ¹⁴In that first fight Jonathan and his officer killed about 20 Philistines.

¹⁵All the Philistine soldiers panicked. Those in the camp and those in the raiding party were frightened. The ground itself shook! God caused the panic.

¹⁶Saul's guards were at Gibeah in the land of Benjamin. They saw the Philistine soldiers running in every direction. ¹⁷Saul said to his army, "Check and find who has left our camp." When they checked, they learned that Jonathan and his officer were gone.

¹⁸So Saul said to Ahijah the priest, "Bring the Holy Box of God." (At that time it was with the Israelites.) ¹⁹While Saul was talking to the priest, the confusion in the Philistine camp was growing. Then Saul said to Ahijah, "Stop. There's not time to pray now!"

²⁰Then Saul and the army with him gathered and entered the battle. They found the Philistines confused, even striking each other with their swords! ²¹Earlier, there were Hebrews who had served the Philistines and had stayed in their camp. They now joined the Israelites with Saul and Jonathan. ²²All the Israelites hidden in the mountains of Ephraim heard that the Philistine soldiers were running away. They too joined the battle and chased the Philistines. ²³So the Lord saved the Israelites that day. And the battle moved on past Beth Aven.

138

GENESIS EXODUS LEVITICUS NUMBERS DEUTERONOMY JOSHUA JUDGES RUTH **1 SAMUEL** 2 SAMUEL 1 KINGS 2 KINGS 1 CHRONICLES 2 CHRONICLES EZRA NEHEMIAH ESTHER JOB PSALMS PROVERBS

1 SAMUEL

David Is Anointed

1 Samuel 16:1-13

Think About This

Samuel wanted Saul to succeed as Israel's king. He was grieving because Saul disobeyed God (1 Samuel 16:1).

The old saying, "Don't judge a book by its cover" comes to mind when reading God's words in 1 Samuel 16:7. The fact that Jesse's first seven sons were tall, muscular and handsome and "looked" like kings didn't mean any of them were God's choice to be king. Saul was tall and powerful, too, but his heart wasn't turned to God. What's on the inside of a person (whether he loves and obeys God) is more important than outward looks.

David was God's choice to be the next king. He was known as a man who followed after God's own heart (see 1 Samuel 13:14) because his faith in God was so strong. After David reigned as king, God was often referred to as the God of David (see Isaiah 38:5).

David wrote many of the psalms in the Bible.

The Israelite people had insisted on having a king to rule them. King Saul was the first king, but he did not serve God. So God would not let him continue to reign. God sent Samuel to Bethlehem to anoint a new king.

Samuel Goes to Bethlehem

16 The Lord said to Samuel, "How long will you continue to feel sorry for Saul? I have rejected him as king of Israel. Fill your container with olive oil and go. I am sending you to Jesse who lives in Bethlehem. I have chosen one of his sons to be king."

²But Samuel said, "If I go, Saul will hear the news. And he will try to kill me."

The Lord said, "Take a young calf with you. Say, 'I have come to offer a sacrifice to the Lord.' ³Invite Jesse to the sacrifice. Then I will show you what to do. You must appoint the one I show you."

⁴Samuel did what the Lord told him to do. When he arrived at Bethlehem, the elders of Bethlehem shook with fear. They met him and asked, "Are you coming in peace?"

⁵Samuel answered, "Yes, I come in peace. I have come to make a sacrifice to the Lord. Make yourselves holy for the Lord and come to the sacrifice with me." Then he made Jesse and his sons holy for the Lord. And he invited them to come to the sacrifice.

⁶When they arrived, Samuel saw Eliab. Samuel thought, "Surely the Lord has appointed this person standing here before him."

⁷But the Lord said to Samuel, "Don't look at how handsome Eliab is. Don't look at how tall he is. I have not chosen him. God does not see the same way people see. People look at the outside of a person, but the Lord looks at the heart."

⁸Then Jesse called Abinadab and told him to pass by Samuel. But Samuel said, "The Lord has not chosen this man either." ⁹Then Jesse had Shammah pass by. But Samuel said, "No, the Lord has not chosen this one." ¹⁰Jesse had seven of his sons pass by Samuel. But Samuel said to him,

139

ECCLESIASTES SONG OF SONGS ISAIAH JEREMIAH LAMENTATIONS EZEKIEL DANIEL HOSEA JOEL AMOS OBADIAH JONAH MICAH NAHUM HABAKKUK ZEPHANIAH HAGGAI ZECHARIAH MALACHI

"The Lord has not chosen any of these."

[11]Then he asked Jesse, "Are these all the sons you have?"

Jesse answered, "I still have the youngest son. He is out taking care of the sheep."

Samuel said, "Send for him. We will not sit down to eat until he arrives."

[12]So Jesse sent and had his youngest son brought in. He was a fine boy, tanned and handsome.

The Lord said to Samuel, "Go! Appoint him. He is the one."

[13]So Samuel took the container of olive oil. Then he poured oil on Jesse's youngest son to appoint him in front of his brothers. From that day on, the Lord's Spirit entered David with power. Samuel then went back to Ramah.

Behind the Story

The people of the town were afraid that Samuel had come to announce some judgment on them (1 Samuel 16:4) because his visit was a surprise.

When Samuel poured the oil on David, the Holy Spirit entered David with power to rule God's people (16:13). So the youngest, least likely of Jesse's sons was chosen to be king. The son who wasn't even worthy to attend the meeting with Samuel—but instead was doing the family work while his brothers attended—was the one chosen.

At the same time the Holy Spirit filled David, he left King Saul (16:14-15) because Saul was no longer God's choice to be leading the people.

David is the second of three kings of the United Kingdom stage of Israel's history. Saul, David and Solomon each ruled for 40 years.

David, a man after God's own heart, was a shepherd. Jesus called himself the good shepherd (see John 10:14).

The Lord's Anointed

A man chosen to be king was anointed by a prophet or a priest. Anointing was done with a special mixture of oil, spices and perfumes. The "recipe" for this oil was top secret, known only by the priests. Some of the ingredients were olive oil, cinnamon and myrrh.

The prophet or priest poured the oil into a vessel made from an animal's horn. Then the person to be anointed knelt before him, and the oil was poured onto his head. This was a sign for all who observed the ceremony that this person was God's choice to be king. He might even be called "the Lord's anointed."

140

GENESIS EXODUS LEVITICUS NUMBERS DEUTERONOMY JOSHUA JUDGES RUTH **1 SAMUEL** 2 SAMUEL 1 KINGS 2 KINGS 1 CHRONICLES 2 CHRONICLES EZRA NEHEMIAH ESTHER JOB PSALMS PROVERBS

1 SAMUEL

David and Goliath

1 Samuel 17:1-51

Words You Should Know

David (DAY-vid)
Israel's greatest king. Jesus is called the "Son of David" because he was born to members of David's family (see Luke 1:69; 2:4; 18:38; Acts 2:29-31; 13:22).

Battle Info

Goliath called for the Israelites to send one man out to fight him (1 Samuel 17:10). This was a common way for armies to battle; the strongest soldier from each side came out and they fought each other. It was believed that each soldier's god would fight for him. The fate of the armies was decided on that battle. Goliath didn't know what he was in for!

Samuel had anointed David to be the next king of Israel. But his kingdom had not yet bugun. Saul was still king, and he led his army into battle with the Philistines. David was too young to be a soldier, but he visited his brothers who served in the army.

17 The Philistines gathered their armies for war. They met at Socoh in Judah. Their camp was at Ephes Dammim between Socoh and Azekah. ²Saul and the Israelites gathered in the Valley of Elah. And they camped there. They took their positions to fight the Philistines. ³The Philistines controlled one hill. The Israelites controlled another. The valley was between them.

⁴The Philistines had a champion fighter named Goliath. He was from Gath. He was about nine feet four inches tall. He came out of the Philistine camp. ⁵He had a bronze helmet on his head. And he wore a coat of scale armor. It was made of bronze and weighed about 125 pounds. ⁶He wore bronze protectors on his legs. And he had a small spear of bronze tied on his back. ⁷The wooden part of his larger spear was like a weaver's rod. And its blade weighed about 15 pounds. The officer who carried his shield walked in front of him.

⁸Goliath stood and shouted to the Israelite soldiers, "Why have you taken positions for battle? I am a Philistine, and you are Saul's servants! Choose a man and send him to fight me. ⁹If he can fight and kill me, we will become your servants. But if I defeat and kill him, you will become our servants." ¹⁰Then he said, "Today I stand and dare the army of Israel! Send one of your men to fight me!" ¹¹When Saul and the Israelites heard the Philistine's words, they were very afraid.

¹²Now David was the son of Jesse, an Ephrathite. Jesse was from Bethlehem in Judah. He had eight sons. In Saul's time Jesse was an old man. ¹³His three oldest sons followed Saul to the war. The first son was Eliab. The second son was

141

ECCLESIASTES SONG OF SONGS ISAIAH JEREMIAH LAMENTATIONS EZEKIEL DANIEL HOSEA JOEL AMOS OBADIAH JONAH MICAH NAHUM HABAKKUK ZEPHANIAH HAGGAI ZECHARIAH MALACHI

Abinadab. And the third son was Shammah. [14]David was the youngest son. Jesse's three oldest sons followed Saul. [15]But David went back and forth from Saul to Bethlehem. There he took care of his father's sheep.

[16]The Philistine Goliath came out every morning and evening. He stood before the Israelite army. This continued for 40 days.

[17]Now Jesse said to his son David, "Take this half bushel of cooked grain. And take ten loaves of bread. Take them to your brothers in the camp. [18]Also take ten pieces of cheese. Give them to the commander of your brothers' group of 1,000 soldiers. See how your brothers are. Bring back something to show me they are all right. [19]Your brothers are with Saul and the army in the Valley of Elah. They are fighting against the Philistines."

[20]Early in the morning David left the sheep with another shepherd. He took the food and left as Jesse had told him. When David arrived at the camp, the army was leaving. They were going out to their battle positions. The soldiers were shouting their war cry. [21]The Israelites and Philistines were lining up their men to face each other in battle.

[22]David left the food with the man who kept the supplies. Then he ran to the battle line and talked to his brothers. [23]While he was talking with them, Goliath came out. He was the Philistine champion from Gath. He shouted things against Israel as usual, and David heard it. [24]When the Israelites saw Goliath, they were very much afraid and ran away.

[25]They said, "Look at this man Goliath. He keeps coming out to speak against Israel. The king will give much money to the man who kills Goliath. He will also give his daughter in marriage to whoever kills him. And his father's family will not have to pay taxes in Israel."

[26]David asked the men who stood near him, "What will be done to reward the man who kills this Philistine? What will be done for whoever takes away the shame from Israel? Goliath is a

Think About This

The two armies were set to battle each other in a valley that was about 15 miles from Bethlehem, David's hometown.

Given Goliath's size and strength, the most likely Israelite to fight him may have been King Saul, who was described as being taller than most men (see 1 Samuel 9:2). However, King Saul did not respond to Goliath's taunts. Neither did any of the other soldiers.

Goliath was insulting King Saul's army with his challenges. He was also insulting God as he challenged him to fight with the Philistine gods. None of the soldiers were willing to fight for God, not even with his power.

FAQs

Q: How big was Goliath?

A: Goliath was over nine feet tall. That's taller than the ceiling in an average room. He had a metal helmet, body armor that weighed 125 pounds, leg armor and two spears. He also had a man who came out with him and carried his shield. David was just a young boy and his weapon was . . . a sling.

142

GENESIS EXODUS LEVITICUS NUMBERS DEUTERONOMY JOSHUA JUDGES RUTH 1 SAMUEL 2 SAMUEL 1 KINGS 2 KINGS 1 CHRONICLES 2 CHRONICLES EZRA NEHEMIAH ESTHER JOB PSALMS PROVERBS

1 SAMUEL

Behind the Story

David brought supplies to his soldier brothers. This was not unusual. More than likely family members were responsible to bring the soldiers food and supplies.

King Saul offered an attractive prize to any soldier who would fight the giant: money, no taxes and his own daughter in marriage (1 Samuel 17:25). Even so, every soldier was too afraid of Goliath to fight him.

David's older brother complains about him. Eliab accuses David of being proud and arrogant (17:28) when it was probably Eliab's own jealousy that made him feel that way.

King Saul knew that he was sending a child out to do a man's job. He tried to put his armor on David to protect him (17:37-39). Of course, it didn't fit. David didn't need it anyway. He had God on his side.

Philistine. He is not circumcised. Why does he think he can speak against the armies of the living God?"

27The Israelites told David what they had been saying. They said, "This is what will be done for the man who kills Goliath."

28David's oldest brother Eliab heard David talking with the soldiers. He became angry with David. He asked David, "Why did you come here? Who's taking care of those few sheep of yours in the desert? I know you are proud. Your attitude is very bad. You came down here just to watch the battle!"

29David asked, "Now what have I done wrong? Can't I even talk?" 30He then turned to other people and asked the same questions. And they gave him the same answer as before. 31Some men heard what David said and told Saul. Then Saul ordered David to be sent to him.

32David said to Saul, "Don't let anyone be discouraged. I, your servant, will go and fight this Philistine!"

33Saul answered, "You can't go out against this Philistine and fight him. You're only a boy. Goliath has been a warrior since he was a young man."

34But David said to Saul, "I, your servant, have been keeping my father's sheep. When a lion or bear came and took a sheep from the flock, 35I would chase it. I would attack it and save the sheep from its mouth. When it attacked me, I caught it by its fur. I would hit it and kill it. 36I, your servant, have killed both a lion and a bear! Goliath, the Philistine who is not circumcised, will be like the lion or bear I killed. He will die because he has stood against the armies of the living God. 37The Lord saved me from a lion and a bear. He will also save me from this Philistine."

Saul said to David, "Go, and may the Lord be with you." 38Saul put his own clothes on David. He put a bronze helmet on David's head and armor on his body. 39David put on Saul's sword and tried to walk around. But he was not used to all the armor Saul had put on him.

He said to Saul, "I can't go in this. I'm not used to it." Then David took it all off. 40He took his stick in his hand. And he chose five smooth stones from a stream. He put them in his pouch and

143

ECCLESIASTES SONG OF SONGS ISAIAH JEREMIAH LAMENTATIONS EZEKIEL DANIEL HOSEA JOEL AMOS OBADIAH JONAH MICAH NAHUM HABAKKUK ZEPHANIAH HAGGAI ZECHARIAH MALACHI

held his sling in his hand. Then he went to meet Goliath.

[41]At the same time, the Philistine was coming closer to David. The man who held his shield walked in front of him. [42]Goliath looked at David. He saw that David was only a boy, tanned and handsome. He looked down at David with disgust. [43]He said, "Do you think I am a dog, that you come at me with a stick?" He used his gods' names to curse David. [44]He said to David, "Come here. I'll feed your body to the birds of the air and the wild animals!"

[45]But David said to him, "You come to me using a sword, a large spear and a small spear. But I come to you in the name of the Lord of heaven's armies. He's the God of the armies of Israel! You have spoken out against him. [46]Today the Lord will give you to me. I'll kill you, and I'll cut off your head. Today I'll feed the bodies of the Philistine soldiers to the birds of the air and the wild animals. Then all the world will know there is a God in Israel! [47]Everyone gathered here will know the Lord does not need swords or spears to save people. The battle belongs to him! And he will help us defeat all of you."

[48]As Goliath came near to attack him, David ran quickly to meet him. [49]He took a stone from his pouch. He put it into his sling and slung it. The stone hit the Philistine on his forehead and sank into it. Goliath fell facedown on the ground.

[50]So David defeated the Philistine with only a sling and a stone! He hit him and killed him. He did not even have a sword in his hand. [51]David ran and stood beside the Philistine. He took Goliath's sword out of its holder and killed him. Then he cut off Goliath's head.

When the Philistines saw that their champion was dead, they turned and ran.

The Sling

The sling David used was made of a leather pocket between two leather cords. A stone that may have weighed as much as two pounds was placed in the pocket. Then the sling cords were held by both hands and twirled around above David's head. When he let go of one cord, the stone flew through the air at great speed and hit Goliath in the head.

Boy Versus Giant

Goliath was insulted when he saw a boy come out to fight him. He thought the Israelites were making fun of him.

David announced that the battle belonged to God (1 Samuel 17:47). That put everything in perspective. He knew that God was fighting for him, and he gave God the credit for the victory.

The force of the stone hitting his head knocked Goliath to the ground. It may have killed him or just stunned him. But David grabbed Goliath's own sword and cut off the giant's head. This was a total insult to the Philistines. The entire Philistine army ran when they saw that their giant soldier had been killed.

Take It to Heart

David's trust in God is an inspirational reminder that God's strength and power are available to all who trust in him. Read Philippians 4:13 to better understand this.

144

GENESIS EXODUS LEVITICUS NUMBERS DEUTERONOMY JOSHUA JUDGES RUTH 1 SAMUEL 2 SAMUEL 1 KINGS 2 KINGS 1 CHRONICLES 2 CHRONICLES EZRA NEHEMIAH ESTHER JOB PSALMS PROVERBS

1 SAMUEL

David and Jonathan

1 Samuel 20:1-42

Words You Should Know

New Moon (NU-moon)
A Jewish feast held on the first day of the month. It was celebrated with animal sacrifices and the blowing of trumpets. It was a way for the Israelites to dedicate the month to the Lord (see Numbers 10:10; 28:14; 1 Samuel 20:5, 24; Psalm 81:3; Ezekiel 46:3-6; Colossians 2:16).

David and Saul

When David was anointed to become king, God's Spirit filled him—and left King Saul (1 Samuel 16:13-14). David quickly became successful, as when he bravely killed Goliath, and King Saul became less successful in all he did.

Not long after Samuel anointed him, David went to live in the palace with King Saul. He played music on his harp to calm the king when he was upset (16:23). King Saul came to love David very much, at least for a while.

David's fame spread quickly after he killed Goliath. He was living in the palace with King Saul who heard how the people admired David. It didn't take long for the king to become very jealous of David.

20 Then David ran away from Naioth in Ramah. He went to Jonathan and asked, "What have I done? What is my crime? How have I sinned against your father so that he's trying to kill me?"

²Jonathan answered, "No! You won't die! See, my father doesn't do anything without first telling me. It doesn't matter if it is very important or just a small thing. Why would he refuse to tell me he wants to kill you? No, it's not true!"

³But David took an oath. He said, "Your father knows very well that I'm your friend. He has said to himself, 'Jonathan must not know about it. If he knows, he will tell David.' But as surely as the Lord lives and as you live, I am very close to death!"

⁴Jonathan said to David, "I'll do anything you want me to do."

⁵So David said, "Look, tomorrow is the New Moon festival. I am supposed to eat with the king. But let me hide in the field until the third evening. ⁶Your father may notice I am gone. If he does, tell him, 'David begged me to let him go to his hometown of Bethlehem. Every year at this time, his family group offers a sacrifice.' ⁷If your father says, 'Fine,' I am safe. But if he becomes angry, you can believe he wants to hurt me. ⁸Jonathan, be kind to me, your servant. You have made an agreement with me before the Lord. If I am guilty, you may kill me yourself! Why hand me over to your father?"

⁹Jonathan answered, "No, never! If I learn that my father plans to harm you, I will warn you!"

¹⁰David asked, "Who will let me know if your father answers you unkindly?"

¹¹Then Jonathan said, "Come, let's go out into the field." So Jonathan and David went together into the field.

¹²Jonathan said to David, "I promise this before the Lord, the God of Israel: At this same time day after tomorrow, I will find out how my father feels. If he feels good toward you, I'll send word to you. I'll let you know. ¹³But my father may mean to hurt you. If so, I will let you know and send you away safely. May the Lord punish me terribly if I don't do this. And may the Lord

145

ECCLESIASTES SONG OF SONGS ISAIAH JEREMIAH LAMENTATIONS EZEKIEL DANIEL HOSEA JOEL AMOS OBADIAH JONAH MICAH NAHUM HABAKKUK ZEPHANIAH HAGGAI ZECHARIAH MALACHI

be with you as he has been with my father. [14]But show me the kindness of the Lord as long as I live. Do this so that I may not die. [15]You must not stop showing your kindness to my family. Don't do this, even when the Lord has destroyed all your enemies from the earth."

[16]So Jonathan made an agreement with David. He said, "May the Lord punish David's enemies." [17]And Jonathan asked David to repeat his promise of love for him. He did this because he loved David as much as he loved himself.

[18]Jonathan said to David, "Tomorrow is the New Moon festival. Your seat will be empty. So my father will notice you're gone. [19]On the third day go to the place where you hid when this trouble began. Wait by the rock Ezel. [20]On the third day I will shoot three arrows to the side of the rock. I will shoot as if I am shooting at a target. [21]Then I will send a boy and tell him to go find the arrows. I may say to him, 'Look, the arrows are on this side of you. Bring them here.' If so, you may come out of hiding. You may do this as surely as the Lord lives because you are safe. There is no danger. [22]But I may say to the boy, 'Look, the arrows are beyond you.' If I do, you must go, because the Lord has sent you away. [23]Remember what we talked about. The Lord is a witness between you and me forever."

[24]So David hid in the field. And when the New Moon festival came, the king sat down to eat. [25]He sat where he always sat, near the wall. Jonathan sat across from him, and Abner sat next to him. But David's place was empty. [26]That day Saul said nothing. He thought, "Maybe something has happened to David so that he is unclean." [27]But

Friendship or Jealousy?

David became good friends with Jonathan, King Saul's son. Jonathan was the prince of Israel and, therefore, in line to be the next king after his father. However, because of Saul's disobedience God had taken the kingship away from Saul's family and given it to David. Jonathan didn't know this at first. He could have been angry or jealous of David when he found out. But he wasn't. He loved David so much that he pledged to be his friend forever (1 Samuel 18:3-4). Even so, his father was growing more jealous of David every day.

Jonathan was unaware of how his father felt about David (20:2). King Saul had promised that he would not hurt David (19:6).

King Saul heard people praising David after he killed Goliath (18:6-7). He became angry and jealous and tried several times to kill David (18:8-9, 11; 19:11, 15).

146

GENESIS EXODUS LEVITICUS NUMBERS DEUTERONOMY JOSHUA JUDGES RUTH 1 SAMUEL 2 SAMUEL 1 KINGS 2 KINGS 1 CHRONICLES 2 CHRONICLES EZRA NEHEMIAH ESTHER JOB PSALMS PROVERBS

1 SAMUEL

Behind the Story

David reminded Jonathan of his pledge to be a lifelong friend (1 Samuel 18:3-4) when he asked for his help.

King Saul must have planned some attack on David at the New Moon Festival. He became very angry when he was told that David was gone (20:30-31).

David and Jonathan came up with a signal that would let David know of King Saul's intentions. It would also protect Jonathan by keeping the king from knowing he had helped David. A servant would fetch arrows from Jonathan's target practice, and by the instructions Jonathan called to him, David would know if he was in danger. However, Jonathan loved his friend so much that he sent the servant away and spoke to David face-to-face. If any of King Saul's supporters had seen this, Jonathan would have been in great danger.

the next day was the second day of the month. And David's place was empty again. So Saul said to Jonathan, "Why hasn't the son of Jesse come to the festival yesterday or today?"

28Jonathan answered, "David begged me to let him go to Bethlehem. 29He said, 'Let me go, because our family has a sacrifice in the town. And my brother has ordered me to be there. Now if I am your friend, please let me go and see my brothers.' That is why he has not come to the king's table."

30Then Saul became very angry with Jonathan. He said, "You son of an evil and disobedient woman! I know you are on the side of David son of Jesse! You bring shame on yourself and on your mother who gave birth to you. 31As long as Jesse's son lives, you'll never be king or have a kingdom. Now send for David and bring him to me. He must die!"

32Jonathan asked his father, "Why should David be killed? What wrong has he done?" 33Then Saul threw his spear at Jonathan, trying to kill him. So Jonathan knew that his father really wanted to kill David. 34Jonathan was very angry and left the table. That second day of the month he refused to eat. He was upset about what his father wanted to do to David.

35The next morning Jonathan went out to the field. He went to meet David as they had agreed. He had a young boy with him. 36Jonathan said to the boy, "Run and find the arrows I shoot."

When he ran, Jonathan shot an arrow beyond him. 37The boy ran to the place where Jonathan's arrow fell. But Jonathan called, "The arrow is beyond you!" 38Then he shouted, "Hurry! Go quickly! Don't stop!" The boy picked up the arrow and brought it back to his master. 39(The boy knew nothing about what this meant. Only Jonathan and David knew.) 40Then Jonathan gave his weapons to the boy. He told him, "Go back to town."

41When the boy left, David came out from the south side of the rock. He bowed facedown on the ground before Jonathan. He did this three times. Then David and Jonathan kissed each other. They cried together, but David cried the most.

42Jonathan said to David, "Go in peace. We have promised by the Lord that we will be friends. We said, 'The Lord will be a witness between you and me, and between our descendants forever.' " Then David left, and Jonathan went back to town.

147

ECCLESIASTES SONG OF SONGS ISAIAH JEREMIAH LAMENTATIONS EZEKIEL DANIEL HOSEA JOEL AMOS OBADIAH JONAH MICAH NAHUM HABAKKUK ZEPHANIAH HAGGAI ZECHARIAH MALACHI

David Hides from Saul

1 Samuel 23:14-18

The Judean Desert

23 ¹⁴David stayed in the protected places in the desert. He also stayed in the hills of the Desert of Ziph. Every day Saul looked for David. But the Lord did not let him take David.

¹⁵David was at Horesh in the Desert of Ziph. He was afraid because Saul was coming to kill him. ¹⁶But Saul's son Jonathan went to David at Horesh. He helped David have stronger faith in God. ¹⁷Jonathan told him, "Don't be afraid. My father won't touch you. You will become king of Israel, and I will be second to you. Even my father Saul knows this." ¹⁸The two of them made an agreement before the Lord. Then Jonathan went home. But David stayed at Horesh.

God's Plan Unfolds

Jonathan didn't know it, but by helping David stay alive, he was playing an important role in God's future plans—a greater plan than just keeping the next king of Israel alive.

David was an ancestor of Jesus. Matthew 1:1 begins with the family history of Jesus. It says, "He came from the family of David."

Later, in the second book of Samuel, God promised David that his family would rule Israel forever. He promised to never take his love and support away from David's family as he had from Saul. God was referring to his own Son, Jesus, who would be born into an earthly family from the line of David. Jesus will rule forever and his kingdom will never end (Isaiah 9:6-7; Luke 1:30-33).

Take It to Heart

God had a plan for David's life. Does he have a plan for yours? Of course he does. Some of his plans are basic and simply require knowing them and obeying them . . . such as the Ten Commandments and the commands to love God with all your heart and love those around you, too (Mark 12:29-31).

How can you find God's specific plans for your life?
Read these verses for some help:

- Psalm 32:8—God will guide you.

- Proverbs 3:5-6—Trusting him is key.

- Jeremiah 29:11—God has a plan for your life.

- James 1:5—Ask God for wisdom.

- 1 John 5:14-15—He will hear your prayers.

148

GENESIS EXODUS LEVITICUS NUMBERS DEUTERONOMY JOSHUA JUDGES RUTH **1 SAMUEL** 2 SAMUEL 1 KINGS 2 KINGS 1 CHRONICLES 2 CHRONICLES EZRA NEHEMIAH ESTHER JOB PSALMS PROVERBS

1 SAMUEL

Behind the Story

David depended on the generosity of farmers to supply food for him and his men. Apparently, some people admired and respected him. Those people helped him gladly. But there must have been some, such as Nabal, who did not care much for David. These people may have remained loyal to King Saul.

David had a band of 600 men. It would not be cheap to give enough food to feed that many hungry men.

Nabal's name means "fool." He lived out the meaning of his name.

Nabal owned thousands of sheep and goats. He would have been a major target for thieves and robbers. David and his men had protected Nabal when they camped near him earlier (1 Samuel 25:15-16, 21).

David and Nabal

1 Samuel 25:4-42

After David left Jonathan, King Saul took an army and tried to find him. David was on the run, hiding from the king. A band of men joined David, so they had to find food and places to sleep.

25 [4]David was in the desert. He heard that Nabal was cutting the wool from his sheep. [5]So he sent ten young men. He told them, "Go to Nabal at Carmel. Greet him for me. [6]Say to Nabal, 'May you and your family have good health! And may all who belong to you have good health. [7]I have heard that you are cutting the wool from your sheep. When your shepherds were with us, we did nothing wrong to them. All the time your shepherds were at Carmel, we stole nothing from them. [8]Ask your servants, and they will tell you. We come at a happy time. So for this reason, be kind to my young men. Please give them anything you can find for them. Please do this for your son David.' "

[9]When the men arrived, they gave the message to Nabal. But Nabal insulted them. [10]He answered them, "Who is David? Who is this son of Jesse? Many slaves are running away from their masters today! [11]I have bread and water. And I have meat that I killed for my servants who cut the wool. But I won't give it to men I don't know."

[12]David's men went back and told him all Nabal had said. [13]Then David said to them, "Put on your swords!" So they put on their swords, and David put on his also. About 400 men went with David. But 200 men stayed with the supplies.

Shearing

Shearing sheep happens every year. The shepherd shaves the wool from the sheep, and it is used to make cloth for blankets or clothing. Shearing does not hurt the sheep.

[14]One of Nabal's servants spoke to Abigail, Nabal's wife. He said, "David sent messengers from the desert to greet our master. But Nabal insulted them. [15]These men were very good to us. They did nothing wrong to us. They stole nothing from us during all the time we were out in the field with them. [16]Night and day they protected us. They were like a wall around us while we were

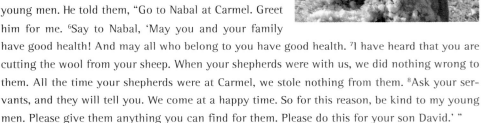

149

ECCLESIASTES SONG OF SONGS ISAIAH JEREMIAH LAMENTATIONS EZEKIEL DANIEL HOSEA JOEL AMOS OBADIAH JONAH MICAH NAHUM HABAKKUK ZEPHANIAH HAGGAI ZECHARIAH MALACHI

with them caring for the sheep. ¹⁷Now think about it, and decide what you can do. Terrible trouble is coming to our master and all his family. Nabal is such a wicked man that no one can even talk to him."

¹⁸Abigail hurried. She took 200 loaves of bread, 2 leather bags full of wine and 5 cooked sheep. She took about a bushel of cooked grain, 100 cakes of raisins and 200 cakes of pressed figs. She put all these on donkeys. ¹⁹Then she told her servants, "Go on. I'll follow you." But she did not tell her husband.

²⁰Abigail rode her donkey and came down into the mountain ravine. There she met David and his men coming down toward her.

²¹David had just said, "It's been useless! I watched over Nabal's property in the desert. I made sure none of his sheep were missing. I did good to him, but he has paid me back with evil. ²²May God punish me terribly if I let just one of Nabal's family live until tomorrow."

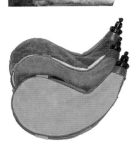

²³When Abigail saw David, she quickly got off her donkey. She bowed facedown on the ground before David. ²⁴She lay at David's feet. She said, "My master, let the blame be on me! Please let me talk to you! Listen to what I say. ²⁵My master, don't pay attention to this worthless man Nabal. He is the same as his name. His name means 'fool,' and he is truly foolish. But I, your servant, didn't see the men you sent. ²⁶The Lord has kept you from killing and punishing people yourself. As surely as the Lord lives and as surely as you live, may your enemies become like Nabal! ²⁷I have brought a gift to you. Please give it to the men who follow you. ²⁸Please forgive my wrong. The Lord will certainly let your family have many kings. He will do this because you fight his battles. As long as you live, people will find nothing bad in you. ²⁹A man might chase you to kill you. But the Lord your God will keep you alive. He will throw away your enemies' lives as he would throw a stone from a sling. ³⁰The Lord will keep all his promises about good things for you. He will make you leader over

Think About This

Sheep shearing took place on a feast day. That was a day when people were generally feeling thankful and, therefore, generous. David sent his men to Nabal on that day expecting generosity.

Nabal insulted David by asking who David was (1 Samuel 25:10). He even suggested that David might be a runaway slave!

Nabal's own servants were afraid that Nabal's rudeness would get them all killed. They told Abigail how kind and helpful David's men had been to them (25:15-16).

Abigail could have had the servants punished for speaking about her husband the way they did. They must have known that she would agree that Nabal was foolish.

150

GENESIS EXODUS LEVITICUS NUMBERS DEUTERONOMY JOSHUA JUDGES RUTH 1 SAMUEL 2 SAMUEL 1 KINGS 2 KINGS 1 CHRONICLES 2 CHRONICLES EZRA NEHEMIAH ESTHER JOB PSALMS PROVERBS

1 SAMUEL

Abigail's Wisdom

David was planning to kill all of Nabal's family (1 Samuel 25:22).

Abigail gathered enough food to feed David's army. She sent the food ahead of her to calm David's anger before she met him.

Abigail asked David's forgiveness for the insults of her husband. She pointed out that everyone knew he was a fool (25:25).

Abigail begged David to control his anger and not seek revenge against Nabal. He had avoided killing people up to this point. Abigail pointed out to David that killing her foolish husband was an act that was beneath a man like David.

Vengeance Is for God

Nabal's heart failed him, and ten days later he died. God took Nabal's life, instead of David killing him.

Abigail's Gift by David Teniers the Elder

Israel. [31]Then you won't feel guilty. You won't have problems about killing innocent people and punishing them yourself. Please remember me when the Lord brings you success."

[32]David answered Abigail, "Praise the Lord, the God of Israel. He sent you to meet me. [33]May you be blessed for your wisdom. You have kept me from killing or punishing people today. [34]As surely as the Lord, the God of Israel, lives, he has kept me from hurting you. If you hadn't come quickly to meet me, no one belonging to Nabal would have lived until tomorrow."

[35]Then David accepted Abigail's gifts. He told her, "Go home in peace. I have heard your words, and I will do what you have asked."

Nabal's Death

[36]When Abigail went back to Nabal, he was in the house. He was eating like a king. He was very drunk and in a good mood. So she told him nothing until the next morning. [37]In the morning he was not drunk. Then his wife told him everything. His heart failed him, and he became like a stone. [38]About ten days later the Lord struck Nabal and caused him to die.

[39]When David heard that Nabal was dead, he said, "Praise the Lord! Nabal insulted me, but the Lord has supported me! He has kept me from doing wrong. And the Lord caused Nabal to die because he did wrong."

Then David sent a message to Abigail. He asked her to become his wife. [40]His servants went to Carmel and spoke to Abigail. They said, "David sent us to take you so you can become his wife."

[41]Abigail bowed facedown on the ground. She said, "I am your servant. I'm ready to serve you. I'm ready to wash the feet of my master's servants." [42]Abigail quickly got on a donkey and went with David's messengers. She had five maids following her. And she became David's wife.

151

ECCLESIASTES SONG OF SONGS ISAIAH JEREMIAH LAMENTATIONS EZEKIEL DANIEL HOSEA JOEL AMOS OBADIAH JONAH MICAH NAHUM HABAKKUK ZEPHANIAH HAGGAI ZECHARIAH MALACHI

Employment in David's Time

By this time in Israel's history, many forms of employment had developed and are even mentioned in Scripture.

Dyers took dull wool, which was cut from the sheep and woven into fabric, then dyed it into beautiful blue, purple and crimson colors. It was used to make blankets, curtains and clothing. They tinted individual threads, instead of whole pieces of fabric, so many different colors could be in one garment. Dye colors came from crushed insects or shellfish.

Pottery shops provided employment for men to make clay bowls, jars and jugs. They used tools to put designs in the clay before it was baked in an oven to set it.

Women were kept busy with daily baking and preparing meals. Grain had to be ground into flour before it could be used to bake bread. The dough had to be kneaded by hand. Sometimes honey or olive oil was added into the dough for flavoring. Bread was baked outside in an oven that was basically a pit lined with clay and filled with coals.

Farming at the Time

Oil was taken from olives by beating the olives with a stone.

The Gezer calendar was divided by agricultural seasons—from "the month to pick olives to the time of summer fruit."

Sheep shearing, trimming wool from the sheep, happened in the middle or at the end of spring.

One sheep could have as much as 10 pounds of wool.

The skin of sheep was used to make tents, which blocked out the wind, cold and rain.

Sheep were considered clean animals, so their milk and meat became a part of the Israelites' diets.

152

GENESIS EXODUS LEVITICUS NUMBERS DEUTERONOMY JOSHUA JUDGES RUTH 1 SAMUEL 2 SAMUEL 1 KINGS 2 KINGS 1 CHRONICLES 2 CHRONICLES EZRA NEHEMIAH ESTHER JOB PSALMS PROVERBS

2 SAMUEL

David Is Made King of Israel

2 Samuel 5:1-25

Michelangelo's David

King Saul died in battle. David could finally stop running for his life. The people of Judah made David king and then, finally, David was made king of all of Israel.

5 Then all the tribes of Israel came to David at Hebron. They said to him, "Look, we are your own family. ²In the past Saul was king over us. But you were the one leading us in battle for Israel. The Lord said to you, 'You will be like a shepherd for my people, the Israelites. You will become their ruler.' "

³All the elders of Israel came to King David at Hebron. Then he made an agreement with them in Hebron in front of the Lord. Then they poured oil on David to make him king over Israel.

Painting by Jean Fouquet

⁴David was 30 years old when he became king. He ruled 40 years. ⁵He was king over Judah in Hebron for 7 years and 6 months. And he was king over all Israel and Judah in Jerusalem for 33 years.

⁶The king and his men went to Jerusalem to attack the Jebusites who lived there. The Jebusites said to David, "You can't come into our city. Even our people who are blind and crippled can stop you." They said this because they thought David could not enter their city. ⁷But David did take the city of Jerusalem with its strong walls. It became the City of David.

⁸That day David said to his men, "To defeat the Jebusites you must go through the water tunnel. Then you can reach those 'crippled' and 'blind' enemies. This is why people say, 'The blind and the crippled cannot enter the palace.' "

⁹So David lived in the city with its strong walls. He called it the City of David. David built more buildings around it. He began where the land was filled in on the east side of the city. He

153

ECCLESIASTES SONG OF SONGS ISAIAH JEREMIAH LAMENTATIONS EZEKIEL DANIEL HOSEA JOEL AMOS OBADIAH JONAH MICAH NAHUM HABAKKUK ZEPHANIAH HAGGAI ZECHARIAH MALACHI

also built more buildings inside the city. [10]He became stronger and stronger, because the Lord of heaven's armies was with him.

[11]Hiram king of the city of Tyre sent messengers to David. He also sent cedar logs, carpenters and men to cut stone. They built a palace for David. [12]Then David knew the Lord really had made him king of Israel. And he knew the Lord had made his kingdom very important. This was because the Lord loved his people, the Israelites.

[13]In Jerusalem David took for himself more slave women and wives. This was after he moved there from Hebron. More sons and daughters were born to David. [14]These are the names of the sons born to David in Jerusalem: Shammua, Shobab, Nathan, Solomon, [15]Ibhar, Elishua, Nepheg, Japhia, [16]Elishama, Eliada and Eliphelet.

David Defeats the Philistines

[17]Now the Philistines heard that David had been made king over Israel. So all the Philistines went to look for him. But when David heard the news, he went down to a safe place. [18]So the Philistines came and camped in the Valley of Rephaim. David asked the Lord, "Should I attack the Philistines? Will you help me defeat them?"

[19]The Lord said to David, "Go! I will certainly help you defeat them."

[20]So David went to Baal Perazim and defeated the Philistines there. David said, "Like a flood of water, the Lord has broken through my enemies." So David named the place Baal Perazim. [21]The Philistines left their idols behind at Baal Perazim. And David and his men carried these idols away.

[22]Once again the Philistines came and camped at the Valley of Rephaim. [23]David prayed to the Lord. This time the Lord told David, "Don't attack the Philistines from the front. Instead, go around them. Attack them opposite the balsam trees. [24]You will hear the sound of marching in the tops of the balsam trees. Then you must act quickly. I, the Lord, will have gone ahead of you and defeated the Philistine army." [25]So David did what the Lord commanded. He defeated the Philistines and chased them all the way from Gibeon to Gezer.

God's Guidance in Battle

David asked God's help and advice before entering the battle. God's instruction to listen to the sound of the rustling in the trees suggests that his army was fighting along with David's men.

Think About This

David had enough military experience to know that surprise is a key element in defeating an enemy. The Jebusites didn't think David could defeat them in a battle but, by sending his men up through the tunnels that were used to bring water into the city, he caught them by surprise, unprepared for battle, and he won.

The tunnels led from a spring at the base of the hill, over 230 feet underground to the city. The tunnels were built so the city could get water, even if it was under attack by an enemy.

Jerusalem became David's capital city. It was centrally located to all the tribes. It was up on a hill with big walls around it, so it would be difficult to capture. The city became famous for the many things that happened there and are recorded in the Bible. The most important thing that happened there was the crucifixion of Jesus.

154

GENESIS EXODUS LEVITICUS NUMBERS DEUTERONOMY JOSHUA JUDGES RUTH 1 SAMUEL 2 SAMUEL 1 KINGS 2 KINGS 1 CHRONICLES 2 CHRONICLES EZRA NEHEMIAH ESTHER JOB PSALMS PROVERBS

2 SAMUEL

David and Mephibosheth

2 Samuel 9:1-13

Behind the Story

When David lived with King Saul and Jonathan, the king had repeatedly tried to kill him. That's why David ended up leaving the palace. When he left, he and Jonathan pledged to be friends forever. They both knew that David would be king one day, and David promised to be kind to Jonathan's family (1 Samuel 20:14-17).

Mephibosheth was afraid when King David sent for him. It would not have been unusual for a king to kill members of the former king's family. Mephibosheth probably thought that David was going to kill him.

Eating at the king's table (2 Samuel 9:7) was not just a one-time meal. David was promising to take care of Mephibosheth the rest of his life.

King Saul and his son Jonathan were both killed in battle. Then David was made king over Israel. He remembered to keep the promise he had made to Jonathan. He promised to take care of Jonathan's family.

David Helps Saul's Family

9 David asked, "Is there anyone still left in Saul's family? I want to show kindness to this person for Jonathan's sake!"

²Now there was a servant named Ziba from Saul's family. So David's servants called Ziba to him. King David said to him, "Are you Ziba?"

He answered, "Yes, I am Ziba, your servant."

TAKING IT TO HEART

Fulfilling Promises

In keeping his promise to be kind, David lived the way God wanted. Check out these verses on loving others:

- **1 Corinthians 16:14**
- **Galatians 5:13**
- **Ephesians 4:2**
- **1 Peter 1:22**
- **1 John 3:11**
- **1 John 4:7**
- **1 John 4:20-21**

³The king asked, "Is there anyone left in Saul's family? I want to show God's kindness to this person."

Ziba answered the king, "Jonathan has a son still living. He is crippled in both feet."

⁴The king asked Ziba, "Where is this son?"

Ziba answered, "He is at the house of Makir son of Ammiel in Lo Debar."

⁵Then King David had servants bring Jonathan's son from the house of Makir son of Ammiel in Lo Debar. ⁶Mephibosheth, Jonathan's son, came before David and bowed facedown on the floor.

David said, "Mephibosheth!"

Mephibosheth said, "I am your servant."

⁷David said to him, "Don't be afraid. I will be kind to you for your father Jonathan's sake. I

155

ECCLESIASTES SONG OF SONGS ISAIAH JEREMIAH LAMENTATIONS EZEKIEL DANIEL HOSEA JOEL AMOS OBADIAH JONAH MICAH NAHUM HABAKKUK ZEPHANIAH HAGGAI ZECHARIAH MALACHI

will give you back all the land of your grandfather Saul. And you will always be able to eat at my table."

[8]Mephibosheth bowed to David again. Mephibosheth said, "You are being very kind to me, your servant! And I am no better than a dead dog!"

[9]Then King David called Saul's servant Ziba. David said to him, "I have given your master's grandson everything that belonged to Saul and his family. [10]You, your sons and your servants will farm the land for Mephibosheth. You will harvest the crops. Then your master's grandson will have food to eat. But Mephibosheth, your master's grandson, will always be able to eat at my table."

(Now Ziba had 15 sons and 20 servants.) [11]Ziba said to King David, "I am your servant. I will do everything my master, the king, commands me."

So Mephibosheth ate at David's table as if he were one of the king's sons. [12]Mephibosheth had a young son named Mica. Everyone in Ziba's family became Mephibosheth's servants. [13]Mephibosheth was crippled in both feet. He lived in Jerusalem and always ate at the king's table.

Seeing Jesus

DISABILITIES IN THE BIBLE

People in Bible times did not have the benefit of the medicines and medical treatment that we enjoy today. When a person was born crippled or became crippled, as Mephibosheth, they were unable to work to support themselves and were doomed to a life of begging. Usually the crippled person sat at the city gates and asked passers-by for a few coins. Some people thought these crippled people had no worth. Jesus didn't believe that. Read these verses to see how he responded to those with disabilities or disease:

- **Matthew 8:1-4**
- **Matthew 12:10-13**
- **Matthew 15:21-28**
- **Matthew 20:30-34**
- **Mark 2:1-12**
- **Mark 7:31-37**
- **Luke 7:1-10**
- **John 9:1-12**

Think About This

Ziba had been Saul's servant. Apparently Ziba was wealthy himself since he had 20 servants.

Mephibosheth was not born crippled. When he was a young boy, his nurse carried him as she ran after hearing of Saul and Jonathan's deaths. She dropped him, and the injuries from the fall left him crippled (2 Samuel 4:4).

David's Mercy

Several times while Saul was pursuing David, he had opportunities to kill the king. David always chose not to do that. He respected life and the position of king (1 Samuel 24:10; 26:9-10).

Take It to Heart

David's kindness to Mephibosheth is an example of God's grace to us. Mephibosheth did nothing to deserve the kindness, and he could in no way repay it. That's true of us, too. Nothing we can do causes us to deserve God's kindness. He gives it because he wants to. There is no way we can repay it.

156

GENESIS EXODUS LEVITICUS NUMBERS DEUTERONOMY JOSHUA JUDGES RUTH 1 SAMUEL 2 SAMUEL **1 KINGS** 2 KINGS 1 CHRONICLES 2 CHRONICLES EZRA NEHEMIAH ESTHER JOB PSALMS PROVERBS

1 KINGS

Solomon's Wisdom

1 Kings 3:1-28

After King David died, his son Solomon became king. Solomon defeated his enemies and began building his own palace and the Temple for God. One night God spoke to him in a dream.

Words You Should Know

Incense (IN-senz)
A spice burned to make a sweet smell. This was done by the priests in the Meeting Tent and the Temple. A special altar was used to burn incense as worship to God. Since the smoke seemed to go up to God, this reminded people of prayer (see Exodus 30:1-10, 34-38; Psalm 141:2; Luke 1:9; Revelation 8:3-4).

Behind the Story

Before he died David gave Solomon some advice on how to live and rule:

He told him to be strong, to be a man of God, to obey God's commands. He also reminded Solomon that God had promised that someone from their family would always rule Israel, as long as they followed and obeyed God (1 Kings 2:2-5).

God often spoke to people in their dreams, when their minds were not filled with the busyness of the day. Solomon had just been giving sacrifices to God, so his heart was focused on God at the time (3:4).

Solomon Asks for Wisdom

3 Solomon made an agreement with the king of Egypt by marrying his daughter. Solomon brought her to Jerusalem. At this time Solomon was still building his palace and the Temple of the Lord. He was also building a wall around Jerusalem. [2]The Temple had not yet been finished. So people were still offering animal sacrifices at altars in many places of worship. [3]Solomon showed that he loved the Lord. He did this by following the commands his father David had given him. But Solomon still used the many places of worship to offer sacrifices and to burn incense.

[4]King Solomon went to Gibeon to offer a sacrifice. He went there because it was the most important place of worship. He offered 1,000 burnt offerings on that altar. [5]While he was at Gibeon, the Lord came to him in a dream during the night. God said, "Ask for anything you want. I will give it to you."

[6]Solomon answered, "You were very kind to your servant, my father David. He obeyed you. He was honest and lived right. And you showed great kindness to him when you allowed his son to be king after him. [7]Lord my God, you have allowed me to be king in my father's place. But I am like a little child. I do not have the wisdom I need to do what I must do. [8]I, your servant, am here among your chosen people. There are too many of them to count. [9]So I ask that you give me wisdom. Then I can rule the people in the right way. Then I will know the difference between right and wrong. Without wisdom, it is impossible to rule this great people of yours."

[10]The Lord was pleased that Solomon had asked him for this. [11]So God said to him, "You did not ask for a long life. And you did not ask for riches for yourself. You did not ask for the death of your enemies. Since you asked for wisdom to make the right decisions, [12]I will give you what you asked. I will give you wisdom and understanding. Your wisdom will be greater than anyone has had in the past. And there will never be anyone in the future like you. [13]Also, I will give you what you did not ask for. You will have riches and honor. During your life no other king will

157

ECCLESIASTES SONG OF SONGS ISAIAH JEREMIAH LAMENTATIONS EZEKIEL DANIEL HOSEA JOEL AMOS OBADIAH JONAH MICAH NAHUM HABAKKUK ZEPHANIAH HAGGAI ZECHARIAH MALACHI

be as great as you. [14]I ask you to follow me and obey my laws and commands. Do this as your father David did. If you do, I will also give you a long life."

[15]Then Solomon woke up. He knew that God had talked to him in the dream. Then he went to Jerusalem and stood before the Box of the Agreement with the Lord. There he gave burnt offerings and fellowship offerings to the Lord. After that, he gave a feast for all of his leaders and officers.

Solomon Makes a Wise Decision

[16]One day two women who were prostitutes came to Solomon. They stood before him. [17]One of the women said, "My master, this woman and I live in the same house. I gave birth to a baby while she was there with me. [18]Three days later this woman also gave birth to a baby. No one else was in the house with us. There were only the two of us. [19]One night this woman rolled over on her baby, and it died. [20]So during the night she took my son from my bed while I was asleep. She carried him to her bed. Then she put the dead baby in my bed. [21]The next morning I got up to feed my baby. But I saw that he was dead! Then I looked at him more closely. I saw that he was not my son."

[22]But the other woman said, "No! The living baby is my son. The dead baby is yours!"

But the first woman said, "No! The dead baby is yours, and the living one is mine!" So the two women argued before the king.

[23]Then King Solomon said, "Each of you says the living baby is your own. And each of you says the dead baby belongs to the other woman."

[24]Then King Solomon sent his servants to get a sword. When they brought it to him, [25]he said, "Cut the living baby into two pieces. Give each woman half of the baby."

[26]The real mother of the living child was full of love for her son. She said to the king, "Please, my master, don't kill him! Give the baby to her!"

But the other woman said, "Neither of us will have him. Cut him into two pieces!"

[27]Then King Solomon said, "Give the baby to the first woman. Don't kill him. She is the real mother."

[28]When the people of Israel heard about King Solomon's decision, they respected him very much. They saw he had wisdom from God to make the right decisions.

Solomon's Name

Solomon's mother was Bathsheba. He was given the name Solomon, but the prophet Nathan said he should be named Jedidiah. That was because the Lord loved him (2 Samuel 12:25).

Think About This

When the Temple was finished, Solomon built a palace for himself. It was a magnificent building which took over 7 years to build.

Solomon's request for wisdom showed that he desired to be a good and fair king to the people.

God was pleased with Solomon's request. It wasn't something that would benefit just him. He gave Solomon even more than he asked for. God promises to provide all the needs of those who seek him (see Matthew 6:33).

Solomon's wisdom told him that the real mother of the child would rather give him up than have him be killed. When she cried out to give the child to the other woman, Solomon knew she was the real mother.

158

GENESIS EXODUS LEVITICUS NUMBERS DEUTERONOMY JOSHUA JUDGES RUTH 1 SAMUEL 2 SAMUEL **1 KINGS** 2 KINGS 1 CHRONICLES 2 CHRONICLES EZRA NEHEMIAH ESTHER JOB PSALMS PROVERBS

1 KINGS

Words You Should Know

Jerusalem
(jeh-ROO-suh-lem)
Sometimes called "Zion" or the "City of David." It was the greatest city in the country of Palestine. It was the center of the Jewish religion because the Temple was there. Jesus was killed on the cross near Jerusalem. The city was destroyed by the Roman army in A.D. 70. Later it was rebuilt in the same place by the Moslems and is a great city today in the Middle East (see 2 Samuel 5:5-7; 2 Chronicles 36:14, 19; Ezra 1:1-11; Luke 2:22-45; 13:34; 24:13-49; Acts 2:5, 14).

Most Holy Place
(most HOL-ee place)
The inner and most special room in the Meeting Tent and the Temple. The Box of the Agreement was kept here. Only the high priest could enter this room, and then only once a year. This was when he sprinkled blood on the lid of the Holy Box to remind the people that their sins needed to be forgiven (see Exodus 26:33-34; Leviticus 16:2-23; 1 Kings 6:16-35; Hebrews 9:3-28).

Solomon Builds the Temple

1 Kings 6:1-38

During David's reign as king, he was heavily involved in battles to defeat Israel's enemies and bring the kingdom together. Solomon's reign as king was devoted to the building of the Temple.

The Western Wall in Modern-Day Jerusalem

6 So Solomon began to build the Temple. This was 480 years after the people of Israel had left Egypt. (This was the fourth year of King Solomon's rule over Israel.) It was the second month, the month of Ziv.

²The Temple was 90 feet long and 30 feet wide. It was 45 feet high. ³The porch in front of the main room of the Temple was 15 feet deep and 30 feet wide. The room ran along the front of the Temple itself. Its width was equal to the width of the Temple. ⁴There were narrow windows in the Temple. These windows were narrow on the outside and larger on the inside. ⁵Then Solomon built some side rooms against the walls of the main room of the Temple. These rooms were built on top of each other. ⁶The rooms on the bottom floor were 7 1/2 feet wide. The rooms on the middle floor were 9 feet wide. The rooms above that were 10 1/2 feet wide. The Temple wall which made the side of each room was thinner than the wall in the room below. The rooms were pushed against the wall but did not have their main beams built into the wall.

⁷The stones were prepared at the same place they were cut from the ground. Only these stones were used to build the Temple. So there was no noise of hammers, axes or any other iron tools at the Temple.

⁸The entrance to the bottom rooms built beside the Temple was on the south side. From there,

Seeing God

God gave David the plans for the Temple (1 Chronicles 28:12) which David gave to Solomon. God cares about the details. Remember he gave Noah specific plans for the boat, too (Genesis 6:14-16).

159

ECCLESIASTES SONG OF SONGS ISAIAH JEREMIAH LAMENTATIONS EZEKIEL DANIEL HOSEA JOEL AMOS OBADIAH JONAH MICAH NAHUM HABAKKUK ZEPHANIAH HAGGAI ZECHARIAH MALACHI

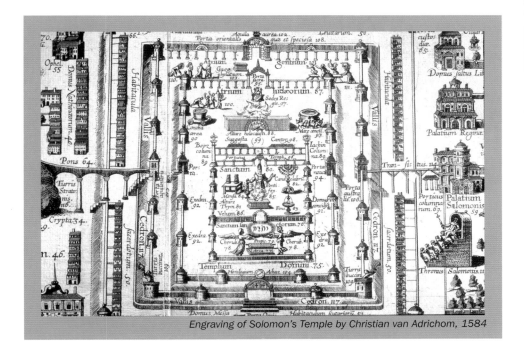

Engraving of Solomon's Temple by Christian van Adrichom, 1584

Think About This

The king of Hiram gave Solomon the cedar and pine logs to be used in building the Temple. In return, Solomon gave Hiram 125,000 bushels of wheat and 115,000 gallons of olive oil each year (1 Kings 5:10-11).

Solomon sent 30,000 men to Lebanon to help with cutting the trees and gathering the wood; 10,000 men were sent each month. They worked for a month then came home for 2 months. Also, 80,000 men worked in the hills cutting stone, and 70,000 men carried the stone to the building site. Another 3,300 men were in charge of the workmen. That means 193,300 men worked on the Temple (5:13-16).

One room was divided from the rest of the Temple. The Most Holy Place was the inside center room where the Box of the Agreement was kept. It was covered with over 20 tons of gold. Two giant gold cherubim, with seven-and-a-half foot wings, stood guard over the Box of the Agreement. The Holy Place was the room around the Most Holy Place. An outer courtyard surrounded it. This was the exact same way the Meeting Tent had been laid out.

stairs went up to the second floor rooms. And from there, they went on to the third floor rooms. [9]Solomon put a roof made from beams and cedar boards on the Temple. So he finished building the Temple. [10]He also finished building the bottom floor that was beside the Temple. It was 7 1/2 feet high. It was attached to the Temple by cedar beams.

[11]The Lord spoke his word to Solomon: [12]"Obey all my laws and commands. If you do, I will do for you what I promised your father David. [13]And I will live among the children of Israel in this Temple you are building. I will never leave the people of Israel."

[14]So Solomon finished building the Temple. [15]The inside walls were covered from floor to ceiling with cedar boards. The floor was made from pine boards. [16]A room 30 feet long was built in the back part of the Temple. It was divided from the rest of the Temple by cedar boards reaching from floor to ceiling. It was called the Most Holy Place. [17]The main room, the room in front of the Most Holy Place, was 60 feet long. [18]Inside the Temple was cedar. It was carved with pictures of flowers and plants. Everything inside was covered with cedar. So a person could not see the stones of the wall.

160

GENESIS EXODUS LEVITICUS NUMBERS DEUTERONOMY JOSHUA JUDGES RUTH 1 SAMUEL 2 SAMUEL 1 KINGS 2 KINGS 1 CHRONICLES 2 CHRONICLES EZRA NEHEMIAH ESTHER JOB PSALMS PROVERBS

1 KINGS

Words You Should Know

Temple (TEM-p'l)
A building where people worship their gods. God told the Jewish people to worship him at the Temple in Jerusalem. This Temple had been built by King Solomon. It was later destroyed by the Babylonians. It was rebuilt by Zerubbabel. That Temple was destroyed by the Roman general, Pompey. Herod built a third Temple which was used in Jesus' time (see 2 Chronicles 2–7; Ezra 3:7-13; Mark 11:15-17; Acts 7:47) .

Behind the Story

David wanted to build the Temple for God himself. But God wouldn't allow him to build it. As a soldier David had shed the blood of his enemies. David gathered the supplies, but the actual building of the Temple was left for Solomon (1 Chronicles 22:7-10).

David gave a lot of money to the Temple construction project (29:4-7). He even had the plans drawn up and gave them to Solomon (28:19).

The Temple Mount

¹⁹He prepared the inner room at the back of the Temple to keep the Box of the Agreement with the Lord. ²⁰This inner room was 30 feet long, 30 feet wide and 30 feet high. Solomon covered this room with pure gold. He built an altar of cedar and covered it also. ²¹He covered the inside of the Temple with pure gold. And he placed gold chains across the front of the inner room. It was covered with gold. ²²So all the inside of the Temple was covered with gold. Also the altar in the Most Holy Place was covered with gold.

²³Solomon made two creatures with wings from olive wood. Each creature was 15 feet tall. They were put in the Most Holy Place. ²⁴Each creature had two wings. Each wing was 7 1/2 feet long. So it was 15 feet from the end of one wing to the end of the other wing. ²⁵The creatures were the same size and shape. ²⁶And each was 15 feet tall. ²⁷These creatures were put beside each other in the Most Holy Place. Their wings were spread out. So one creature's wing touched one wall. The other creature's wing touched the other wall. And their wings

FAQs

Q: Where was the original Temple built?

A: Solomon's Temple was the first of three temples built in Israel's history. It was built on Mount Moriah, north of Old Jerusalem. It sat higher than the rest of the city. This was the place where God had asked Abraham to sacrifice Isaac. Araunah's threshing floor was also on Mount Moriah. David had purchased this place when a terrible plague spread across the land (due to his disobedience), and it stopped at Araunah's threshing floor (2 Samuel 24). Acts of worship had already taken place on Mount Moriah, so it was fitting that the Temple be built there.

The Dome of the Rock mosque is on Mount Moriah now.

161

ECCLESIASTES SONG OF SONGS ISAIAH JEREMIAH LAMENTATIONS EZEKIEL DANIEL HOSEA JOEL AMOS OBADIAH JONAH MICAH NAHUM HABAKKUK ZEPHANIAH HAGGAI ZECHARIAH MALACHI

touched each other in the middle of the room. [28]The two creatures were covered with gold.

[29]All the walls around the Temple were carved. They were carved with pictures of creatures with wings, palm trees and flowers. This was true for both the main room and the inner room. [30]The floors of both rooms were covered with gold.

[31]Doors made from olive wood were put at the entrance to the Most Holy Place. The doors were made to fit into an area with five sides. [32]Creatures with wings, palm trees and

flowers were carved on the two olive wood doors. Then the doors were covered with gold. And the creatures and the palm trees were covered with gold. [33]At the entrance to the main room there was a door frame. It was square and was made of olive wood. [34]Two doors were made from pine. Each door had two parts so that the doors folded. [35]The doors were covered with pictures of creatures with wings, palm trees and flowers. And all of the carvings were covered with gold. The gold was smoothed over the carvings.

[36]The inner courtyard was built and enclosed with walls. The walls were made of three rows of cut stones and one row of cedar boards.

[37]Work began on the Temple in Ziv, the second month. This was during the fourth year Solomon ruled over Israel. [38]The Temple was finished during the eleventh year Solomon ruled. It was finished in the eighth month, the month of Bul. It was finished exactly as it was planned. Solomon had worked seven years to build the Temple.

Hebrew Calendar

The Jews had two different calendars. The Festival Calendar year began in the spring. The Gezer Calendar, used for planting and harvesting, began in the autumn.

Festival Calendar Year

Abib (our April)

Ziv

Sivan

Tammuz

Ab

Elul

Ethanim

(1st month of Gezer Calendar)

Bul

Chislev

Tebeth

Shebat

Adar

Temple Dedication

When the Temple was finished, Solomon dedicated it to God in front of all the people. He offered sacrifices of 22,000 bulls and 120,000 sheep. This is the largest offering recorded in the Bible. He also offered grain offerings and burnt offerings (1 Kings 8:63-64).

Solomon held a great feast that lasted 14 days (2 Chronicles 7:9). Solomon prayed, asking God to come into his Temple. He asked that the influence of the Temple would include sinners being judged; that the sins of Israel would be forgiven; and that the heathen would be judged (1 Kings 8:31-32).

When he finished praying, fire came down from heaven and burned up the offerings, and God's glory filled the Temple. This was probably a thick, dark cloud that filled the Temple. This showed the people that God approved of his Temple and accepted it as his home.

162

GENESIS EXODUS LEVITICUS NUMBERS DEUTERONOMY JOSHUA JUDGES RUTH 1 SAMUEL 2 SAMUEL **1 KINGS** 2 KINGS 1 CHRONICLES 2 CHRONICLES EZRA NEHEMIAH ESTHER JOB PSALMS PROVERBS

1 KINGS

Queen of Sheba

1 Kings 10:1-10, 13

Behind the Story

The hard questions the Queen of Sheba asked Solomon were probably riddles that would show his wisdom as he figured out the answers. More than likely this type of thing happened often, as news of Solomon's wisdom spread. People would come to test it. This may have led to Jerusalem being a center of intellectual discussions during Solomon's reign.

Solomon's reputation of wisdom and wealth was spread around the known world by his navy, which sailed to foreign lands. The Queen of Sheba would also have known of him because Sheba was a trade center where caravans passed through on their way to Damascus and other cities. Solomon's fame spread on land and sea!

More than likely those who told of Solomon's wealth and wisdom gave credit to God for all he had. That's why the queen praised God.

Solomon kept peace with neighboring nations by marrying princesses from them. He concentrated his energies on building his wealth by trading with other nations. Soon everyone knew of Solomon's wisdom and wealth.

The Queen of Sheba Visits Solomon

10 Now the queen of Sheba heard about Solomon's fame. So she came to test him with hard questions. ²She traveled to Jerusalem with a very large group of servants. There were many camels carrying spices, jewels and much gold. She came to Solomon and talked with him about all that she had in mind. ³Solomon answered all her questions. Nothing was too hard for him to explain to her. ⁴The queen of Sheba learned that Solomon was very wise. She saw the palace he had built. ⁵She saw his many officers and the food on his table. She saw the palace servants and their good clothes. She was shown the servants who served him at feasts. And she was shown the whole burnt offerings he made in the Temple of the Lord. All these things amazed her.

⁶So she said to King Solomon, "I heard in my own country about your achievements and wisdom. And all of it is true. ⁷I could not believe it then. But now I have come and seen it with my own eyes. I was not told even half of it! Your wisdom and wealth are much greater than I had heard. ⁸Your men and officers are very lucky! In always serving you, they are able to hear your wisdom! ⁹Praise the Lord your God! He was pleased to make you king of Israel. The Lord has constant love for Israel. So he made you king to keep justice and to rule fairly."

FAQs

Q: Where was the country of Sheba?

A: Sheba was a country about 1,000 miles from Palestine. More than likely it was the area which is today's Yemen.

¹⁰Then the queen of Sheba gave the king about 9,000 pounds of gold. She also gave him many spices and jewels. No one since that time has brought more spices into Israel than the queen of Sheba gave King Solomon.

¹³King Solomon gave the queen of Sheba many gifts. He gave her gifts that a king would give to another ruler. Then he gave her whatever else she wanted and asked for. After this, she and her servants went back to her own country.

163

ECCLESIASTES SONG OF SONGS ISAIAH JEREMIAH LAMENTATIONS EZEKIEL DANIEL HOSEA JOEL AMOS OBADIAH JONAH MICAH NAHUM HABAKKUK ZEPHANIAH HAGGAI ZECHARIAH MALACHI

Solomon's Wealth
1 Kings 10:14-29

10 ¹⁴Every year King Solomon received about 50,000 pounds of gold. ¹⁵Besides that he also received gold from the traders and merchants. And he received gold from the kings of Arabia and governors of the land.

¹⁶King Solomon made 200 large shields of hammered gold. Each shield contained about seven and one-half pounds of gold. ¹⁷He also made 300 smaller shields of hammered gold. They each contained about three and three-fourths pounds of gold. The king put them in the Palace of the Forest of Lebanon.

¹⁸Then King Solomon built a large throne of ivory. And he covered it with pure gold. ¹⁹There were six steps leading up to the throne. The back of the throne was round at the top. There were armrests on both sides of the chair. And beside each armrest was a statue of a lion. ²⁰Twelve lions stood on the six steps. There was one lion at each end of each step. Nothing like this had ever been made for any other kingdom. ²¹All of Solomon's drinking cups were made of gold. All of the dishes in the Palace of the Forest of Lebanon were pure gold. Nothing was made from silver. In Solomon's time people did not think silver was valuable.

²²King Solomon also had many trading ships at sea, along with Hiram's ships. Every three years the ships returned. They brought back gold, silver, ivory, apes and baboons.

²³So Solomon had more riches and wisdom than all the other kings on earth. ²⁴People everywhere wanted to see King Solomon. They wanted to hear the wisdom God had given him. ²⁵Every year everyone who came brought a gift. They brought things made of gold and silver, along with clothes, weapons, spices, horses and mules.

²⁶So Solomon had many chariots and horses. He had 1,400 chariots and 12,000 chariot soldiers. He kept some in special cities for the chariots. And he kept some with him in Jerusalem. ²⁷In Jerusalem silver was as common as stones while Solomon was king. Cedar trees were as common as the fig trees growing on the mountain slopes. ²⁸Solomon brought in horses from Egypt and Kue. His traders bought them in Kue and brought them to Israel. ²⁹A chariot from Egypt cost about 15 pounds of silver. And a horse cost about 3 3/4 pounds of silver. The traders also sold horses and chariots to the kings of the Hittites and the Arameans.

Think About This

Solomon became wealthy by trading with other nations. He opened trade routes to far away nations that Israel had never dealt with before. He also collected taxes from caravans of traders who passed through his kingdom on their way to other lands.

Solomon had more gold than could be measured. He had 1,400 chariots, which cost about $400 each. He had 12,000 soldiers to man those chariots. He had a huge fleet of ships (1 Kings 9:26-28; 10:22). His own throne was built from ivory and covered with gold (10:18). However, all of his wealth didn't keep Solomon close to God. Even his gift of wisdom didn't hold him close to God. He turned away from following God (11:1-13). Sometimes being wealthy makes it harder to depend on God and trust him. Jesus said, "It would be easier for a camel to go through the eye of a needle than for a rich person to enter the kingdom of God" (Luke 18:25).

164

GENESIS EXODUS LEVITICUS NUMBERS DEUTERONOMY JOSHUA JUDGES RUTH 1 SAMUEL 2 SAMUEL **1 KINGS** 2 KINGS 1 CHRONICLES 2 CHRONICLES EZRA NEHEMIAH ESTHER JOB PSALMS PROVERBS

1 KINGS

Elijah's Work

1 Kings 17:1-24

Words You Should Know

Elijah (e-LIE-juh)
A man who spoke for God in the Old Testament. He was a prophet about 800 years before Jesus was born (see 1 Kings 17–21; 2 Kings 1–2; Matthew 16:14; 17:3-4; 27:47; Luke 1:17; James 5:17).

Prophet (PRAH-fet)
Means "messenger" or one who speaks for someone else. With God's help, a prophet was able to tell the people God's message correctly. Sometimes prophets told what would happen in the future. A woman who spoke God's message was called a prophetess (see 2 Kings 22:14; Luke 2:36). Several books of the Old Testament were written by prophets, including Jeremiah, Amos, Jonah and Micah (see 2 Kings 6:12-16; 17:12-13; Matthew 2:5-6; Luke 16:29-31; 24:25-27; Romans 1:2; 1 Corinthians 12:28-31; 1 Peter 1:10-12).

Elijah Stops the Rain

17 Now Elijah was a prophet from the town of Tishbe in Gilead. Elijah said to King Ahab, "I serve the Lord, the God of Israel. As surely as the Lord lives, I tell you the truth. No rain or dew will fall during the next few years unless I command it."

²Then the Lord spoke his word to Elijah: ³"Leave this place. Go east and hide near Kerith Ravine. It is east of the Jordan River. ⁴You may drink from the brook. And I have commanded ravens to bring you food there." ⁵So Elijah did what the Lord told him to do. He went to Kerith Ravine, east of the Jordan, and lived there. ⁶The birds brought Elijah bread and meat every morning and every evening. And he drank water from the brook.

⁷After a while the brook dried up because there was no rain. ⁸Then the Lord spoke his word to Elijah, ⁹"Go to Zarephath in Sidon. Live there. I have commanded a widow there to take care of you."

¹⁰So Elijah went to Zarephath. When he reached the town gate, he saw a widow there. She was gathering wood for a fire. Elijah asked her, "Would you bring me a little water in a cup? I would like to have a drink." ¹¹As she was going to get his water, Elijah said, "Please bring me a piece of bread, too."

¹²The woman answered, "As surely as the Lord your God lives, I tell you the truth. I have no bread. I have only a handful of flour in a jar. And I have only a little olive oil in a jug. I came here to gather some wood. I will take it home and cook our last meal. My son and I will eat it and then die from hunger."

¹³Elijah said to her, "Don't worry. Go home and cook your food as you have said. But first make a small loaf of bread from the flour you have. Bring it to me. Then cook something for yourself and your son. ¹⁴The Lord, the God of Israel, says, 'That jar of flour will never become empty. The jug will always have oil in it. This will continue until the day the Lord sends rain to the land.' "

¹⁵So the woman went home. And she did what Elijah told her to do. So Elijah, the woman and her son had enough food every day. ¹⁶The jar of flour and the jug of oil were never empty. This happened just as the Lord, through Elijah, said it would.

165

ECCLESIASTES SONG OF SONGS ISAIAH JEREMIAH LAMENTATIONS EZEKIEL DANIEL HOSEA JOEL AMOS OBADIAH JONAH MICAH NAHUM HABAKKUK ZEPHANIAH HAGGAI ZECHARIAH MALACHI

Elijah Brings a Boy Back to Life

[17] Some time later the son of the woman who owned the house became sick. He grew worse and worse. Finally he stopped breathing. [18] So the woman said to Elijah, "You are a man of God. What have you done to me? Did you come here to remind me of my sin? Did you come here to kill my son?"

[19] Elijah said to her, "Give me your son." So Elijah took the boy from her and carried him upstairs. Elijah laid the boy on the bed in the room where he was staying. [20] Then he prayed to the Lord. He said, "Lord my God, this widow is letting me stay in her house. Why have you done this terrible thing to her? Why have you caused her son to die?" [21] Then Elijah lay on top of the boy three times. Elijah prayed to the Lord, "Lord my God, let this boy live again!"

[22] The Lord answered Elijah's prayer. The boy began breathing again, and he was alive. [23] Elijah carried the boy downstairs. He gave the boy to his mother and said, "See! Your son is alive!"

[24] The woman said to Elijah, "Now I know you really are a man from God. I know that the Lord truly speaks through you!"

Divided Kingdom

Miniature from the Nuremburg Bible, 1483

After Solomon died, the kingdom split in half because his son Rehoboam wouldn't repeal taxes his father had put on the people. Ten tribes pulled away and started their own kingdom. They made one of Solomon's other sons, Jeroboam, their king. He set up his own system of worship and appointed his own priests. Then there was a northern and a southern kingdom. None of the kings of the northern kingdom honored God. They all did evil and worshiped the false gods Jeroboam had set up. Ahab was one of those kings. His wife, Jezebel, influenced him to turn away from God even more than he already had.

Behind the Story

Elijah announced to King Ahab that there would be no rain until he commanded it. This was a punishment because of King Ahab's sin of worshiping false gods instead of the one true God.

God had sent Elijah to the mountains to hide from King Ahab, who was angry about the drought. God sent ravens to bring Elijah food (1 Kings 17:6). Then he sent him to a poor widow who would provide food for him. God tested Elijah's faith in him to provide all his needs.

This miracle was an answer to Elijah's prayer. It began a time of great miracles in the land, as God used Elijah and Elisha to show his power.

It also shows the power which is available through prayer (see James 5:16).

Resurrections

Elijah's miracle of bringing the widow's son back to life is the first of eight resurrections recorded in the Bible. The others were: two by Elisha (2 Kings 4:32-35; 13:21); three by Jesus (Matthew 9:23-26; Luke 7:12-15; John 11:41-44); one by Peter (Acts 9:37-41) and one by Paul (Acts 20:9-12).

166

GENESIS EXODUS LEVITICUS NUMBERS DEUTERONOMY JOSHUA JUDGES RUTH 1 SAMUEL 2 SAMUEL 1 KINGS 2 KINGS 1 CHRONICLES 2 CHRONICLES EZRA NEHEMIAH ESTHER JOB PSALMS PROVERBS

1 KINGS

Words You Should Know

Baal (BAY-al)
A false god of the Canaanites
(see 1 Kings 18:17-40; Jeremiah
11:13).

Asherah (as-SHIR-ah)
The name of a false goddess of
the people of Canaan. She was
thought to be the wife of the
false god Baal (see Judges 3:7;
1 Kings 15:13; 2 Kings 21:7;
2 Chronicles 15:16).

Behind the Story

Elijah was sent to the nation of
Israel at a time when the leaders
had repeatedly turned their backs
on God. Of course, the people
were following their leaders. The
current leaders, King Ahab and
his wife Jezebel, were leading
the people to worship the false
god Baal. They killed God's
prophets and brought in Baal's
prophets from Jezebel's homeland. That's when God sent Elijah
to stop them.

Elijah and the Prophets of Baal

1 Kings 18:1-39

Elijah had declared that no rain would fall in the land until he said so. That came true by God's power. King Ahab, who didn't believe in God, was very angry at Elijah. If he found him, he would kill him.

18 During the third year without rain, the Lord spoke his word to Elijah. The Lord said, "Go and meet King Ahab. I will soon send rain." ²So Elijah went to meet Ahab.

By this time there was no food in Samaria. ³So King Ahab sent for Obadiah. Obadiah was in charge of the king's palace. (Obadiah was a true follower of the Lord. ⁴One time Jezebel was killing all the Lord's prophets. So Obadiah took 100 of them and hid them in two caves. He put 50 in one cave and 50 in another cave. And he brought them food and water.) ⁵King Ahab said to Obadiah, "Let's look at every spring and valley in the land. Maybe we can find enough grass to keep our horses and mules alive. Then we will not have to kill our animals." ⁶So each one chose a part of the country to search. Ahab went in one direction. Obadiah went in another direction.

⁷While Obadiah was walking along, Elijah met him. Obadiah knew who Elijah was. So he bowed down to the ground before Elijah. He said, "Elijah? Is it really you, master?"

⁸Elijah answered, "Yes. Go tell your master the king that I am here."

⁹Then Obadiah said, "If I tell Ahab that, he will kill me! I have done nothing wrong that I should be killed! ¹⁰As surely as the Lord your God lives, the king has looked everywhere for you! He has sent people to every country to look for you. If the ruler said you were not there, that was not enough. Ahab then forced the ruler to swear you could not be found in his country. ¹¹Now you want me to go to my master and tell him, 'Elijah is here'? ¹²The Spirit of the Lord may carry you to some other place after I leave. If I go tell King Ahab you are here, he will come. If he doesn't find you, he will kill me! I have followed the Lord since I was a boy. ¹³Haven't you heard

167

ECCLESIASTES SONG OF SONGS ISAIAH JEREMIAH LAMENTATIONS EZEKIEL DANIEL HOSEA JOEL AMOS OBADIAH JONAH MICAH NAHUM HABAKKUK ZEPHANIAH HAGGAI ZECHARIAH MALACHI

what I did? When Jezebel was killing the Lord's prophets, I hid 100 of them. I put 50 prophets in one cave and 50 prophets in another cave. I brought them food and water. ¹⁴Now you want me to go and tell the king you are here. He will kill me!"

¹⁵Elijah answered, "I serve the Lord of heaven's armies. As surely as the Lord lives, I will stand before Ahab today."

Modern View from Mount Carmel

¹⁶So Obadiah went to Ahab and told him where Elijah was. Then Ahab went to meet Elijah.

¹⁷When he saw Elijah, he said, "Is it you—the biggest troublemaker in Israel?"

¹⁸Elijah answered, "I have not caused trouble in Israel. You and your father's family have caused all this trouble. You have not obeyed the Lord's commands. You have followed the Baals. ¹⁹Now tell all Israel to meet me at Mount Carmel. Also bring the 450 prophets of Baal there. And bring the 400 prophets of Asherah, who eat at Jezebel's table."

²⁰So Ahab called all the Israelites and those prophets to Mount Carmel. ²¹Elijah stood before the people. He said, "How long will you try to serve both Baal and the Lord? If the Lord is the true God, follow him. But if Baal is the true God, follow him!"

But the people said nothing.

²²Elijah said, "I am the only prophet of the Lord here. But there are 450 prophets of Baal. ²³So bring two bulls. Let the prophets of Baal choose one bull. Let them kill it and cut it into pieces. Then let them put the meat on the wood. But they are not to set fire to it. Then I will do the same with the other bull. And I will put it on the wood. But I will not set fire to it. ²⁴You prophets of Baal, pray to your god. And I will pray to the Lord. The god who answers the prayer will set fire to his wood. He is the true God."

All the people agreed that this was a good idea.

²⁵Then Elijah said to the prophets of Baal, "There are many of you. So you go first. Choose a bull and prepare it. Pray to your god, but don't start the fire."

²⁶So they took the bull that was given to them and prepared it. They prayed to Baal from morning until noon. They shouted, "Baal, answer us!" But there was no sound. No one answered. They danced around the altar they had built.

²⁷At noon Elijah began to make fun of them. He

168

GENESIS EXODUS LEVITICUS NUMBERS DEUTERONOMY JOSHUA JUDGES RUTH 1 SAMUEL 2 SAMUEL **1 KINGS** 2 KINGS 1 CHRONICLES 2 CHRONICLES EZRA NEHEMIAH ESTHER JOB PSALMS PROVERBS

1 KINGS

Behind the Story

Nothing the prophets did got Baal's attention. The practice of cutting themselves was a normal part of their worship.

Once the prophets of Baal gave up, Elijah used a different altar to make his offering. It was one that had been used before to give an offering to God. He stayed away from the altar of Baal.

Elijah's use of the 12 stones for the 12 tribes (1 Kings 18:31) reminded the people how God had taken care of them through so many hard times. It reminded them that he was the God of the northern kingdom, as well as the southern kingdom. Elijah mentioned the God of Abraham, Isaac and Israel to remind the people of the covenant God had made with Abraham. Even though the people had turned away from him for a time, he was still their God.

Elijah had water poured on the sacrifice three times. It was thoroughly soaked, which made the fact that the fire consumed it even more amazing.

said, "Pray louder! If Baal really is a god, maybe he is thinking. Or maybe he is busy or traveling! Maybe he is sleeping so you will have to wake him!" ²⁸So the prophets prayed louder. They cut themselves with swords and spears until their blood flowed. (This was the way they worshiped.)

²⁹The afternoon passed, and the prophets continued to act wildly. They continued until it was time for the evening sacrifice. But no voice was heard. Baal did not answer. No one paid attention.

³⁰Then Elijah said to all the people, "Now come to me." So they gathered around him. Elijah rebuilt the altar of the Lord because it had been torn down. ³¹He took 12 stones. He took 1 stone for each of the 12 tribes. These 12 tribes were named for the 12 sons of Jacob. (Jacob was the man the Lord had called Israel.) ³²Elijah used these stones to rebuild the altar in honor of the Lord. Then he dug a small ditch around it. It was big enough to hold about 13 quarts of seed. ³³Elijah put the wood on the altar. He cut the bull into pieces and laid them on the wood. Then he said, "Fill four jars with water. Put the water on the meat and on the wood."

³⁴Then Elijah said, "Do it again." And they did it again.

Then he said, "Do it a third time." And they did it the third time. ³⁵So the water ran off of the altar and filled the ditch.

³⁶It was time for the evening sacrifice. So the prophet Elijah went near the altar. He prayed, "Lord, you are the God of Abraham, Isaac and Israel. I ask you now to prove that you are the God of Israel. And prove that I am your servant. Show these people that you commanded me to do all these things. ³⁷Lord, answer my prayer. Show these people that

169

ECCLESIASTES SONG OF SONGS ISAIAH JEREMIAH LAMENTATIONS EZEKIEL DANIEL HOSEA JOEL AMOS OBADIAH JONAH MICAH NAHUM HABAKKUK ZEPHANIAH HAGGAI ZECHARIAH MALACHI

you, Lord, are God. Then the people will know that you are bringing them back to you."

[38]Then fire from the Lord came down. It burned the sacrifice, the wood, the stones and the ground around the altar. It also dried up the water in the ditch. [39]When all the people saw this, they fell down to the ground. They cried, "The Lord is God! The Lord is God!"

False Gods

Some of the false gods that nations around the Israelites worshiped crept into the lives of God's people and turned them away from the one true God.

Some of these gods were:

Baal who was called the Storm God. Read about him in 1 Kings 18:18-46.

Ashtoreth who was the goddess of love and beauty. Read about her in 1 Kings 11:5, 33.

Chemosh was the god of war. Read about him in 1 Kings 11:7, 33.

Dagon was the god of agriculture. Read about him in 1 Samuel 5:2-7.

Elijah Versus Moses

- **Both of these prophets were called by God to rescue his people.**
  Read about Moses in Exodus 3:7-10; Elijah announces his purpose in 1 Kings 17:1.

- **God performed supernatural miracles for both prophets, in order to protect the people or bring them back to him.**
  Read about Moses and the Red Sea in Exodus 14:21-28, and Elijah on Mount Carmel in 1 Kings 18:36-39.

- **Both received special care from God.**
  Read about God providing food for Moses and the Israelites in Exodus 16:4-5, and God sending birds to feed Elijah in 1 Kings 17:2-6.

Think About This

Elijah's prayer in 1 Kings 18:37 has two requests. First, he wanted all the people there—the prophets of Baal and the people who were watching—to know that the Lord alone is God. Second, he asked that the people would know that God would bring them back to worshiping him. God doesn't get angry and walk away when his people sin. He waits for them to come back to him.

God's response was very decisive. He sent fire that burned up not only the sacrifice, but also the altar itself, the ground around it and all the water that had been poured on the altar. There was no doubt about God's response.

Once again, as they did each time God did a miracle for them, the people fell down and worshiped him. But, as usual, their faith in God and obedience to him would be short-lived.

170

GENESIS EXODUS LEVITICUS NUMBERS DEUTERONOMY JOSHUA JUDGES RUTH 1 SAMUEL 2 SAMUEL 1 KINGS 2 KINGS 1 CHRONICLES 2 CHRONICLES EZRA NEHEMIAH ESTHER JOB PSALMS PROVERBS

1 KINGS

Elijah at Mount Sinai

1 Kings 19:1-18

Behind the Story

Elijah ran from King Ahab and Queen Jezebel. In fact, he ran far away. The trip from Mount Carmel to Mount Sinai was about 200 miles. It took him over 40 days and nights to walk that distance (1 Kings 19:8).

Elijah was so discouraged that he prayed to die. He thought he was the only man left who served God. Two other God-followers in Scripture prayed to die: Moses (Numbers 11:11-15) and Job (Job 6:8-9).

God knew that Elijah just needed some rest and care. He sent his special caregivers—angels —to take care of Elijah.

Many amazing things happened at Mount Sinai before this. The Israelites camped there shortly after they left Egypt. It was on Mount Sinai that Moses received the Ten Commandments from God. Also, the people built God's Meeting Tent there.

When God burned up the offering on Mount Carmel in front of the prophets of Baal, those prophets took off running. Elijah chased them and killed every single one of them. King Ahab wasn't very happy about that. So he sent out men to capture Elijah.

19 King Ahab told Jezebel everything Elijah had done. Ahab told her how Elijah had killed all the prophets with a sword. ²So Jezebel sent a messenger to Elijah. Jezebel said, "By this time tomorrow I will kill you. I will kill you as you killed those prophets. If I don't succeed, may the gods punish me terribly."

³When Elijah heard this, he was afraid. So he ran away to save his life. He took his servant with him. When they came to Beersheba in Judah, Elijah left his servant there. ⁴Then Elijah walked for a whole day into the desert. He sat down under a bush and asked to die. Elijah prayed, "I have had enough, Lord. Let me die. I am no better than my ancestors." ⁵Then Elijah lay down under the tree and slept.

Suddenly an angel came to him and touched him. The angel said, "Get up and eat." ⁶Elijah saw near his head a loaf baked over coals and a jar of water. So he ate and drank. Then he went back to sleep.

⁷Later the Lord's angel came to him a second time. The angel touched him and said, "Get up and eat. If you don't, the journey will be too hard for you." ⁸So Elijah got up and ate and drank. The food made him strong enough to walk for 40 days and nights. He walked to Mount Sinai, the mountain of God. ⁹There Elijah went into a cave and stayed all night.

Then the Lord spoke his word to him: "Elijah! Why are you here?"

¹⁰Elijah answered, "Lord, God of heaven's armies, I have always served you the best I could. But the people of Israel have broken their agreement with you. They have destroyed your altars. They have killed your prophets with swords. I am the only prophet left. And now they are trying to kill me, too!"

¹¹Then the Lord said to Elijah, "Go. Stand in front of me on the mountain. I will pass by you." Then a very strong wind blew. It caused the mountains to break apart. It broke apart large rocks in front of the Lord. But the Lord was not in the wind. After the wind, there was an earthquake. But the Lord was not in the earth-

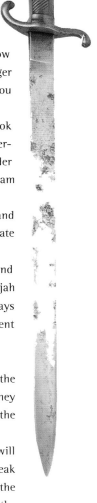

171

ECCLESIASTES SONG OF SONGS ISAIAH JEREMIAH LAMENTATIONS EZEKIEL DANIEL HOSEA JOEL AMOS OBADIAH JONAH MICAH NAHUM HABAKKUK ZEPHANIAH HAGGAI ZECHARIAH MALACHI

quake. [12]After the earthquake, there was a fire. But the Lord was not in the fire. After the fire, there was a quiet, gentle voice. [13]When Elijah heard it, he covered his face with his coat. He went out and stood at the entrance to the cave.

Then a voice said to him, "Elijah! Why are you here?"

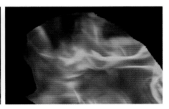

[14]Elijah answered, "Lord, God of heaven's armies, I have always served you the best I could. But the people of Israel have broken their agreement with you. They have destroyed your altars. They have killed your prophets with swords. I am the only prophet left. And now they are trying to kill me, too."

[15]The Lord said to him, "Go back on the road that leads to the desert around Damascus. Enter that city. There pour olive oil on Hazael to make him king over Aram. [16]Then pour oil on Jehu son of Nimshi to make him king over Israel. Next, pour oil on Elisha son of Shaphat from Abel Meholah. He will be a prophet in your place. [17]Jehu will kill anyone who escapes from Hazael's sword. And Elisha will kill anyone who escapes from Jehu's sword. [18]But I have left 7,000 people living in Israel. Those 7,000 have never bowed down before Baal. Their mouths have never kissed his idol."

Elisha Becomes a Prophet

[19]So Elijah left there and found Elisha son of Shaphat. He was plowing a field with a team of oxen. There were 11 teams ahead of him. Elisha was plowing with the twelfth team of oxen. Elijah came up to Elisha. Elijah took off his coat and put it on Elisha. [20]Then Elisha left his oxen and ran to follow Elijah. Elisha said, "Let me kiss my father and my mother good-bye. Then I will go with you."

Elijah answered, "That is fine. Go back. I won't stop you."

[21]So Elisha went back. He took his pair of oxen and killed them. He used the wooden yoke for the fire. Then he cooked the meat and gave it to the people. And they ate it. Then Elisha went and followed Elijah and became his helper.

Think About This

Elijah's discouragement came from feeling that he alone was standing for God. He needed God's encouragement that he wasn't alone.

God passed by Elijah as he stood on the mountain.

He first passed by in a strong wind that broke apart the mountain (1 Kings 18:11). It was powerful and impressive. But God's voice wasn't in it.

Second, there was an earthquake, one of the most powerful natural disasters on earth. But God didn't speak from it.

Next there was a fire, but God's voice wasn't in it, either (18:12).

Finally, Elijah heard a quiet voice, almost a whisper (18:12-13). That was God speaking to him. Elijah had to ignore the spectacular and noisy. He had to be still and quiet to hear God's voice.

God told Elijah that there were still other believers in the land. He was not alone after all.

172

GENESIS EXODUS LEVITICUS NUMBERS DEUTERONOMY JOSHUA JUDGES RUTH 1 SAMUEL 2 SAMUEL 1 KINGS 2 KINGS 1 CHRONICLES 2 CHRONICLES EZRA NEHEMIAH ESTHER JOB PSALMS PROVERBS

2 KINGS

Elijah Is Taken to Heaven

2 Kings 2:1-18

God had spoken to Elijah in a still quiet voice to tell him he was not alone. He sent him to anoint new kings. He also told him to anoint Elisha to be a prophet. After that Elisha would not leave Elijah's side.

2 It was near the time for the Lord to take Elijah. He was going to take him by a whirlwind up into heaven. Elijah and Elisha were at Gilgal. ²Elijah said to Elisha, "Please stay here. The Lord has told me to go to Bethel."

But Elisha said, "As the Lord lives, and as you live, I won't leave you." So they went down to Bethel. ³A group of the prophets at Bethel came to Elisha. They said to him, "Do you know the Lord will take your master away from you today?"

Elisha said, "Yes, I know. But don't talk about it."

⁴Elijah said to him, "Stay here, because the Lord has sent me to Jericho."

But Elisha said, "As the Lord lives, and as you live, I won't leave you."

So they went to Jericho. ⁵A group of the prophets at Jericho came to Elisha. They said, "Do you know that the Lord will take your master away from you today?"

Elisha answered, "Yes, I know. But don't talk about it."

⁶Elijah said to Elisha, "Stay here. The Lord has sent me to the Jordan River."

Elisha answered, "As the Lord lives, and as you live, I won't leave you."

So the two of them went on. ⁷Fifty men from a group of the prophets came. They stood far from where Elijah and Elisha were by the Jordan. ⁸Elijah took off his coat. Then he rolled it up and hit the water. The water divided to the right and to the left. Then Elijah and Elisha crossed over on dry ground.

173

ECCLESIASTES SONG OF SONGS ISAIAH JEREMIAH LAMENTATIONS EZEKIEL DANIEL HOSEA JOEL AMOS OBADIAH JONAH MICAH NAHUM HABAKKUK ZEPHANIAH HAGGAI ZECHARIAH MALACHI

⁹After they had crossed over, Elijah said to Elisha, "What can I do for you before I am taken from you?"

Elisha said, "Leave me a double share of your spirit."

¹⁰Elijah said, "You have asked a hard thing. But if you see me when I am taken from you, it will be yours. If you don't, it won't happen."

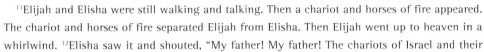

¹¹Elijah and Elisha were still walking and talking. Then a chariot and horses of fire appeared. The chariot and horses of fire separated Elijah from Elisha. Then Elijah went up to heaven in a whirlwind. ¹²Elisha saw it and shouted, "My father! My father! The chariots of Israel and their horsemen!" Elisha did not see him anymore. Elisha grabbed his own clothes and tore them to show how sad he was.

¹³He picked up Elijah's coat that had fallen from him. Then Elisha returned and stood on the bank of the Jordan. ¹⁴Elisha hit the water with Elijah's coat. He said, "Where is the Lord, the God of Elijah?" When he hit the water, it divided to the right and to the left. Then Elisha crossed over.

¹⁵A group of the prophets at Jericho were watching. They said, "Elisha now has the spirit Elijah had." They came to meet him. And they bowed down to the ground before him. ¹⁶They said to him, "There are 50 strong men with us! Please let them go and look for your master. Maybe the Spirit of the Lord has taken Elijah up and set him down. He may be on some mountain or in some valley."

But Elisha answered, "No. Don't send them."

¹⁷The group of prophets begged Elisha until he hated to refuse them anymore. Then he said, "Send them." So they sent 50 men who looked for three days. But they could not find Elijah. ¹⁸Then they came back to Elisha at Jericho where he was staying. He said to them, "I told you not to go, didn't I?"

Think About This

Elisha's request to get a double portion of Elijah's spirit was a request to be a man who followed God as Elijah did. It was actually a humble request to serve God.

The coat that Elijah dropped as he was taken up to heaven would be similar to outer coats of today. It was made by hand from animal hair that was woven into thread. Coats were valuable because they took so long to make. They were not just thrown away, but were patched and reused. Coats were used to keep warm and as pillows. When spread over another person, it was a sign that the coat's owner would care for that person. If it was placed on another's shoulders, it was a sign that authority was being transferred or given to that person. When Elisha picked up Elijah's coat, authority and power were transferred to him as God's prophet.

Seeing God

The fire blazing on the chariot and horse indicated God's presence. He came to bring his servant, Elijah, to heaven. What an honor for Elijah!

174

GENESIS EXODUS LEVITICUS NUMBERS DEUTERONOMY JOSHUA JUDGES RUTH 1 SAMUEL 2 SAMUEL 1 KINGS **2 KINGS** 1 CHRONICLES 2 CHRONICLES EZRA NEHEMIAH ESTHER JOB PSALMS PROVERBS

2 KINGS

Words You Should Know

Miracles (MEER-ih-k'ls)
A Latin word that means "wonderful thing." Miracles are special signs to show God's power. In the Old Testament God used miracles to rescue his people. Jesus did miracles to prove that he was God's Son. The Bible tells us of many miracles. The sick were healed, the blind were given sight, the crippled were able to walk and people could speak languages they had never studied. Sometimes people were even brought back to life after they had died. The best miracle was Jesus' coming back to life after he was killed on the cross. (See Nehemiah 9:17; Psalm 77:11, 14; Matthew 28:5-7; Luke 23:8; John 2:1-11; 3:2; 20:30-31; Acts 4:16-22; 8:13.)

Elisha

2 Kings 4:1-37

After Elijah was taken to heaven, Elisha became God's prophet to the Israelites. With the power of God's Spirit, he immediately began doing miracles.

A Widow Asks Elisha for Help

4 The wife of a man from a group of the prophets came to Elisha. She said, "Your servant, my husband, is dead! You know he honored the Lord. But now the man he owes money to is coming to take my two boys. He will make them his slaves!"

²Elisha answered, "How can I help you? Tell me, what do you have in your house?"

The woman said, "I don't have anything there except a pot of oil."

³Then Elisha said, "Go and get empty jars from all your neighbors. Don't ask for just a few. ⁴Then you must go into your house and close the door. Only you and your sons will be there. Then pour oil into all the jars. Set the full ones to one side."

175

ECCLESIASTES SONG OF SONGS ISAIAH JEREMIAH LAMENTATIONS EZEKIEL DANIEL HOSEA JOEL AMOS OBADIAH JONAH MICAH NAHUM HABAKKUK ZEPHANIAH HAGGAI ZECHARIAH MALACHI

[5]She left Elisha and shut the door. Only she and her sons were in the house. As they brought the jars to her, she poured the oil. [6]When the jars were all full, she said to her son, "Bring me another jar."

But he said, "There are no more jars." Then the oil stopped flowing.

[7]She went and told Elisha. Elisha said to her, "Go. Sell the oil and pay what you owe. You and your sons can live on what is left."

The Shunammite Woman

[8]One day Elisha went to Shunem. An important woman lived there. She begged Elisha to stay and eat. So every time Elisha passed by, he stopped there to eat. [9]The woman said to her husband, "I know that Elisha is a holy man of God. He passes by our house all the time. [10]Let's make a small room on the roof. Let's put a bed in the room for Elisha. And we can put a table, a chair and a lampstand there. Then when he comes by, he can stay there."

Shunem was presumably in Galilee, pictured above.

[11]One day Elisha came to the woman's house. He went to his room and rested. [12]He said to his servant Gehazi, "Call the Shunammite."

When the servant called her, she stood in front of him. [13]Elisha told his servant, "Now say to her, 'You have gone to all this trouble for us. What can I do for you? Do you want me to speak to the king or the commander of the army for you?' "

The woman answered, "I live among my own people."

[14]Elisha said, "But what can we do for her?"

Gehazi answered, "She has no son, and her husband is old."

[15]Then Elisha said, "Call her." So he called her, and she stood in the doorway. [16]Then Elisha said, "About this time next year, you will hold a son in your arms."

The woman said, "No, master, man of God. Don't lie to me!"

[17]But the woman became pregnant. And she gave birth to a son at that time the next year as Elisha had told her.

Think About This

Widows in Elisha's time were in serious trouble with no one to provide for them financially. They often lost everything when their husbands died. Later, Christians were taught that taking care of widows and orphans showed their faith in God (James 1:27).

It was not uncommon for people to be taken into slavery as payment for a debt owed.

This was a test of faith for the widow. As many jars as she brought would be filled by oil. This miracle provided for her immediate need—paying the debt to protect her sons. It also provided for future needs. She could sell the rest of the oil and use that money to buy food for her family.

The Shunammite woman was a contrast to the poor widow. This woman was wealthy. She and her husband owned their own home and had enough money to build a room for Elisha.

Elisha's friendship with this woman is similar to Elijah's friendship with the widow who gave him food (1 Kings 17:8-16).

176

GENESIS EXODUS LEVITICUS NUMBERS DEUTERONOMY JOSHUA JUDGES RUTH 1 SAMUEL 2 SAMUEL 1 KINGS 2 KINGS 1 CHRONICLES 2 CHRONICLES EZRA NEHEMIAH ESTHER JOB PSALMS PROVERBS

2 KINGS

Behind the Story

Elisha's room was on the roof. Houses had flat tops, and the roof was often used as part of the living space. He would have had his own entrance from a staircase that went up the outside of the house.

Elisha wanted to do something kind for the woman who had been so kind to him. She didn't ask him for the child; the idea came from Elisha's servant, Gehazi. It was a disgrace for a woman to have no children, especially a son to carry on the family name.

When her son died, the woman laid him on Elisha's bed. There may have been two reasons for this. One was to hide his death from servants and neighbors until she could talk to Elisha. Second, she knew God could help Elisha raise her son back to life.

Again, this experience is similar to Elijah's with the widow who gave him food. In both stories, the woman's son dies. In both stories, the prophet prays for help and stretches out on top of the boy. In both stories, God restores the boy to life (1 Kings 17:8-16).

[18]The child grew. One day he went out to his father, who was with the men harvesting grain. [19]The boy said to his father, "My head! My head!"

The father said to his servant, "Carry him to his mother!" [20]The servant took him to his mother. He lay on his mother's lap until noon. Then he died. [21]She took him up and laid him on Elisha's bed. Then she shut the door and went out.

[22]She called to her husband. She said, "Send me one of the servants and one of the donkeys. Then I can go quickly to the man of God and come back."

[23]The woman's husband said, "Why do you want to go to him today? It isn't the New Moon or the Sabbath day."

She said, "It will be all right."

[24]Then she saddled the donkey and said to her servant, "Lead on. Don't slow down for me unless I tell you." [25]So she went to Elisha at Mount Carmel.

He saw her coming from far away. So he said to his servant Gehazi, "Look, there's the Shunammite woman! [26]Run to meet her! Say to her, 'Are you all right? Is your husband all right? Is the child all right?' "

She answered, "Everything is all right."

[27]Then she came to Elisha at the hill. She caught hold of his feet. Gehazi came near to pull her away. But Elisha said to him, "Let her alone. She's very upset, and the Lord has not told me about it. He has hidden it from me."

[28]She said, "Master, I didn't tell you I wanted a son. I told you, 'Don't fool me.' "

[29]Then Elisha said to Gehazi, "Get ready. Take my walking stick in your hand and go quickly. If you meet anyone, don't greet him. If anyone greets you, don't answer him. Lay my walking stick on the face of the boy."

[30]But the child's mother said, "As surely as the Lord lives and as you live, I won't leave you!" So he got up and followed her.

[31]Gehazi went on ahead. He laid the walking stick on the child's face. But the child did not talk or move. Then Gehazi went back to meet Elisha. He told Elisha, "The child has not awakened."

[32]Elisha came into the house. There was the child, lying dead on his bed. [33]When Elisha entered the room, he shut the door. Only he and the child were in the room. Then Elisha prayed to the

177

ECCLESIASTES SONG OF SONGS ISAIAH JEREMIAH LAMENTATIONS EZEKIEL DANIEL HOSEA JOEL AMOS OBADIAH JONAH MICAH NAHUM HABAKKUK ZEPHANIAH HAGGAI ZECHARIAH MALACHI

Old Testament Miracles

Miracle	Person Involved	Scripture
Parting of the Red Sea	Moses	Exodus 14:21-31
Parting of the Jordan River	Joshua	Joshua 3:7-17
Jericho's Walls Fall	Joshua	Joshua 6:1-27
Killing of Philistines	Samson	Judges 15:15-17
Defeat of Goliath	David	1 Samuel 17:1-51
Three years of drought	Elijah	1 Kings 17:1-6
Endless flour	Elijah	1 Kings 17:13-16
Raising of widow's son	Elijah	1 Kings 17:17-24
Defeat of Baal's prophets	Elijah	1 Kings 18:1-40
Oil for a widow	Elisha	2 Kings 4:1-7
Raising of boy to life	Elisha	2 Kings 4:32-37
Healing of Naaman	Elisha	2 Kings 5:1-19

Lord. [34]He went to the bed and lay on the child. He put his mouth on the child's mouth. He put his eyes on the child's eyes and his hands on the child's hands. He stretched himself out on top of the child. Then the child's skin became warm. [35]Elisha turned away and walked around the room. Then he went back and put himself on the child again. Then the child sneezed seven times and opened his eyes.

[36]Elisha called Gehazi and said, "Call the Shunammite!" And he did. When she came, Elisha said, "Pick up your son." [37]She came in and fell at Elisha's feet. She bowed facedown to the floor. Then she picked up her son and went out.

Think About This

The woman's pain and grief were overwhelming. She pointed out to Elisha that she had not told him she wanted a child (2 Kings 4:28). It hurt more to have a child and lose him than it had hurt to not have children.

The boy was not restored to life because Elisha touched his eyes and mouth. He came back to life because Elisha prayed. It is only God's power that can do a miracle.

Read these verses about the strength that comes from God's power:

- Psalm 18:1
- Psalm 27:14
- Psalm 29:11
- 2 Corinthians 12:9
- Philippians 3:10
- Philippians 4:13

178

GENESIS EXODUS LEVITICUS NUMBERS DEUTERONOMY JOSHUA JUDGES RUTH 1 SAMUEL 2 SAMUEL 1 KINGS 2 KINGS 1 CHRONICLES 2 CHRONICLES EZRA NEHEMIAH ESTHER JOB PSALMS PROVERBS

2 KINGS

Naaman Is Healed

2 Kings 5:1-14

Words You Should Know

Leprosy (LEH-prah-see)
A name for some bad skin diseases, called a "harmful skin disease" in this story. A person with leprosy was called a leper and had to live outside the city. When other people came by, the lepers had to warn them by crying out, "Unclean, unclean!" (Leviticus 13:45-46; 2 Kings 5:1-27; 2 Chronicles 26:19-23; Matthew 8:1-3; Luke 17:11-19).

Think About This

Even though the little girl had been captured and taken away from her parents, it seems that Naaman and his wife treated her well. She seemed to care very much for them (2 Kings 5:3).

The king sent a letter with Naaman to introduce him to the king of Israel. However, it just made the king suspicious. He wondered if the Arameans were looking for another reason to attack Israel.

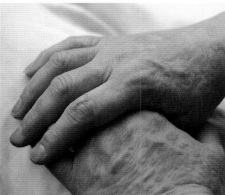

Elisha's fame spread as he did miracles and taught the people about God. The people recognized that God was with him.

5 Naaman was commander of the army of the king of Aram. He was a great man to his master. He had much honor because the Lord had used him to give victory to Aram. He was a mighty and brave man. But he had a harmful skin disease.

²The Arameans had gone out to steal from the Israelites. And they had taken a little girl as a captive from Israel. This little girl served Naaman's wife. ³She said to her mistress, "I wish that my master would meet the prophet who lives in Samaria. He would heal Naaman of his disease."

⁴Naaman went to the king. He told him what the girl from Israel had said. ⁵The king of Aram said, "Go now. And I will send a letter to the king of Israel." So Naaman left and took about 750 pounds of silver. He also took about 150 pounds of gold and ten changes of clothes with him.

⁶He brought the letter to the king of Israel. It read, "I am sending my servant Naaman to you. I'm sending him so you can heal him of his skin disease."

⁷The king of Israel read the letter. Then he tore his clothes to show how upset he was. He said, "I'm not God! I can't kill and make alive again! Why does this man send someone with a harmful skin disease for me to heal? You can see that the king of Aram is trying to start trouble with me!"

⁸Elisha, the man of God, heard that the king of Israel had torn his clothes. So he sent a message to the king. It said, "Why have you become so upset

FAQs

Who were the Arameans?

Aram was another name for Syria. Israel and Syria fought each other for over 100 years. The most important thing the Arameans gave the world was the language of Aramaic, which became a common language of the Jewish people.

179

ECCLESIASTES SONG OF SONGS ISAIAH JEREMIAH LAMENTATIONS EZEKIEL DANIEL HOSEA JOEL AMOS OBADIAH JONAH MICAH NAHUM HABAKKUK ZEPHANIAH HAGGAI ZECHARIAH MALACHI

that you tore your clothes? Let Naaman come to me. Then he will know there is a prophet in Israel!" [9]So Naaman went with his horses and chariots to Elisha's house. And he stood outside the door.

[10]Elisha sent a messenger to Naaman. The messenger said, "Go and wash in the Jordan River seven times. Then your skin will be healed, and you will be clean."

[11]Naaman became angry and left. He said, "I thought Elisha would surely come out and stand before me. I thought he would call on the name of the Lord his God. I thought he would wave his hand over the place and heal the disease! [12]Abana and Pharpar, the rivers of Damascus, are better than all the waters of Israel! Why can't I wash in them and become clean?" So Naaman went away very angry.

[13]But Naaman's servants came near and talked to him. They said, "My father, if the prophet had told you to do some great thing, wouldn't you have done it? Doesn't it make more sense just to do it? After all, he only told you, 'Wash, and you will be clean.' " [14]So Naaman went down and dipped in the Jordan seven times. He did just as Elisha had said. Then Naaman's skin became new again. It was like the skin of a little boy. And Naaman was clean!

TAKING IT TO HEART

Humility

Naaman nearly missed the miracle of being healed because of his pride. He thought he deserved better treatment than Elisha gave him. He got a lesson in being humble before God and man.

Behind the Story

Naaman must have had a mild case of leprosy. It doesn't appear that he had been forced to leave his home or the presence of his family.

Elisha asked the king to send Naaman to him. But then he didn't go out to meet him. Perhaps he didn't want to be exposed to the disease Naaman had because that would limit his own ministry to others. Another reason may have been that he wanted Naaman to know it was God who healed him, not the words or touch of Elisha.

Elisha's instruction for Naaman to wash seven times in the Jordan River in order to be healed required Naaman's complete obedience—six times was not enough.

Naaman's servants advised him to obey Elisha's command. They must have believed in God's power to heal their master.

Once Naaman was healed, he believed in God. Second Kings 5:15 records his word: "I now know there is no God in all the earth except in Israel."

180

GENESIS EXODUS LEVITICUS NUMBERS DEUTERONOMY JOSHUA JUDGES RUTH 1 SAMUEL 2 SAMUEL 1 KINGS 2 KINGS 1 CHRONICLES 2 CHRONICLES EZRA NEHEMIAH ESTHER JOB PSALMS PROVERBS

ESTHER

Esther's Courage

Esther 2:17-18; 3:8-11; 7:1-7

Behind the Story

King Xerxes searches for a new queen after getting angry at Queen Vashti. He holds a contest to find the most beautiful girl in his country (Esther 2:1-4).

Esther was brought to the palace by her cousin, Mordecai. She was beautiful, and all who met her liked her (2:7, 9, 17).

After Esther became queen, one of the king's servants, Haman, was promoted to a high rank. Everyone bowed down when Haman came by . . . everyone except Mordecai. Since Mordecai was Jewish, Haman got very angry at all the Jews. He got the king's permission to have all the Jews in the land destroyed (3:13).

However, Haman did not know that Esther was Jewish. She had not told anyone, not even the king. Mordecai asked her to help her people. He told her that this might be the very reason she had become queen (4:13-14).

No one knows who wrote the book of Esther. It is one of two books in the Bible that have no mention of God at all. It takes place during the time that King Xerxes ruled in Persia which was from 486-465 B.C.

Esther Is Made Queen

2 ¹⁷The king was pleased with Esther more than with any of the other virgins. And he liked her more than any of the others. So King Xerxes put a royal crown on Esther's head. And he made her queen in place of Vashti. ¹⁸Then the king gave a great banquet for Esther. He invited all his important men and royal officers. He announced a holiday in all the empire. And he was generous and gave everyone a gift.

Haman Plans to Destroy the Jews

3 ⁸Then Haman said to King Xerxes, "There is a certain group of people in all the areas of your kingdom. They are scattered among the other people. They keep themselves separate. Their customs are different from those of all the other people. And they do not obey the king's laws. It is not right for you to allow them to continue living in your kingdom. ⁹If it pleases the king, let an order be given to destroy those people. Then I will pay 375 tons of silver to those who do the king's business. They will put it into the royal treasury."

181

ECCLESIASTES SONG OF SONGS ISAIAH JEREMIAH LAMENTATIONS EZEKIEL DANIEL HOSEA JOEL AMOS OBADIAH JONAH MICAH NAHUM HABAKKUK ZEPHANIAH HAGGAI ZECHARIAH MALACHI

[10]So the king took his signet ring off and gave it to Haman. Haman son of Hammedatha, the Agagite, was the enemy of the Jews. [11]Then the king said to Haman, "The money and the people are yours. Do with them as you please."

Haman Is Hanged

7 So the king and Haman went in to eat with Queen Esther. [2]They were drinking wine. And the king said to Esther on this second day also, "What are you asking for? I will give it to you. What is it you want? I will give you as much as half of my kingdom."

[3]Then Queen Esther answered, "My king, I hope you are pleased with me. If it pleases you, let me live. This is what I ask. And let my people live, too. This is what I want. [4]I ask this because my people and I have been sold to be destroyed. We are to be killed and completely wiped out. If we had been sold as male and female slaves, I would have kept quiet. That would not be enough of a problem to bother the king."

[5]Then King Xerxes asked Queen Esther, "Who is he? Where is he? Who has done such a thing?"

[6]Esther said, "A man who is against us! Our enemy is this wicked Haman!"

Then Haman was filled with terror before the king and queen. [7]The king was very angry. He got up, left his wine and went out into the palace garden. But Haman stayed inside to beg Queen Esther to save his life. He could see that the king had already decided to kill him.

> ### Seeing Jesus
>
> Esther was willing to risk her life to save her people. When Mordecai asked for her help, she said, "I will go to the king. . . . And if I die, I die." This same devotion was heard from Jesus in the Garden of Gethsemane. He knew he was about to die, and yet he prayed, "Father . . . do what you want, not what I want" (Luke 22:42).

Behind the Story (cont.)

While Haman made plans to kill Mordecai and the Jews, the king discovered that Mordecai had saved the king's life one time. He wanted to honor Mordecai. He asked Haman how to honor someone. Haman thought he was the one who would be honored. He was very angry when he found out it was Mordecai (6:1-14).

Esther invited the king and Haman to dinner. After they had eaten, she told the king that Haman planned to kill her and all her people (7:4-6).

The king was very angry. He ordered that Haman be hung on the platform where he had planned to kill Mordecai (7:9-10).

Esther's courage helped to save the Jewish people.

The Other Books of History:

Chronicles Info

- 1 and 2 Chronicles, Ezra and Nehemiah were originally all one book.

- 1 Chronicles focuses on the life of David. It retells much of what is recorded in 1 Samuel.

- 2 Chronicles recalls Solomon's life and the rulers of Judah.

- 2 Chronicles has the same information as 1 and 2 Kings.

- 1 and 2 Chronicles end at the same point in Israel's history where the previous twelve books end.

- 1 and 2 Chronicles were written between 450-400 B.C.

Nehemiah Info

Nehemiah had the job of choosing the king's wine then tasting it before the king did to make certain it wasn't poisoned.

Nehemiah's mission as governor was to rebuild the walls around the city of Jerusalem.

1 CHRONICLES

First Chronicles retells the story of the nation of Israel told in the previous books. Tradition says that Ezra is the author. The fact that these stories are retold in Chronicles emphasizes their importance and means that the writer wanted the Israelites to pay attention to them.

2 CHRONICLES

This book is a hopeful word to Israel that God has not forgotten them. The whole nation was in captivity to Babylon, and they needed hope that God would rescue them. Ezra is usually thought to be the author. One reason is that there are many lists in this book, just as there are in the book of Ezra.

EZRA

In this book, Ezra records the return of the people to the Promised Land after their captivity in Babylon. Even though life is difficult for them, Ezra reminds them of God's constant faithfulness to them. It was written in about 440 B.C.

NEHEMIAH

Once again, Ezra is considered to be the author of this book which tells the story of Nehemiah, the one who served wine to the king of Babylon. He left that job to become governor of Jerusalem.

POETRY

Five books make up the Poetry section of the Old Testament. They are:

Job
Psalms
Proverbs
Ecclesiastes
Song of Songs

Several different authors contributed to these books. The common thread throughout them is an ancient style of poetry. The words don't rhyme as you might expect. Ancient Hebrew poetry set ideas together. Sometimes a thought was stated, and the next sentence emphasized it even more. Sometimes, as in Proverbs, the first statement was positive, and the second statement was an opposite statement.

The time in Israel's history when the books of poetry were written was a time of literary growth and achievement.

- Job looks at God's providence in human suffering.
- Psalms is a book of praise to God.
- Proverbs records many of the wise sayings of the time.
- Ecclesiastes expresses thoughts on the meaning of life.
- Song of Songs celebrates married love.

184

GENESIS EXODUS LEVITICUS NUMBERS DEUTERONOMY JOSHUA JUDGES RUTH 1 SAMUEL 2 SAMUEL 1 KINGS 2 KINGS 1 CHRONICLES 2 CHRONICLES EZRA NEHEMIAH ESTHER JOB **PSALMS** PROVERBS

PSALMS

Behind the Book

The book of Psalms was written over a thousand-year period by several different writers. The known authors are David, Asaph, the sons of Korah, Solomon, Ethan and Moses. Fifty psalms were anonymously written.

Individual psalms were written as a response to God's work in a person's life. The words come straight from the heart.

There are 150 psalms in the whole book.

Several psalms end a thought or phrase with the word "Selah." This word probably means "pause" or "reflect," and seems to have been used in a similar way as the word "Amen" is used today.

Books of Poetry: PSALMS

Psalms is a wonderful collection of songs and prayers that express a deep relationship with God. The psalmist often cries out to God for help and at other times praises him with beautiful poetry. The psalms were sung by the Jewish people as they worshiped God. So Psalms could be considered a hymnbook.

God's Works and Word

Psalm 19

For the director of music. A song of David.

19 The heavens tell the glory of God.
And the skies announce what
his hands have made.
²Day after day they tell the story.
Night after night they tell it again.
³They have no speech or words.
They don't make any sound to be heard.
⁴But their message goes out through all the world.
It goes everywhere on earth.
The sky is like a home for the sun.
⁵ The sun comes out like a bridegroom
from his bedroom.
It rejoices like an athlete eager to run a race.
⁶The sun rises at one end of the sky,
and it follows its path to the other end.
Nothing hides from its heat.

185

ECCLESIASTES SONG OF SONGS ISAIAH JEREMIAH LAMENTATIONS EZEKIEL DANIEL HOSEA JOEL AMOS OBADIAH JONAH MICAH NAHUM HABAKKUK ZEPHANIAH HAGGAI ZECHARIAH MALACHI

⁷The Lord's teachings are perfect.
    They give new strength.
The Lord's rules can be trusted.
    They make plain people wise.
⁸The Lord's orders are right.
    They make people happy.
The Lord's commands are pure.
    They light up the way.
⁹It is good to respect the Lord.
    That respect will last forever.
The Lord's judgments are true.
    They are completely right.
¹⁰They are worth more than gold,
    even the purest gold.
They are sweeter than honey,
    even the finest honey.
¹¹They tell your servant what to do.
    Keeping them brings great reward.

¹²No one can see all his own mistakes.
    Forgive me for my secret sins.
¹³Keep me from the sins that I want to do.
    Don't let them rule me.
Then I can be pure
    and free from the greatest of sins.

¹⁴I hope my words and thoughts please you.
    Lord, you are my Rock, the one who saves me.

Psalm Themes

The psalms can be divided into categories by their themes:

Songs of Repentance are cries of sorrow for disobeying God and asking for his help.

Songs of Praise are given for all God has done.

Wisdom Songs teach about God and living for him.

Messianic Songs are sung about Jesus and anticipate his coming.

Songs of Ascent are sung by the people as they travel to Jerusalem. They speak of God's care for his people and his power and glory.

Imprecatory Psalms are cries for God to punish the enemies of his people.

186

GENESIS EXODUS LEVITICUS NUMBERS DEUTERONOMY JOSHUA JUDGES RUTH 1 SAMUEL 2 SAMUEL 1 KINGS 2 KINGS 1 CHRONICLES 2 CHRONICLES EZRA NEHEMIAH ESTHER JOB **PSALMS** PROVERBS

PSALMS

The Best-Known Psalm

Psalm 23 sings of great trust in God. David wrote this song, which has become one of the best-loved psalms in the Bible.

This psalm shows great confidence that God will take care of his people (his sheep) regardless of their circumstances in life.

This psalm looks forward to Jesus coming to earth. He is the Great Shepherd.

This psalm does not say that God will take away bad things or change circumstances. But it does promise that God will be close beside his people as they go through hard times.

This psalm makes promises of God's care and the joy of being with him not just in this life but it speaks of eternity and being with him in heaven.

The Lord the Shepherd

Psalm 23

A song of David.

23 The Lord is my shepherd.
I have everything I need.
²He gives me rest in green pastures.
    He leads me to calm water.
³He gives me new strength.
 For the good of his name,
    he leads me on paths that are right.
⁴Even if I walk
    through a very dark valley,
 I will not be afraid
    because you are with me.
 Your rod and your shepherd's staff comfort me.

⁵You prepare a meal for me
    in front of my enemies.
 You pour oil of blessing on my head.
    You give me more than I can hold.
⁶Surely your goodness and love will be with me
    all my life.
 And I will live in the house of the Lord forever.

187

ECCLESIASTES SONG OF SONGS ISAIAH JEREMIAH LAMENTATIONS EZEKIEL DANIEL HOSEA JOEL AMOS OBADIAH JONAH MICAH NAHUM HABAKKUK ZEPHANIAH HAGGAI ZECHARIAH MALACHI

The Majesty of God

Psalm 93

93 The Lord is king. He is clothed with majesty.
The Lord is clothed in majesty
and armed with strength.
The world is set,
and it cannot be moved.
[2]Lord, your kingdom was set up long ago.
You are everlasting.

[3]Lord, the seas rise up.
The seas raise their voice.
The seas lift up their pounding waves.
[4]The sound of the water is loud.
The ocean waves are powerful.
But the Lord above is much greater.

[5]Lord, your laws will stand forever.
Your Temple will be holy forevermore.

A Praise Psalm

Psalm 93 focuses on God's king-ship. It points out that God will reign forever.

The Canaanites lived in the Prom-ised Land when the Israelites captured it. The Canaanites had many "gods" who ruled for a short time and then, for various reasons, lost power to another god. In contrast, the true God rules eternally.

If you have ever stood near the ocean on a stormy day, you will understand the word-picture in verses 3 and 4. The sea is indeed powerful, but the Lord God is almighty.

Psalm 93 is somewhat unique because the praise to God focuses simply on who God is, not on things he has done for the writer.

Psalms to Read

When you are scared—3, 27, 46, 91, 118

When you are thankful—136, 138

To worship God—8, 19, 29, 150

When you are tempted—38, 141

When you need wisdom—1, 16, 19, 64

188

GENESIS EXODUS LEVITICUS NUMBERS DEUTERONOMY JOSHUA JUDGES RUTH 1 SAMUEL 2 SAMUEL 1 KINGS 2 KINGS 1 CHRONICLES 2 CHRONICLES EZRA NEHEMIAH ESTHER JOB PSALMS **PROVERBS**

PROVERBS

Books of Poetry: PROVERBS

Behind the Book

Proverbs talks to people about living in obedience to God in their everyday lives. It gives advice on relating to other people in a way that will please God.

Proverbs 15 teaches us how to get along with others. The simple message of these verses is to treat others as you would like to be treated.

Good communication is basic to a good relationship, whether it is with family members or friends.

The book of Proverbs was written by several different people. One of them was King Solomon, to whom God gave great wisdom and riches. Proverbs is a collection of sayings which give very practical advice on how to live life. One of the key verses to understanding Proverbs is found in 3:13: "Happy is the person who finds wisdom. And happy is the person who gets understanding."

Wisdom and Foolishness

Proverbs 15:1-33

15 A gentle answer will calm a person's anger.
But an unkind answer will cause more anger.

²Wise people use knowledge when they speak.
But fools speak only foolishness.

³The Lord's eyes see everything that happens.
He watches both evil and good people.

⁴As a tree gives us fruit, healing words give us life.
But evil words crush the spirit.

⁵A foolish person rejects his father's correction.
But anyone who accepts correction is wise.

⁶There is much wealth in the houses of good people.
But evil people are paid only with trouble.

189

ECCLESIASTES SONG OF SONGS ISAIAH JEREMIAH LAMENTATIONS EZEKIEL DANIEL HOSEA JOEL AMOS OBADIAH JONAH MICAH NAHUM HABAKKUK ZEPHANIAH HAGGAI ZECHARIAH MALACHI

⁷With their words wise people spread knowledge.
  But there is no knowledge in the thoughts of the foolish.

⁸The Lord hates the sacrifice that the wicked person offers.
  But he is pleased with an honest person's prayer.

⁹The Lord hates what evil people do.
  But he loves those who do what is right.

¹⁰The person who quits doing what is right will really be punished.
  The one who hates to be corrected will die.

¹¹The Lord knows what is happening where the dead people are.
  So he can surely know what living people are thinking.

¹²A person who laughs at wisdom does not like to be corrected.
  He will not ask advice from the wise.

¹³Happiness makes a person smile.
  But sadness breaks a person's spirit.

¹⁴Smart people want more knowledge.
  But a foolish person just wants more foolishness.

¹⁵Every day is hard for those who suffer.
  But a happy heart makes it like a continual feast.

¹⁶It is better to be poor and respect the Lord
  than to be wealthy and have much trouble.

¹⁷It is better to eat vegetables with those who love you
  than to eat meat with those who hate you.

Verses Explained

Notice the contrast in 15:5: A wise person accepts correction while a fool rejects it.

Verse 8 points out that a wicked person can make sacrifices to God, but still not please him because God looks at the heart. God is pleased with the prayers of a person who is being honest before him.

Death is no mystery to the Lord. If he knows what is happening with those who are dead, how much more must he know about what is happening in the hearts of people on earth (15:11).

This proverb clearly teaches that there is a choice to make of which path to take for your life. The path of wisdom brings joy and happiness. The path of foolishness brings pain, sorrow and, finally, death.

Being loved and accepted is more important than having all the stuff that goes with a fancy life. That is clear from verse 17!

190

GENESIS EXODUS LEVITICUS NUMBERS DEUTERONOMY JOSHUA JUDGES RUTH 1 SAMUEL 2 SAMUEL 1 KINGS 2 KINGS 1 CHRONICLES 2 CHRONICLES EZRA NEHEMIAH ESTHER JOB PSALMS **PROVERBS**

PROVERBS

Words and Deeds

Have you ever been told to "Count to ten before you lose your temper"? That idea might have come from Proverbs 15:18.

You should not take advice from just anybody. However, the smart person listens to wise people and takes their advice (15:22).

How good does it make you feel to get an encouraging word or hear that you have done something well? Verse 23 reinforces that and reminds you to say kind and encouraging things to others.

Solomon devoted many of the proverbs to the topic of words. See James 3 for more instructions on speaking kindly and wisely to others.

Verse 25 speaks of God protecting widows. Throughout Scripture we learn that God takes care of the defenseless and helpless.

[18]A person who quickly gets angry causes trouble.
But a person who controls his temper stops a quarrel.

[19]A lazy person's life is as difficult as walking through a patch of thorns.
But an honest person's life is as easy as walking down a
smooth highway.

[20]A wise son makes his father happy.
But a foolish person hates his mother.

[21]A man without wisdom enjoys being foolish.
But a man with understanding does what is right.

[22]Plans fail without good advice.
But plans succeed when you get advice from many others.

[23]People enjoy giving good answers!
Saying the right word at the right time is so pleasing!

[24]A wise person does things that will make his life better.
He avoids whatever would cause his death.

[25]The Lord will tear down the proud person's house.
But he will protect the property of a widow.

[26]The Lord hates evil thoughts.
But he is pleased with kind words.

[27]A greedy person brings trouble to his family.
But the person who can't be paid to do wrong will live.

191

ECCLESIASTES SONG OF SONGS ISAIAH JEREMIAH LAMENTATIONS EZEKIEL DANIEL HOSEA JOEL AMOS OBADIAH JONAH MICAH NAHUM HABAKKUK ZEPHANIAH HAGGAI ZECHARIAH MALACHI

²⁸Good people think before they answer.

But the wicked simply give evil answers.

²⁹The Lord does not listen to the wicked.

But he hears the prayers of those who do right.

³⁰Good news makes you feel better.

Your happiness will show in your eyes.

³¹A wise person pays attention to correction

that will improve his life.

³²A person who refuses correction hates himself.

But a person who accepts correction gains understanding.

³³Respect for the Lord will teach you wisdom.

If you want to be honored, you must not be proud.

Think About This

Proverbs is the Old Testament sister to the book of James in the New Testament.

First Kings 4:32 states that Solomon wrote 3,000 proverbs. The book of Proverbs contains only a portion of those.

Proverbs gives advice on everything from keeping a good reputation (22:1) to conducting business fairly (11:1). It also covers marriage (18:22), friendship (17:17), kind words (15:1), wisdom (3:14), self-control (16:32) and many other practical truths.

In Proverbs you can read about six things God hates (6:16-19), four things hard to understand (30:18-19) and four little but wise things (30:24-28).

Parallelism

Some of the proverbs are written in a form called synonomous parallelism. That means that a statement is made, then the second line says the same thing again in a slightly different way. For example, 1:2 says of the Proverbs: "They teach wisdom and self-control. They give understanding." The second line gives more information about what is stated in the first line.

Antithetical parallelism is also found in Proverbs. In that case the second line of the verse expresses a contrasting or opposite thought. Some examples are 15:2 and 15:21.

192

GENESIS EXODUS LEVITICUS NUMBERS DEUTERONOMY JOSHUA JUDGES RUTH 1 SAMUEL 2 SAMUEL 1 KINGS 2 KINGS 1 CHRONICLES 2 CHRONICLES EZRA NEHEMIAH ESTHER JOB PSALMS PROVERBS

ECCLESIASTES

Behind the Book

If Solomon wrote the book of Ecclesiastes, it was probably written toward the end of his life when he had come back to God after worshiping false gods for a time.

It is easier to understand this book when you read the end first. Ecclesiastes 12:13 says, "Here is my final advice: Honor God and obey his commands. This is the most important thing people can do." Everything else written about in this book comes down to that advice. Nothing is more important than obeying God.

Ecclesiastes 3 gives 14 pairs of opposites to show that everything in the world is actually in God's hands. He controls the order of things, such as the seasons (3:1). He also gives us wisdom to know when to speak up and when to be silent (3:7).

Books of Poetry: ECCLESIASTES

Ecclesiastes is one of the hardest books in the Bible to understand. Most experts believe that Solomon wrote this book. It asks many questions about the meaning of life and proclaims that life is completely meaningless without God.

There Is a Time for Everything

Ecclesiastes 3:1-8

3 There is a right time for everything.
Everything on earth has its special season.
²There is a time to be born
and a time to die.
There is a time to plant
and a time to pull up plants.
³There is a time to kill
and a time to heal.
There is a time to destroy
and a time to build.
⁴There is a time to cry
and a time to laugh.
There is a time to be sad
and a time to dance.

193

ECCLESIASTES SONG OF SONGS ISAIAH JEREMIAH LAMENTATIONS EZEKIEL DANIEL HOSEA JOEL AMOS OBADIAH JONAH MICAH NAHUM HABAKKUK ZEPHANIAH HAGGAI ZECHARIAH MALACHI

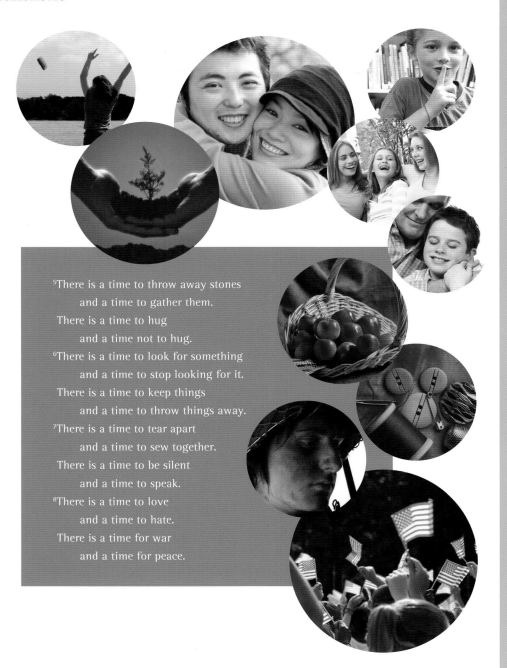

5There is a time to throw away stones
and a time to gather them.
There is a time to hug
and a time not to hug.
6There is a time to look for something
and a time to stop looking for it.
There is a time to keep things
and a time to throw things away.
7There is a time to tear apart
and a time to sew together.
There is a time to be silent
and a time to speak.
8There is a time to love
and a time to hate.
There is a time for war
and a time for peace.

Think About This

King Solomon had many wives who were from the countries around Israel. He married these women to insure that he would have peace with their nations. However, they brought their false gods into his life, and he began worshiping them. Ecclesiastes was written after he returned to God. He wanted to show that there was no meaning in life apart from God.

Ecclesiastes is one of the books called Wisdom Literature because it gives instructions for right living. The writer wants to warn the reader to avoid making the same mistakes he made in trying to live apart from God.

The Other Books of Poetry:

JOB PSALMS PROVERBS ECCLESIASTES SONG OF SONGS

JOB

No one knows for certain who wrote Job. However, the book focuses on one man's suffering and his response of faithful trust in God. It doesn't give any real answers about why there is suffering, but it does assure us of God's presence throughout the hard times in life.

The Fountain of Job

Job's three friends and his wife suggest to him why the terrible events have come into his life. All their advice was wrong. In the end, all that mattered was that Job trusted God—no matter what.

Job's problems happen because God allows Satan to test Job. Satan wants to see if Job will turn away from God. He doesn't.

SONG OF SONGS

This book is a collection of love poems considered to have been written by Solomon. It celebrates the love of a husband and wife. Though Solomon had many wives, the one written about in this book was his true love.

THE PROPHETS

The section of the Old Testament known as the Prophets contains seventeen books. The first five are called the Major Prophets. The other twelve are called the Minor Prophets. Generally, the books are arranged in chronological order, with the earliest prophets first. The writings of the prophets covers about 400 years in Israel's history.

Prophecy is sometimes defined as "predicting the future," but it is really more than that. Prophets did sometimes warn about future judgments, but they also challenged the people to live for God. They encouraged the people and even kings and rulers to obey God.

The Major Prophets are:

Isaiah, Jeremiah, Lamentations, Ezekiel and Daniel.

The Minor Prophets are:

Hosea, Joel, Amos, Obadiah, Jonah, Micah, Nahum, Habakkuk, Zephaniah, Haggai, Zechariah and Malachi.

These 17 books were written by 16 prophets. Jeremiah wrote both his book and Lamentations.

Any of the Major Prophets are longer than all of the Minor Prophets put together.

The prophets wrote during the time of the fall of the Hebrew nation—when the people turned away from God and were punished.

196

GENESIS EXODUS LEVITICUS NUMBERS DEUTERONOMY JOSHUA JUDGES RUTH 1 SAMUEL 2 SAMUEL 1 KINGS 2 KINGS 1 CHRONICLES 2 CHRONICLES EZRA NEHEMIAH ESTHER JOB PSALMS PROVERBS

ISAIAH

Words You Should Know

Messiah (muh-SYE-uh)
A Hebrew word for "appointed one" or "one chosen by God." The Greek word for Messiah is "Christ." Christians believe that Jesus is the Messiah or Christ (John 1:41; 4:25).

Savior (SAVE-yor)
Someone who saves people from danger. The name Jesus means "savior." Jesus is the Savior of the people of this world. His life, death and resurrection made it possible for people to be saved from punishment and death for their sins (see Luke 2:11; John 4:42; Ephesians 5:23; Philippians 3:20; Titus 1:4; 1 John 4:14).

God's Suffering Servant

Isaiah 53:1-12

Isaiah is called the Messianic Prophet because he wrote about the Messiah—the Savior God would send to rescue his people. Isaiah's name means "The Lord Saves." Of all the prophets, Isaiah most clearly writes of God's plan to save his people.

53 Who would have believed what we heard?
Who saw the Lord's power in this?
²He grew up like a small plant before the Lord.
He was like a root growing in a dry land.
He had no special beauty or form to make us notice him.
There was nothing in his appearance to make us desire him.
³He was hated and rejected by people.
He had much pain and suffering.
People would not even look at him.
He was hated, and we didn't even notice him.

⁴But he took our suffering on him
and felt our pain for us.
We saw his suffering.
We thought God was punishing him.
⁵But he was wounded for the wrong things we did.
He was crushed for the evil things we did.
The punishment, which made us well, was given to him.
And we are healed because of his wounds.
⁶We all have wandered away like sheep.
Each of us has gone his own way.
But the Lord has put on him the punishment
for all the evil we have done.

197

ECCLESIASTES SONG OF SONGS **ISAIAH** JEREMIAH LAMENTATIONS EZEKIEL DANIEL HOSEA JOEL AMOS OBADIAH JONAH MICAH NAHUM HABAKKUK ZEPHANIAH HAGGAI ZECHARIAH MALACHI

⁷He was beaten down and punished.
　　But he didn't say a word.
He was like a lamb being led to be killed.
　　He was quiet, as a sheep is quiet while
　　　its wool is being cut.
　　He never opened his mouth.
⁸Men took him away roughly and unfairly.
　　He died without children to continue
　　　his family.
　He was put to death.
　　He was punished for the sins of my people.
⁹He was buried with wicked men.
　　He died with the rich.
He had done nothing wrong
　　He had never lied.

¹⁰But it was the Lord who decided
　　to crush him and make him suffer.
　　So the Lord made his life a penalty offering.
　But he will see his descendants and live a
　　　long life.
　　He will complete the things the Lord wants
　　　him to do.
¹¹He will suffer many things in his soul.
　　But then he will see life and be satisfied.
　My good servant will make many people right with God.
　　He carried away their sins.
¹²For this reason I will make him a great man among
　　　people.
　　He will share in all things with those who are strong.
He willingly gave his life.
　　He was treated like a criminal.
But he carried away the sins of many people.
　　And he asked forgiveness for those who sinned.

Seeing Jesus

Jesus fulfills Isaiah's prophecies:

- He will be rejected (53:1, 3); see John 12:37-38.

- He will bear our sins (53:4); see Romans 4:25.

- He will be our substitute (53:6, 8); see 2 Corinthians 5:21.

- He will justify man's sin (53:10-11); see Romans 5:15-19.

The Suffering Savior

Isaiah 53 speaks of Jesus coming to earth. Note that verse 3 states that he will be rejected by men. He had much pain and suffering. These words were written hundreds of years before Jesus was born. He knew when he came to earth that his life here would be difficult, but he chose to come anyway. He said, "I give my life for the sheep" (John 10:15).

Every person who has ever lived is a sinner. Isaiah 53:6 confirms that. Romans 3:23 restates it: "All people have sinned and are not good enough for God's glory." Jesus came because we needed his sacrifice for our sins in order to enter God's heaven someday.

198

GENESIS EXODUS LEVITICUS NUMBERS DEUTERONOMY JOSHUA JUDGES RUTH 1 SAMUEL 2 SAMUEL 1 KINGS 2 KINGS 1 CHRONICLES 2 CHRONICLES EZRA NEHEMIAH ESTHER JOB PSALMS PROVERBS

DANIEL

Behind the Book

Daniel is divided into two parts. The first part is about Daniel's life and work; the second part records the visions Daniel had and the prophecies he gave.

Israel wasn't captured just because Babylon was bigger or stronger. This was part of God's punishment for Israel's disobedience.

Daniel Taken Captive

Daniel 1:1-21

King Nebuchadnezzar of Babylon captured the Israelites and took them into captivity. He had a plan that some of the strong, healthy, handsome Jewish boys could be trained to work as servants in his palace. Daniel was one of those boys.

Daniel Taken to Babylon

1 Nebuchadnezzar king of Babylon came to Jerusalem and surrounded it with his army. This happened during the third year that Jehoiakim was king of Judah. ²The Lord allowed Nebuchadnezzar to capture Jehoiakim king of Judah. Nebuchadnezzar also took some of the things from the Temple of God. He carried them to Babylonia and put them in the temple of his gods.

³Then King Nebuchadnezzar gave an order to Ashpenaz, his chief officer. He told Ashpenaz to bring some of the men from Judah into his house. He wanted them to be from important families. And he wanted those who were from the family of the king of Judah. ⁴King Nebuchadnezzar wanted only healthy, young, Israelite men. These men were not to have anything wrong with their bodies. They were to be handsome and well educated. They were to be able to learn and understand things. He wanted those who were able to serve in his palace. Ashpenaz was to teach them the language and writings of the Babylonians. ⁵The king gave the young men a certain amount of food and wine every day. That was the same kind of food that the king ate. They were to be trained for three years. Then the young men would become servants of the king of Babylon. ⁶Among those young men were some from the people of Judah. These were Daniel, Hananiah, Mishael and Azariah.

⁷Then Ashpenaz, the chief officer, gave them Babylonian names. Daniel's new name was Belteshazzar. Hananiah's was Shadrach. Mishael's was Meshach. And Azariah's new name was Abednego.

FAQs

Q: Why would Daniel turn down good food?

A: The food offered to the boys had not been prepared or cooked according to the rules given by Moses. Also, the meat probably had been dedicated to the idols of Babylon. If Daniel ate this food, he would be acknowledging the idols of Babylon.

199

ECCLESIASTES SONG OF SONGS ISAIAH JEREMIAH LAMENTATIONS EZEKIEL **DANIEL** HOSEA JOEL AMOS OBADIAH JONAH MICAH NAHUM HABAKKUK ZEPHANIAH HAGGAI ZECHARIAH MALACHI

⁸Daniel decided not to eat the king's food and wine because that would make him unclean. So he asked Ashpenaz for permission not to make himself unclean in this way.

⁹God made Ashpenaz want to be kind and merciful to Daniel. ¹⁰But Ashpenaz said to Daniel, "I am afraid of my master, the king. He ordered me to give you this food and drink. If you don't eat this food, you will begin to look worse than other young men your age. The king will see this. And he will cut off my head because of you."

¹¹Ashpenaz had ordered a guard to watch Daniel, Hananiah, Mishael and Azariah. ¹²Daniel said to the guard, "Please give us this test for ten days: Don't give us anything but vegetables to eat and water to drink. ¹³Then after ten days compare us with the other young men who eat the king's food. See for yourself who looks healthier. Then you judge for yourself how you want to treat us, your servants."

¹⁴So the guard agreed to test them for ten days. ¹⁵After ten days they looked very healthy. They looked better than all of the young men who ate the king's food. ¹⁶So the guard took away the king's special food and wine. He gave Daniel, Hananiah, Mishael and Azariah vegetables instead.

¹⁷God gave these four men wisdom and the ability to learn. They learned many kinds of things people had written and studied. Daniel could also understand all kinds of visions and dreams.

¹⁸The end of the three years came. And Ashpenaz brought all of the young men to King Nebuchadnezzar. ¹⁹The king talked to them. He found that none of the young men were as good as Daniel, Hananiah, Mishael and Azariah. So those four young men became the king's servants. ²⁰Every time the king asked them about something important, they showed much wisdom and understanding. He found they were ten times better than all the fortune-tellers and magicians in his kingdom. ²¹So Daniel continued to be the king's servant until the first year Cyrus was king.

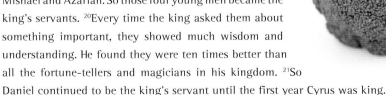

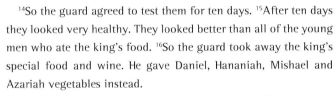

Think About This

Babylon was the wealthy capital of the most powerful empire of its day. It was located about 50 miles southwest of where Baghdad, Iraq is today.

Daniel and his friends were teenagers from royal or well-to-do families. They were educated and, therefore, bright enough to learn all that the king wanted them to know.

Daniel's name means "God is Judge." His Babylonian name, Belteshazzar, means "Bel's prince." The changing of the boys' names may have been meant to brainwash them into becoming Babylonian.

God provided for Daniel and his friends by making them stronger and healthier than all the other boys. He rewarded them for staying pure and not eating the king's food.

200

GENESIS EXODUS LEVITICUS NUMBERS DEUTERONOMY JOSHUA JUDGES RUTH 1 SAMUEL 2 SAMUEL 1 KINGS 2 KINGS 1 CHRONICLES 2 CHRONICLES EZRA NEHEMIAH ESTHER JOB PSALMS PROVERBS

DANIEL

The Fiery Furnace

Daniel 3:1-30

Daniel and his friends, Shadrach, Meshach and Abednego, went through the training program and became servants of Nebuchadnezzar. However, they held tightly to their faith in God, and even when threatened with death they refused to let go of it.

The Gold Idol and Blazing Furnace

3 Now King Nebuchadnezzar had a gold statue made. That statue was 90 feet high and 9 feet wide. He set up the statue on the plain of Dura in the area of Babylon. [2]Then the king called the important leaders: the governors, assistant governors, captains of the soldiers, people who advised the king, keepers of the treasury, judges, rulers and all other officers in his kingdom. He wanted these men to come to the special service for the statue he had set up. [3]So they all came for the special service. And they stood in front of the statue that King Nebuchadnezzar had set up. [4]Then the man who made announcements for the king spoke in a loud voice. He said, "People, nations and men of every language, this is what you are commanded to do: [5]You will hear the sound of the horns, flutes, lyres, zithers, harps, pipes and all the other musical instruments. When this happens, you must bow down and worship the gold statue. This is the one King Nebuchadnezzar has set up. [6]Everyone must bow down and worship this

gold statue. Anyone who doesn't will be quickly thrown into a blazing furnace."

[7]Now people, nations and men who spoke every language were there. And they heard the sound of the horns, flutes, lyres, zithers, pipes and all the other musical instruments. So they bowed down and worshiped the gold statue that King Nebuchadnezzar had set up.

[8]Then some Babylonians came up to

Behind the Story

Daniel isn't mentioned in this story. But these three friends were the same boys who refused to eat the king's food during their training program. Now they refuse to bow down and worship the king's gold statue. Their faith in God remains firm, even after living in Babylon and being influenced to worship their gods.

Just before this event, King Nebuchadnezzar had some dreams which none of his wise men could explain. God gave Daniel the wisdom and understanding to explain what the dreams meant. The king was very happy and said, "Truly, I know your God is the greatest of all gods. And he is the Lord of all kings" (Daniel 2:47). Apparently he didn't really mean those words.

Daniel, Shadrach, Meshach and Abednego had been in Babylon about 20 years when this incident happened.

201

ECCLESIASTES SONG OF SONGS ISAIAH JEREMIAH LAMENTATIONS EZEKIEL DANIEL HOSEA JOEL AMOS OBADIAH JONAH MICAH NAHUM HABAKKUK ZEPHANIAH HAGGAI ZECHARIAH MALACHI

the king. They began speaking against the men of Judah. ⁹They said to King Nebuchadnezzar, "Our king, live forever! ¹⁰Our king, you gave a command. You said that everyone would hear the horns, lyres, zithers, harps, pipes and all the other musical instruments. Then they would have to bow down and worship the gold statue. ¹¹Anyone who wouldn't do this was to be thrown into a blazing furnace. ¹²Our king, there are some men of Judah who did not pay attention to your order. You made them important officers in the area of Babylon. Their names are Shadrach, Meshach and Abednego. They do not serve your gods. And they do not worship the gold statue you have set up."

¹³Nebuchadnezzar became very angry. He called for Shadrach, Meshach and Abednego. So those men were brought to the king. ¹⁴And Nebuchadnezzar said, "Shadrach, Meshach and Abednego, is it true that you do not serve my gods? And is it true that you did not worship the gold statue I have set up? ¹⁵Now, you will hear the sound of the horns, flutes, lyres, zithers, harps, pipes and all the other musical instruments. And you must be ready to bow down and worship

the statue I made. That will be good. But if you do not worship it, you will be thrown quickly into the blazing furnace. Then no god will be able to save you from my power!"

¹⁶Shadrach, Meshach and Abednego answered the king. They said, "Nebuchadnezzar, we do not need to defend ourselves to you. ¹⁷You can throw us into the blazing furnace. The God we serve is able to save us from the furnace and your power. If he does this, it is good. ¹⁸But even if God does not save us, we want you, our king, to know this: We will not serve your gods. We will not worship the gold statue you have set up."

¹⁹Then Nebuchadnezzar was furious with Shadrach, Meshach and Abednego. He ordered the furnace to be heated seven times hotter than usual. ²⁰Then he commanded some of the strongest soldiers in his army to tie up Shadrach, Meshach and Abednego. The king told the soldiers to throw them into the blazing furnace.

²¹So Shadrach, Meshach and Abednego were tied up and thrown into the blazing furnace. They were still wearing their robes, trousers, turbans and other clothes. ²²The king was very angry when he gave the command. And the furnace was made very hot. The fire was so hot that the

Think About This

Shadrach, Meshach and Abednego knew that the punishment for refusing to bow down and worship the statue would be death. They chose death rather than worshiping something other than the real God. They believed that God would protect them —either he would protect them from the fire or take them to heaven to be with him.

Normally criminals were stripped of their clothing before being executed. However, these three men were thrown into the furnace wearing all their clothing (3:21). Apparently the king was so angry that the executions were carried out immediately, without any of the normal preparations.

The fire was so hot that some of the men who were on the outside —the ones throwing them into the furnace—were killed by the heat (3:22).

202

GENESIS EXODUS LEVITICUS NUMBERS DEUTERONOMY JOSHUA JUDGES RUTH 1 SAMUEL 2 SAMUEL 1 KINGS 2 KINGS 1 CHRONICLES 2 CHRONICLES EZRA NEHEMIAH ESTHER JOB PSALMS PROVERBS

DANIEL

God's Protection

Shadrach, Meshach and Abednego should have been immediately consumed by the flames. Instead, only the ropes that they were tied with burned. The king saw them walking around inside the huge furnace (3:25).

When the king saw them walking around inside the furnace, he also saw a fourth man with them. He recognized this man as being from God (3:25).

Not only were Shadrach, Meshach and Abednego saved from being harmed by the fire; they came out not even smelling like smoke! When God protects his children, he protects them completely.

For the second time, King Nebuchadnezzar praises God. He allows them to worship God, but doesn't declare God to be above any of the many gods the Babylonians worshiped (3:29).

flames killed the strong soldiers who took Shadrach, Meshach and Abednego there. ²³Firmly tied, Shadrach, Meshach and Abednego fell into the blazing furnace.

²⁴Then King Nebuchadnezzar was very surprised and jumped to his feet. He asked the men who advised him, "Didn't we tie up only three men? Didn't we throw them into the fire?"

They answered, "Yes, our king."

²⁵The king said, "Look! I see four men. They are walking around in the fire. They are not tied up, and they are not burned. The fourth man looks like a son of the gods."

²⁶Then Nebuchadnezzar went to the opening of the blazing furnace. He shouted, "Shadrach, Meshach and Abednego, come out! Servants of the Most High God, come here!"

So Shadrach, Meshach and Abednego came out of the fire. ²⁷When they came out, the princes, assistant governors, governors and royal advisers crowded around them. They saw that the fire had not harmed their bodies. Their hair was not burned. Their robes were not burned. And they didn't even smell like smoke.

²⁸Then Nebuchadnezzar said, "Praise the God of Shadrach, Meshach and Abednego. Their God has sent his angel and saved his servants from the fire! These three men trusted their God. They refused to obey my command. And they were willing to die rather than serve or worship any god other than their own. ²⁹So I now make this law: The people of any nation or language must not say anything against the God of Shadrach, Meshach and Abednego. Anyone who does will be torn apart. And his house will be turned into a pile of stones. No other god can save his people like this." ³⁰Then the king promoted Shadrach, Meshach and Abednego in the area of Babylon.

God in Three Persons

Today we know that God is three different persons, God the Father, God the Son (Jesus) and God the Holy Spirit. This wasn't really understood until Jesus came. He said that he was the Son of God, and he taught about the Holy Spirit who would come after he left the earth. However, there are times in the Old Testament when appearances by God prepare the people for learning about the Trinity. The "man" in the furnace is a good example. Some other appearances include the man who told Abraham and Sarah they would have a son (Genesis 18:1-15); the presence of God in the burning bush (Exodus 3:1-6); and the pillars of cloud and fire that led the Israelites out of Egypt (Exodus 13:21-22). God's Spirit is mentioned about 80 times in the Old Testament.

203

ECCLESIASTES SONG OF SONGS ISAIAH JEREMIAH LAMENTATIONS EZEKIEL **DANIEL** HOSEA JOEL AMOS OBADIAH JONAH MICAH NAHUM HABAKKUK ZEPHANIAH HAGGAI ZECHARIAH MALACHI

The Writing on the Wall
Daniel 5:1-8, 13-14, 17, 25-31

5 King Belshazzar gave a big banquet for 1,000 royal guests. And he drank wine with them. ²As Belshazzar was drinking his wine, he gave an order to his servants. He told them to bring the gold and silver cups that his ancestor Nebuchadnezzar had taken from the Temple in Jerusalem. King Belshazzar wanted his royal guests to drink from those cups. He also wanted his wives and his slave women to drink from them. ³So they brought the gold cups. They had been taken from the Temple of God in Jerusalem. And the king and his royal guests, his wives and his slave women drank from them. ⁴As they were drinking, they praised their gods. Those gods were made from gold, silver, bronze, iron, wood and stone.

⁵Then suddenly a person's hand appeared. The fingers wrote words on the plaster on the wall. This was near the lampstand in the royal palace. The king watched the hand as it wrote.

⁶King Belshazzar was very frightened. His face turned white, and his knees knocked together. He could not stand up because his legs were too weak. ⁷The king called for the magicians and wise men to be brought to him. He said to the wise men of Babylon, "I will give a reward to anyone who can read this writing and explain it. I will give him purple clothes fit for a king. I will put a gold chain around his neck. And I will make him the third highest ruler in the kingdom."

⁸So all the king's wise men came in. But they could not read the writing. And they could not tell the king what it meant.

¹³So they brought Daniel to the king. The king said to him, "Is your name Daniel? Are you one of the captives my father the king brought from Judah? ¹⁴I have heard that the spirit of the gods is in you. And I have heard that you are very wise and have knowledge and understanding.

¹⁷Then Daniel answered the king, "You may keep your gifts for yourself. Or you may give those rewards to someone else. I will read the writing on the wall for you. And I will explain to you what it means.

²⁵"These are the words that were written on the wall: 'Mene, mene, tekel, parsin.'

²⁶"This is what these words mean: Mene: God has counted the days until your kingdom will end. ²⁷Tekel: You have been weighed on the scales and found not good enough. ²⁸Parsin: Your kingdom is being divided. It will be given to the Medes and the Persians."

²⁹Then Belshazzar gave an order for Daniel to be dressed in purple clothes. A gold chain was put around his neck. And he was announced to be the third highest ruler in the kingdom. ³⁰That very same night Belshazzar, king of the Babylonian people, was killed. ³¹A man named Darius the Mede became the new king. Darius was 62 years old.

Think About This

Belshazzar was probably the grandson of King Nebuchadnezzar.

King Belshazzar was using the gold cups that had been taken from the Temple in Jerusalem (5:3-4). These were holy things, only to be used in worship. He was allowing them to be used at a party where false gods were being worshiped.

What Does it "Mene"?

The mysterious words that the hand wrote on the wall were weights of measure. *Mene* meant "numbered"; *Tekel* meant "weighed"; *Parsin* meant "divided." Babylon had been "weighed . . . and found not good enough." God was going to destroy it. This prophecy came true that very night, when the king died and the Medes and Persians captured Babylon.

God had already helped Daniel interpret dreams for King Nebuchadnezzar several times. King Belshazzar trusted what Daniel said. Daniel was about 80 years old when this event took place.

204

GENESIS EXODUS LEVITICUS NUMBERS DEUTERONOMY JOSHUA JUDGES RUTH 1 SAMUEL 2 SAMUEL 1 KINGS 2 KINGS 1 CHRONICLES 2 CHRONICLES EZRA NEHEMIAH ESTHER JOB PSALMS PROVERBS

DANIEL

Daniel and the Lions

Daniel 6:1-23

When Darius the Mede captured Babylon, he kept Daniel in a place of authority as a governor. Some of the other governors and men in authority didn't like that a Jewish man had so much power. They looked for ways to get Daniel in trouble.

Words You Should Know

Signet ring (SIG-net ring)
A ring worn by a king or another important person. It had the king's seal on it. He would stamp things with this ring to show that he owned them. The stamp was like a signature (see Genesis 41:42; Esther 3:10; 8:2-10).

Seal
A tool with a design or picture carved on it. Kings pressed this seal into wax which was placed on important papers to close them. If the seal was broken it showed that someone else had looked at the papers. A seal also showed who owned something. Sometimes these seals were worn as rings (1 Kings 21:8; 2 Corinthians 1:22).

6 Darius thought it would be a good idea to choose 120 governors. They would rule through all of his kingdom. [2]And he chose three men as supervisors over those 120 governors. Daniel was one of these three supervisors. The king set up these men so that he would not be cheated. [3]Daniel showed that he could do the work better than the other supervisors and the governors. Because of this, the king planned to put Daniel in charge of the whole kingdom. [4]So the other supervisors and the governors tried to find reasons to accuse Daniel. But he went on doing the business of the government. And they could not find anything wrong with him. So they could not accuse him of doing anything wrong. Daniel was trustworthy. He was not lazy and did not cheat the king. [5]Finally these men said, "We will never find any reason to accuse Daniel. But we must find something to complain about. It will have to be about the law of his God."

[6]So the supervisors and the governors went as a group to the king. They said: "King Darius, live forever! [7]The supervisors, assistant governors, governors, the people who advise you and the captains of the soldiers have all agreed on something. We think the king should make this law that everyone would have to obey: No one should pray to any god or man except to you, our king. This should be done for the next 30 days. Anyone who doesn't obey will be thrown into

the lions' den. [8]Now, our king, make the law. Write it down so it cannot be changed. The laws of the Medes and Persians cannot be canceled." [9]So King Darius made the law and had it written.

[10]When Daniel heard that the new law had been written, he went to his house. He went to his upstairs room. The windows of that room opened toward Jerusalem. Three times each day Daniel got down on his knees and prayed. He prayed and thanked God, just as he always had done.

[11]Then those men went as a group and found Daniel. They saw him praying and asking God for help. [12]So they went to

205

ECCLESIASTES SONG OF SONGS ISAIAH JEREMIAH LAMENTATIONS EZEKIEL **DANIEL** HOSEA JOEL AMOS OBADIAH JONAH MICAH NAHUM HABAKKUK ZEPHANIAH HAGGAI ZECHARIAH MALACHI

the king. They talked to him about the law he had made. They said, "Didn't you write a law that says no one may pray to any god or man except you, our king? Doesn't it say that anyone who disobeys during the next 30 days will be thrown into the lions' den?"

The king answered, "Yes, I wrote that law. And the laws of the Medes and Persians cannot be canceled."

[13]Then those men spoke to the king. They said, "Daniel is one of the captives from Judah. And he is not paying attention to the law you wrote. Daniel still prays to his God three times every day." [14]The king became very upset when he heard this. He decided he had to save Daniel. He worked until sunset trying to think of a way to save him.

[15]Then those men went as a group to the king. They said, "Remember, our king, the law of the Medes and Persians. It says that no law or command given by the king can be changed."

[16]So King Darius gave the order. They brought Daniel and threw him into the lions' den. The king said to Daniel, "May the God you serve all the time save you!" [17]A big stone was brought. It was put over the opening of the lions' den. Then the king used his signet ring to put his special seal on the rock. And he used the rings of his royal officers to put their seals on the rock also. This showed that no one could move that rock and bring Daniel out. [18]Then King Darius went back to his palace. He did not eat that night. He did not have any entertainment brought to entertain him. And he could not sleep.

[19]The next morning King Darius got up at dawn. He hurried to the lions' den. [20]As he came near the den, he was worried. He called out to Daniel. He said, "Daniel, servant of the living God! Has your God that you always worship been able to save you from the lions?"

Painting by Peter Paul Rubens

[21]Daniel answered, "My king, live forever! [22]My God sent his angel to close the lions' mouths. They have not hurt me, because my God knows I am innocent. I never did anything wrong to you, my king."

[23]King Darius was very happy. He told his servants to lift Daniel out of the lions' den. So they lifted him out and did not find any injury on him. This was because Daniel had trusted in his God.

Behind the Story

Daniel's enemies knew that he prayed to God every day. They tricked King Darius into making the law, knowing that Daniel would break it (Daniel 6:5, 7-8).

Once a law had been decreed, it could not be changed, not even by the king himself.

The lions' den was a hole in the ground, wide at the bottom and narrow at the top. A large stone covered the opening, and the king sealed it so no one could let Daniel out (6:17).

When the king realized he had been tricked, he tried to find a way to save Daniel, but he couldn't. Before putting Daniel in with the lions, he expressed hope that Daniel's God would save him (6:16).

Daniel's faith and obedience to God got him into trouble and out of trouble. God showed once again that he honors those who honor and obey him.

206

GENESIS EXODUS LEVITICUS NUMBERS DEUTERONOMY JOSHUA JUDGES RUTH 1 SAMUEL 2 SAMUEL 1 KINGS 2 KINGS 1 CHRONICLES 2 CHRONICLES EZRA NEHEMIAH ESTHER JOB PSALMS PROVERBS

JONAH

Jonah Obeys

Jonah 1:1–3:5

God gave the prophet Jonah one message. The message in this prophetic book boils down to one line: "Nineveh will be destroyed in forty days." However, Jonah wasn't fond of the people in Nineveh, so he didn't want to warn them of the coming destruction.

God Calls and Jonah Runs

Think About This

Nineveh was about 500 miles from Jonah's hometown, Tarshish. But he was apparently quite familiar with Nineveh's evil ways.

The message of Jonah concerns the prophet's disobedience. God gave him a job to do, and he disobeyed. It's impossible to love God without obeying him. First John 5:3 says, "Loving God means obeying his commands."

Note two things: Jonah could not hide from God, and God controls nature. He caused the great wind to come up and frighten the sailors.

Jesus referred to Jonah's experience in Matthew 12:39-41 as he taught about his own resurrection.

1 The Lord spoke his word to Jonah son of Amittai: ²"Get up, go to the great city of Nineveh and preach against it. I see the evil things they do."

³But Jonah got up to run away from the Lord. He went to the city of Joppa. There he found a ship that was going to the city of Tarshish. Jonah paid for the trip and went aboard. He wanted to go to Tarshish to run away from the Lord.

⁴But the Lord sent a great wind on the sea. This wind made the sea very rough. So the ship was in danger of breaking apart. ⁵The sailors were afraid. Each man cried to his own god. The men began throwing the cargo into the sea. This would make the ship lighter so it would not sink.

But Jonah had gone down into the ship to lie down. He fell fast asleep. ⁶The captain of the ship came and said, "Why are you sleeping? Get up! Pray to your god! Maybe your god will pay attention to us. Maybe he will save us!"

⁷Then the men said to each other, "Let's throw lots to see who caused these troubles to happen to us."

So the men threw lots. The lot showed that the trouble had happened because of Jonah. ⁸Then the men said to Jonah, "Tell us what you have done. Why has this terrible thing happened to us? What is your job? Where do you come from? What is your country? Who are your people?"

⁹Then Jonah said to them, "I am a Hebrew. I fear the Lord, the God of heaven. He is the God who made the sea and the land."

¹⁰Then the men were very afraid. They asked Jonah, "What terrible thing did you do?" They

207

ECCLESIASTES SONG OF SONGS ISAIAH JEREMIAH LAMENTATIONS EZEKIEL DANIEL HOSEA JOEL AMOS OBADIAH **JONAH** MICAH NAHUM HABAKKUK ZEPHANIAH HAGGAI ZECHARIAH MALACHI

knew Jonah was running away from the Lord because Jonah had told them.

¹¹The wind and the waves of the sea were becoming much stronger. So the men said to Jonah, "What should we do to you to make the sea calm down?"

¹²Jonah said to them, "Pick me up, and throw me into the sea. Then it will calm down. I know it is my fault that this great storm has come on you."

¹³Instead, the men tried to row the ship back to the land. But they could not. The wind and the waves of the sea were becoming much stronger.

Jonah's Punishment

¹⁴So the men cried to the Lord, "Lord, please don't let us die because of taking this man's life. Please don't think we are guilty of killing an innocent man. Lord, you have caused all this to happen. You wanted it this way." ¹⁵Then the men picked up Jonah and threw him into the sea. So the sea became calm. ¹⁶Then they began to fear the Lord very much. They offered a sacrifice to the Lord. They also made promises to him.

¹⁷And the Lord caused a very big fish to swallow Jonah. Jonah was in the stomach of the fish three days and three nights.

2 While Jonah was in the stomach of the fish, he prayed to the Lord his God. Jonah said,

²"I was in danger.

So I called to the Lord,
   and he answered me.
 I was about to die.
   So I cried to you,
   and you heard my voice.
³You threw me into the sea.
   I went down, down into the deep sea.
 The water was all around me.
   Your powerful waves flowed over me.
⁴I said, 'I was driven out of your presence.
   But I hope to see your Holy Temple again.'
⁵The waters of the sea closed over me.
   I was about to die.
 The deep sea was all around me.
   Seaweed wrapped around my head.
⁶I went down to where the mountains of the sea start to rise.

Words You Should Know

Lots (lots)
Sticks, stones or pieces of bone thrown like dice to decide something. Often God controlled the result of the lots to let the people know what he wanted them to do (see Numbers 26:55-56; Proverbs 18:18; Luke 23:34; Acts 1:26).

The Choices

The sailors didn't want to throw Jonah into the sea. They didn't want to be responsible for his death. Jonah knew he had disobeyed God and was willing to take the punishment (Jonah 1:12).

God didn't want Jonah to die —only to obey. The great fish protected Jonah from drowning and gave him time to think about his disobedience.

Jonah confessed his disobedience in the prayer of Jonah 2 and promised to obey. God had the fish spit him out onto dry land. God gave Jonah a second chance to obey him.

208

GENESIS EXODUS LEVITICUS NUMBERS DEUTERONOMY JOSHUA JUDGES RUTH 1 SAMUEL 2 SAMUEL 1 KINGS 2 KINGS 1 CHRONICLES 2 CHRONICLES EZRA NEHEMIAH ESTHER JOB PSALMS PROVERBS

JONAH

Behind the Story

Jonah served God as a mission-ary. But he tried very hard to stop God's plan from moving forward. He did not want God to save the people of Nineveh.

God's second chance for Jonah did not change God's plan. Jonah had the same message to preach to Nineveh as God had originally given him.

Nineveh was a huge city, but the three-day walk Jonah took prob-ably included the area around Nineveh, too.

The putting on of rough cloth was to show how sad they were and that they were grieving or mourning over their sins before God.

In Nineveh

The people of Nineveh still had 40 days to repent before God would destroy the city. The people heard Jonah's prophecy and repented. God spared the city, just as Jonah had feared. However, their belief in God didn't last. The city was eventu-ally destroyed in 612 B.C.

I thought I was locked in this prison forever.
But you saved me from death,
    Lord my God.

[7]"When my life had almost gone,
    I remembered the Lord.
Lord, I prayed to you.
    And you heard my prayers in your Holy Temple.

[8]"People who worship useless idols
    give up their loyalty to you.
[9]Lord, I will praise and thank you
    while I give sacrifices to you.
I will make promises to you.
    And I will do what I promise.
Salvation comes from the Lord!"

[10]Then the Lord spoke to the fish. And the fish spit Jonah out of its stomach onto the dry land.

God Calls and Jonah Obeys

3 Then the Lord spoke his word to Jonah again. The Lord said, [2]"Get up. Go to the great city Nineveh. Preach against it what I tell you."

[3]So Jonah obeyed the Lord. He got up and went to Nineveh. It was a very large city. It took a person three days just to walk across it. [4]Jonah entered the city. When he had walked for one day, he preached to the people. He said, "After 40 days, Nineveh will be destroyed!"

[5]The people of Nineveh believed in God. They announced they would stop eating for a while. They put on rough cloth to show how sad they were. All the people in the city wore the cloth. People from the most important to the least important did this.

The Other Books of Prophets:

MAJOR PROPHETS, along with Isaiah and Daniel:
ISAIAH JEREMIAH LAMENTATIONS EZEKIEL DANIEL

JEREMIAH

Jeremiah was a prophet during around 640 B.C. The northern kingdom of Judah had been destroyed because of their failure to obey God. Jeremiah tried to stop the same thing from happening to the southern kingdom of Israel. He begged the people to return to God. The people would not listen to him, and he felt that he alone was standing for God. Jeremiah is known as the "weeping prophet." He prophesied during the last 40 years of Judah's existence.

LAMENTATIONS

Lamentations is filled with the pain of a broken heart over the destruction of Jerusalem and the sinfulness of God's people. The book is made up of five acrostic poems, where each successive line begins with the next letter of the Hebrew alphabet. Tradition says that Jeremiah wrote these poems telling of the pain and loss that the Israelites felt as captives in Babylon.

EZEKIEL

Ezekiel prophesied at the same time as Jeremiah, but his message went to the Jews who were in Babylon. He was given messages from God for the people from about 591 to 570 B.C. The book of Ezekiel gives many dates which have helped to fix certain circumstances in history. Ezekiel's message was that God's purpose is always to bring his people back to worshiping and obeying him.

The Other Books of Prophets:

MINOR PROPHETS, along with Jonah:

■ HOSEA JOEL AMOS OBADIAH JONAH MICAH NAHUM HABAKKUK ZEPHANIAH HAGGAI ZECHARIAH MALACHI

HOSEA

Hosea's ministry began around 785 B.C. His purpose in writing was to warn the people against sin. He also wanted to encourage the people to know that God's love would always win, no matter how difficult life became. He contrasted Israel's unfaithfulness to God with God's complete love for them.

JOEL

Joel's message to the people concerned the day of coming judgment. This judgment hadn't happened yet, so there was still time to stop sinning and obey God. This little book has only 3 chapters, but it packs a powerful message.

AMOS

Amos was a prophet from the southern kingdom who went to the northern kingdom to warn them that God was going to punish them for their sins. God told him what sins to point out to the people. No one paid attention to Amos, and about 40 years later, the northern kingdom was destroyed.

OBADIAH

Obadiah contains only 21 verses. The prophet proclaims that God has had enough of Edom attacking Jerusalem. He is going to punish the Edomites for what they have done to his people. About 4 years after Edom destroyed Jerusalem, Edom itself was destroyed.

MICAH

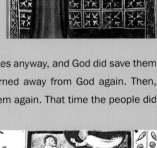

Micah continued the prophets' theme of warning the people to stop sinning or suffer serious problems. However, his message included the confidence that God would restore the nation. Micah's ministry began in about 740 B.C. He wrote to both Israel and Judah. One king who ruled during Micah's time was a very good king. His name was Hezekiah.

NAHUM

Nahum is the second prophet called to warn Nineveh of the consequences of their sin. Jonah didn't want God to save the people of Nineveh. But he preached to the Ninevites anyway, and God did save them when they repented. However, the people of Nineveh turned away from God again. Then, about 100 years after Jonah, God sent Nahum to warn them again. That time the people did not listen, and God destroyed Nineveh with a flood.

HABAKKUK

Habakkuk's ministry was during the reign of King Josiah. Habakkuk is unique from the other prophets because he questioned God. He asked how God could allow the people to continue sinning and disobeying him. God assured him that the Babylonians would capture the people and that would be their punishment. Habakkuk urged God to act quickly so the people would be purified and return to worshiping him.

The Other Books of Prophets:
More MINOR PROPHETS:

HOSEA JOEL AMOS OBADIAH JONAH MICAH NAHUM HABAKKUK ZEPHANIAH HAGGAI ZECHARIAH MALACHI

ZEPHANIAH

Zephaniah ministered at the same time as Jeremiah, during the reign of King Josiah, the last good king who obeyed God. Zephaniah's mission was to warn Judah that judgment was coming. He had a word of hope for the people, though, reminding them of God's great love for them.

HAGGAI

Haggai preached four sermons encouraging the Jews to finish rebuilding God's Temple in Jerusalem. His sermons were given in 520 B.C. He reminded the people that God would help them with the work and provide what they needed.

ZECHARIAH

Zechariah preached at the same time as Haggai and often on the same topic: to finish building the Temple. This book is also filled with several visions that predict the end of time on earth. They are repeated in the book of Revelation.

MALACHI

Malachi is the last book in the Old Testament. It was written about 400 B.C. Malachi encouraged the people of Jerusalem to honor God. The people insisted that they did honor him, so Malachi got detailed about how they ignored God, disobeyed him, and even lived like he wasn't important.

THE GOSPELS

The Gospels begin the New Testament, a collection of 27 books that tell the story of Jesus' life and ministry on earth and how his followers continued that ministry when he went back to heaven.

The New Testament books are divided into four different groups:

- **The Gospels**

- **The Acts**

- **The Letters of Paul**

- **General Letters**
  (written by various men)

The Gospels are four books: **Matthew, Mark, Luke and John.**
These books tell the story of Jesus' life on earth, recording his teachings, stories and miracles—four different perspectives on the same man's life.

The New Testament shows us how understanding and living out our purpose on this earth is related to knowing and understanding Jesus. The Gospels cover almost 35 years of history—about the same amount of time that Jesus lived on earth.

THE GOSPELS

THE GOSPELS AS ONE STORY

Why did God give us four Gospels? Why do we need four versions of the same story? Because four different writers give four different perspectives on the life of Jesus. Each writer came from a different background and had a different personality, so he noticed different things about Jesus.

In Matthew Jesus is presented as King.
This book was written primarily to the Jews.
In Mark Jesus is presented as Servant.
This book was written to the Romans.
In Luke Jesus is presented as Man.
This book was written to the Greeks.
In John Jesus is presented as God.
This book was written for everyone.

The first three Gospels, Matthew, Mark and Luke, are called the "synoptic gospels" because they give a synopsis, or overview, of Jesus' life. The Gospel of John records more of Jesus' work.

It is important to read all four Gospels for a complete understanding of Jesus' life and ministry while he was here on earth.

Interesting Facts

The Gospels record:

- **36** miracles of Jesus;
- **38** parables of Jesus;
- **37** prophecies Jesus fulfilled; and
- more than **35** names of Jesus.

In the days of Jesus there were three areas in Israel:

- **Galilee,** which was in the north;
- **Samaria,** which was in the middle; and
- **Judea,** which was in the south.

Seeing Jesus

Read John 1:1-5. Jesus was with God before time began. He was the Creator of the world. He is the light of life. These verses establish who Jesus is and how important he is to God's plan.

A HARMONY OF GOSPEL STORIES

TIMELINE OF THESE STORIES OF JESUS' LIFE AND MINISTRY

EVENT	MATTHEW	MARK	LUKE	JOHN
Birth and Childhood of Jesus				
John the Baptist's Birth			1:5-25, 57-64	
Announcement of Jesus' Birth			1:26-38	
Birth of Jesus	1:18-25		2:1-21	
Presented in the Temple			2:26-38	
The Wise Men Come	2:1-12			
Egypt and Childhood	2:13-19		2:41-52	
Early Ministry				
Jesus' Baptism	3:17-18	1:9-11	3:21-22	
Jesus' Temptation	4:1-11	1:12-13	4:1-13	
Jesus Chooses Followers		1:14-20; 3:13-19		1:35-51
The Wedding Miracle				2:1-11
Jesus Cleans the Temple				2:12-25
Jesus and Nicodemus				3:1-21
The Woman at the Well				4:1-42
Four Friends' Faith	9:1-8	2:1-12	5:17-26	
The Tax Collector		2:13-17		
Ministry and Parables				
Sermon on the Mount	5:1-20, 5:21–7:29		6:17-49	
Jesus' Works	8:1-17		7:1-10	
Jesus' Stories	13:1-52	4:1-34	8:4-16; 13:18-21	
Jesus Stops a Storm	8:18-27	4:35-41	8:22-25	
Jesus Heals	9:18-26	5:21-43	8:40-56	
Feeding of the 5,000	14:13-21	6:30-44	9:10-17	6:1-15
Walking on Water	14:22-36	6:45-52		6:16-21
Jesus with Moses	17:1-9	9:2-10	9:28-36	
Ministry in Galilee				
The Good Samaritan			10:25-37	
Mary and Martha			10:38-42	
Going to and Staying at Jerusalem				
The Lost Things			15:1-32	
Raising Lazarus				11:28-44
Zacchaeus			19:1-10	
A Woman Anoints Jesus	26:6-13	14:3-9	7:36-50	12:1-8
Palm Sunday	21:1-11	11:1-10	19:28-40	12:12-16
Three Servants	25:14-29		19:11-27	
Foot Washing				13:1-20
The Lord's Supper	26:17-25	14:22-31	22:14-20	13:21-35
Garden of Gethsemane	26:36-46	14:32-50	22:39-46	17:1–18:1
Crucifixion, Resurrection and Ascension				
Peter's Denial and the Trial	26:69-75	14:66–15:20	22:54-64	18:12-27
The Crucifixion	27:27-61	15:21-47	23:26-56	19:17-42
The Tomb	27:62-66			
The Resurrection	28:1-10	16:1-11	24:1-12	20:1-18
The Road to Emmaus		16:12-13	24:13-35	
The Ascension		16:14-20	24:50-53	

Verses in **black** are included in this book; verses in gray are other passages where the same story is recorded.

216

MATTHEW MARK LUKE JOHN **ACTS ROMANS 1 CORINTHIANS 2 CORINTHIANS GALATIANS EPHESIANS PHILIPPIANS COLOSSIANS 1 THESSALONIANS**

THE GOSPELS

Birth and Childhood of Jesus

Words You Should Know

Herod (HEH-rud)
The name of four different rulers in the New Testament.

Herod I was king of Palestine from 40 B.C. to about 4 B.C. He tried to kill the baby Jesus because Jesus was called a "king." Herod thought Jesus was an earthly king and would take away his throne (see Matthew 2:1-16; Luke 1:5).

Virgin (VUR-jin)
A woman or girl who has not had sexual relations (see Genesis 24:16; Deuteronomy 22:15-28; Isaiah 7:14; Matthew 1:23; Luke 1:34).

Two Special Babies

Luke 1:5-38

The Jews expected God to send the Messiah, the one he had promised to them. An angel appeared to two people to start this plan in motion.

Zechariah and Elizabeth

1 5During the time Herod ruled Judea, there was a priest named Zechariah. He belonged to Abijah's group. Zechariah's wife came from the family of Aaron. Her name was Elizabeth. 6Zechariah and Elizabeth truly did what God said was good. They did everything the Lord commanded and told people to do. They were without fault in keeping his law. 7But Zechariah and Elizabeth had no children. Elizabeth could not have a baby; and both of them were very old.

8Zechariah was serving as a priest before God for his group. It was his group's time to serve. 9According to the custom of the priests, he was chosen to go into the Temple of the Lord and burn incense. 10There were a great many people outside praying at the time the incense was offered. 11Then, on the right side of the incense table, an angel of the Lord came and stood before Zechariah. 12When he saw the angel, Zechariah was confused and frightened. 13But the angel said to him, "Zechariah, don't be afraid. Your prayer has been heard by God. Your wife, Elizabeth, will give birth to a son. You will name him John. 14You will be very happy. Many people will be happy because of his birth. 15John will be a great man for the Lord. He will never drink wine or beer. Even at the time John is born, he will be filled with the Holy Spirit. 16He will help many people of Israel return to the Lord their God. 17He himself will go first before the Lord. John will be powerful in spirit like Elijah. He will make peace between fathers and their children. He will bring those who are not obeying God back to the right way of thinking. He will make people ready for the coming of the Lord."

18Zechariah said to the angel, "How can I know that what you say is true? I am an old man, and my wife is old, too."

19The angel answered him, "I am Gabriel. I stand before God. God sent me to talk to you and to tell you this good news. 20Now, listen! You will not be able to talk until the day these things happen. You will lose your speech because you did not believe what I told you. But these things will really happen."

217

2 THESSALONIANS 1 TIMOTHY 2 TIMOTHY TITUS PHILEMON HEBREWS JAMES 1 PETER 2 PETER 1 JOHN 2 JOHN 3 JOHN JUDE REVELATION

²¹Outside, the people were still waiting for Zechariah. They were surprised that he was staying so long in the Temple. ²²Then Zechariah came outside, but he could not speak to them. So they knew that he had seen a vision in the Temple. Zechariah could not speak. He could only make signs to them. ²³When his time of service as a priest was finished, he went home.

²⁴Later, Zechariah's wife, Elizabeth, became pregnant. She did not go out of her house for five months. Elizabeth said, ²⁵"Look what the Lord has done for me! My people were ashamed of me, but now the Lord has taken away that shame."

The Virgin Mary

²⁶⁻²⁷During Elizabeth's sixth month of pregnancy, God sent the angel Gabriel to a virgin who lived in Nazareth, a town in Galilee. She was engaged to marry a man named Joseph from the family of David. Her name was Mary. ²⁸The angel came to her and said, "Greetings! The Lord has blessed you and is with you."

²⁹But Mary was very confused by what the angel said. Mary wondered, "What does this mean?"

³⁰The angel said to her, "Don't be afraid, Mary, because God is pleased with you. ³¹Listen! You will become pregnant. You will give birth to a son, and you will name him Jesus. ³²He will be great, and people will call him the Son of the Most High. The Lord God will give him the throne of King David, his ancestor. ³³He will rule over the people of Jacob forever. His kingdom will never end."

³⁴Mary said to the angel, "How will this happen? I am a virgin!"

³⁵The angel said to Mary, "The Holy Spirit will come upon you, and the power of the Most High will cover you. The baby will be holy. He will be called the Son of God. ³⁶Now listen! Elizabeth, your relative, is very old. But she is also pregnant with a son. Everyone thought she could not have a baby, but she has been pregnant for six months. ³⁷God can do everything!"

³⁸Mary said, "I am the servant girl of the Lord. Let this happen to me as you say!" Then the angel went away.

Behind the Story

Zechariah served for one week each year at the Temple. Burning the incense in the holy place was something a priest did only one time in his career.

As common as angel appearances seem to readers of Scripture, they must have been an awesome sight because they nearly always said, "Do not be afraid" (Luke 1:13).

Zechariah and Elizabeth are another example of a couple who were too old (by human standards) to have a baby. However, God intervened and gave them the child they wanted so much.

John would be a prophet who told people to stop sinning and that Jesus would be born.

Gabriel (1:19) is one of two angels named in the Bible. The other is Michael (see Daniel 10:13, 21; Revelation 12:7).

THE GOSPELS

Birth and Childhood of Jesus

Words You Should Know

Joseph of Nazareth
The husband of Mary, Jesus' mother. He was a carpenter. He may have died when Jesus was a young man because he is not mentioned after Jesus' childhood. The New Testament says he was "a good man" (see Matthew 1:18-25; 2:13-23).

Bethlehem (BETH-le-hem) "House of bread." It is a small town five miles from Jerusalem in the country of Judea. It was the hometown of King David in the Old Testament. Jesus was born there (see Matthew 2:1; Luke 2:15-18).

Births of John and Jesus

Luke 1:57-64; 2:1-21

Painting by Botticelli

The two babies Gabriel announced to Zechariah and Mary were born about 6 months apart. The birth of the second baby, Jesus, would change the world forever.

The Birth of John

1 ⁵⁷When it was time for Elizabeth to give birth, she had a boy. ⁵⁸Her neighbors and relatives heard how good the Lord was to her, and they rejoiced.

⁵⁹When the baby was eight days old, they came to circumcise him. They wanted to name him Zechariah because this was his father's name. ⁶⁰But his mother said, "No! He will be named John."

⁶¹The people said to Elizabeth, "But no one in your family has this name!" ⁶²Then they made signs to his father, "What would you like to name him?"

⁶³Zechariah asked for something to write on. Then he wrote, "His name is John." Everyone was surprised. ⁶⁴Then Zechariah could talk again. He began to praise God.

Birth of Jesus

2 At that time, Augustus Caesar sent an order to all people in the countries that were under Roman rule. The order said that they must list their names in a register. ²This was the first registration taken while Quirinius was governor of Syria. ³And everyone went to their own towns to be registered.

⁴So Joseph left Nazareth, a town in Galilee. He went to the town of Bethlehem in Judea. This

town was known as the town of David. Joseph went there because he was from the family of David. ⁵Joseph registered with Mary because she was engaged to marry him. (Mary was now pregnant.) ⁶While Joseph and Mary were in Bethlehem, the time came for her to have the baby. ⁷She gave birth to her first son. There were no rooms left in the inn. So she wrapped the baby with cloths and laid him in a box where animals are fed.

Some Shepherds Hear About Jesus

[8]That night, some shepherds were in the fields nearby watching their sheep. [9]An angel of the Lord stood before them. The glory of the Lord was shining around them, and suddenly they became very frightened. [10]The angel said to them, "Don't be afraid, because I am bringing you some good news. It will be a joy to all the people. [11]Today your Savior was born in David's town. He is Christ, the Lord. [12]This is how you will know him: You will find a baby wrapped in cloths and lying in a feeding box."

[13]Then a very large group of angels from heaven joined the first angel. All the angels were praising God, saying:

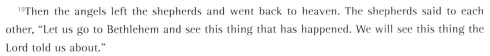

> [14]"Give glory to God in heaven,
>
> > and on earth let there be peace to the people who
> >
> > > please God."

[15]Then the angels left the shepherds and went back to heaven. The shepherds said to each other, "Let us go to Bethlehem and see this thing that has happened. We will see this thing the Lord told us about."

[16]So the shepherds went quickly and found Mary and Joseph. [17]And the shepherds saw the baby lying in a feeding box. Then they told what the angels had said about this child. [18]Everyone was amazed when they heard what the shepherds said to them. [19]Mary hid these things in her heart; she continued to think about them. [20]Then the shepherds went back to their sheep, praising God and thanking him for everything that they had seen and heard. It was just as the angel had told them.

[21]When the baby was eight days old, he was circumcised, and he was named Jesus. This name had been given by the angel before the baby began to grow inside Mary.

A Voice in the Wilderness

John the Baptist's work was to tell people that they were sinners and they needed to stop sinning and start obeying God. He announced that someone was coming who  would teach them more about God. He was talking about Jesus. John was called "the Baptist" because when people wanted to follow God more closely, he baptized them with water.

Think About This

Luke was a doctor, so it is fitting that his Gospel is the only one that records the actual birth of Jesus.

The trip from Nazareth to Bethlehem would have taken Mary and Joseph about 3 days.

Mary wrapped baby Jesus tightly in cloths (Luke 2:7). This was done to keep the infant's arms and legs straight.

When the angel announced Jesus' birth to the shepherds, three titles were used: Savior, Christ and Lord. These three titles summarize Jesus' life and work (2:11).

The shepherds stayed in the fields at night with their sheep to protect them from wild animals and from being stolen.

Jesus' birth is called the Virgin Birth because Mary had not had sexual relations with any man. She became pregnant by the power of God's Spirit. This fulfilled a prophecy given in Isaiah 7:14 that the Messiah would be born of a virgin.

220

MATTHEW MARK LUKE JOHN ACTS ROMANS 1 CORINTHIANS 2 CORINTHIANS GALATIANS EPHESIANS PHILIPPIANS COLOSSIANS 1 THESSALONIANS

THE GOSPELS

Birth and Childhood of Jesus

Behind the Story

Joseph and Mary took Jesus to Jerusalem to present him to God. This was something a faithful Jewish person would do. It shows that they loved God and wanted to obey him.

Simeon had been waiting for God to send the Messiah who would save Israel from its enemies. God brought Simeon to the Temple at the right time to see Jesus. The Holy Spirit showed him that Jesus was the one he had been waiting for.

Simeon became a prophet when he predicted to Mary the things that would happen in Jesus' life (Luke 2:34-35).

God also allowed Anna, a faithful woman who worshiped God with all her heart, to recognize Jesus as the Messiah. She talked about Jesus to everyone she saw. So, from the time Jesus was born, the shepherds, Simeon and Anna began telling people that the Savior had been born.

Presented in the Temple

Luke 2:26-38

Mary knew that her Son, Jesus, was special because Gabriel had told her so. From the moment he was born, more things happened to confirm that Jesus was God's Son.

2 [26]The Holy Spirit told Simeon that he would not die before he saw the Christ promised by the Lord. [27]The Spirit led Simeon to the Temple. Mary and Joseph brought the baby Jesus to the Temple to do what the law said they must do. [28]Then Simeon took the baby in his arms and thanked God:

[29]"Now, Lord, you can let me, your servant,
    die in peace as you said.
[30]I have seen your Salvation with my own eyes.
[31]   You prepared him before all people.
[32]He is a light for the non-Jewish people to see.
    He will bring honor to your people, the Israelites."

[33]Jesus' father and mother were amazed at what Simeon had said about him. [34]Then Simeon blessed them and said to Mary, "Many in Israel will fall and many will rise because of this child. He will be a sign from God that many people will not accept. [35]The things they think in secret will be made known. And the things that will happen will make your heart sad, too."

Anna Sees Jesus

[36]Anna, a prophetess, was there at the Temple. She was from the family of Phanuel in the tribe of Asher. Anna was very old. She had once been married for seven years. [37]Then her husband died and she lived alone. She was now 84 years old. Anna never left the Temple. She worshiped God by going without food and praying day and night. [38]She was standing there at that time, thanking God. She talked about Jesus to all who were waiting for God to free Jerusalem.

The Wise Men Come

Matthew 2:1-12

Wise men in a country far from Judea saw a special star, or a star that glowed especially bright. They knew this star meant that a special king had been born. They wanted to worship this king and give him presents.

2 Jesus was born in the town of Bethlehem in Judea during the time when Herod was king. After Jesus was born, some wise men from the east came to Jerusalem. [2]They asked, "Where is the baby who was born to be the king of the Jews? We saw his star in the east. We came to worship him."

[3]When King Herod heard about this new king of the Jews, he was troubled. And all the people in Jerusalem were worried too. [4]Herod called a meeting of all the leading priests and teachers of the law. He asked them where the Christ would be born. [5]They answered, "In the town of Bethlehem in Judea. The prophet wrote about this in the Scriptures:

[6]'But you, Bethlehem, in the land of Judah,
 you are important among the rulers of Judah.
A ruler will come from you.
 He will be like a shepherd for my people,
  the Israelites.' "   Micah 5:2

Gold, Myrrh and Frankincense

[7]Then Herod had a secret meeting with the wise men from the east. He learned from them the exact time they first saw the star. [8]Then Herod sent the wise men to Bethlehem. He said to them, "Go and look carefully to find the child. When you find him, come tell me. Then I can go worship him too."

[9]The wise men heard the king and then left. They saw the same star they had seen in the east. It went before them until it stopped above the place where the child was. [10]When the wise men saw the star, they were filled with joy. [11]They went to the house where the child was and saw him with his mother, Mary. They bowed down and worshiped the child. They opened the gifts they brought for him. They gave him treasures of gold, frankincense, and myrrh. [12]But God warned the wise men in a dream not to go back to Herod. So they went home to their own country by a different way.

Words You Should Know

Wise men, or "magi"
A name for men who studied the stars. Some wise men followed a star from the East and brought gifts to Jesus when he was born.

The visit of the wise men did not take place in the stable, as is often pictured. Their arrival was at least several months, if not a couple of years, after Jesus' birth.

Frankincense
(FRANK-in-senz)
A very expensive, sweet-smelling perfume. It comes from inside the terebinth tree that grows in the country of Arabia. Some wise men gave frankincense to Jesus when he was born (see Exodus 30:34; Revelation 18:13).

Myrrh (MUR)
A sweet-smelling liquid taken from certain trees and shrubs. It was used as perfume and a pain reliever. It was one of the gifts the wise men gave Jesus when he was born (see Genesis 37:25; 43:11; Proverbs 7:17; Mark 15:23; John 19:39).

222

■MATTHEW MARK LUKE JOHN ■ ACTS ROMANS 1 CORINTHIANS 2 CORINTHIANS GALATIANS EPHESIANS PHILIPPIANS COLOSSIANS 1 THESSALONIANS

THE GOSPELS

Birth and Childhood of Jesus

Jesus Goes to Egypt

Matthew 2:13-19

An angel warned the wise men in a dream that Herod wanted to hurt baby Jesus, so they should not tell him where the baby was. They went home a different way, so they wouldn't see Herod again.

Jesus' Parents Take Him to Egypt

Think About This

From the first angel's visit to tell Mary that she would have a baby, there were five more angel messages about baby Jesus and how to protect him. Read Matthew 1:20; 2:12-13, 19, 22.

Matthew is the only Gospel which records the wise men's visit and Joseph taking Mary and Jesus to Egypt.

Herod believed he could kill the new king, which the wise men had told him about, by killing all the boy children in Bethlehem. God protected Jesus because Jesus had work to do here on earth.

When they returned from Egypt, an angel told Joseph to go to Nazareth, his hometown, because Jesus would be safer there than in Bethlehem.

2 ^{13}After they left, an angel of the Lord came to Joseph in a dream. The angel said, "Get up! Take the child and his mother and escape to Egypt. Herod will start looking for the child to kill him. Stay in Egypt until I tell you to return."

^{14}So Joseph got up and left for Egypt during the night with the child and his mother. ^{15}Joseph stayed in Egypt until Herod died. This was to make clear the full meaning of what the Lord had said through the prophet. The Lord said, "I called my son out of Egypt."

Herod Kills the Baby Boys

^{16}When Herod saw that the wise men had tricked him, he was very angry. So he gave an order to kill all the baby boys in Bethlehem and in all the area around Bethlehem who were two years old or younger. This was in keeping with the time he learned from the wise men. ^{17}So what God had said through the prophet Jeremiah came true:

^{18}"A sound was heard in Ramah.
  It was painful crying and much sadness.
Rachel cries for her children,
  and she cannot be comforted,
  because her children are dead."
        Jeremiah 31:15

Joseph and Mary Return

^{19}After Herod died, an angel of the Lord came to Joseph in a dream. This happened while Joseph was in Egypt. ^{20}The angel said, "Get up! Take the child and his mother and go to Israel. The people who were trying to kill the child are now dead."

Jesus as a Boy

Luke 2:41-52

After the family returned to Nazareth, Joseph taught Jesus how to be a carpenter. When Jesus was 12, he went with Mary and Joseph to Jerusalem to celebrate the Passover. They did this every year, but something unusual happened this particular year.

2 41Every year Jesus' parents went to Jerusalem for the Passover Feast. 42When Jesus was 12 years old, they went to the feast as they always did. 43When the feast days were over, they went home. The boy Jesus stayed behind in Jerusalem, but his parents did not know it. 44Joseph and Mary traveled for a whole day. They thought that Jesus was with them in the group. Then they began to look for him among their family and friends, 45but they did not find him. So they went back to Jerusalem to look for him there. 46After three days they found him. Jesus was sitting in the Temple with the religious teachers, listening to them and asking them questions. 47All who heard him were amazed at his understanding and wise answers. 48When Jesus' parents saw him, they were amazed. His mother said to him, "Son, why did you do this to us? Your father and I were very worried about you. We have been looking for you."

49Jesus asked, "Why did you have to look for me? You should have known that I must be where my Father's work is!" 50But they did not understand the meaning of what he said.

51Jesus went with them to Nazareth and obeyed them. His mother was still thinking about all that had happened. 52Jesus continued to learn more and more and to grow physically. People liked him, and he pleased God.

FAQs

Q: How did Jesus have such understanding?

A: Jesus was not teaching the Law. He was asking questions and talking with the teachers about it, perhaps even learning more about their understanding of the Law. This is the first time the Bible indicates that Jesus may have known he had a different relationship with God from anyone else. He knew that God was his Father.

Words You Should Know

Passover Feast
(PASS-o-ver FEEST)
An important holy day for the Jews in the spring of each year. They ate a special meal on this day to remind them that God had freed them from being slaves in Egypt. Jesus was killed at Passover time (see Exodus 12:27; Numbers 9:1-14; Joshua 5:10; Matthew 26:2, 17-19).

Behind the Story

Attendance by Jewish men was required at the three religious festivals each year—Passover, Pentecost and the Feast of Tabernacles.

People traveled to Jerusalem in caravans—groups of people walking together—for safety and for companionship. Jesus may have walked with some other boys or with cousins not with Joseph and Mary.

Jesus would have begun learning the Old Testament Law at age 5. By age 12, a Jewish boy was expected to obey the Law. At age 13, he was considered an adult.

The teachers Jesus was talking to were rabbis who were trained to know the Law.

THE GOSPELS

Early Ministry

Jesus' Temptation

Mark 1:9-11; Matthew 4:1-11

Words You Should Know

Devil (DEV-'l)
"One who accuses." In the New Testament, the devil is often called Satan or Beelzebul. He is a spirit and the enemy of God and man (see John 13:2; Ephesians 4:27; 6:10-17).

Satan (SAY-t'n)
In Hebrew means "enemy." It is a name for the devil, the enemy of God and man (see 1 Chronicles 21:1; Job 1:6-12; Luke 10:18-19; Acts 5:3; 26:18).

Temptation
(temp-TAY-shun)
The devil's trying to get us to do something wrong. God has promised to help us when we are tempted, so we can choose to do the right thing (see 1 Corinthians 10:13; Hebrews 2:18; 4:15-16; James 1:12-14).

Follower (FAHL-o-wer)
A person who is learning from someone. Jesus' followers are those who believe and obey his teaching.

Jesus was 30 years old when his ministry began. He asked his cousin, John the Baptist, to baptize him. God declared that Jesus was his Son and that he loved him very much. Not long after that, the Holy Spirit took Jesus into the desert where Satan tempted him.

Jesus Is Baptized

1 ⁹At that time Jesus came from the town of Nazareth in Galilee to the place where John was. John baptized Jesus in the Jordan River. ¹⁰When Jesus was coming up out of the water, he saw heaven open. The Holy Spirit came down on him like a dove. ¹¹A voice came from heaven and said: "You are my Son and I love you. I am very pleased with you."

The Temptation of Jesus

4 Then the Spirit led Jesus into the desert to be tempted by the devil. ²Jesus ate nothing for 40 days and nights. After this, he was very hungry. ³The devil came to Jesus to tempt him. The devil said, "If you are the Son of God, tell these rocks to become bread."

⁴Jesus answered, "It is written in the Scriptures, 'A person does not live only by eating bread. But a person lives by everything the Lord says.' "

⁵Then the devil led Jesus to the holy city of Jerusalem. He put Jesus on a very high place of the Temple. ⁶The devil said, "If you are the Son of God, jump off. It is written in the Scriptures,

'He has put his angels in charge of you.
   They will catch you with their hands.
And you will not hit your foot on a rock.' "

Psalm 91:11-12

⁷Jesus answered him, "It also says in the Scriptures, 'Do not test the Lord your God.' "

[8]Then the devil led Jesus to the top of a very high mountain. He showed Jesus all the kingdoms of the world and all the great things that are in those kingdoms. [9]The devil said, "If you will bow down and worship me, I will give you all these things."

[10]Jesus said to the devil, "Go away from me, Satan! It is written in the Scriptures, 'You must worship the Lord your God. Serve only him!' "

[11]So the devil left Jesus. And then some angels came to Jesus and helped him.

TAKING IT TO HEART

How Did Jesus Fight Temptation?

1. He had read God's Word.

2. He knew God's Word well enough to quote it to Satan.

3. He was sure that he would always put God first.

Jesus Chooses Some Followers
Mark 1:14-20; 3:13-19

1 [14]After John was put in prison, Jesus went into Galilee and preached the Good News from God. [15]Jesus said, "The right time has come. The kingdom of God is near. Change your hearts and lives and believe the Good News!"

[16]When Jesus was walking by Lake Galilee, he saw Simon and Simon's brother, Andrew. They were fishermen and were throwing a net into the lake to catch fish. [17]Jesus said to them, "Come and follow me. I will make you fishermen for men." [18]So Simon and Andrew immediately left their nets and followed him.

[19]Jesus continued walking by Lake Galilee. He saw two more brothers, James and John, the sons of Zebedee. They were in their boat, preparing their nets to catch fish. [20]Their father Zebedee and the men who worked for him were in the boat with the brothers. When Jesus saw the brothers, he called them to come with him. They left their father and followed Jesus.

3 [13]Then Jesus went up on a hill and called some men to come to him. These were the men Jesus wanted, and they went up to him. [14]Jesus chose 12 men and called them apostles. He wanted these 12 to be with him, and he wanted to send them to other places to preach. [15]He also wanted them to have the power to force demons out of people. [16]These are the 12 men he chose: Simon (Jesus gave him the name Peter); [17]James and John, the sons of Zebedee (Jesus gave them the name Boanerges, which means "Sons of Thunder"); [18]Andrew, Philip, Bartholomew, Matthew, Thomas, James the son of Alphaeus, Thaddaeus, Simon the Zealot, [19]and Judas Iscariot. Judas is the one who gave Jesus to his enemies.

Think About This

Three different times a voice from heaven spoke to Jesus. The first time was at Jesus' baptism. Read of the other two in Mark 9:7 and John 12:28.

It was not Satan who led Jesus into the desert; it was the Holy Spirit.

Jesus' temptation helps him identify with us when we are tempted to disobey God or do wrong things.

Satan tempted Jesus to avoid all the suffering and pain that was ahead of him if he lived out God's plan. Jesus resisted the temptation. He came to earth to make a way for people to come to God, and he wouldn't do anything to stop that plan.

The temptation took place right after Jesus was baptized. Satan often attacks believers after something good has happened—something for which they may praise God. His goal is to pull people away from God.

The 12 men chosen were Jesus' apostles—his special students who traveled with him, saw his miracles and listened to his teachings.

226

MATTHEW MARK LUKE JOHN ACTS ROMANS 1 CORINTHIANS 2 CORINTHIANS GALATIANS EPHESIANS PHILIPPIANS COLOSSIANS 1 THESSALONIANS

THE GOSPELS

Early Ministry

Behind the Story

A wedding celebration often lasted for a whole week. It would have been very embarrassing for the bridegroom to run out of wine at the party.

Jesus told his mother that his time had not yet come, meaning that it was not time for him to do miracles. She then told the servants to do whatever Jesus said. Mary wasn't certain what Jesus would do. She would accept whatever he said.

The water Jesus changed into wine was in jars that were filled with special water, used for required cleansing before and after meals. This water was not for drinking.

Usually the best wine was served first and the cheaper wine served later, when the guests didn't pay as much attention. The wine Jesus made was the best.

The Wedding Miracle

John 2:1-11

Jesus called twelve men to be his apostles. He began teaching them about living for God. The first miracle they saw him do was at a wedding.

The Wedding at Cana

2 Two days later there was a wedding in the town of Cana in Galilee. Jesus' mother was there. ²Jesus and his followers were also invited to the wedding. ³When all the wine was gone, Jesus' mother said to him, "They have no more wine."

⁴Jesus answered, "Dear woman, why come to me? My time has not yet come."

⁵His mother said to the servants, "Do whatever he tells you to do."

⁶In that place there were six stone water jars. The Jews used jars like these in their washing ceremony. Each jar held about 20 or 30 gallons.

⁷Jesus said to the servants, "Fill the jars with water." So they filled the jars to the top.

⁸Then he said to them, "Now take some out and give it to the master of the feast."

So the servants took the water to the master. ⁹When he tasted it, the water had become wine. He did not know where the wine came from. But the servants who brought the water knew. The master of the wedding called the bridegroom ¹⁰and said to him, "People always serve the best wine first. Later, after the guests have been drinking a lot, they serve the cheaper wine. But you have saved the best wine till now."

¹¹So in Cana of Galilee, Jesus did his first miracle. There he showed his glory, and his followers believed in him.

Jesus Cleans the Temple

John 2:12-25

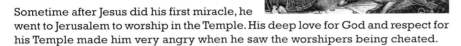

Sometime after Jesus did his first miracle, he went to Jerusalem to worship in the Temple. His deep love for God and respect for his Temple made him very angry when he saw the worshipers being cheated.

Jesus in the Temple

12 [12]Then Jesus went to the town of Capernaum with his mother, brothers and his followers. They all stayed in Capernaum for a few days. [13]But it was almost time for the Jewish Passover Feast. So Jesus went to Jerusalem. [14]In the Temple he found men selling cattle, sheep, and doves. He saw others sitting at tables, exchanging money. [15]Jesus made a whip out of cords. Then he forced all these men, with the sheep and cattle, to leave the Temple. He turned over the tables and scattered the money of the men who were exchanging it. [16]Then he said to those who were selling pigeons, "Take these things out of here! Don't make my Father's house a place for buying and selling!"

[17]When this happened the followers remembered what was written in the Scriptures: "My strong love for your Temple completely controls me."

[18]The Jews said to Jesus, "Show us a miracle for a sign. Prove that you have the right to do these things."

[19]Jesus answered, "Destroy this temple, and I will build it again in three days."

[20]The Jews answered, "Men worked 46 years to build this Temple! Do you really believe you can build it again in three days?"

[21](But the temple Jesus meant was his own body. [22]After Jesus was raised from death, his followers remembered that Jesus had said this. Then they believed the Scripture and the words Jesus said.)

[23]Jesus was in Jerusalem for the Passover Feast. Many people believed in him because they saw the miracles he did. [24]But Jesus did not believe in them because he knew them all. [25]He did not need anyone to tell him about people. Jesus knew what was in a person's mind.

Behind the Story

People came to the Temple to worship God. They had to offer animal sacrifices and often bought the sacrifices there. The people selling the animals were charging unfair prices and cheating the people. Jesus was not objecting to the system of sacrificing, but to the people being cheated when they came to worship.

The ones handling the money were exchanging Jewish coins for foreign money—usually Roman coins which were not accepted to buy the animals. Those exchanging money were cheating the people, too.

Jesus called the Temple "my Father's house," which was a claim that he was the Messiah.

When Jesus said that he would rebuild the temple in three days, he was talking about his own body. He was referring to his death and resurrection. After the resurrection, Jesus' followers believed the words he had said.

228

MATTHEW MARK LUKE JOHN ACTS ROMANS 1 CORINTHIANS 2 CORINTHIANS GALATIANS EPHESIANS PHILIPPIANS COLOSSIANS 1 THESSALONIANS

THE GOSPELS

Early Ministry

Jesus and Nicodemus
John 3:1-21

Jesus quickly became known. He turned water into wine at a wedding. Then he turned over the money tables in the Temple. One high Jewish official had questions he wanted to ask Jesus.

Words You Should Know

Pharisees (FARE-uh-seez) "The separate people." They were a Jewish religious group who followed the religious laws and customs very strictly. Jesus often spoke against the Pharisees for their religious teachings and traditions. Many of the Pharisees did not like Jesus because he did not follow all of their rules (see Matthew 5:20; 23:23-36; Mark 7:1-13; Luke 18:9-14).

Behind the Story

Jesus' answers to Nicodemus' questions explain the process of salvation for all people. The only way to heaven is to be "born again," which only happens through the power of the Holy Spirit when a person trusts Christ as his Savior.

Nicodemus came to talk to Jesus at night. He may have been afraid of what his important Jewish friends would think about him talking with Jesus.

3 There was a man named Nicodemus who was one of the Pharisees. He was an important Jewish leader. ²One night Nicodemus came to Jesus. He said, "Teacher, we know that you are a teacher sent from God. No one can do the miracles you do, unless God is with him."

³Jesus answered, "I tell you the truth. Unless you are born again, you cannot be in God's kingdom."

⁴Nicodemus said, "But if a man is already old, how can he be born again? He cannot enter his mother's body again. So how can he be born a second time?"

⁵But Jesus answered, "I tell you the truth. Unless you are born from water and the Spirit, you cannot enter God's kingdom. ⁶A person's body is born from his human parents. But a person's spiritual life is born from the Spirit. ⁷Don't be surprised when I tell you, 'You must all be born again.' ⁸The wind blows where it wants to go. You hear the wind blow. But you don't know where the wind comes from or where it is going. It is the same with every person who is born from the Spirit."

⁹Nicodemus asked, "How can all this be possible?"

¹⁰Jesus said, "You are an important teacher in Israel. But you still don't understand these things? ¹¹I tell you the truth. We talk about what we know. We tell about what we have seen. But you don't accept what we tell you. ¹²I have told you about things here on earth, but you do not believe me. So surely you will not believe me if I tell you about the things of heaven! ¹³The only one who has ever gone up to heaven is the One who came down from heaven—the Son of Man.

[14]"Moses lifted up the snake in the desert. It is the same with the Son of Man. The Son of Man must be lifted up too. [15]Then everyone who believes in him can have eternal life.

[16]"For God loved the world so much that he gave his only Son. God gave his Son so that whoever believes in him may not be lost, but have eternal life. [17]God did not send his Son into the world to judge the world guilty, but to save the world through him. [18]He who believes in God's Son is not judged guilty. He who does not believe has already been judged guilty, because he has not believed in God's only Son. [19]People are judged by this fact: I am the Light from God that has come into the world. But men did not want light. They wanted darkness because they were doing evil things. [20]Everyone who does evil hates the light. He will not come to the light because it will show all the evil things he has done. [21]But he who follows the true way comes to the light. Then the light will show that the things he has done were done through God."

The Deity of Jesus

When Jesus was on earth, he was completely human like any other person. He was also still completely God. This is hard to understand, but it is important that Jesus became a man. Because of that, he understands what life is like on this earth.

It is also important that he is God:

- The angels declared that he was God's Son in Luke 1:26-33.

- God announced that Jesus was his Son in Matthew 3:16-17.

- The miracles he did showed he had power that wasn't human. See John 20:30-31.

- He lived a sinless life. See Luke 23:41.

- Even the demons knew he was God. See Matthew 8:28-29.

Think About This

Nicodemus was a teacher of the Law. He should have understood the prophecies about the Messiah better than he did.

John 3:15 is the first time eternal life is mentioned in the Bible.

John 3:16 is a famous verse that explains God's plan to make a way for people to come to him. It tells how very much God loves all people, regardless of what nation or country they are from. If Jesus had not come, people would die without being able to enter heaven. He made the way possible.

See Romans 5:8 to for more understanding of God's love.

Jesus is the Light of the World (John 3:19). Also see John 1:7-9; 8:12 and 9:5. He reveals peoples' sins—the things they may want to hide in the darkness. It is a person's choice to come into the light, to turn away from sin and accept Jesus as Savior.

230

MATTHEW MARK LUKE JOHN ACTS ROMANS 1 CORINTHIANS 2 CORINTHIANS GALATIANS EPHESIANS PHILIPPIANS COLOSSIANS 1 THESSALONIANS

THE GOSPELS

Early Ministry

The Woman at the Well

John 4:1-42

Words You Should Know

Baptizing (BAP-tize-ing)
From a Greek word that in New Testament times meant to dip or immerse. Baptism as practiced by Christians was in water. Baptism reminds us of Jesus' death, burial and rising to live again. It shows our death to sin and our being raised to new life with Christ (see Acts 2:38, 41; 8:36-39; 10:47-48; 16:15, 33; 18:8; Romans 6:3-4).

Samaritan (suh-MEHR-ih-t'n)
A person from the area of Samaria in Palestine. Samaria was between Galilee and Judea. These people were only part Jewish, so the Jews did not accept them. They hated the Samaritans. But Jesus showed love and concern for the Samaritans. One story that Jesus told is known as the story of "the good Samaritan" (Luke 10:30-37). Also see John 4:1-42.

Nomadic Well

After Jesus talked with Nicodemus, he returned to Galilee. However, he didn't take the normal route to get there. He went through Samaria, which was a place that most Jewish people avoided. Jews and Samaritans did not like each other. However, Jesus had a reason for going through Samaria.

Jesus and a Samaritan Woman

4 The Pharisees heard that Jesus was making and baptizing more followers than John. ²(But really Jesus himself did not baptize people. His followers did the baptizing.) Jesus knew that the Pharisees had heard about him. ³So he left Judea and went back to Galilee. ⁴On the way he had to go through the country of Samaria.

⁵In Samaria Jesus came to the town called Sychar. This town is near the field that Jacob gave to his son Joseph. ⁶Jacob's well was there. Jesus was tired from his long trip. So he sat down beside the well. It was about noon. ⁷A Samaritan woman came to the well to get some water. Jesus said to her, "Please give me a drink." ⁸(This happened while Jesus' followers were in town buying some food.)

⁹The woman said, "I am surprised that you ask me for a drink. You are a Jew and I am a Samaritan." (Jews are not friends with Samaritans.)

¹⁰Jesus said, "You don't know what God gives. And you don't know who asked you for a drink. If you knew, you would have asked me, and I would have given you living water."

¹¹The woman said, "Sir, where will you get that living water? The well is very deep, and you have nothing to get water with. ¹²Are you greater than Jacob, our father? Jacob is the one who gave us this well. He drank from it himself. Also, his sons and flocks drank from this well."

¹³Jesus answered, "Every person who drinks this water will be thirsty again. ¹⁴But whoever drinks the water I give will never be thirsty again. The water I give will become a spring of water flowing inside him. It will give him eternal life."

¹⁵The woman said to him, "Sir, give me this water. Then I will never be thirsty again. And I will not have to come back here to get more water."

[16]Jesus told her, "Go get your husband and come back here."

[17]The woman answered, "But I have no husband."

Jesus said to her, "You are right to say you have no husband. [18]Really you have had five husbands. But the man you live with now is not your husband. You told the truth."

[19]The woman said, "Sir, I can see that you are a prophet. [20]Our fathers worshiped on this mountain. But you Jews say that Jerusalem is the place where people must worship."

[21]Jesus said, "Believe me, woman. The time is coming when you will not have to be in Jerusalem or on this mountain to worship the Father. [22]You Samaritans worship what you don't understand. We Jews understand what we worship. Salvation comes from the Jews. [23]The time is coming when the true worshipers will worship the Father in spirit and truth. That time is now here. And these are the kinds of worshipers the Father wants. [24]God is spirit. Those who worship God must worship in spirit and truth."

[25]The woman said, "I know that the Messiah is coming." (Messiah is the One called Christ.) "When the Messiah comes, he will explain everything to us."

[26]Then Jesus said, "He is talking to you now. I am he."

[27]Just then his followers came back from town. They were surprised because they saw Jesus talking with a woman. But none of them asked, "What do you want?" or "Why are you talking with her?"

[28]Then the woman left her water jar and went back to town. She said to the people, [29]"A man told me everything I have ever done. Come see him. Maybe he is the Christ!" [30]So the people left the town and went to see Jesus.

[31]While the woman was away, the followers were begging him, "Teacher, eat something!"

[32]But Jesus answered, "I have food to eat that you know nothing about."

[33]So the followers asked themselves, "Did somebody already bring Jesus some food?"

Think About This

Notice the contrast between Jesus' talk with Nicodemus, an educated Jewish official, and the Samaritan woman, who was immoral and from a group that was despised by the Jews. In both cases, Jesus knew what was in the person's heart.

Jesus did not have to go through Samaria. He chose to. Jesus wanted all people to know about God, so he went through Samaria in order to tell the Samaritans about God and show them that he loved them.

The woman did not understand Jesus' spiritual message. She thought he was talking about actual water like she drew from the well.

Because Jesus could tell the woman about her life, she knew that he was a prophet. She tried to shift the conversation away from her life. But Jesus would not let her. He wanted to be sure she understood about God.

Jesus said that true worshipers worship in spirit and in truth. They don't insist on a lot of rules to keep. They worship from the heart.

232

MATTHEW MARK LUKE JOHN ACTS ROMANS 1 CORINTHIANS 2 CORINTHIANS GALATIANS EPHESIANS PHILIPPIANS COLOSSIANS 1 THESSALONIANS

THE GOSPELS

Early Ministry

Behind the Story

The apostles didn't understand why Jesus wasn't hungry. He explained that what satisfied him was doing God's will—not just knowing it, but doing it.

In John 4:35 Jesus challenged his apostles, as he challenges all believers, to see that there are still many people who haven't accepted Jesus into their hearts. He gave the apostles a chance to have a part in telling people about him. He wanted them to get their focus off of themselves.

Jesus is the Savior of the world (4:42). He didn't come only to save all the Jews, but all who would believe in him.

As soon as the woman understood who Jesus was, she rushed into town to tell others. She was excited about meeting Jesus and wanted everyone to know him.

³⁴Jesus said, "My food is to do what the One who sent me wants me to do. My food is to finish the work that he gave me to do. ³⁵You say, 'Four more months to wait before we gather the grain.' But I tell you, open your eyes. Look at the fields that are ready for harvesting now. ³⁶Even now, the one who harvests the crop is being paid. He is gathering crops for eternal life. So now the one who plants can be happy along with the one who harvests. ³⁷It is true when we say, 'One person plants, but another harvests the crop.' ³⁸I sent you to harvest a crop that you did not work for. Others did the work, and you get the profit from their work."

³⁹Many of the Samaritans in that town believed in Jesus. They believed because of what the woman said: "He told me everything I have ever done." ⁴⁰The Samaritans came to Jesus and begged him to stay with them. So he stayed there two days. ⁴¹Many more believed because of the things he said.

⁴²They said to the woman, "First we believed in Jesus because of what you told us. But now we believe because we heard him ourselves. We know that this man really is the Savior of the world."

Seeing Jesus

Jesus was able to tell the woman at the well all about her life. He knew everything about it. He knows all about everyone's life. Things you do and thoughts you have can be hidden from other people, but not from Jesus. He knows what you do and what you think. But, just as he loved the Samaritan woman, he loves you and will forgive any and all of your sins. Read Psalm 139 to see how well he knows you and how much he loves you.

Life in Jesus' Time

The Land of Galilee

Gentle hills covered with flowers, golden wheat and barley filled the land of Galilee. Farmers walked the fields with a sickle in hand to harvest the crops. The great Sea of Galilee was filled with fish, which were caught and sold around the area. Many people depended on fishing to earn their living.

Towns

Herod Antipas governed Galilee. He was a son of Herod the Great. Each town had at least one synagogue, which was the center of community life. Synagogue leaders handled the community's financial affairs and settled differences between members.

The Synagogue at Capernaum in Galilee

Boys and Girls

Boys were taken to synagogue by their fathers and started learning Hebrew traditions and studying the Law when they were six or seven years old. When a boy turned 13, he was considered to be a man and had to strictly follow the rules of the Law. He learned to read and write—using the Torah as his study text.

Boys married at 18 years of age, and girls usually around the age of 12 1/2. Marriages were arranged by parents, and a price was paid from the father of the bride to the family of the groom. There was a year of "betrothal," or engagement, before the marriage. During the year of engagement the agreement couldn't be broken, except through a letter of divorce. If the boy died, the girl was considered a widow.

234

MATTHEW MARK LUKE JOHN ACTS ROMANS 1 CORINTHIANS 2 CORINTHIANS GALATIANS EPHESIANS PHILIPPIANS COLOSSIANS 1 THESSALONIANS

THE GOSPELS

Early Ministry

Four Friends' Faith

Mark 2:1-12

Everywhere Jesus went crowds followed him. People brought their sick loved ones and wanted him to heal them. One time he came home to Capernaum, where he stayed with Peter, and a crowd gathered to hear him teach. The house was so full that not even one more person could get inside.

Behind the Story

Houses were built so that the roof was flat. There were usually stairs leading up the outside of the house to the roof. Some homes even used the roof as another room where people slept when it was too hot to sleep inside. The house in this story probably did not have that kind of roof. It would not have been strong enough to support a room. The roof would have been made of sun-baked bricks and straw.

Some teachers of the Law followed Jesus around to listen to his teaching, but not because they agreed with him. They tried to find ways that he disobeyed God or taught wrong things. When Jesus said he could forgive the paralyzed man's sin, he was claiming to be God. Only God can forgive sin. The religious teachers didn't like this claim. But Jesus told the man to get up and walk, and the man did.

Jesus Heals a Paralyzed Man

2 A few days later, Jesus came back to Capernaum. The news spread that he was home. ²So many people gathered to hear him preach that the house was full. There was no place to stand, not even outside the door. Jesus was teaching them. ³Some people came, bringing a paralyzed man to Jesus. Four of them were carrying the paralyzed man. ⁴But they could not get to Jesus because of the crowd. So they went to the roof above Jesus and made a hole in the roof. Then they lowered the mat with the paralyzed man on it. ⁵Jesus saw that these men had great faith. So he said to the paralyzed man, "Young man, your sins are forgiven."

⁶Some of the teachers of the law were sitting there. They saw what Jesus did, and they said to themselves, ⁷"Why does this man say things like that? He is saying things that are against God. Only God can forgive sins."

⁸At once Jesus knew what these teachers of the law were thinking. So he said to them, "Why are you thinking these things? ⁹Which is easier: to tell this paralyzed man, 'Your sins are forgiven,' or to tell him, 'Stand up. Take your mat and walk'? ¹⁰But I will prove to you that the Son of Man has authority on earth to forgive sins." So Jesus said to the paralyzed man, ¹¹"I tell you, stand up. Take your mat and go home." ¹²Immediately the paralyzed man stood up. He took his mat and walked out while everyone was watching him.

The people were amazed and praised God. They said, "We have never seen anything like this!"

Jesus Chooses a Tax Collector

Mark 2:13-17

The religious leaders watched everything Jesus did. When he started associating with people who were sinners, the religious leaders criticized him more than ever.

Painting by William Hole

2 [13]Jesus went to the lake again. A crowd followed him there, and he taught them. [14]While he was walking beside the lake, he saw a tax collector named Levi son of Alphaeus. Levi was sitting in the tax office. Jesus said to him, "Follow me." And Levi stood up and followed Jesus.

[15]Later that day, Jesus ate at Levi's house. There were many tax collectors and "sinners" eating there with Jesus and his followers. Many people like this followed Jesus. [16]The teachers of the law who were Pharisees saw Jesus eating with the tax collectors and "sinners." They asked his followers, "Why does he eat with tax collectors and sinners?"

[17]Jesus heard this and said to them, "Healthy people don't need a doctor. It is the sick who need a doctor. I did not come to invite good people. I came to invite sinners."

An Unexpected Messiah

Jesus didn't fit the idea the Pharisees had for what the Messiah would be like. They thought he would be a king and would keep all their rules perfectly. Jesus was born in a manger. The first people to see him were simple shepherds. He identified with the ones other people wouldn't have anything to do with—tax collectors, lepers, crippled people. He didn't keep all of the Pharisee's laws. But he taught about God and lived a life of love.

Behind the Story

Tax collectors were hated by the people. They collected heavy taxes from the people to build roads for the Romans. Many of them cheated the people by collecting extra money, which they kept for themselves. Tax collectors could not serve as witnesses or judges and were not allowed into the synagogues.

Matthew, who was also called Levi, was probably collecting taxes for the Romans.

When Jesus was criticized for eating with the tax collectors, he pointed out that people who are well don't need a doctor. He came to help those who were sick. The religious teachers kept strict rules; they never would have associated with the tax collectors. They thought anyone who didn't do what they said was a terrible sinner. They loved their rules more than they loved people. Jesus came for everyone.

236

MATTHEW MARK LUKE JOHN ACTS ROMANS 1 CORINTHIANS 2 CORINTHIANS GALATIANS EPHESIANS PHILIPPIANS COLOSSIANS 1 THESSALONIANS

THE GOSPELS

Ministry and Parables

The Beatitudes

In the Sermon on the Mount, Jesus taught how a person who is living for God should live his life. He was speaking to his apostles, but what he taught applies to people today, too.

The sermon begins with the Beatitudes (Matthew 5:1-12). These verses describe people who are needy, humble, pure, peaceful, merciful and have other character qualities that help them to be happy or blessed.

None of these were qualities of the Pharisees. Jesus showed that the Pharisees didn't live in a way that pleased God. They just kept laws which were very strict and negative. Jesus taught his followers about the blessings or good things that come from obeying God.

Jesus also pointed out that people who live the way he taught will be criticized and hurt by those who don't understand them. Pharisees criticized him for not keeping their rules. People had also criticized the Old Testament prophets.

Sermon on the Mount

Matthew 5:1-20

Jesus taught about God to the crowds of people who followed him everywhere. Once he took his apostles up on a mountain away from the crowds and taught them. This is known as the Sermon on the Mount.

A Hillside Above the Sea of Galilee

Jesus Teaches the People

5 Jesus saw the crowds who were there. He went up on a hill and sat down. His followers came to him. ²Jesus taught the people and said:

³"Those people who know they have great spiritual needs are happy.

The kingdom of heaven belongs to them.

⁴Those who are sad now are happy.

God will comfort them.

⁵Those who are humble are happy.

The earth will belong to them.

⁶Those who want to do right more than anything else are happy.

God will fully satisfy them.

⁷Those who give mercy to others are happy.

Mercy will be given to them.

⁸Those who are pure in their thinking are happy.

They will be with God.

⁹Those who work to bring peace are happy.

God will call them his sons.

¹⁰Those who are treated badly for doing good are happy.

The kingdom of heaven belongs to them.

¹¹"People will say bad things about you and hurt you. They will lie and say all kinds of evil things about you because you follow me. But when they do these things to you, you are happy.

[12]Rejoice and be glad. You have a great reward waiting for you in heaven. People did the same evil things to the prophets who lived before you.

You Are like Salt and Light

[13]"You are the salt of the earth. But if the salt loses its salty taste, it cannot be made salty again. It is good for nothing. It must be thrown out for people to walk on.

[14]"You are the light that gives light to the world. A city that is built on a hill cannot be hidden. [15]And people don't hide a light under a bowl. They put the light on a lampstand. Then the light shines for all the people in the house. [16]In the same way, you should be a light for other people. Live so that they will see the good things you do. Live so that they will praise your Father in heaven.

Jerusalem

The Importance of the Law

[17]"Don't think that I have come to destroy the law of Moses or the teaching of the prophets. I have not come to destroy their teachings but to do what they said. [18]I tell you the truth. Nothing will disappear from the law until heaven and earth are gone. The law will not lose even the smallest letter or the smallest part of a letter until all has happened. [19]Whoever refuses to obey any command and teaches other people not to obey that command will be the least important in the kingdom of heaven. But whoever obeys the law and teaches other people to obey the law will be great in the kingdom of heaven. [20]I tell you that you must do better than the teachers of the law and the Pharisees. If you are not better than they are, you will not enter the kingdom of heaven.

A Page from the Hebrew Torah (The Law)

Salt and Light

Jesus used two illustrations to show that people who lived for God could make a difference in the world.

Salt makes people thirsty. These God-followers would make people thirsty to know God by the way they lived. But if they let sin creep into their lives, they would not be useful—just as salt that has other things mixed with it is no good for seasoning (Matthew 5:13).

A person living the way God wants will shine as brightly as a **light** does in darkness. The light a God-follower has is a light that reflects who God is (5:14). That means it is important to stay close to God and live so others will see his light.

Jesus and the Law

Jesus did not intend to replace the Law that Moses taught, the one the Jews knew. This was what the Pharisees had accused him of. He was completing the Law by obeying it perfectly and explaining the way of salvation. He had great respect for the Law.

238

MATTHEW MARK LUKE JOHN ACTS ROMANS 1CORINTHIANS 2CORINTHIANS GALATIANS EPHESIANS PHILIPPIANS COLOSSIANS 1THESSALONIANS

THE GOSPELS

Ministry and Parables

Painting by James Tissot

Think About This

This is the first time in the New Testament that a person is healed of a skin disease. Jesus knew the priests would pay attention to this man because this had never happened before.

It is significant that Jesus touched the man. The disease the man had was very contagious. Jesus could have caught it by touching him, and he could have healed him by just saying, "Be healed."

Matthew 8:5-13 tells about a man who was not Jewish. He was a Gentile army officer who had a lot of authority. Jesus was amazed by the amount of faith this man had. The Scriptures record only one other time that Jesus was amazed (see Mark 6:6). This officer's faith was stronger than the faith of many of the Israelites. This showed that faith in God and the promise of heaven was not just for the Jewish people. Anyone can come to faith in God.

Jesus' Works

Matthew 8:1-17

When Jesus and his apostles came down from the mountain, big crowds of people followed him everywhere to hear him teach and to see what he would do next.

Jesus Heals a Sick Man

8 When Jesus came down from the hill, great crowds followed him. [2]Then a man sick with a harmful skin disease came to Jesus. The man bowed down before him and said, "Lord, you have the power to heal me if you want."

[3]Jesus touched the man and said, "I want to heal you. Be healed!" And immediately the man was healed from his skin disease. [4]Then Jesus said to him, "Don't tell anyone about what happened. But go and show yourself to the priest. And offer the gift that Moses commanded for people who are made well. This will show people that you are healed."

Jesus Heals a Soldier's Servant

[5]Jesus went to the city of Capernaum. When he entered the city, an army officer came to Jesus and begged for help. [6]The officer said, "Lord, my servant is at home in bed. He can't move his body and is in much pain."

[7]Jesus said to the officer, "I will go and heal him."

[8]The officer answered, "Lord, I am not good enough for you to come into my house. All you need to do is command that my servant be healed, and he will be healed. [9]I myself am a man under the authority of other men. And I have soldiers

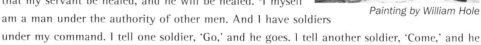

Painting by William Hole

under my command. I tell one soldier, 'Go,' and he goes. I tell another soldier, 'Come,' and he comes. I say to my servant, 'Do this,' and my servant obeys me."

[10]When Jesus heard this, he was amazed. He said to those who were with him, "I tell you the truth. This man has more faith than any other person I have found, even in Israel. [11]Many people will come from the east and from the west. They will sit and eat with Abraham, Isaac, and Jacob in the kingdom of heaven. [12]And those people who should have the kingdom will be thrown outside into the darkness. In that place people will cry and grind their teeth with pain."

[13]Then Jesus said to the officer, "Go home. Your servant will be healed just as you believed he would." And at that same time his servant was healed.

Jesus Heals Many People

[14]Jesus went to Peter's house. There Jesus saw that Peter's mother-in-law was in bed with a high fever. [15]Jesus touched her hand, and the fever left her. Then she stood up and began to serve Jesus.

[16]That evening people brought to Jesus many who had demons. Jesus spoke and the demons left them. Jesus healed all the sick. [17]He did these things to make come true what Isaiah the prophet said:

> "He took our suffering on him.
>   And he felt our pain for us."   *Isaiah 53:4*

Painting by William Hole

Faith and Power

The army officer had such great faith in Jesus that he believed Jesus could just speak the words and his servant would be healed. He didn't believe Jesus had to come and touch the servant. His faith was so strong that he believed his servant was healed, even though he couldn't see that for himself.

Personal faith is the only way to please God. It is not possible to please God or be a Christian just because your parents are Christians. It's a personal decision. See Acts 16:31.

Not only did Jesus have the power to heal diseases, he had power over demons. Demons were evil spirits from the devil. Sometimes demons lived in people. Jesus could make the demons come out.

The healings and forcing out of demons showed that Jesus was the Messiah. He fulfilled the prophecies written long before he was born.

The World at the Time

The Roman Empire

The Roman Empire was powerful and strong. It began around 60 B.C. and continued throughout New Testament times. Rome occupied the land of Israel and controlled the lives of all who lived there. The nation of Israel had become one province or state called Palestine. Then it was divided into smaller sections, such as Galilee and Samaria. The Roman rulers hated Christians and made their lives very difficult. The Romans did bring a stable currency. They also built good roads and encouraged trade between nations. They didn't know it, but they were actually helping the spread of Christianity.

A Roman Road

240

MATTHEW MARK LUKE JOHN **ACTS** ROMANS 1 CORINTHIANS 2 CORINTHIANS GALATIANS EPHESIANS PHILIPPIANS COLOSSIANS 1 THESSALONIANS

THE GOSPELS

Ministry and Parables

Words You Should Know

Parables (PARE-uh-b'ls)
Stories that teach a lesson by comparing two things. Jesus often used parables to teach the people. Some examples of parables can be found in Mark 12:1-12, Luke 10:29-37 and Luke 15:1-32.

Behind the Story

The rabbis or religious teachers of the day taught the people by telling stories. Their stories were much simpler than the ones Jesus taught. Jesus taught 38 different stories or parables that were about God's kingdom. He used stories that were about things his listeners would understand, such as farming, fishing, weddings and shepherds.

His stories taught about forgiveness, faith, prayer, the church, salvation and following God.

Jesus' Stories
Matthew 13:1-52

Sometimes when he was teaching, Jesus told stories to explain things about the kingdom of God. These stories are called parables. People who did not care about God or want to live for him could not understand the meaning of the stories.

The Sea of Galilee with Capernaum in the Background

A Story About Planting Seed

13 That same day Jesus went out of the house and sat by the lake. ²Large crowds gathered around him. So Jesus got into a boat and sat, while the people stayed on the shore. ³Then Jesus used stories to teach them many things. He said: "A farmer went out to plant his seed. ⁴While he was planting, some seed fell by the road. The birds came and ate all that seed. ⁵Some seed fell on rocky ground, where there wasn't enough dirt. That seed grew very fast, because the ground was not deep. ⁶But when the sun rose, the plants dried up because they did not have deep roots. ⁷Some other seed fell among thorny weeds. The weeds grew and choked the good plants. ⁸Some other seed fell on good ground where it grew and became grain. Some plants made 100 times more grain. Other plants made 60 times more grain, and some made 30 times more grain. ⁹Let those with ears use them and listen!"

Why Jesus Used Stories to Teach

[10]The followers came to Jesus and asked, "Why do you use stories to teach the people?"

[11]Jesus answered, "Only you can know the secret truths about the kingdom of heaven. Other people cannot know these secret truths. [12]The person who has something will be given more. And he will have all he needs. But the person who does not have much, even what he has will be taken from him. [13]This is why I use stories to teach the people: They see, but they don't really see. They hear, but they don't really understand. [14]So they show that the things Isaiah said about them are true:

'You will listen and listen, but you will not understand.

   You will look and look, but you will not learn.

[15]For these people have become stubborn.

   They do not hear with their ears.

   And they have closed their eyes.

  Otherwise they might really understand

   what they see with their eyes

   and hear with their ears.

   They might really understand in their minds.

   If they did this, they would come back to me and be forgiven.'

Isaiah 6:9-10

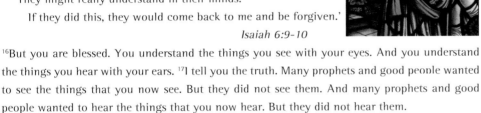

[16]But you are blessed. You understand the things you see with your eyes. And you understand the things you hear with your ears. [17]I tell you the truth. Many prophets and good people wanted to see the things that you now see. But they did not see them. And many prophets and good people wanted to hear the things that you now hear. But they did not hear them.

Jesus Explains the Seed Story

[18]"So listen to the meaning of that story about the farmer. [19]What is the seed that fell by the road? That seed is like the person who hears the teaching about the kingdom but does not understand it. The Evil One comes and takes away the things that were planted in that person's heart. [20]And what is the seed that fell on rocky ground? That seed is like the person who hears the teaching and quickly accepts it with joy. [21]But he does not let the teaching go deep into his life. He keeps it only a short time. When trouble or persecution comes because of the teaching he accepted, then he quickly gives up. [22]And what is the seed that fell among the thorny weeds? That seed is like the person who hears the teaching but lets worries about this life and love of

Think About This

Jesus' followers questioned why he told stories instead of just teaching. Jesus told them that the message he was bringing was for people who believed he was God's Son and wanted to know more about God.

See 1 Corinthians 2:9-12 for more understanding of this.

Jesus explained the story of the sower and seed to his apostles. The first soil represented someone whose heart was too hard to receive God's Word. The second soil represented people who made a decision to follow God, but didn't pray or study his Word, so their roots didn't go down deep. The third soil represented those who understood God's Word, but let the worries of life choke it out. The fourth soil represented a person who wanted to know God and lived in a way that pleased him.

This story shows that when you respond to God's Word, it changes you and helps your faith to grow stronger.

THE GOSPELS

Ministry and Parables

Behind the Story

Jesus told another story that explained what the kingdom of God is like. Once again he used a farming illustration.

This one was about weeds being planted in with a good crop. The kind of weeds Jesus referred to actually look a lot like wheat, but of course are not. Some people, Jesus taught, will act like they love God; they will know the right words to say and the right things to do, but their hearts will not belong to him. They will be fake.

The mustard seed parable uses the example of the tiniest seed known at that time. When this tiny seed is planted it grows into a tree that can get as tall as 15 feet! The message of this parable is that God's kingdom began small—with just a few people —but would quickly grow to a large kingdom.

money stop that teaching from growing. So the teaching does not produce fruit in that person's life. ²³But what is the seed that fell on the good ground? That seed is like the person who hears the teaching and understands it. That person grows and produces fruit, sometimes 100 times more, sometimes 60 times more, and sometimes 30 times more."

A Story About Wheat and Weeds

²⁴Then Jesus told them another story. He said, "The kingdom of heaven is like a man who planted good seed in his field. ²⁵That night, when everyone was asleep, his enemy came and planted weeds among the wheat. Then the enemy went away. ²⁶Later, the wheat grew and heads of grain grew on the wheat plants. But at the same time the weeds also grew. ²⁷Then the man's servants came to him and said, 'You planted good seed in your field. Where did the weeds come from?' ²⁸The man answered, 'An enemy planted weeds.' The servants asked, 'Do you want us to pull up the weeds?' ²⁹The man answered, 'No, because when you pull up the weeds, you might also pull up the wheat. ³⁰Let the weeds and the wheat grow together until the harvest time. At harvest time I will tell the workers this: First gather the weeds and tie them together to be burned. Then gather the wheat and bring it to my barn.' "

Stories of Mustard Seed and Yeast

³¹Then Jesus told another story: "The kingdom of heaven is like a mustard seed. A man plants the seed in his field. ³²That seed is the smallest of all seeds. But when it grows, it is one of the largest garden plants. It becomes a tree, big enough for the wild birds to come and make nests in its branches."

³³Then Jesus told another story: "The kingdom of heaven is like yeast that a woman mixes into a big bowl of flour. The yeast makes all the dough rise."

³⁴Jesus used stories to tell all these things to the people. He always used stories to teach people. ³⁵This is as the prophet said:

"I will speak using stories;
   I will tell things that have been secret since the world was
      made."

Psalm 78:2

Jesus Explains About the Wheat and Weeds

³⁶Then Jesus left the crowd and went into the house. His followers came to him and said, "Explain to us the meaning of the story about the weeds in the field."

³⁷Jesus answered, "The man who planted the good seed in the field is the Son of Man. ³⁸The field is the world. And the good seed are all of God's children in the kingdom. The weeds are those people who belong to the Evil One. ³⁹And the enemy who planted the bad seed is the devil. The harvest time is the end of the age. And the workers who gather are God's angels.

⁴⁰"The weeds are pulled up and burned in the fire. It will be this way at the end of the age. ⁴¹The Son of Man will send out his angels. They will gather out of his kingdom all who cause sin and all who do evil. ⁴²The angels will throw them into the blazing furnace. There the people will cry and grind their teeth with pain. ⁴³Then the good people will shine like the sun in the kingdom of their Father. Let those with ears use them and listen!

Stories of a Treasure and a Pearl

⁴⁴"The kingdom of heaven is like a treasure hidden in a field. One day a man found the treasure, and then he hid it in the field again. The man was very happy to find the treasure. He went and sold everything that he owned to buy that field.

⁴⁵"Also, the kingdom of heaven is like a man looking for fine pearls. ⁴⁶One day he found a very valuable pearl. The man went and sold everything he had to buy that pearl.

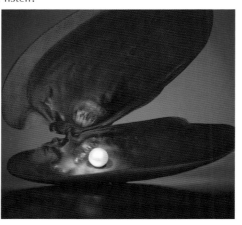

Behind the Story

The story of the yeast has the same message: the kingdom of heaven will grow. When yeast is mixed into dough, the dough will grow bigger. God's kingdom will grow because Christians are like yeast. They spread the message of God's love, others hear it and believe and the kingdom gets larger.

Jesus went into the house (Matthew 13:36) before explaining the weeds story. The explanation was just for those who were serious about understanding God's kingdom.

The story of the hidden treasure emphasizes the importance of the kingdom of heaven and the treasure it is to those who discover it.

The story of the pearl tells how Jesus came to give his life so people who believe in him can live with him forever. Nothing is more valuable that knowing him.

All of the stories Jesus told here are about the kingdom of heaven. He wanted his followers to understand that nothing should be more important to them than God's kingdom.

244

MATTHEW MARK LUKE JOHN ACTS ROMANS 1 CORINTHIANS 2 CORINTHIANS GALATIANS EPHESIANS PHILIPPIANS COLOSSIANS 1 THESSALONIANS

THE GOSPELS

Ministry and Parables

Fishers of Men

The story of the fishing net speaks of the responsibilities of Christians. When a big net is dropped into a lake and dragged along the bottom, it picks up anything and everything that it surrounds. Then the fisherman goes through the things in the net and throws out the junk —fish that are not edible or rocks or sticks that the net has picked up. This is like the kingdom of heaven because Christians share the Good News of God's love with everyone. Some will believe, and some will not. Some may even pretend to believe. But someday the angels will go through the "catch" and throw out the ones who aren't real. This is the angels' job, not the human's job.

Jesus asked his apostles if they understood his stories. They said they did, so they were expected to get to work.

A Story of a Fishing Net

47"Also, the kingdom of heaven is like a net that was put into the lake. The net caught many different kinds of fish. 48When it was full, the fishermen pulled the net to the shore. They sat down and put all the good fish in baskets. Then they threw away the bad fish. 49It will be this way at the end of the age. The angels will come and separate the evil people from the good people. 50The angels will throw the evil people into the blazing furnace. In that place the people will cry and grind their teeth with pain."

51Jesus asked his followers, "Do you understand all these things?"

Etching of a Painting by Raphael

They answered, "Yes, we understand."

52Then Jesus said to them, "So every teacher of the law who has been taught about the kingdom of heaven is like the owner of a house. He has both new things and old things saved in his house. And he brings out both those new things and old things."

TAKING IT TO HEART

The Parables and You

What should the parables mean to you? They mean that it's not acceptable to be "Christian" when you are at church or with your church friends, but act any old way you want when you're at school or with non-Christian friends. Christians should stand out from the crowd by the way they love others, and by being honest, obedient and respectful. Read Matthew 16:24-26 for encouragement.

Jesus Stops a Storm

Mark 4:35-41

One day Jesus had been teaching the crowds. At the end of the day, Jesus and his apostles got into a boat to cross the lake. He was tired and fell asleep right away. When a big storm came up, Jesus used the opportunity to show that he is the God of nature and has power over it.

4 ³⁵That evening, Jesus said to his followers, "Come with me across the lake." ³⁶He and the followers left the people there. They went in the boat that Jesus was already sitting in. There were also other boats with them. ³⁷A very strong wind came up on the lake. The waves began coming over the sides and into the boat. It was almost full of water. ³⁸Jesus was at the back of the boat, sleeping with his head on a pillow. The followers went to him and woke him. They said, "Teacher, do you care about us? We will drown!"

³⁹Jesus stood up and commanded the wind and the waves to stop. He said, "Quiet! Be still!" Then the wind stopped, and the lake became calm.

⁴⁰Jesus said to his followers, "Why are you afraid? Do you still have no faith?"

⁴¹The followers were very afraid and asked each other, "What kind of man is this? Even the wind and the waves obey him!"

Think About This

The lake in this story is the Lake of Galilee. Jesus spent much time around the Lake of Galilee. It is 13 miles long and about 8 miles wide. Storms often come up very quickly on this lake. Lake Galilee is 700 feet below sea level, but surrounded on three sides by mountains that are several thousand feet above sea level. It is not unusual for violent storms to blow up with no warning on this lake.

Jesus' ability to calm the storm shows his deity—that he is God. He could control what he created.

Jesus' apostles had been with him for a while. They had heard him teach and seen him do miracles, but when he calmed the storm, they were terrified. They still didn't quite understand that he was God.

246

MATTHEW MARK LUKE JOHN ACTS ROMANS 1 CORINTHIANS 2 CORINTHIANS GALATIANS EPHESIANS PHILIPPIANS COLOSSIANS 1 THESSALONIANS

THE GOSPELS

Ministry and Parables

Jesus Heals
Mark 5:21-43

After Jesus crossed over the lake, he was again met by a crowd of people who wanted him to do things for them. Two of these people had very strong faith. Jesus used these situations to show his power to all who were there.

Jesus Gives Life to a Dead Girl and Heals a Sick Woman

5 ²¹Jesus went in the boat back to the other side of the lake. There, a large crowd gathered around him. ²²A ruler from the synagogue, named Jairus, came to that place. Jairus saw Jesus and bowed before him. ²³The ruler begged Jesus again and again. He said, "My little daughter is dying. Please come and put your hands on her. Then she will be healed and will live." ²⁴So Jesus went with the ruler, and many people followed Jesus. They were pushing very close around him.

²⁵A woman was there who had been bleeding for the past 12 years. ²⁶She had suffered very much. Many doctors had tried to help her. She had spent all the money she had, but she was not improving. She was getting worse. ²⁷When the woman heard about Jesus, she followed him with the people and touched his coat. ²⁸The woman thought, "If I can even touch his coat, that will be enough to heal me." ²⁹When she touched his coat, her bleeding stopped. She could feel in her body that she was healed.

Painting by C.F. Vos

³⁰At once Jesus felt power go out from him. So he stopped and turned around. Then he asked, "Who touched my clothes?"

³¹The followers said, "There are so many people pushing against you! And you ask, 'Who touched me?' "

³²But Jesus continued looking around to see who had touched him. ³³The woman knew that she was healed. So she came and bowed at Jesus' feet. Shaking with fear, she told him the whole story. ³⁴Jesus said to the woman, "Dear woman, you are made well because you believed. Go in peace. You will have no more suffering."

³⁵Jesus was still speaking to her when some men came from the house of Jairus, the synagogue ruler. The men said, "Your daughter is dead. There is now no need to bother the teacher."

Words You Should Know

Faith (FAYTH)
Belief and trust. People who have great faith in God do what he says to do, even when they do not understand why. They do it because they believe in him and trust him. Faith in Jesus means believing he is the Son of God and trusting in him (see 2 Chronicles 20:20; Habakkuk 2:4; Matthew 8:5-10; Luke 8:22-25; Romans 4:16–5:2; Hebrews 11:1-40).

Behind the Story

Jairus was a synagogue official. Not all the religious leaders hated Jesus. Jairus begged Jesus over and over to come to his home and save the little girl. Jesus always felt compassion for people who were hurting, and he started out to go with Jairus. However, he was interrupted by the knowledge or feeling that power had gone out from him.

³⁶But Jesus paid no attention to what the men said. He said to the synagogue ruler, "Don't be afraid; only believe."

³⁷Jesus let only Peter, James, and John the brother of James go with him to Jairus's house. ³⁸They came to the house of the synagogue ruler, and Jesus found many people there crying loudly. There was much confusion. ³⁹Jesus entered the house and said to the people, "Why are you crying and making so much noise? This child is not dead. She is only asleep." ⁴⁰But they only laughed at Jesus. He told all the people to leave. Then he went into the room where the child

Painting by J.J. Tissot

was. He took the child's father and mother and his three followers into the room with him. ⁴¹Then he took hold of the girl's hand and said to her, "Talitha, koum!" (This means, "Little girl, I tell you to stand up!") ⁴²The girl stood right up and began walking. (She was 12 years old.) The father and mother and the followers were amazed. ⁴³Jesus gave the father and mother strict orders not to tell people about this. Then he told them to give the girl some food.

Feeding the 5,000
Matthew 14:13-21

14 ¹³When Jesus heard what happened to John, Jesus left in a boat. He went to a lonely place by himself. But when the crowds heard about it, they followed him on foot from the towns. ¹⁴When Jesus arrived, he saw a large crowd. He felt sorry for them and healed those who were sick.

¹⁵Late that afternoon, his followers came to Jesus and said, "No one lives in this place. And it is already late. Send the people away so they can go to the towns and buy food for themselves."

¹⁶Jesus answered, "They don't need to go away. You give them some food to eat."

¹⁷The followers answered, "But we have only five loaves of bread and two fish."

¹⁸Jesus said, "Bring the bread and the fish to me." ¹⁹Then he told the people to sit down on the grass. He took the five loaves of bread and the two fish. Then he looked to heaven and thanked God for the food. Jesus divided the loaves of bread. He gave them to his followers, and they gave the bread to the people. ²⁰All the people ate and were satisfied. After they finished eating, the followers filled 12 baskets with the pieces of food that were not eaten. ²¹There were about 5,000 men there who ate, as well as women and children.

Think About This

Jesus was interrupted by a woman who believed she could be healed just by touching the hem of his robe. And she was. However, Jesus knew immediately that power had gone out from him. The woman was not healed because of some kind of magic clothing; she was healed by Jesus' divine power.

Jesus went on to Jairus's home, even though the little girl had died. This is one of three times that Jesus brought someone back to life.

Matthew 14:14 says that Jesus felt sorry for the people. Jesus often felt great compassion for those who needed to know God. He also felt compassion for those who were sad or in pain.

Jesus met the physical need (hunger) of all the people, and there was more than enough food left over for the apostles. This is the only miracle recorded in all four Gospels.

248

MATTHEW MARK LUKE JOHN ACTS ROMANS 1 CORINTHIANS 2 CORINTHIANS GALATIANS EPHESIANS PHILIPPIANS COLOSSIANS 1 THESSALONIANS

THE GOSPELS

Ministry and Parables

Walking on Water

Matthew 14:22-33

After feeding the 5,000, Jesus sent his followers across the lake. This gave them a chance to get away from the crowd and think about what they had just seen. Jesus stayed behind for some time alone with God.

Jesus Walks on the Water

14 [22]Then Jesus made his followers get into the boat. He told them to go ahead of him to the other side of the lake. Jesus stayed there to tell the people they could go home. [23]After he said good-bye to them, he went alone up into the hills to pray. It was late, and Jesus was there alone. [24]By this time, the boat was already far away on the lake. The boat was having trouble because of the waves, and the wind was blowing against it.

[25]Between three and six o'clock in the morning, Jesus' followers were still in the boat. Jesus came to them. He was walking on the water. [26]When the followers saw him walking on the water,

they were afraid. They said, "It's a ghost!" and cried out in fear.

[27]But Jesus quickly spoke to them. He said, "Have courage! It is I! Don't be afraid."

[28]Peter said, "Lord, if that is really you, then tell me to come to you on the water."

[29]Jesus said, "Come."

And Peter left the boat and walked on the water to Jesus. [30]But when Peter saw the wind and the waves, he became afraid and began to sink. He shouted, "Lord, save me!"

[31]Then Jesus reached out his hand and caught Peter. Jesus said, "Your faith is small. Why did you doubt?"

[32]After Peter and Jesus were in the boat, the wind became calm. [33]Then those who were in the boat worshiped Jesus and said, "Truly you are the Son of God!"

Think About This

Matthew is the only Gospel that records Peter walking on water. Peter's courage and faith in Jesus made him one of only two men that are recorded to ever have walked on water. Jesus is the other one.

Peter waited for Jesus to call him before he jumped out of the boat. As soon as Jesus called, Peter jumped out of the boat onto the water. As long as he kept his eyes on Jesus, he was fine. But when he looked around at the wind and waves, his faith wavered and he sank.

After getting in the boat, Jesus calmed the storm. The apostles worshiped him and believed that he was the Son of God.

Jesus with Moses and Elijah

Luke 9:28-36

Several times Jesus took Peter, James and John with him so they could witness important events. He must have believed that those three would learn from what they saw. One time he took them up on a mountain with him, and they had an incredible experience.

9 28About eight days after Jesus said these things, he took Peter, James, and John and went up on a mountain to pray. 29While Jesus was praying, his face was changed, and his clothes became shining white. 30Then two men were talking with Jesus. The men were Moses and Elijah. 31They appeared in heavenly glory, talking with Jesus about his death which would happen in Jerusalem. 32Peter and the others were asleep. But they woke up and saw the glory of Jesus. They also saw the two men who were standing with him. 33When Moses and Elijah were about to leave, Peter said, "Master, it is good that we are here. We will put three tents here—one for you, one for Moses, and one for Elijah." (Peter did not know what he was saying.)

34While Peter was saying these things, a cloud came down all around them. Peter, James, and John became afraid when the cloud covered them. 35A voice came from the cloud. The voice said, "This is my Son. He is the One I have chosen. Obey him."

36When the voice finished speaking, only Jesus was there. Peter, James, and John said nothing. At that time they told no one about what they had seen.

Depictions of the Transfiguration by Three Artists: William Hole, Theophanes and Raphael.

Behind the Story

Moses and Elijah appearing with Jesus showed that he was the Messiah they had been waiting for.

God's words here are the same words he spoke when Jesus was baptized by John the Baptist (see Matthew 3:17). He wanted the apostles to obey Jesus.

Note that the apostles had fallen asleep, even though Jesus had chosen them to accompany him. They also fell asleep in the Garden of Gethsemane when Jesus wanted them to be praying (Matthew 26:36-46).

THE GOSPELS

Ministry in Galilee

More Stories of Jesus

Luke 10:25–11:4

The Good Samaritan

Painting by H. Copping

10 ²⁵Then a teacher of the law stood up. He was trying to test Jesus. He said, "Teacher, what must I do to get life forever?"

²⁶Jesus said to him, "What is written in the law? What do you read there?"

²⁷The man answered, "Love the Lord your God. Love him with all your heart, all your soul, all your strength, and all your mind." Also, "You must love your neighbor as you love yourself."

²⁸Jesus said to him, "Your answer is right. Do this and you will have life forever."

²⁹But the man wanted to show that the way he was living was right. So he said to Jesus, "And who is my neighbor?"

³⁰To answer this question, Jesus said, "A man was going down the road from Jerusalem to Jericho. Some robbers attacked him. They tore off his clothes and beat him. Then they left him lying there, almost dead. ³¹It happened that a Jewish priest was going down that road. When the priest saw the man, he walked by on the other side of the road. ³²Next, a Levite came there. He went over and looked at the man. Then he walked by on the other side of the road. ³³Then a Samaritan traveling down the road came to where the hurt man was lying. He saw the man and felt very sorry for him. ³⁴The Samaritan went to him and poured olive oil and wine on his wounds and bandaged them. He put the hurt man on his own donkey and took him to an inn. At the inn, the Samaritan took care of him. ³⁵The next day, the Samaritan brought out two silver coins and gave them to the innkeeper. The Samaritan said, 'Take care of this man. If you spend more money on him, I will pay it back to you when I come again.' "

³⁶Then Jesus said, "Which one of these three men do you think was a neighbor to the man who was attacked by the robbers?"

³⁷The teacher of the law answered, "The one who helped him."

Jesus said to him, "Then go and do the same thing he did!"

Behind the Story

The teacher of the law was trying to test Jesus with his question. Jesus turned things right back to him by asking him two questions about the Law. The teacher quoted Deuteronomy 6:5. But he wouldn't let Jesus go. He asked, "Who is my neighbor?" He thought there were some groups of people he wouldn't have to treat so kindly.

Jews hated Samaritans. They thought the people of Samaria were below them in every way.

It would have been expected for the priest or Levite to be the ones to help the hurt man because they were religious people. However, it was the Samaritan who was the good person who helped the man.

The lesson is to love others without judging them. Do not love only people who are like you. Help those who need help, regardless of their social status.

WALTER PAYTON
Running Back, 1975-87

WALTER PAYTON

Running Back, Chicago Bears
Height: 5'10" Weight: 202 lbs.
Born: 7/25/54, Columbia, MS; Died: 11/1/99

JOHN IACONO

- In 1987, Payton retired as the leading rusher in NFL history (16,726 yards) and the career record holder for combined net yards (21,803). He rushed for at least 1,200 yards 10 times in his 13-season career.
- Payton was named NFL MVP in 1977. He rushed for 275 yards in a game against the Minnesota Vikings that season, setting an NFL record that stood for 23 years.

What was Payton's nickname?

Answer: Sweetness

Career Totals	Games	Att	Yds	TD
13 Seasons	190	3,838	16,726	110

CARD #219
WALTER IOOSS, JR.

Mary and Martha

10 ³⁸While Jesus and his followers were traveling, Jesus went into a town. A woman named Martha let Jesus stay at her house. ³⁹Martha had a sister named Mary. Mary was sitting at Jesus' feet and listening to him teach. ⁴⁰Martha became angry because she had so much work to do. She went in and said, "Lord, don't you care that my sister has left me alone to do all the work? Tell her to help me!"

⁴¹But the Lord answered her, "Martha, Martha, you are getting worried and upset about too many things. ⁴²Only one thing is important. Mary has chosen the right thing, and it will never be taken away from her."

Painting by H. Semiradsky

QUOTING JESUS

The Lord's Prayer

Jesus Teaches About Prayer

11 One time Jesus was praying in a place. When he finished, one of his followers said to him, "John taught his followers how to pray. Lord, please teach us how to pray, too."

²Jesus said to them, "When you pray, say:
'Father, we pray that your name will always be kept holy.
We pray that your kingdom will come.
³Give us the food we need for each day.
⁴Forgive us the sins we have done,
because we forgive every person who has done wrong to us.
And do not cause us to be tested.' "

Painting by J.J. Tissot

Priorities

Martha was caught up in the work of having dinner guests. She let the work consume her, while Mary focused her attention on spending time with Jesus. Housework and cooking are not bad things, but Martha paid more attention to them than she did to Jesus. This story is like the lesson in Deuteronomy 4:29: "You will find [God] if you look. But you must look for him with your whole being."

Prayer

The Lord's Prayer is the model Jesus gave to teach his followers how to pray. It has six elements:

First, we should address God as Father, which shows intimacy and respect.

Then, Jesus said to pray for God's name to be kept holy and for his kingdom to come. These two requests honor God.

The last three concern the one praying. The request for food addresses the daily needs of living. Next is the need for daily forgiveness from God. Last is the request to be shielded from temptation. God does not tempt his children, but he will protect them from it.

252

■MATTHEW MARK LUKE JOHN ■ACTS ROMANS 1 CORINTHIANS 2 CORINTHIANS GALATIANS EPHESIANS PHILIPPIANS COLOSSIANS 1 THESSALONIANS

The Lost Things

Luke 15:1-32

Crowds of people gathered around Jesus to hear him teach about God's kingdom. He often taught by telling stories that were in settings with which the people could identify. The stories about lost things taught how much God loves his children.

Behind the Stories

These stories are found only in Luke's Gospel. Jesus told them to explain why he associated with tax collectors and other undesirable people. All three tell about something being lost and the absolute joy when the lost item was found.

In the story of the one lost sheep, Jesus compares the joy of the shepherd at finding that one lost sheep with the celebration in heaven when just one sinner comes to Jesus. Jesus talked with the tax collectors and outcasts of society in the hope that even just one of them would come to understand the kingdom of heaven.

The lost coin was equal to a whole day's wages for a common worker. The point is that every person is important and valuable to Jesus.

A Lost Sheep and a Lost Coin

15 Many tax collectors and "sinners" came to listen to Jesus. ²The Pharisees and the teachers of the law began to complain: "Look! This man welcomes sinners and even eats with them!"

³Then Jesus told them this story: ⁴"Suppose one of you has 100 sheep, but he loses 1 of them. Then he will leave the other 99 sheep alone and go out and look for the lost sheep. The man will keep on searching for the lost sheep until he finds it. ⁵And when he finds it, the man is very happy. He puts it on his shoulders ⁶and goes home. He calls to his friends and neighbors and says, 'Be happy with me because I found my lost sheep!' ⁷In the same way, I tell you there is much joy in heaven when 1 sinner changes his heart. There is more joy for that 1 sinner than there is for 99 good people who don't need to change.

⁸"Suppose a woman has ten silver coins, but she loses one of them. She will light a lamp and clean the house. She will look carefully for the coin until she finds it. ⁹And when she finds it, she will call her friends and neighbors and say, 'Be happy with me because I have found the coin that I lost!' ¹⁰In the same way, there is joy before the angels of God when 1 sinner changes his heart."

The Son Who Left Home

¹¹Then Jesus said, "A man had two sons. ¹²The younger son said to his father, 'Give me my share of the property.' So the father divided the property between his two sons. ¹³Then the younger son gathered up all that was his and left. He traveled far away to another country. There

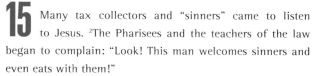

253

2 THESSALONIANS 1 TIMOTHY 2 TIMOTHY TITUS PHILEMON HEBREWS JAMES 1 PETER 2 PETER 1 JOHN 2 JOHN 3 JOHN JUDE REVELATION

he wasted his money in foolish living. ¹⁴He spent everything that he had. Soon after that, the land became very dry, and there was no rain. There was not enough food to eat anywhere in the country. The son was hungry and needed money. ¹⁵So he got a job with one of the citizens there. The man sent the son into the fields to feed pigs. ¹⁶The son was so hungry that he was willing to eat the food the pigs were eating. But no one gave him anything. ¹⁷The son realized that he had been very foolish. He thought, 'All of my father's servants have plenty of food. But I am here, almost dying with hunger. ¹⁸I will leave and return to my father. I'll say to him: Father, I have sinned against God and against you. ¹⁹I am not good enough to be called your son. But let me be like one of your servants.' ²⁰So the son left and went to his father.

Painting by B.E. Murillo

The Son Returns

"While the son was still a long way off, his father saw him coming. He felt sorry for his son. So the father ran to him, and hugged and kissed him. ²¹The son said, 'Father, I have sinned against God and against you. I am not good enough to be called your son.' ²²But the father said to his servants, 'Hurry! Bring the best clothes and put them on him. Also, put a ring on his finger and sandals on his feet. ²³And get our fat calf and kill it. Then we can have a feast and celebrate! ²⁴My son was dead, but now he is alive again! He was lost, but now he is found!' So they began to celebrate.

²⁵"The older son was in the field. As he came closer to the house, he heard the sound of music and dancing. ²⁶So he called to one of the servants and asked, 'What does all this mean?' ²⁷The servant said, 'Your brother has come back. Your father killed the fat calf to eat because your brother came home safely!' ²⁸The older son was angry and would not go in to the feast. So his father went out and begged him to come in. ²⁹The son said to his father, 'I have served you like a slave for many years! I have always obeyed your commands. But you never even killed a young goat for me to have a feast with my friends. ³⁰But your other son has wasted all your money on prostitutes. Then he comes home, and you kill the fat calf for him!' ³¹The father said to him, 'Son, you are always with me. All that I have is yours. ³²We had to celebrate and be happy because your brother was dead, but now he is alive. He was lost, but now he is found.' "

The Prodigal Son

The story of the lost son had a strong message for the Pharisees who were listening to Jesus. The contrast between the younger and older son is important. The Pharisees were like the older son who stayed home and kept all the rules. The younger son was like the sinners who were throwing their lives away—but Jesus spent time with them and forgave them, just as the father in the story did.

When the son came home, the father ran to him and hugged and kissed him, before the boy even had a chance to apologize. He threw a big party and celebrated that his lost son had come home.

This is a picture of the joy in heaven when just one person comes to know God.

The father begged his older son to celebrate, too, but he complained that he had never had a party. He obeyed his father, but only out of obligation. He didn't really love him or have a relationship with him. This is a picture of the Pharisees and the way they viewed God.

THE GOSPELS

Going to and Staying at Jerusalem

Behind the Story

Mary and Martha sent for Jesus as soon as their brother got sick (John 11:3).

Jesus loved Martha, Mary and Lazarus (11:5).

The system of burial was much different from today. The body of the dead person was placed in a cave, covered with spices and perfumes. A stone was rolled in front of the cave opening, and the body was left to decay. Eventually, the bones were put in a small jar on a shelf in the cave. That way, one cave could be used for burying an entire family.

Why did Jesus cry? He knew he was going to bring Lazarus back to life. He cried for the pain his friends had been through. He cried because of the unbelief of the people who did not trust him.

Jesus Brings Lazarus Back to Life

John 11:28-44

Jesus had visited the home of Mary, Martha and their brother, Lazarus. They were his friends, and he cared about them very much. When Lazarus got sick, Jesus could have come and healed him. But he let Lazarus die, and then Jesus taught an amazing lesson.

Painting by William Hole

Jesus Cries

11 28 After Martha said this, she went back to her sister Mary. She talked to Mary alone. Martha said, "The Teacher is here and he is asking for you." 29 When Mary heard this, she got up quickly and went to Jesus. 30 Jesus had not yet come into the town. He was still at the place where Martha had met him. 31 The Jews were with Mary in the house, comforting her. They saw Mary stand and leave quickly. They followed her, thinking that she was going to the tomb to cry there. 32 But Mary went to the place where Jesus was. When she saw him, she fell at his feet and said, "Lord, if you had been here, my brother would not have died."

33 Jesus saw that Mary was crying and that the Jews who came with her were crying, too. Jesus felt very sad in his heart and was deeply troubled. 34 He asked, "Where did you bury him?"

"Come and see, Lord," they said.

35 Jesus cried.

36 So the Jews said, "See how much he loved him."

37 But some of them said, "If Jesus healed the eyes of the blind man, why didn't he keep Lazarus from dying?"

Jesus Raises Lazarus

38 Again Jesus felt very sad in his heart. He came to the tomb. The tomb was a cave with a large stone covering the entrance. 39 Jesus said, "Move the stone away."

Martha said, "But, Lord, it has been four days since he died.

255

2 THESSALONIANS 1 TIMOTHY 2 TIMOTHY TITUS PHILEMON HEBREWS JAMES 1 PETER 2 PETER 1 JOHN 2 JOHN 3 JOHN JUDE REVELATION

Seeing Jesus

Jesus used Lazarus's death to teach people to trust him because he has power over death. He said, "I am the resurrection and the life. He who believes in me will . . . never die" (John 11:25-26). All who believe will be alive in heaven, even though they die on this earth.

There will be a bad smell." Martha was the sister of the dead man.

⁴⁰Then Jesus said to her, "Didn't I tell you that if you believed, you would see the glory of God?"

⁴¹So they moved the stone away from the entrance. Then Jesus looked up and said, "Father, I thank you that you heard me. ⁴²I know that you always hear me. But I said these things because of the people here around me. I want them to believe that you sent me." ⁴³After Jesus said this, he cried out in a loud voice, "Lazarus, come out!" ⁴⁴The dead man came out. His hands and feet were wrapped with pieces of cloth, and he had a cloth around his face.

Zacchaeus

Luke 19:1-10

19 Jesus was going through the city of Jericho. ²In Jericho there was a man named Zacchaeus. He was a wealthy, very important tax collector. ³He wanted to see who Jesus was, but he was too short to see above the crowd. ⁴He ran ahead to a place where he knew Jesus would come. He climbed a sycamore tree so he could see Jesus. ⁵When Jesus came to that place, he looked up and saw Zacchaeus in the tree. He said to him, "Zacchaeus, hurry and come down! I must stay at your house today."

⁶Zacchaeus came down quickly. He was pleased to have Jesus in his house. ⁷All the people saw this and began to complain, "Look at the kind of man Jesus stays with. Zacchaeus is a sinner!"

⁸But Zacchaeus said to the Lord, "I will give half of my money to the poor. If I have cheated anyone, I will pay that person back four times more!"

⁹Jesus said, "Salvation has come to this house today. This man truly belongs to the family of Abraham. ¹⁰The Son of Man came to find lost people and save them."

Think About This

Zacchaeus was the chief tax collector. That means he was like a boss of the tax collectors. He was hated by the people because he charged them more taxes than they owed; then he kept money for himself. The crowd was not happy that Jesus was going to Zacchaeus's house.

Jesus knew Zacchaeus's name. He called him by name to get him to come down from the tree.

After talking with Jesus, Zacchaeus decided not to cheat people anymore. In fact, he said he would pay back four times more than he had stolen. This was much more than the Law required for robbers to repay.

Jesus' experience with Zacchaeus was an example of his purpose in coming to earth—to find and save lost people, just as the stories of the lost coin, lost sheep and lost son had taught (see Luke 15:1-32).

256

MATTHEW MARK LUKE JOHN ACTS ROMANS 1 CORINTHIANS 2 CORINTHIANS GALATIANS EPHESIANS PHILIPPIANS COLOSSIANS 1 THESSALONIANS

THE GOSPELS

Going to and Staying at Jerusalem

A Woman with Perfume for Jesus

Mark 14:3-9

Jesus was a guest at the home of Simon. A young woman came into Simon's house and poured perfume on Jesus' feet. She did this to show how much she loved him. This happened about a week before Jesus died.

Words You Should Know

Alabastar (AL-a-bas-ter)
A light-colored stone with streaks or stripes through it. Perfume was often kept in beautiful containers made of alabaster (see Matthew 26:7; Luke 7:37-38).

Nard (nar-d)
An expensive perfume. It cost so much because it had to be imported from India (see Song of Songs 4:13; John 12:3).

Behind the Story

It is believed that the woman who anointed Jesus in this story was Mary, the sister of Martha and Lazarus. She understood what the apostles did not—that Jesus would soon die. She was preparing his body for death and burial.

Judas was the loudest critic of the woman pouring the expensive perfume on Jesus' feet (see John 12:4-6).

14 ³Jesus was in Bethany. He was at dinner in the house of Simon, who had a harmful skin disease. While Jesus was there, a woman came to him. She had an alabaster jar filled with very expensive perfume, made of pure nard. The woman opened the jar and poured the perfume on Jesus' head.

⁴Some of those who were there saw this and became angry. They complained to each other, saying, "Why waste that perfume? ⁵It was worth a full year's work. It could be sold, and the money could be given to the poor." They spoke to the woman sharply.

Painting by J.J. Tissot

Loving Jesus

It is impossible to actually repay Jesus for his great sacrifice of dying for our sins. There is nothing we can give him, except our love and obedience. Jesus' death made it possible for us to know God personally and be able to talk with him and read his Word. The only way to thank Jesus is to love and obey him completely.

⁶Jesus said, "Don't bother the woman. Why are you troubling her? She did a beautiful thing for me. ⁷You will always have the poor with you. You can help them anytime you want. But you will not always have me. ⁸This woman did the only thing she could do for me. She poured perfume on my body. She did this before I die to prepare me for burial. ⁹I tell you the truth. The Good News will be told to people in all the world. And in every place it is preached, what this woman has done will be told. And people will remember her."

Palm Sunday

Luke 19:28-40

Jesus went to Jerusalem for what would be the last week of his life on earth. Much of what he did during that week showed evidence that he was the Messiah. This was the first time Jesus allowed himself to be publicly called Messiah.

Jesus Enters Jerusalem as a King

19 [28]After Jesus said this, he went on toward Jerusalem. [29]Jesus came near Bethphage and Bethany, towns near the hill called the Mount of Olives. Then he sent out two of his followers. [30]He said, "Go into the town you can see there. When you enter it, you will find a colt tied there. No one has ever ridden this colt. Untie it, and bring it here to me. [31]If anyone asks you why you are taking it, say, 'The Master needs it.' "

[32]The two followers went into town. They found the colt just as Jesus told them. [33]The followers untied it, but the owners of the colt came out. They asked the followers, "Why are you untying our colt?"

[34]The followers answered, "The Master needs it." [35]So they brought it to Jesus. They threw their coats on the colt's back and put Jesus on it. [36]As Jesus rode toward Jerusalem, the followers spread their coats on the road before him.

[37]Jesus was coming close to Jerusalem. He was already near the bottom of the Mount of Olives. The whole crowd of followers was very happy. They began shouting praise to God for all the powerful works they had seen. They said,

[38]"God bless the king who comes in the name of the Lord!
   There is peace in heaven and glory to God!"

Psalm 118:26

[39]Some of the Pharisees said to Jesus, "Teacher, tell your followers not to say these things!"

[40]But Jesus answered, "I tell you, if my followers don't say these things, then the stones will cry out."

Think About This

When Jesus rode into the city on a donkey, he was fulfilling the prophecy of Zechariah 9:9 that the Messiah would enter Jerusalem that way.

Jesus was coming to Jerusalem to celebrate Passover and the Feast of Unleavened Bread. These two celebrations recalled when God saved the people.

The actions of the crowd to spread their coats on the road in front of Jesus was a sign of respect for him. Apparently, they understood the significance of the prophecy he was fulfilling. He was the Messiah they had been waiting for.

The Pharisees also understood the significance of Jesus doing what the prophets had said. That's why they told him to make the crowds stop praising him.

258

MATTHEW MARK LUKE JOHN ACTS ROMANS 1 CORINTHIANS 2 CORINTHIANS GALATIANS EPHESIANS PHILIPPIANS COLOSSIANS 1 THESSALONIANS

THE GOSPELS

Going to and Staying at Jerusalem

Behind the Story

This is one of the stories Jesus told to remind his followers that one day they would have to answer to God—for how they spent their time, how they used the gifts God gave them and how well they shared God's love with others.

God gives all people abilities and talents. He expects them to use these gifts to share his love with others and build his kingdom on earth.

Each person is responsible only for himself and will answer to God for how he has served him and used the abilities God has given him.

The master gave the servants plenty of time to do good things with the money he gave them. He was gone for quite a while.

A Story About Three Servants

Matthew 25:14-29

Jesus taught this lesson in the Temple, but later his apostles asked him to explain it. His message concerns when the kingdom of God comes and how well prepared God's servants should be.

25 [14]"The kingdom of heaven is like a man who was going to another place for a visit. Before he left, he talked with his servants. The man told them to take care of his things while he was gone. [15]He decided how much each servant would be able to care for. He gave one servant five bags of money. He gave another servant two bags of money. And he gave a third servant one bag of money. Then the man left. [16]The servant who got five bags went quickly to invest the money. The five bags of money earned five more. [17]It was the same with the servant who had two bags of money. He invested the money and earned two more. [18]But the servant who got one bag of money went out and dug a hole in the ground. Then he hid his master's money in the hole.

[19]"After a long time the master came home. He asked the servants what they did with his money. [20]The servant who got five bags of money brought five more bags to the master. The servant said, 'Master, you trusted me to care for five bags of money. So I used your five bags to earn five more.' [21]The master answered, 'You did well. You are a good servant who can be trusted. You did well with small things. So I will let you care for much greater things. Come and share my happiness with me.'

Be Prepared

The Bible teaches that no one knows when Jesus will come back and take all his followers to heaven, to be part of God's kingdom. Therefore, we should always be serving and obeying him so we will be ready for his return.

[22]"Then the servant who got two bags of money came to the master. The servant said, 'Master, you gave me two bags of money to care for. So I used your two bags to earn two more.' [23]The master answered, 'You did well. You are a good servant who can be trusted. You did well with small things. So I will let you care for much greater things. Come and share my happiness with me.'

[24]"Then the servant who got one bag of money came to the master. The servant said, 'Master, I knew that you were a hard man. You harvest things you did not plant. You gather crops where you did not sow any seed. [25]So I was afraid. I went and hid your money in the ground. Here is the bag of money you gave me.' [26]The master answered, 'You are a bad and lazy servant! You say you knew that I harvest things I did not plant, and that I gather crops where I did not sow any seed? [27]So you should have put my money in the bank. Then, when I came home, I would get my money back with interest.'

[28]"So the master told his other servants, 'Take the bag of money from that servant and give it to the servant who has ten bags of money. [29]Everyone who uses what he has will get more. He will have much more than he needs. But the one who does not use what he has will have everything taken away from him.'"

QUOTING JESUS

The Great Commandment

"The most important command is this: 'Listen, people of Israel! The Lord our God, he is the only Lord. Love the Lord your God. Love him with all your heart, all your soul, all your mind, and all your strength.' The second most important command is this: 'Love your neighbor as you love yourself.' These two commands are the most important commands."

—Mark 12:29-31

Think About This

The first two servants were rewarded for investing the money and earning more. This is an example of God's pleasure when people use their talents and gifts to tell others about his love and encourage them to know God better.

The third servant just hid the money his master gave him. This is an example of someone who uses his talents and abilities only for himself, such as to make money but not to do things for God.

The first two servants were given more responsibility and were honored by their master. The third servant was thrown out of the master's service. This is an example of a person who does not really know God in his heart and, therefore, does not serve him. That person will be sent from God's presence and will not be able to enter heaven.

The great commandment Jesus gave in Mark 12:29-31 gives a simple explanation of how to please God.

260

MATTHEW MARK LUKE JOHN ACTS ROMANS 1 CORINTHIANS 2 CORINTHIANS GALATIANS EPHESIANS PHILIPPIANS COLOSSIANS 1 THESSALONIANS

THE GOSPELS

Going to and Staying at Jerusalem

Foot Washing

John 13:1-20

Behind the Story

People traveled from town to town or house to house, along dusty roads, wearing only sandals. The custom was that when a guest entered a home, one of the servants would wash the dust from that person's feet. A person bathed before attending a party or a feast, then needed only his feet washed to be considered clean again. It is important to note that this was usually the job of the lowliest servant—not something Jesus would have been expected to do.

Jesus knew the time was near for him to leave this world and return to heaven. He loved his followers so much that he gave them an example of real humility and service to one another.

Jesus knew that Judas was going to betray him, although it was Judas's own choice to do so. Even knowing what Judas was planning to do, Jesus still chose to wash Judas's feet.

The time of Jesus' arrest and death was drawing close. The events of this story happened on the very night that Jesus was arrested. He had an important lesson to teach them about serving one another.

Jesus Washes His Followers' Feet

13 It was almost time for the Jewish Passover Feast. Jesus knew that it was time for him to leave this world and go back to the Father. He had always loved those who were his own in the world, and he loved them all the way to the end.

²Jesus and his followers were at the evening meal. The devil had already persuaded Judas Iscariot to turn against Jesus. (Judas was the son of Simon.) ³Jesus knew that the Father had given him power over everything. He also knew that he had come from God and was going back to God. ⁴So during the meal Jesus stood up and took off his outer clothing. Taking a towel, he wrapped it around his waist. ⁵Then he poured water into a bowl and began to wash the followers' feet. He dried them with the towel that was wrapped around him.

⁶Jesus came to Simon Peter. But Peter said to Jesus, "Lord, are you going to wash my feet?"

⁷Jesus answered, "You don't understand what I am doing now. But you will understand later."

⁸Peter said, "No! You will never wash my feet."

Jesus answered, "If I don't wash your feet, then you are not one of my people."

⁹Simon Peter answered, "Lord, after you wash my feet, wash my hands and my head, too!"

¹⁰Jesus said, "After a person has had a bath, his whole body is clean. He needs only to wash his feet. And you men are clean, but not all of you." ¹¹Jesus knew who would turn against him. That is why Jesus said, "Not all of you are clean."

¹²When he had finished washing their feet, he put on his clothes and sat down again.

TAKING IT TO HEART

A SERVANT LEADER

Jesus really wanted his followers (and all who read this story) to understand that a real leader is one who serves others. No job is too lowly, no person too undesirable to be served. A true follower of Jesus will follow his example of serving others. The strength to do this comes from staying close to him by reading his Word and praying.

Jesus asked, "Do you understand what I have just done for you? [13]You call me 'Teacher' and 'Lord.' And this is right, because that is what I am. [14]I, your Lord and Teacher, have washed your feet. So you also should wash each other's feet. [15]I did this as an example for you. So you should do as I have done for you. [16]I tell you the truth. A servant is not greater than his master. A messenger is not greater than the one who sent him.

[17]If you know these things, you will be happy if you do them.

[18]"I am not talking about all of you. I know those I have chosen. But what the Scripture said must happen: 'The man who ate at my table has now turned against me.' [19]I am telling you this now before it happens. Then when it happens you will believe that I am he. [20]I tell you the truth. Whoever accepts anyone I send also accepts me. And whoever accepts me also accepts the One who sent me."

QUOTING JESUS

The Vine and the Branches

"I am the true vine; my Father is the gardener. He cuts off every branch of mine that does not produce fruit. And he trims and cleans every branch that produces fruit so that it will produce even more fruit. You are already clean because of the words I have spoken to you. Remain in me, and I will remain in you. No branch can produce fruit alone. It must remain in the vine. It is the same with you. You cannot produce fruit alone. You must remain in me.

"I am the vine, and you are the branches. If a person remains in me and I remain in him, then he produces much fruit. But without me he can do nothing."

—John 15:1-5

Think About This

This foot washing was a symbol of the spiritual cleansing that happens when a person accepts Jesus and confesses his sins, which are then washed away. Once a person does this, he is made clean. Then he only needs cleansing by confessing his sins and asking forgiveness for them on a daily basis.

Peter complained about Jesus doing the work of a servant, but he didn't offer to take Jesus' place. This action of Jesus taught humility—which meant not to consider yourself better than anyone else or too good to serve another person.

Jesus' actions here silenced his followers arguments about which of them would be the greatest in heaven (see Luke 9:46-48).

Jesus quoted Psalm 41:9 in John 13:18, referring to Judas who had been with him for his entire ministry, but still did not believe in him.

262

MATTHEW MARK LUKE JOHN ACTS ROMANS 1 CORINTHIANS 2 CORINTHIANS GALATIANS EPHESIANS PHILIPPIANS COLOSSIANS 1 THESSALONIANS

THE GOSPELS

Going to and Staying at Jerusalem

The Last Supper

Matthew 26:17-25; Mark 14:22-31

This was the last meal Jesus shared with his followers. Afterward, he was arrested.

Words You Should Know

Feast of Unleavened Bread (Feest of Un-lev-end Bred)
Also called Passover. It was held to remember how God helped the Israelites in Egypt. He saved them from the one who brought death that passed over their families. And God led them out of slavery. For seven days they ate bread made without yeast and did only certain types of work (see Exodus 12:14-20; Numbers 28:16-25; Deuteronomy 16:1-8).

Mount of Olives (Mount of Ol-ivs)
A hill covered with olive trees near Jerusalem. The Garden of Gethsemane is on one side of the Mount of Olives. Jesus was praying there when the Roman soldiers came to arrest him. Some of the same olive trees that were in the garden when Jesus was on earth may still be there today (see 2 Samuel 15:30; Luke 22:39-53; Acts 1:12).

Jesus Eats the Passover Feast

26 ¹⁷On the first day of the Feast of Unleavened Bread, the followers came to Jesus. They said, "We will prepare everything for you to eat the Passover Feast. Where do you want to have the feast?"

¹⁸Jesus answered, "Go into the city to a certain man. Tell him that the Teacher says, 'The chosen time is near. I will have the Passover Feast with my followers at your house.'" ¹⁹The followers did what Jesus told them to do, and they prepared the Passover Feast.

²⁰In the evening Jesus was sitting at the table with his 12 followers. ²¹They were all eating. Then Jesus said, "I tell you the truth. One of you 12 will turn against me."

²²This made the followers very sad. Each one said to Jesus, "Surely, Lord, I am not the one who will turn against you. Am I?"

²³Jesus answered, "The man who has dipped his hand with me into the bowl is the one who will turn against me. ²⁴The Son of Man will die. The Scriptures say this will happen. But how terrible it will be for the person who gives the Son of Man to be killed. It would be better for him if he had never been born."

²⁵Then Judas said to Jesus, "Teacher, surely I am not the one. Am I?" (Judas is the one who would give Jesus to his enemies.)

Jesus answered, "Yes, it is you."

263

2 THESSALONIANS 1 TIMOTHY 2 TIMOTHY TITUS PHILEMON HEBREWS JAMES 1 PETER 2 PETER 1 JOHN 2 JOHN 3 JOHN JUDE REVELATION

The Lord's Supper

14 ²²While they were eating, Jesus took some bread. He thanked God for it and broke it. Then he gave it to his followers and said, "Take it. This bread is my body."

²³Then Jesus took a cup. He thanked God for it and gave it to the followers. All the followers drank from the cup.

²⁴Then Jesus said, "This is my blood which begins the new agreement that God makes with his people. This blood is poured out for many. ²⁵I tell you the truth. I will not drink of this fruit of the vine again until that day when I drink it new in the kingdom of God."

²⁶They sang a hymn and went out to the Mount of Olives.

Jesus' Followers Will All Leave Him

²⁷Then Jesus told the followers, "You will all lose your faith in me. It is written in the Scriptures:

'I will kill the shepherd,

and the sheep will scatter.'

Zechariah 13:7

²⁸But after I rise from death, I will go ahead of you into Galilee."

²⁹Peter said, "All the other followers may lose their faith. But I will not."

³⁰Jesus answered, "I tell you the truth. Tonight you will say you don't know me. You will say this three times before the rooster crows twice."

Mount of Olives

³¹But Peter answered strongly, "I will never say that I don't know you! I will even die with you!" And all the other followers said the same thing.

Think About This

In Mark 14:22-24, Jesus instituted the Lord's Supper or Communion, which Christian churches observe today. Read more about it in Matthew 26:26-29 and Luke 22:14-20. The Lord's Supper is a time when Christians remember Christ's sacrifice for them.

Jesus predicted that all of his close friends would desert him when he was arrested, in order to avoid being arrested themselves. Peter boldly claimed that he would never lose his faith. Mark is the only Gospel that tells us Peter would deny he knew Jesus three times, before the rooster crowed twice. Peter's claims indicate that he thought he was stronger than the others. Jesus' prediction caused Peter once again to claim that he would never deny Jesus. The words Peter used, as recorded in the Greek, are found only in this place in the New Testament. Peter was certain that he would never deny Jesus.

Even though Jesus knew his friends would deny him, he promised that he would be with them again after his death (Mark 14:28).

264

MATTHEW MARK LUKE JOHN ACTS ROMANS 1 CORINTHIANS 2 CORINTHIANS GALATIANS EPHESIANS PHILIPPIANS COLOSSIANS 1 THESSALONIANS

THE GOSPELS

Going to and Staying at Jerusalem

Garden of Gethsemane

Mark 14:32-50

From the room where they ate their last meal together, Jesus and his followers went to a garden to pray. Jesus knew that he was about to be arrested and killed. His followers did not understand what was going to happen.

Words You Should Know

Gethsemane

(geth-SEM-uh-nee)
A garden of olive trees just outside Jerusalem. It was at the bottom of the Mount of Olives. The night before Jesus was killed, he prayed in this garden. Jesus was there when Judas brought the soldiers to arrest him (see Matthew 26:36-50).

Abba (AB-uh)

A child's word for "father" in the Aramaic language. Early Christians used this word in speaking to God. This shows how close we can feel to him (see Romans 8:15; Galatians 4:6).

Behind the Story

Jesus wanted his closest friends with him (Mark 14:33) to support him and pray with him, just as we need friends to support and encourage us. He told them how upset he was, hoping they would understand and also pray while he prayed. However, all three of them fell asleep.

Jesus Prays Alone

14 32Jesus and his followers went to a place called Gethsemane. He said to his followers, "Sit here while I pray." 33Jesus told Peter, James, and John to come with him. Then Jesus began to be very sad and troubled. 34He said to them, "I am full of sorrow. My heart is breaking with sadness. Stay here and watch."

35Jesus walked a little farther away from them. Then he fell on the ground and prayed. He prayed that, if possible, he would not have this time of suffering. 36He prayed, "Abba, Father! You can do all things. Let me not have this cup of suffering. But do what you want, not what I want."

37Then Jesus went back to his followers. He found them asleep. He said to Peter, "Simon, why are you sleeping? You could not stay awake with me for one hour? 38Stay awake and pray that you will not be tempted. Your spirit wants to do what is right, but your body is weak."

³⁹Again Jesus went away and prayed the same thing. ⁴⁰Then he went back to the followers. Again he found them asleep because their eyes were very heavy. And they did not know what to say to Jesus.

⁴¹After Jesus prayed a third time, he went back to his followers. He said to them, "You are still sleeping and resting? That's enough! The time has come for the Son of Man to be given to sinful people. ⁴²Get up! We must go. Here comes the man who has turned against me."

The Garden of Gethsemane

Jesus Is Arrested

⁴³While Jesus was still speaking, Judas came up. Judas was 1 of the 12 followers. He had many people with him. They were sent from the leading priests, the teachers of the law, and the Jewish elders. Those with Judas had swords and clubs.

⁴⁴Judas had planned a signal for them. He had said, "The man I kiss is Jesus. Arrest him and guard him while you lead him away." ⁴⁵So Judas went to Jesus and said, "Teacher!" and kissed him. ⁴⁶Then the men grabbed Jesus and arrested him. ⁴⁷One of the followers standing near drew his sword. He struck the servant of the high priest with the sword and cut off his ear.

⁴⁸Then Jesus said, "You came to get me with swords and clubs as if I were a criminal. ⁴⁹Every day I was with you teaching in the Temple. You did not arrest me there. But all these things have happened to make the Scriptures come true." ⁵⁰Then all of Jesus' followers left him and ran away.

Think About This

Jesus' prayer in Mark 14:36 was not a request to stop his arrest and death, but an acknowledgement that he would be separated from God as he bore the sins of the whole world on his shoulders. Still, he was willing to go through with the plan because of his love for God and his love for all mankind.

Judas came to the garden with about 600 men. He showed them which man was Jesus by kissing him.

John 18:10 tells us that Peter used a sword to cut off a man's ear. Luke adds that Jesus healed the man's ear (Luke 22:51).

Jesus did not resist being arrested. But he did point out that they could have arrested him any time, even in the Temple. However, the church leaders knew that arresting Jesus in a crowd might cause a riot.

Just as Jesus had predicted, every one of his followers ran away when things got tough.

THE GOSPELS

Crucifixion,
Resurrection
and Ascension

Peter's Denial and the Trial

Mark 14:66–15:20

St. Peter by W.H. Hunt

They took Jesus to the Sanhedrin—the Jewish court. Peter followed and stayed in the Temple courtyard outside the place where Jesus was.

Words You Should Know

The Sanhedrin

Made up of the high priest, chief priests and scribes (experts who knew God's Law). It was supposed to carry out justice. Jesus' trial was held during the night so that, once they found him guilty, they could turn him over to the Roman courts to be killed. Jewish courts had lost the authority to give death sentences.

Barabbas (bah-RAB-us)

"Son of a father." He was a robber who had murdered someone in Jerusalem. He was in jail when Jesus was on trial. It was the time of year when a criminal would be freed from prison. The people cried out to have Barabbas freed and Jesus killed on the cross. Pilate, the Roman governor, did as they demanded (see Matthew 27:16-26).

Model of the Temple with Its Courts

Peter Says He Doesn't Know Jesus

14 [66]Peter was still in the courtyard when a servant girl of the high priest came there. [67]She saw Peter warming himself at the fire. She looked closely at him.

Then the girl said, "You were with Jesus, that man from Nazareth."

[68]But Peter said that he was never with Jesus. He said, "I don't know or understand what you are talking about." Then Peter left and went toward the entrance of the courtyard.

[69]The servant girl saw Peter there. Again she said to the people who were standing there, "This man is one of those who followed Jesus." [70]Again Peter said that it was not true.

A short time later, some people were standing near Peter. They said, "We know you are one of those who followed Jesus. You are from Galilee, too."

[71]Then Peter began to curse. He said, "I swear that I don't know this man you're talking about!"

[72]As soon as Peter said this, the rooster crowed the second time. Then Peter remembered what Jesus had told him: "Before the rooster crows twice, you will say three times that you don't know me." Then Peter was very sad and began to cry.

Pilate Questions Jesus

15 Very early in the morning, the leading priests, the Jewish elders, the teachers of the law, and all the Jewish council decided what to do with Jesus. They tied him, led him away, and turned him over to Pilate, the governor.

[2]Pilate asked Jesus, "Are you the king of the Jews?"

267

2 THESSALONIANS 1 TIMOTHY 2 TIMOTHY TITUS PHILEMON HEBREWS JAMES 1 PETER 2 PETER 1 JOHN 2 JOHN 3 JOHN JUDE REVELATION

Jesus answered, "Yes, I am."

[3]The leading priests accused Jesus of many things. [4]So Pilate asked Jesus another question. He said, "You can see that these people are accusing you of many things. Why don't you answer?"

[5]But Jesus still said nothing. Pilate was very surprised at this.

Pilate Tries to Free Jesus

[6]Every year at the Passover time the governor would free one person from prison. He would free any person the people wanted him to free. [7]At that time, there was a man named Barabbas in prison. He was a rebel and had committed murder during a riot. [8]The crowd came to Pilate and asked him to free a prisoner as he always did.

[9]Pilate asked them, "Do you want me to free the king of the Jews?" [10]Pilate knew that the leading priests had given Jesus to him because they were jealous of Jesus. [11]And the leading priests had persuaded the people to ask Pilate to free Barabbas, not Jesus.

[12]Pilate asked the crowd again, "So what should I do with this man you call the king of the Jews?"

[13]They shouted, "Kill him on a cross!"

[14]Pilate asked, "Why? What wrong has he done?"

But they shouted louder and louder, "Kill him on a cross!"

[15]Pilate wanted to please the crowd. So he freed Barabbas for them. And Pilate told the soldiers to beat Jesus with whips. Then he gave Jesus to the soldiers to be killed on a cross.

[16]Pilate's soldiers took Jesus into the governor's palace (called the Praetorium). They called all the other soldiers together. [17]They put a purple robe on Jesus. Then they used thorny branches to make a crown. They put it on his head. [18]Then they called out to him, "Hail, King of the Jews!" [19]The soldiers beat Jesus on the head many times with a stick. They also spit on him. Then they made fun of him by bowing on their knees and worshiping him. [20]After they finished making fun of him, the soldiers took off the purple robe and put his own clothes on him again. Then they led Jesus out of the palace to be killed on a cross.

Think About This

Peter was identified as being from Galilee by the way he spoke.

Out of fear for his own life, he emphatically denied any association with Jesus three times—just as Jesus said he would.

Several "witnesses" testified against Jesus. However, their stories did not match so their testimonies were dismissed.

Jesus was brought to Pilate, the Roman governor, and tried for treason. Pilate did not agree that Jesus was guilty, but the chief priests had agitated the crowd to insist on Jesus' death. Pilate didn't want the crowd angry at him or to risk losing his position, so he freed Barabbas, who had rioted against Rome, and then condemned Jesus to death.

Pilate ordered Jesus beaten, thinking perhaps the crowd would have pity on him and beg for the beating to stop. They did not.

The soldiers dressed Jesus as a king to mock him, because he was called King of the Jews.

268

MATTHEW MARK LUKE JOHN ACTS ROMANS 1 CORINTHIANS 2 CORINTHIANS GALATIANS EPHESIANS PHILIPPIANS COLOSSIANS 1 THESSALONIANS

THE GOSPELS

Crucifixion, Resurrection and Ascension

The Crucifixion

Mark 15:21-47; Matthew 27:62-66

Pilate sentenced Jesus to death by crucifixion, even though he found Jesus not guilty. Crucifixion was one of the cruelest forms of killing a person. However, Jesus' pain was not just physical; it was also spiritual and emotional, as he took the sins of the whole world upon himself.

Jesus Is Killed on a Cross

15 [21]There was a man from Cyrene coming from the fields to the city. The man was Simon, the father of Alexander and Rufus. The soldiers forced Simon to carry the cross for Jesus. [22]They led Jesus to the place called Golgotha. (Golgotha means the Place of the Skull.) [23]At Golgotha the soldiers tried to give Jesus wine to drink. This wine was mixed with myrrh. But he refused to drink it. [24]The soldiers nailed Jesus to a cross. Then they divided his clothes among themselves. They threw lots to decide which clothes each soldier would get.

[25]It was nine o'clock in the morning when they nailed Jesus to the cross. [26]There was a sign with the charge against Jesus written on it. The sign read: "THE KING OF THE JEWS." [27]They also put

Behind the Story

When a man was condemned to death on a cross, he had to carry the crossbeam, which weighed about 100 pounds, to the crucifixion. However, Jesus was so weak from being beaten, the soldiers forced Simon to carry the cross.

Golgotha is often referred to as "Calvary," which comes from the Latin word for skull.

According to tradition, a drink was provided to those about to be killed, which acted as a sedative to dull the pain of their crucifixion. Jesus refused the drink.

two robbers on crosses beside Jesus, one on the right, and the other on the left. [28][And the Scripture came true that says, "They put him with criminals."] [29]People walked by and insulted Jesus. They shook their heads, saying, "You said you could destroy the Temple and build it again in three days. [30]So save yourself! Come down from that cross!"

[31]The leading priests and the teachers of the law were also there. They made fun of Jesus just as the other people did. They said among themselves, "He saved other people, but he can't save himself. [32]If he is really the Christ, the king of Israel, then let him come down from the cross now. We will see this, and then we will believe in him." The robbers who were being killed on the crosses beside Jesus also insulted him.

Jesus Dies

[33]At noon the whole country became dark. This darkness lasted for three hours. [34]At three o'clock Jesus cried in a loud voice, "Eloi, Eloi, lama sabachthani." This means, "My God, my God, why have you left me alone?"

[35]Some of the people standing there heard this. They said, "Listen! He is calling Elijah."

[36]One man there ran and got a sponge. He filled the sponge with vinegar and tied it to a stick. Then he used the stick to give the sponge to Jesus to drink from it. The man said, "We should wait now and see if Elijah will come to take him down from the cross."

[37]Then Jesus cried in a loud voice and died.

[38]When Jesus died, the curtain in the Temple split into two pieces. The tear started at the top and tore all the way to the bottom. [39]The army officer that was standing there before the cross saw what happened when Jesus died. The officer said, "This man really was the Son of God!"

[40]Some women were standing at a distance from the cross, watching. Some of these women were Mary Magdalene, Salome, and Mary the mother of James and Joseph. (James was her youngest son.) [41]These were the women who followed Jesus in Galilee and cared for him. Many other women were also there who had come with Jesus to Jerusalem.

Think About This

When the soldiers threw lots for Jesus' clothing, they didn't know they were fulfilling what had been predicted in Psalm 22:18.

Similarly, when Jesus was crucified between two robbers, that action fulfilled the prophecy of Isaiah 53:12.

Death by crucifixion usually came from exhaustion and thirst. It often took two or three days for the victim to die. Jesus died in about 6 hours.

Luke's version of the Crucifixion tells us that one of the robbers crucified alongside Jesus asked Jesus to remember him when he came into his kingdom. Jesus promised to do so (Luke 23:39-43).

Jesus' words in Mark 15:34 show his agony at being abandoned by God while he bore the sins of the world. God could not look on that sin, so he turned away from Jesus.

The tearing of the Temple veil meant that God was now available to everyone. No longer were sacrifices of animals needed to approach him. The sacrifice of Jesus' life was the final sacrifice needed.

270

MATTHEW MARK LUKE JOHN ACTS ROMANS 1 CORINTHIANS 2 CORINTHIANS GALATIANS EPHESIANS PHILIPPIANS COLOSSIANS 1 THESSALONIANS

THE GOSPELS

Crucifixion, Resurrection and Ascension

Behind the Story

Joseph of Arimathea was courageous to ask to bury Jesus, because he was a member of the Sanhedrin who condemned Jesus to death. By asking to bury Jesus, he was showing that he didn't agree with the rest of the council.

Joseph must have been wealthy to have owned a stone cave to be used as a tomb. He probably believed that it was important for a person to be buried on the same day he died. Also, since the next day was the Sabbath, Jesus could not have been buried then.

Nicodemus helped Joseph prepare the body for burial by putting about 75 pounds of spices and perfumes on it (see John 19:31-42).

The tomb was sealed, probably with the official Roman seal of wax. That way, if anyone had tampered with the tomb or tried to move the stone, it would have been obvious.

Jesus Is Buried

42This was Preparation Day. (That means the day before the Sabbath day.) It was becoming dark. 43A man named Joseph from Arimathea was brave enough to go to Pilate and ask for Jesus' body. Joseph was an important member of the Jewish council. He was one of the people who wanted the kingdom of God to come. 44Pilate wondered if Jesus was already dead. Pilate called the army officer who guarded Jesus and asked him if Jesus had already died. 45The officer told Pilate that he was dead. So Pilate told Joseph he could have the body. 46Joseph bought some linen cloth, took the body down from the cross and wrapped it in the linen. He put the body in a tomb that was cut in a wall of rock. Then he closed the tomb by rolling a very large stone to cover the entrance. 47And Mary Magdalene and Mary the mother of Joseph saw the place where Jesus was laid.

The Tomb of Jesus Is Guarded

27 62That day was the day called Preparation Day. The next day, the leading priests and the Pharisees went to Pilate. 63They said, "Sir, we remember that while that liar was still alive he said, 'After three days I will rise from death.' 64So give the order for the tomb to be guarded closely till the third day. His followers might come and steal the body. Then they could tell the people that he has risen from death. That lie would be even worse than the first one."

65Pilate said, "Take some soldiers and go guard the tomb the best way you know." 66So they all went to the tomb and made it safe from thieves. They did this by sealing the stone in the entrance and then putting soldiers there to guard it.

The Passion of Jesus Christ

Jesus left the glory of heaven and the presence of his Father to come to earth. This was God's plan to make a way possible for people to have a personal relationship with God and someday be in heaven with him.

Jesus was both God and man while he was on earth. He taught how to live for God and how to live with one another. He healed sick people in God's name, and he raised dead people back to life.

Even though he did not sin at all, the church leaders hated him and arranged for his arrest. He was tried and condemned to death by crucifixion—the cruelest form of murder. He was nailed to the cross, where he hung for 6 hours. At the point of his death, the sins of all mankind were laid on him, and God turned his face away from his beloved Son.

Jesus was buried, but on the third day after his death, he came back to life—showing that he forever has victory over death!

All who believe in Jesus, confess their sins and accept him as Lord and Savior can live forever with him in heaven!

272

MATTHEW MARK LUKE JOHN ACTS ROMANS 1 CORINTHIANS 2 CORINTHIANS GALATIANS EPHESIANS PHILIPPIANS COLOSSIANS 1 THESSALONIANS

THE GOSPELS

Crucifixion, Resurrection and Ascension

The Resurrection

Mark 16:1-11

The church leaders thought they had won when Jesus was crucified. Jesus' followers were sad and discouraged. But neither group realized that God's story wasn't finished. Three days after he died, Jesus was alive again!

Behind the Story

The women who came to the tomb obviously did not expect Jesus to rise from the dead, even though he had told his followers he would.

The spices were poured on to cover the smell of a decaying body. It was an act of love and care for the dead person.

The women were concerned about how to move the stone. They may not have known that a Roman seal had been put on the tomb. Matthew 28:2-3 says there was an earthquake and an angel rolled the stone away from the entrance.

The young man who sat on the stone was an angel, a messenger from God, to tell the women that the crucified one was now the risen one!

The women were instructed to tell Jesus' friends that he would meet them in Galilee. This is the same thing he told them at the Last Supper (see Mark 14:28).

Jesus Rises from Death

16 The day after the Sabbath day, Mary Magdalene, Mary the mother of James, and Salome bought some sweet-smelling spices to put on Jesus' body. ²Very early on that day, the first day of the week, the women were on their way to the tomb. It was soon after sunrise. ³They said to each other, "There is a large stone covering the entrance of the tomb. Who will move the stone for us?"

⁴Then the women looked and saw that the stone was already moved. The stone was very large, but it was moved away from the entrance. ⁵The women entered the tomb and saw a young man wearing a white robe. He was sitting on the right side, and the women were afraid.

⁶But the man said, "Don't be afraid. You are looking for Jesus from Nazareth, the one who was killed on a cross. He has risen from death. He is not here. Look, here is the place they laid him. ⁷Now go and tell his followers and Peter, 'Jesus is going into Galilee. He will be there before you. You will see him there as he told you before.' "

⁸The women were confused and shaking with fear. They left the tomb and ran away. They did not tell anyone about what happened, because they were afraid.

Some Followers See Jesus

⁹Jesus rose from death early on the first day of the week. He showed himself first to Mary Magdalene. One time in the past, he had forced seven demons to leave Mary. ¹⁰After Mary saw Jesus, she went and told his followers. They were very sad and were crying. ¹¹But Mary told them that Jesus was alive. She said that she had seen him, but the followers did not believe her.

Think About This

Mary Magdalene saw the risen Jesus, but did not recognize him until he spoke her name. In fact, she thought he was the gardener who might have moved Jesus' body (see John 20:14-16).

Jesus' followers had forgotten that he had told them several times he would die but then come back to life. (Read Luke 9:18-22 for one of those times.)

Jesus appeared to his 11 followers later that day. (Judas had killed himself after Jesus was arrested.) Jesus scolded them for not believing the women's report that he was alive.

The fact that Jesus came back to life shows that he has victory over death. As his followers, Christians will also have victory over death and live in heaven with him forever.

By his death and resurrection, Jesus fulfilled what had been written about the Messiah in Isaiah 53.

274

■ MATTHEW MARK LUKE JOHN ■ ACTS ROMANS 1 CORINTHIANS 2 CORINTHIANS GALATIANS EPHESIANS PHILIPPIANS COLOSSIANS 1 THESSALONIANS

THE GOSPELS

Crucifixion, Resurrection and Ascension

Behind the Story

Cleopas's comment that this "stranger" must be the only one who didn't know what had happened in Jerusalem shows that Jesus was well known, and everyone was talking about his death.

The two men were still sad, so they either didn't understand or didn't believe that Jesus had risen from the dead.

The men were followers of Jesus, but they thought he was going to save Israel and set up a new kingdom on earth. Jesus reminded them that the Old Testament prophets had written that the Messiah would suffer, not come to earth and set up a kingdom. The men needed to understand that all the things that had happened to Jesus fulfilled the prophecies about the Messiah.

On the Road to Emmaus

Luke 24:13-35

Painting by William Hole

Later that day, two people were walking to the village of Emmaus when, suddenly, Jesus was there walking with them. They didn't recognize him right away.

24 [13]That same day two of Jesus' followers were going to a town named Emmaus. It is about seven miles from Jerusalem. [14]They were talking about everything that had happened. [15]While they were discussing these things, Jesus himself came near and began walking with them. [16](They were not allowed to recognize Jesus.) [17]Then he said, "What are these things you are talking about while you walk?"

The two followers stopped. Their faces were very sad. [18]The one named Cleopas answered, "You must be the only one in Jerusalem who does not know what just happened there."

[19]Jesus said to them, "What are you talking about?"

The followers said, "It is about Jesus of Nazareth. He was a prophet from God to all the people. He said and did many powerful things. [20]Our leaders and the leading priests gave him up to be judged and killed. They nailed him to a cross. [21]But we were hoping that he would free the Jews. It is now the third day since this happened. [22]And today some women among us told us some amazing things. Early this morning they went to the tomb, [23]but they did not find his body there. They came and told us that they had seen a vision of angels. The angels said that Jesus was alive! [24]So some of our group went to the tomb, too. They found it just as the women said, but they did not see Jesus."

[25]Then Jesus said to them, "You are foolish and slow to realize what is true. You should believe everything the prophets said. [26]They said that the Christ must suffer these things before he enters his glory." [27]Then Jesus began to explain everything that had been written about himself in the Scriptures. He started with Moses, and then he talked about what all the prophets had said about him.

[28]They came near the town of Emmaus, and Jesus acted as if he did not plan to stop there. [29]But they begged him, "Stay with us. It is late; it is almost night." So he went in to stay with them.

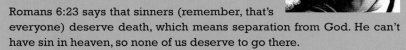
TAKING IT TO HEART

Have You Recognized Jesus?

The Romans Road to Salvation

Romans 3:23 points out that everyone sins. Every single person does things that are disobedient to God—thoughts, actions and words.

Romans 6:23 says that sinners (remember, that's everyone) deserve death, which means separation from God. He can't have sin in heaven, so none of us deserve to go there.

Romans 10:9-10 says that if we confess that Jesus is Lord and believe it in our hearts, we will be saved. That's because Jesus took the payment for our sins when he died on the cross.

Romans 10:13 states that anyone—absolutely anyone—who calls on the name of Jesus will be saved.

Pray like this:

Dear God,
I confess that I am a sinner. I'm sorry for my sins. I believe that Jesus is your Son and that he died for my sins and rose from the grave. Please, Jesus, forgive my sins and come into my heart. I want to trust you as my Savior and Lord. Amen.

³⁰Jesus sat down with them and took some bread. He gave thanks for the food and divided it. Then he gave it to them. ³¹And then, they were allowed to recognize Jesus. But when they saw who he was, he disappeared. ³²They said to each other, "When Jesus talked to us on the road, it felt like a fire burning in us. It was exciting when he explained the true meaning of the Scriptures."

Painting by Caravaggio

³³So the two followers got up at once and went back to Jerusalem. There they found the 11 apostles and others gathered. ³⁴They were saying, "The Lord really has risen from death! He showed himself to Simon."

³⁵Then the two followers told what had happened on the road. They talked about how they recognized Jesus when he divided the bread.

Think About This

The men had heard the women's report that an angel said Jesus was alive. They knew some of his followers had gone to the tomb and found it empty. However, the apostles (and these men) needed to see Jesus for themselves before they would believe he was actually alive.

As Jesus blessed the bread, their eyes were opened, and they knew they had been speaking with the risen Christ. Before that moment they had no idea who they were talking to.

Immediately the two men went to find the apostles to report that they had seen Jesus. However, the apostles were already talking about Simon seeing Jesus. They were all beginning to believe that he was alive. By now, the women, the two men on the road and Simon had all seen him. The pain and hopelessness in their hearts was turning to joy and hope!

276

MATTHEW MARK LUKE JOHN ACTS ROMANS 1 CORINTHIANS 2 CORINTHIANS GALATIANS EPHESIANS PHILIPPIANS COLOSSIANS 1 THESSALONIANS

THE GOSPELS

Crucifixion,
Resurrection
and Ascension

The Ascension

Mark 16:14-20

Behind the Story

Returning to heaven was the logical conclusion to Jesus' earthly ministry. He left the glory of heaven, became a man and lived on earth as God and man. When his work here was finished, he returned to the glory of heaven where he was once again with his Father.

When he returned to heaven, Jesus sat at the right side of his Father, a place of honor and authority.

Luke 24:50-53 records that Jesus ascended to heaven from Bethany, which is on the Mount of Olives. Those who saw this miracle were filled with joy and praised God.

Jesus appeared to his apostles while they were all together in one room. He gave the instructions for their future work, then he returned to heaven.

Jesus Talks to the Apostles

16 ¹⁴Later Jesus showed himself to the 11 followers while they were eating. He criticized them because they had little faith. They were stubborn and refused to believe those who had seen him after he had risen from death.

¹⁵Jesus said to the followers, "Go everywhere in the world. Tell the Good News to everyone. ¹⁶Anyone who believes and is baptized will be saved. But he who does not believe will be judged guilty. ¹⁷And those who believe will be able to do these things as proof: They will use my name to force demons out of people. They will speak in languages they never learned. ¹⁸They will pick up snakes without being hurt. And they will drink poison without being hurt. They will touch the sick, and the sick will be healed."

¹⁹After the Lord Jesus said these things to the followers, he was carried up into heaven. There, Jesus sat at the right side of God. ²⁰The followers went everywhere in the world and told the Good News to people. And the Lord helped them. The Lord proved that the Good News they told was true by giving them power to work miracles.

The Great Commission

Jesus' earthly job was finished, so he returned to heaven. But the job of sharing the story of God's love for all people and his plan of salvation was not finished. Jesus "commissioned" his followers to carry on the work. He gave them the authority and promised the power they needed to do it.

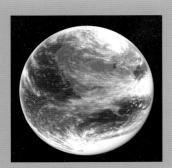

Matthew 28:18-20:

Then Jesus came to them and said, "All power in heaven and on earth is given to me. So go and make followers of all people in the world. Baptize them in the name of the Father and the Son and the Holy Spirit. Teach them to obey everything that I have told you. You can be sure that I will be with you always. I will continue with you until the end of the world."

This command to share Christ's story was not just for the men and women who saw Jesus return to heaven. It is the command to all believers for all time. The offer of salvation is not just for the Jewish nation, but for all the nations of the world (see Acts 1:8).

Think About This

Only Mark and Luke record the story of Jesus' ascension to heaven. It is also found in Acts 1:9-11, where the apostles watched as a cloud covered Jesus as he returned to heaven. They looked toward the sky until two angels appeared and asked them why they were staring at the empty sky. The angels repeated his promise that he will return one day in the same way he left. Jesus had already promised his followers that he would come back one day and take them to be with him in heaven (see John 14:2).

Seeing Jesus

Jesus' commission to his followers is also recorded in Luke 24:47-48 and John 20:21. It is God's desire for the whole world to know of his love.

There are many other things that Jesus did. If every one of them were written down, I think the whole world would not be big enough for all the books that would be written.

—John 21:25

The Gospel Writers

Four men lived and walked with Jesus. They heard him teach and saw him do miracles. Since they all wrote about it, there are four different perspectives and viewpoints of Jesus' work on earth.

Matthew

Matthew was a tax collector. He was educated and familiar with systems of accounting and record-keeping. There are more references to money in Matthew's Gospel than any of the others.

Matthew wrote to the Hebrews and showed Jesus to be the King.

Mark

The Jewish name of this writer was Mark, but his Roman name was John. He was from Jerusalem and was a cousin to Barnabas who traveled with Paul on some of his missionary journeys. Much of Mark's Gospel is filled with information given to him from Peter.

Mark wrote to the Romans and showed Jesus to be a Servant.

Luke

Luke was a doctor and may be the only non-Jewish author of a New Testament book. He may have become a Christian after Jesus' ascension. The writer of Luke says that he was not an eye-witness of the things he writes about, but he gives a complete look at Christ's life, beginning with his birth. Luke was a friend and traveling companion of Paul.

Luke wrote to the Greeks and showed Jesus to be a perfect Man.

John

John is known as the "follower Jesus loved." He was one of the 12 apostles—Jesus' closest friends. John's book explains how to find eternal life and is a condensed version of the Bible. It is often given to unbelievers or new believers to read, because it explains Jesus' work so completely.

John wrote to the entire world and showed Jesus to be Mighty God.

THE ACTS OF THE APOSTLES

10 BC	0	5 AD	10 AD	15 AD	20 AD	25 AD	30 AD	35 AD	40 AD	50 AD	60AD	70 AD	80 AD	90 AD

The Gospels end with Jesus giving his followers a job to do: Spread the Good News around the world.

Acts is the story of how they began following Jesus' command.

Acts records the birth of Christianity and the beginning of the church as the Good News spread throughout the Roman Empire. It was actually the work of the Holy Spirit through these men. The Holy Spirit is mentioned over 70 times in this book.

Luke is generally considered to be the author of Acts, though the writer is not identified. The opening chapters focus on Peter and his obedience to Jesus' command. Much of the rest of the book

records details of Paul's ministry. It was written around 60 A.D., probably from Rome and covers about 30 years of the growth of the church.

Important Themes:

- The Holy Spirit empowering the believers.
- The spread of Christianity from Jerusalem to Rome.
- The battle between good and evil, as Satan tries to stop the spread of the Good News.

The Main Characters:

Chapters 1–12
Peter, with John, Stephen and Philip

Chapters 13–28
Paul with Barnabas, Silas, Mark, Timothy and Luke

280

MATTHEW MARK LUKE JOHN **ACTS** ROMANS 1 CORINTHIANS 2 CORINTHIANS GALATIANS EPHESIANS PHILIPPIANS COLOSSIANS 1 THESSALONIANS

ACTS

The Coming of the Holy Spirit

Acts 2:1-42

Words You Should Know

Holy Spirit (HO-lee SPIH-rit)
One of the three persons of God. The other two persons are God the Father and God the Son (Jesus). The Holy Spirit lives in Christians today. He is also called the Spirit of Christ, the Spirit of God, and the Comforter (see Genesis 1:2; John 3:5-8; 16:13-15; Acts 5:32; Romans 5:5; 8:9-16; 2 Peter 1:20-21).

Pentecost (PEN-tee-cost)
"Fifty"—Pentecost was a Jewish feast day celebrating the summer harvest. It took place 50 days after the Passover Feast. The apostles began telling the Good News on Pentecost after Jesus died (see Acts 20:16; 1 Corinthians 16:8).

Apostle (uh-POS-'l)
A Greek word that means "someone who is sent off." Jesus gave the name to the 12 men he chose as his special followers. He sent them to tell the Good News about him to the whole world. Later, after Judas killed himself, Matthias became an apostle (see Matthew 10:1-4; Mark 3:14-19; Acts 1:2-26; 1 Corinthians 15:8-10).

Christ rose from the dead, appeared to his followers, talked with them, ate with them and touched them. He gave them the Great Commission before he returned to heaven. His friends waited in Jerusalem for the special gift he promised them, the gift of the Holy Spirit, God's presence, to live in them.

2 When the day of Pentecost came, they were all together in one place. ²Suddenly a noise came from heaven. It sounded like a strong wind blowing. This noise filled the whole house where they were sitting. ³They saw something that looked like flames of fire. The flames were separated and stood over each person there. ⁴They were all filled with the Holy Spirit, and they began to speak different languages. The Holy Spirit was giving them the power to speak these languages.

> **FAQ**
>
> **Q:** What is the baptism of the Holy Spirit?
>
> **A:** God gives the Holy Spirit to believers to equip and empower the church for the mission of sharing the Good News with the whole world. The Spirit is given to all believers at the time of their salvation (Acts 2:38).

⁵There were some religious Jews staying in Jerusalem who were from every country in the world. ⁶When they heard this noise, a crowd came together. They were all surprised, because each one heard them speaking in his own language. ⁷They were completely amazed at this. They said, "Look! Aren't all these men that we hear speaking from Galilee? ⁸But each of us hears them in his own language. How is this possible? We are from different places: ⁹Parthia, Media, Elam, Mesopotamia, Judea, Cappadocia, Pontus, Asia, ¹⁰Phrygia, Pamphylia, Egypt, the areas of Libya near Cyrene, Rome ¹¹(both Jews and those who had become Jews), Crete and Arabia. But we hear these men telling in our own languages about the great things God

has done!" [12]They were all amazed and confused. They asked each other, "What does this mean?"

[13]But others were making fun of them, saying, "They have had too much wine."

Peter Speaks to the People

[14]But Peter stood up with the 11 apostles. In a loud voice he spoke to the crowd: "My fellow Jews, and all of you who are in Jerusalem, listen to me. Pay attention to what I have to say. [15]These men are not drunk, as you think; it is only nine o'clock in the morning! [16]But Joel the prophet wrote about what is happening here today:

[17]'God says: In the last days

I will give my Spirit freely to all kinds of people.

Your sons and daughters will prophesy.

Your old men will dream dreams.

Your young men will see visions.

[18]At that time I will give my Spirit

even to my servants, both men and women.

And they will prophesy.

[19]I will show miracles

in the sky and on the earth:

blood, fire and thick smoke.

[20]The sun will become dark.

The moon will become red as blood.

And then the great and glorious day of the Lord will come.

[21]Then anyone who asks the Lord for help will be saved.'   *Joel 2:28-32*

The Apostle Peter

[22]"Men of Israel, listen to these words: Jesus from Nazareth was a very special man. God clearly showed this to you by the miracles, wonders, and signs God did through him. You all know this, because it happened right here among you. [23]Jesus was given to you, and you killed him. With the help of evil men you nailed him to a cross. But God knew all this would happen. This was God's plan which he had made long ago. [24]God raised Jesus from death. God set him free from the pain of death. Death could not hold him. [25]For David said this about him:

'I keep the Lord before me always.

Because he is close by my side,

I will not be hurt.

Think About This

The book of Acts was written by Luke, the physician. He also wrote the Gospel of Luke, and he traveled with Paul on some of his missionary journeys.

The presence of God was often noted by fire. God spoke to Moses from a burning bush, he led the Israelites with a pillar of fire and he consumed Elijah's offering on Mt. Carmel with fire.

Peter, who had denied knowing Jesus three times, was the first apostle to preach a sermon (Acts 2:14-40) about Christ's work. His sermon covers the Good News message of Christ's work, death and resurrection.

Peter's sermon began with God's promise, from the Old Testament book of Joel, that God would send his Spirit to all people.

Acts 2:22-24 reveals that Christ's death and resurrection were within God's plan to make salvation available to all of mankind. It was God's power that raised Jesus to life.

282

MATTHEW MARK LUKE JOHN **ACTS** ROMANS 1 CORINTHIANS 2 CORINTHIANS GALATIANS EPHESIANS PHILIPPIANS COLOSSIANS 1 THESSALONIANS

ACTS

Behind the Story

Jesus had promised the Holy Spirit to his followers in John 14:16-17.

The people listening to Peter's sermon were upset by what they heard about themselves. They wanted to know what to do.

Peter told them to repent, which means to change your outlook, or to have a change of heart and direction in your life. He wanted them to stop sinning and follow Jesus.

Peter was not teaching that baptism was necessary in order to be saved. Baptism is a public statement that sins have been forgiven because of Christ's death and resurrection.

That day the brand-new church that began with a few more than 12 members swelled to over 3,000 members.

The new believers began immediately to learn the apostles' teaching. They wanted to know more about their new relationship with God.

²⁶So I am glad, and I rejoice.

Even my body has hope.

²⁷This is because you will not leave me in the grave.

You will not let your Holy One rot.

²⁸You will teach me God's way to live.

Being with you will fill me with joy.'   *Psalm 16:8-11*

²⁹"Brothers, I can tell you truly about David, our ancestor. He died and was buried. His grave is still here with us today. ³⁰David was a prophet and knew what God had said. God had promised David that he would make a person from David's family a king just as he was. ³¹David knew this before it happened. That is why he said:

'He was not left in the grave.

His body did not rot.'

David was talking about the Christ rising from death. ³²So Jesus is the One who God raised from death! And we are all witnesses to this. ³³Jesus was lifted up to heaven and is now at God's right side. The Father has given the Holy Spirit to Jesus as he promised. So now Jesus has poured out that Spirit. This is what you see and hear. ³⁴David was not the one who was lifted up to heaven. But he said:

'The Lord said to my Lord:

Sit by me at my right side,

³⁵   until I put your enemies under your control.'   *Psalm 110:1*

³⁶"So, all the people of Israel should know this truly: God has made Jesus both Lord and Christ. He is the man you nailed to the cross!"

³⁷When the people heard this, they were sick at heart. They asked Peter and the other apostles, "What shall we do?"

³⁸Peter said to them, "Change your hearts and lives and be baptized, each one of you, in the name of Jesus Christ for the forgiveness of your sins. And you will receive the gift of the Holy Spirit. ³⁹This promise is for you. It is also for your children and for all who are far away. It is for everyone the Lord our God calls to himself."

⁴⁰Peter warned them with many other words. He begged them, "Save yourselves from the evil of today's people!" ⁴¹Then those people who accepted what Peter said were baptized. About 3,000 people were added to the number of believers that day. ⁴²They spent their time learning the apostles' teaching. And they continued to share, to break bread, and to pray together.

Philip Teaches an Ethiopian

Acts 8:26-39

8 ²⁶An angel of the Lord spoke to Philip. The angel said, "Get ready and go south. Go to the road that leads down to Gaza from Jerusalem—the desert road." ²⁷So Philip got ready and went. On the road he saw a man from Ethiopia, a eunuch. He was an important officer in the service of Candace, the queen of the Ethiopians. He was responsible for taking care of all her money. He had gone to Jerusalem to worship, and ²⁸now he was on his way home. He was sitting in his chariot and reading from the book of Isaiah, the prophet. ²⁹The Spirit said to Philip, "Go to that chariot and stay near it."

³⁰So Philip ran toward the chariot. He heard the man reading from Isaiah, the prophet. Philip asked, "Do you understand what you are reading?"

³¹He answered, "How can I understand? I need someone to explain it to me!" Then he invited Philip to climb in and sit with him. ³²The verse of Scripture that he was reading was this:

"He was like a sheep being led to be killed.

He was quiet, as a sheep is quiet while its wool is being cut.
He said nothing.
³³ He was shamed and was treated unfairly.
He died without children to continue his family.

His life on earth has ended."   *Isaiah 53:7-8*

Painting by C.F. Vos

³⁴The officer said to Philip, "Please tell me, who is the prophet talking about? Is he talking about himself or about someone else?" ³⁵Philip began to speak. He started with this same Scripture and told the man the Good News about Jesus.

³⁶While they were traveling down the road, they came to some water. The officer said, "Look! Here is water! What is stopping me from being baptized?" ³⁷[Philip answered, "If you believe with all your heart, you can." The officer said, "I believe that Jesus Christ is the Son of God."] ³⁸Then the officer commanded the chariot to stop. Both Philip and the officer went down into the water, and Philip baptized him. ³⁹When they came up out of the water, the Spirit of the Lord took Philip away; the officer never saw him again. The officer continued on his way home, full of joy.

Words You Should Know

Eunuch (U-nuk)
A man who cannot have sexual relations. In the Bible eunuchs were often high officers in royal palaces or armies (see 2 Kings 9:32; Esther 2:3; Isaiah 56:3-5).

Behind the Story

The Lord told Philip to go, and Philip didn't question him at all. He got up and went. We should always be ready to obey God, and we should respond immediately when he asks us to do something.

It was common for people to read aloud, so Philip easily heard the part of Scripture the man was reading.

The eunuch did not understand that the passage from Isaiah was talking about Jesus. Philip taught him about Jesus, and the man immediately believed and wanted to be baptized.

Philip was God's tool to make the Scripture understandable to this man and then to baptize him. Then God miraculously took Philip away from the man so he might do more work for God.

284

MATTHEW MARK LUKE JOHN **ACTS** ROMANS 1 CORINTHIANS 2 CORINTHIANS GALATIANS EPHESIANS PHILIPPIANS COLOSSIANS 1 THESSALONIANS

ACTS

Saul Is Converted

Acts 9:1-19

*The Golan Heights,
Between Israel and Damascus*

Behind the Story

Saul was a Pharisee, a very religious man who felt that the Christians had turned away from God and were no longer following his teaching. He was determined to wipe out the church to stop the wrong teaching he thought the new Christians were giving.

Saul had a vision, not a dream. The people with him heard the voice, too. Saul, however, saw Jesus in the light that blinded him (Acts 9:17). After this he was called an apostle—one who has seen the Lord. Saul's name was changed to Paul after his conversion to Christianity.

Paul is responsible for much of the spread of Christianity during that time and for writing many of the New Testament books.

Luke is telling the story of Saul's conversion here; but it is so important, Paul tells it again in Acts 22:6-16 and 26:12-18 when he is preaching.

It was a well-known fact that Saul had given his life to persecuting Christians. He wanted to frighten people away from following Christ. When Saul finally believed in Jesus, he turned his life around and gave all his energy to bringing people to Christ.

Painting by Caravaggio

9 In Jerusalem Saul was still trying to frighten the followers of the Lord by saying he would kill them. So he went to the high priest ²and asked him to write letters to the synagogues in the city of Damascus. Saul wanted the high priest to give him the authority to find people in Damascus who were followers of Christ's Way. If he found any there, men or women, he would arrest them and bring them back to Jerusalem.

³So Saul went to Damascus. As he came near the city, a bright light from heaven suddenly flashed around him. ⁴Saul fell to the ground. He heard a voice saying to him, "Saul, Saul! Why are you doing things against me?"

⁵Saul said, "Who are you, Lord?"

The voice answered, "I am Jesus. I am the One you are trying to hurt. ⁶Get up now and go into the city. Someone there will tell you what you must do."

⁷The men traveling with Saul stood there, but they said nothing. They heard the voice, but they saw no one. ⁸Saul got up from the ground. He opened his eyes, but he could not see. So the men with Saul took his hand and led him into Damascus. ⁹For three days Saul could not see, and he did not eat or drink.

¹⁰There was a follower of Jesus in Damascus named Ananias. The Lord spoke to Ananias in a vision, "Ananias!"

Ananias answered, "Here I am, Lord."

[11]The Lord said to him, "Get up and go to the street called Straight Street. Find the house of Judas. Ask for a man named Saul from the city of Tarsus. He is there now, praying. [12]Saul has seen a vision. In it a man named Ananias comes to him and lays his hands on him. Then he sees again."

[13]But Ananias answered, "Lord, many people have told me about this man and the terrible things he did to your people in Jerusalem. [14]Now he has come here to Damascus. The leading priests have given him the power to arrest everyone who worships you."

[15]But the Lord said to Ananias, "Go! I have chosen Saul for an important work. He must tell about me to non-Jews, to kings, and to the people of Israel. [16]I will show him how much he must suffer for my name."

[17]So Ananias went to the house of Judas. He laid his hands on Saul and said, "Brother Saul, the Lord Jesus sent me. He is the one you saw on the road on your way here. He sent me so that you can see again and be filled with the Holy Spirit." [18]Immediately, something that looked like fish scales fell from Saul's eyes. He was able to see again! Then Saul got up and was baptized. [19]After eating some food, his strength returned.

The Beginning of the Church

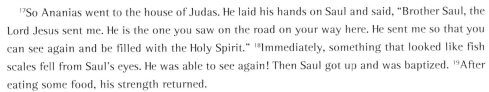

After Jesus' ascension, the church began to grow in Jerusalem. Following Peter's sermon on the Day of Pentecost, 3,000 people believed. Then Paul's ministry began. As it grew, he took the Good News beyond Jerusalem on his missionary journeys, and the church grew in the world as it was known at that time.

Think About This

Ananias had heard of Saul and was afraid of him. He questioned God's direction for him to go to Saul.

When God restated that Ananias should go, he obeyed.

Obedience is very important in serving God, even when his direction doesn't seem to make sense. Remember that he sees the bigger plan of what he asks us to do and how it fits in with what others are doing to serve him. God asks for obedience from his followers and for their trust in him (see John 14:23 and 1 John 5:3).

Saul's ministry was to preach to the Gentiles, people who were not Jewish. In Romans 11:13 Paul called himself the "apostle to the non-Jews."

When the scales fell from Saul's eyes (Acts 9:18) his physical sight was restored. His spiritual sight had changed, too. He no longer wanted to persecute Christians. Instead, he was immediately baptized.

286

MATTHEW MARK LUKE JOHN **ACTS** ROMANS 1 CORINTHIANS 2 CORINTHIANS GALATIANS EPHESIANS PHILIPPIANS COLOSSIANS 1 THESSALONIANS

ACTS

Saul's Early Ministry

Acts 9:19-31

Behind the Story

Saul came to Damascus with a letter from the high priest giving him permission to search for Christians and arrest them (Acts 9:1-2). The synagogue leaders in Damascus were confused by Saul's behavior when he began preaching about Christ.

Saul's work for Jesus was just as passionate as his work against him had been. The Jews were instantly angered by Saul's new beliefs, and they made plans to kill him.

The Christians in Damascus saved Saul's life by lowering him over the city wall in a basket. The walls had window openings in them so they lowered him from one of those. If they had been caught helping Saul, their actions would have brought persecution and punishment, at the very least. At the worst, they would have been killed.

Saul, who hated Christians, became a believer and began preaching and teaching about Jesus. People who had known him before were confused by this change. Some of Saul's old friends were angry about it.

Saul Preaches in Damascus

9 Saul stayed with the followers of Jesus in Damascus for a few days. [20]Soon he began to preach about Jesus in the synagogues, saying, "Jesus is the Son of God!"

[21]All the people who heard him were amazed. They said, "This is the man who was in Jerusalem. He was trying to destroy those who trust in this name! He came here to do the same thing. He

The Synagogue at Capernaum

came here to arrest the followers of Jesus and take them back to the leading priests."

[22]But Saul became more and more powerful. His proofs that Jesus is the Christ were so strong that the Jews in Damascus could not argue with him.

Saul Escapes from Damascus

[23]After many days, the Jews made plans to kill Saul. [24]They were watching the city gates day and night. They wanted to kill him, but Saul learned about their plan. [25]One night some followers of Saul helped him leave the city. They lowered him in a basket through an opening in the city wall.

Saul in Jerusalem

²⁶Then Saul went to Jerusalem. He tried to join the group of followers, but they were all afraid of him. They did not believe that he was really a follower. ²⁷But Barnabas accepted Saul and took him to the apostles. Barnabas told them that Saul had seen the Lord on the road. He explained how the Lord had spoken to Saul. Then he told them how boldly Saul had preached in the name of Jesus in Damascus.

²⁸And so Saul stayed with the followers. He went everywhere in Jerusalem, preaching boldly in the name of Jesus. ²⁹He would often talk and argue with the Jews who spoke Greek. But they were trying to kill him. ³⁰When the brothers learned about this, they took Saul to Caesarea. From there they sent him to Tarsus.

³¹The church everywhere in Judea, Galilee, and Samaria had a time of peace. With the help of the Holy Spirit, the group became stronger. The believers showed that they respected the Lord by the way they lived. Because of this, the group of believers grew larger and larger.

Peter in Joppa
Acts 9:36-42

9 ³⁶In the city of Joppa there was a follower named Tabitha. (Her Greek name, Dorcas, means "a deer.") She was always doing good and helping the poor. ³⁷While Peter was in Lydda, Tabitha became sick and died. Her body was washed and put in a room upstairs. ³⁸The followers in Joppa heard that Peter was in Lydda. (Lydda is near Joppa.) So they sent two men to Peter. They begged him, "Hurry, please come to us!" ³⁹Peter got ready and went with them. When he arrived, they took him to the upstairs room. All the widows stood around Peter, crying. They showed him the shirts and coats that Tabitha had made when she was still alive. ⁴⁰Peter sent everyone out of the room. He kneeled and prayed. Then he turned to the body and said, "Tabitha, stand up!" She opened her eyes, and when she saw Peter, she sat up. ⁴¹He gave her his hand and helped her up. Then he called the saints and the widows into the room. He showed them Tabitha; she was alive! ⁴²People everywhere in Joppa learned about this, and many believed in the Lord.

Think About This

The Christians in Jerusalem were afraid that Saul's conversion was not real. They were afraid he was pretending to be a Christian just to get in with them, so he could arrest them.

Saul went to Tarsus, his hometown. It was about 300 miles north of Jerusalem. It was a well-known city where a university was located.

The peace that the church enjoyed wasn't because of Saul. The emperor of Rome, Tiberius, died, and the new emperor, Caligula, wanted to do things that the Jews didn't like. So their focus was on fighting him, not the Christians.

Tabitha's body was washed in preparation for burial. This was a custom of both the Jews and the Greeks.

Peter was able to raise Tabitha back to life by the power of God through the Holy Spirit, who came to believers after Jesus went back to heaven (Acts 1:8).

288

MATTHEW MARK LUKE JOHN **ACTS** ROMANS 1 CORINTHIANS 2 CORINTHIANS GALATIANS EPHESIANS PHILIPPIANS COLOSSIANS 1 THESSALONIANS

ACTS

Peter and Cornelius

Acts 10:1-48

Behind the Story

This story is an important turning point in the growth of the church. Christians had been sharing the story of Jesus only with Jews, up to this point. Peter's vision to go to Caesarea meant that he would be teaching Gentiles, people who were not Jewish. This helped to spread Christianity outside the Jewish world and began to make it known worldwide.

Cornelius was a God-fearer. The group of people who lived in his house believed in one God and attended synagogue, but they didn't believe in all that the Jews believed. Cornelius possibly didn't know the whole story of Jesus' death and resurrection.

Cornelius, an officer in the Roman army, was in charge of 100 men. He had power and authority.

Peter had been traveling on missionary journeys, teaching about Christ. He would not have gone to Caesarea if God had not told him to go.

10 At Caesarea there was a man named Cornelius. He was an officer in the Italian group of the Roman army. ²Cornelius was a religious man. He and all the other people who lived in his house worshiped the true God. He gave much of his money to the poor and prayed to God often. ³One afternoon about three o'clock, Cornelius saw a vision clearly. In the vision an angel of God came to him and said, "Cornelius!"

⁴Cornelius stared at the angel. He became afraid and said, "What do you want, Lord?"

The angel said, "God has heard your prayers. He has seen what you give to the poor. And God remembers you. ⁵Send some men now to Joppa to bring back a man named Simon. Simon is also called Peter. ⁶Simon is staying with a man, also named Simon, who is a leatherworker. He has a house beside the sea." ⁷Then the angel who spoke to Cornelius left. Cornelius called two of his servants and a soldier. The soldier was a religious man who worked for Cornelius. ⁸Cornelius explained everything to these three men and sent them to Joppa.

⁹The next day as they came near Joppa, Peter was going up to the roof to pray. It was about noon. ¹⁰Peter was hungry and wanted to eat. But while the food was being prepared, he had a vision. ¹¹He saw heaven opened and something coming down. It looked like a big sheet being lowered to earth by its four corners. ¹²In it were all kinds of animals, reptiles, and birds. ¹³Then a voice said to Peter, "Get up, Peter; kill and eat."

¹⁴But Peter said, "No, Lord! I have never eaten food that is unholy or unclean."

¹⁵But the voice said to him again, "God has made these things clean. Don't call them 'unholy'!" ¹⁶This happened three times. Then the sheet was taken back to heaven.

¹⁷While Peter was wondering what this vision meant, the men Cornelius sent had found Simon's house. They were standing at the gate. ¹⁸They asked, "Is Simon Peter staying here?"

¹⁹Peter was still thinking about the vision. But the Spirit said to him, "Listen! Three men are

looking for you. ²⁰Get up and go downstairs. Go with them and don't ask questions. I have sent them to you."

²¹So Peter went down to the men. He said, "I am the man you are looking for. Why did you come here?"

²²They said, "A holy angel spoke to Cornelius, an army officer. He is a good man; he worships God. All the Jewish people respect him. The angel told Cornelius to ask you to his house so that he can hear what you have to say." ²³Peter asked the men to come in and spend the night.

The next day Peter got ready and went with them. Some of the brothers from Joppa joined him. ²⁴On the following day they came to Caesarea. Cornelius was waiting for them. He had called together his relatives and close friends. ²⁵When Peter entered, Cornelius met him. He fell at Peter's feet and worshiped him. ²⁶But Peter helped him up, saying, "Stand up! I too am only a man." ²⁷Peter went on talking with Cornelius as they went inside. There Peter saw many people together. ²⁸He said, "You people understand that it is against our Jewish law for a Jew to associate with or visit anyone who is not a Jew. But God has shown me that I should not call any person 'unholy' or 'unclean.' ²⁹That is why I did not argue when I was asked to come here. Now, please tell me why you sent for me."

³⁰Cornelius said, "Four days ago, I was praying in my house. It was at this same time— three o'clock in the afternoon. Suddenly, there was a man standing before me wearing shining clothes. ³¹He said, 'Cornelius! God has heard your prayer. He has seen what you give to the poor. And God remembers you. ³²So send some men to Joppa and ask Simon Peter to come. Peter is staying in the house of a man, also named Simon, who is a leatherworker. His house is beside the sea.' ³³So I sent for you immediately, and it was very good of you to come. Now we are all here before God to hear everything the Lord has commanded you to tell us."

Cornelius Inscription

Think About This

Cornelius's vision came at about 3:00, a traditional time of Jewish prayer. His observance of prayer and his generosity to the poor show that he tried to please God.

Peter went to the roof to pray. The flat roof of the homes provided a place to get away from things, like food preparation, and to be alone with God.

Peter's dream of being told to eat the animals, reptiles and birds was contrary to Jewish law. These creatures were not "clean" and, therefore, not permissible to eat.

Peter refused God's order to eat these animals. Peter had refused to obey once before, when Jesus wanted to wash his feet (see John 13:8).

Peter refused because the Law given to Moses outlined which animals were permissible to eat and which ones were not (see Leviticus 11). God's response to Peter's refusal was that only God decides what is clean and unclean. See Mark 7:14-23.

290

MATTHEW MARK LUKE JOHN ACTS ROMANS 1 CORINTHIANS 2 CORINTHIANS GALATIANS EPHESIANS PHILIPPIANS COLOSSIANS 1 THESSALONIANS

ACTS

Behind the Story

The Holy Spirit prepared Peter for the arrival of three men (Acts 10:19).

After Peter and Cornelius talked, Peter realized what God was trying to teach him in his dream. The sermon Peter gave wiped away all the prejudices between Jews and Gentiles. It made clear that Christianity was for all people—anyone who believed in Jesus Christ. The Jews were God's chosen people and had received many of his blessings and promises. However, God wanted the message of his love for all people to spread throughout the entire world.

Peter quickly outlined all of Christ's life and work. As a result, the Gentile people who were listening believed, and the Holy Spirit came down on them. The presence of the Spirit showed equality between Jews and Gentiles.

Peter's Speech

³⁴Peter began to speak: "I really understand now that to God every person is the same. ³⁵God accepts anyone who worships him and does what is right. It is not important what country a person comes from. ³⁶You know that God has sent his message to the people of Israel. That message is the Good News that peace has come through Jesus Christ. Jesus is the Lord of all people! ³⁷You know what has happened all over Judea. It began in Galilee after John preached to the people about baptism. ³⁸You know about Jesus from Nazareth. God made him the Christ by giving him the Holy Spirit and power. You know how Jesus went everywhere doing good. He healed those who were ruled by the devil, for God was with Jesus. ³⁹We saw all the things that Jesus did in Judea and in Jerusalem. But they killed him by nailing him to a cross. ⁴⁰Yet, on the third day, God raised Jesus to life and caused him to be seen. ⁴¹But he was not seen by all the people. Only the witnesses that God had already chosen saw him, and we are those witnesses. We ate and drank with him after he was raised from death. ⁴²He told us to preach to the people and to tell them that he is the one whom God chose to be the judge of the living and the dead. ⁴³Everyone who believes in Jesus will be forgiven. God will forgive his sins through Jesus. All the prophets say this is true."

Non-Jews Receive the Holy Spirit

⁴⁴While Peter was still saying this, the Holy Spirit came down on all those who were listening. ⁴⁵The Jewish believers who came with Peter were amazed that the gift of the Holy Spirit had been given even to the non-Jewish people. ⁴⁶These Jewish believers heard them speaking in different languages and praising God. Then Peter said, ⁴⁷"Can anyone keep these people from being baptized with water? They have received the Holy Spirit just as we did!" ⁴⁸So Peter ordered that they be baptized in the name of Jesus Christ. Then they asked Peter to stay with them for a few days.

Seeing God

THE TRINITY

This term refers to the three persons of God. He is God the Father, God the Son (Jesus) and God the Holy Spirit. The Holy Spirit lives in believers, helping them to obey God and know him. He came to believers when Jesus returned to heaven.

291

The Early Church

The birth of the early church is recorded only in the book of Acts.

After Jesus' resurrection, the believers secretly met together in homes. They were persecuted by the Jewish authorities and thrown out of the Temple. However, the church began to grow, and new Christian communities were established in Antioch, Damascus, Samaria and a few other towns.

Because of the persecution, the believers had to help one another. Acts 4:34-35 says that they sold all they had and used the money to help anyone who had a need. They met together every day, ate together and worshiped together, and the church grew.

Churches in Greece, Europe and Scandinavia

The Worldwide Church

Because of Peter's vision and the lesson he learned from it, believers became obedient to share the Good News with the whole world. Jesus had instructed them to do this in Acts 1:8, when he told them to go into the whole world. Paul followed up on it in Romans 3:29-30, when he said that God is the God of the Gentiles, too.

292

MATTHEW MARK LUKE JOHN **ACTS** ROMANS 1 CORINTHIANS 2 CORINTHIANS GALATIANS EPHESIANS PHILIPPIANS COLOSSIANS 1 THESSALONIANS

ACTS

Peter in Jail

Acts 12:1-18

Not long after Peter met with Cornelius and understood that God's desire was for Gentiles to become believers, Herod Agrippa I began to persecute believers. He killed James, the brother of John, and threw Peter into jail. But God knew what was happening.

Herod Agrippa Hurts the Church

12 During that same time King Herod began to do terrible things to some who belonged to the church. ²He ordered James, the brother of John, to be killed by the sword. ³Herod saw that the Jews liked this, so he decided to arrest Peter, too. (This happened during the time of the Feast of Unleavened Bread.)

⁴After Herod arrested Peter, he put him in jail and handed him over to be guarded by 16 soldiers. Herod planned to bring Peter before the people for trial after the Passover Feast. ⁵So Peter was kept in jail. But the church kept on praying to God for him.

Peter Leaves the Jail

⁶The night before Herod was to bring him to trial, Peter was sleeping. He was between two soldiers, bound with two chains. Other soldiers were guarding the door of the jail. ⁷Suddenly, an angel of the Lord stood there. A light shined in the room. The angel touched Peter on the side and woke him up. The angel said, "Hurry! Get up!" And the chains

A Fresco by Raphael

fell off Peter's hands. ⁸The angel said to him, "Get dressed and put on your sandals." And so Peter did this. Then the angel said, "Put on your coat and follow me." ⁹So the angel went out, and Peter followed him. Peter did not know if what the angel was doing was real. He thought he might be seeing a vision. ¹⁰They went past the first and the second guard. They came to the iron gate that separated them from the city. The gate opened itself for them. They went through the gate and

Detail of Fresco

Words You Should Know

Herod Agrippa I
The king of Palestine for about three years (A.D. 41-44). He was the grandson of Herod I. He had the apostle James killed and the apostle Peter arrested. He did it to please the Jews who hated Jesus' followers. Later, this man was eaten by worms and died because he let the people treat him like a god (see Acts 12:1-23).

Persecute (PUR-seh-cute)
To hurt people. Christians in New Testament times were often persecuted. Saul persecuted Christians by dragging them from their homes, putting them in jail and killing them (see Matthew 5:11-12; Acts 8:1-4; Galatians 6:12; 1 Peter 3:13-15).

James
The first of the apostles to die because of his faith. Being killed by the sword meant that he was beheaded.

walked down a street. And the angel suddenly left him.

[11]Then Peter realized what had happened. He thought, "Now I know that the Lord really sent his angel to me. He rescued me from Herod and from all the things the Jewish people thought would happen."

[12]When he realized this, he went to the home of Mary. She was the mother of John. (John was also called Mark.) Many people were gathered there, praying. [13]Peter knocked on the outside door. A servant girl named Rhoda came to answer it. [14]She recognized Peter's voice, and she was very happy. She even forgot to open the door. She ran inside and told the group, "Peter is at the door!"

[15]They said to her, "You are crazy!" But she kept on saying that it was true. So they said, "It must be Peter's angel."

[16]Peter continued to knock. When they opened the door, they saw him and were amazed. [17]Peter made a sign with his hand to tell them to be quiet. He explained how the Lord led him out of the jail. And he said, "Tell James and the other believers what happened." Then he left to go to another place.

The World at the Time
Prisons

Prisoners were put in prison at this time just to wait for the day of their execution. Prisoners were not kept in prison for long periods of time as a form of punishment. Many prisoners were beaten or tortured, and they were not given enough food to eat nor water to drink.

An Ancient Prison in Philippi

Herod Agrippa I was actually in prison a few times himself before he became the king of Samaria. One time he was released from prison, but still chained at the wrist to a guard in his own house.

Behind the Story

Peter's only crime was that he preached about Jesus.

The believers were together praying for Peter to be spared from death. Since Herod Agrippa I knew that the Jews were pleased when he killed James, they knew he was planning to kill Peter, too.

Yet when Rhoda told them that their prayers were answered and Peter was outside the door, they thought she had lost her mind.

God sent his angel to free Peter from prison. Peter knew without a doubt that it was God who had saved him. He told the believers who were praying for him that God had saved him, and their faith was strengthened, too.

When a prisoner escaped, his guards were killed in his place; so the 16 men who were guarding Peter were probably killed by Herod Agrippa I.

The James mentioned in Acts 12:17 was probably the brother of Jesus.

Believers should support each other by praying for each others' needs. See Ephesians 6:18.

294

MATTHEW MARK LUKE JOHN ACTS ROMANS 1 CORINTHIANS 2 CORINTHIANS GALATIANS EPHESIANS PHILIPPIANS COLOSSIANS 1 THESSALONIANS

ACTS

Paul and Silas in Jail

Acts 16:16-34

Paul was traveling on his second missionary journey and came to the city of Philippi. There he met a girl who had an evil spirit (or demon) living in her. He commanded the spirit to come out of her, and that made her owners angry. They had been using the girl to make money. So Paul and Silas were beaten and thrown into jail.

Words You Should Know

Demon (DEE-mun)
An evil spirit from the devil. Sometimes a demon lived in a person. But Jesus has more power than demons and can make them come out of people (see Deuteronomy 32:17; Psalm 106:37; Matthew 12:22; Luke 8:26-39).

Behind the Story

People paid the owners of this girl because she could tell fortunes. When Paul made the evil spirit leave the girl, her owners knew they were going to lose a lot of money.

Paul wasn't upset because the girl kept saying they were servants of God. He was upset because the people believed everything she said.

Paul and Silas were beaten and imprisoned without a trial, even though Paul was a Roman citizen. That was against the law.

The prisoners enjoyed hearing Paul and Silas sing songs to God.

16 ¹⁶Once, while we were going to the place for prayer, a servant girl met us. She had a special spirit in her. She earned a lot of money for her owners by telling fortunes. ¹⁷This girl followed Paul and us. She said loudly, "These men are servants of the Most High God! They are telling you how you can be saved!"

¹⁸She kept this up for many days. This bothered Paul, so he turned and said to the spirit, "By the power of Jesus Christ, I command you to come out of her!" Immediately, the spirit came out.

¹⁹The owners of the servant girl saw this. These men knew that now they could not use her to make money. So they grabbed Paul and Silas and dragged them before the city rulers in the marketplace. ²⁰Here they brought Paul and Silas to the Roman rulers and said, "These men are Jews and are making trouble in our city. ²¹They are teaching things that are not right for us as Romans to do."

²²The crowd joined the attack against them. The Roman officers tore the clothes of Paul and Silas and had them beaten with rods again and again. ²³Then Paul and Silas were thrown into jail. The jailer was ordered to guard them carefully. ²⁴When he heard this order, he put them far inside the jail. He pinned down their feet between large blocks of wood.

²⁵About midnight Paul and Silas were praying and singing songs to God. The other prisoners were listening to them. ²⁶Suddenly, there was a big earthquake. It was so strong that it shook the foundation of the jail. Then all the doors of the jail

295

2 THESSALONIANS 1 TIMOTHY 2 TIMOTHY TITUS PHILEMON HEBREWS JAMES 1 PETER 2 PETER 1 JOHN 2 JOHN 3 JOHN JUDE REVELATION

broke open. All the prisoners were freed from their chains. ²⁷The jailer woke up and saw that the jail doors were open. He thought that the prisoners had already escaped. So he got his sword and was about to kill himself. ²⁸But Paul shouted, "Don't hurt yourself! We are all here!"

²⁹The jailer told someone to bring a light. Then he ran inside. Shaking with fear, he fell down

before Paul and Silas. ³⁰Then he brought them outside and said, "Men, what must I do to be saved?"

³¹They said to him, "Believe in the Lord Jesus and you will be saved—you and all the people in your house." ³²So Paul and Silas told the message of the Lord to the jailer and all the people in his house. ³³At that hour of the night the jailer took Paul and Silas and washed their wounds. Then he and all his people were baptized immediately. ³⁴After this the jailer took Paul and Silas home and gave them food. He and his family were very happy because they now believed in God.

TAKING IT TO HEART

Worship During Hard Times

It's easy to praise God when everything is going great and you're healthy and happy. However, it's also easy to get lazy about your faith and stop growing and depending on God when things are going well. When life is hard and you must depend on God and trust him alone, faith grows stronger.

Read these verses about suffering and faith:

- Psalm 22:24
- Psalm 23:4
- Isaiah 41:10
- John 14:1
- Romans 5:3-4
- 2 Corinthians 1:5
- James 1:3-4

Think About This

The earthquake was strong enough to break open all the doors of the jail and to break free all the chains, but none of the prisoners were killed.

The jailer started to kill himself because he knew he would be killed by his superiors if any of the prisoners escaped.

The jailer was amazed that the prisoners were still there, and he gave God credit for that. He wanted to be saved immediately. Paul told him that all he had to do was believe in Jesus.

The jailer and all the people in his house were baptized that night. Baptism is an act of obedience after salvation and shows publicly the desire for new life in Christ.

The jailer took Paul and Silas to his home. He washed their wounds and fed and cared for them. This was an amazing thing for a Roman jailer to do for prisoners.

296

MATTHEW MARK LUKE JOHN **ACTS** ROMANS 1 CORINTHIANS 2 CORINTHIANS GALATIANS EPHESIANS PHILIPPIANS COLOSSIANS 1 THESSALONIANS

ACTS

Paul's Travels

Acts 17:1-34

Behind the Story

This was Paul's third missionary journey and may have lasted as long as five years. Paul traveled on the Egnatian Way, a road that crossed Greece from east to west. Major cities were located about a day's travel apart.

Thessalonica had a population close to 200,000 and was about 100 miles from Philippi.

Paul talked with the Jews on three different Sabbath days, but he stayed in Thessalonica longer than three weeks. He taught the Gentiles after that. Other passages indicate that, while he was in Thessalonica, the Philippian church sent him money (Philippians 4:15-16). He also had to get a job while he was there (1 Thessalonians 2:9), so he must have been there longer than three weeks.

Paul and Silas's teaching caused some Jews to become believers (Acts 17:4). Paul could teach them Old Testament prophecies of the Messiah, then show how Christ fulfilled those prophecies.

When Paul and Silas were released from prison, Paul went on to the large city of Thessalonica. He preached in the synagogue there. Some Jews got angry at him and caused so much trouble that he had to leave town. They followed him to Berea and continued to cause trouble.

Paul and Silas in Thessalonica

17 Paul and Silas traveled through Amphipolis and Apollonia and came to Thessalonica. In that city there was a Jewish synagogue. ²Paul went into the synagogue as he always did. On each Sabbath day for three weeks, Paul talked with the Jews about the Scriptures. ³He explained and proved that the Christ must die and then rise from death. He said, "This Jesus I am telling you about is the Christ." ⁴Some of the Jews were convinced and joined Paul and Silas. Many of the Greeks who worshiped the true God and many of the important women joined them.

Old Road near Thessalonica, Greece

Ancient Marketplace in Greece

⁵But the Jews became jealous. They got some evil men from the marketplace, formed a mob and started a riot. They ran to Jason's house, looking for Paul and Silas. The men wanted to bring Paul and Silas out to the people. ⁶But they did not find them. So they dragged Jason and some other believers to the leaders of the city. The people were yelling, "These men have made trouble everywhere in the world. And now they have come here too! ⁷Jason is keeping them in his house. All of them do things against the laws of Caesar. They say that there is another king called Jesus."

[8]When the people and the leaders of the city heard these things, they became very upset. [9]They made Jason and the others put up a sum of money. Then they let the believers go free.

Paul and Silas Go to Berea

[10]That same night the believers sent Paul and Silas to Berea. There Paul and Silas went to the Jewish synagogue. [11]These Jews were better than the Jews in Thessalonica. They were eager to hear the things Paul and Silas said. These Jews in Berea studied the Scriptures every day to find out if these things were true. [12]So, many of them believed. Many important Greek men and women also believed. [13]But when the Jews in Thessalonica learned that Paul was preaching the word of God in Berea, they came there, too. They

Reading the Torah (Jewish Scriptures)

upset the people and made trouble. [14]So the believers quickly sent Paul away to the coast. But Silas and Timothy stayed in Berea. [15]The men who took Paul went with him to Athens. Then they carried a message from Paul back to Silas and Timothy. It said, "Come to me as soon as you can."

Paul in Athens

[16]Paul was waiting for Silas and Timothy in Athens. He was troubled because he saw that the city was full of idols. [17]In the synagogue, he talked with the Jews and the Greeks who worshiped the true God. He also talked every day with people in the marketplace.

[18]Some of the Epicurean and Stoic philosophers argued with him. Some of them said, "This man doesn't know what he is talking about. What is he trying to say?" Paul was telling them the Good News of Jesus' rising from death. They said, "He seems to be telling us about some other gods." [19]They got Paul and took him to a meeting of the Areopagus. They said, "Please explain to us this new idea that you have been teaching. [20]The things you are saying are new to us. We want to know what this teaching means." [21](All the people of Athens and those from other countries always used their time talking about all the newest ideas.)

FAQs

Q: Why did these Jews make trouble for Paul?

A: Basically because they were afraid. Paul was teaching things they did not agree with and that frightened them. Also, they were jealous of Paul and the many people who followed him.

Think About This

The Jews who got angry with Paul were upset because he was teaching the Good News which contradicted their religious beliefs.

They accused Paul of making trouble around the whole world.

The money Jason paid (Acts 17:9) was to be a promise that Paul wouldn't cause anymore trouble. So Paul and Silas left for Berea, which was about 50 miles away.

The Jews in Berea were more noble and perhaps more educated than the Jews in Thessalonica. They were interested in what Paul was teaching. But then the Jews from Thessalonica showed up to make more trouble. So, once again, Paul left. But Timothy and Silas stayed behind to help the new church grow.

298

MATTHEW MARK LUKE JOHN **ACTS** ROMANS 1 CORINTHIANS 2 CORINTHIANS GALATIANS EPHESIANS PHILIPPIANS COLOSSIANS 1 THESSALONIANS

ACTS

At the Areopagus

Paul met with the most educated men in Athens. Because he was also educated and familiar with the philosophy and writings they studied, he could discuss those things with them. From that discussion he went right into the message of the Good News. Some accepted Christ and became believers.

Paul pointed out that they had an altar built to an unknown god; they didn't even know the name of the god they worshiped. These men of Greece had no knowledge of the Hebrew Scriptures, so Paul began his message with the fact that God made everything and has control over everything. God doesn't live in a temple or at an altar. He has no physical needs and should not be worshiped as a man, but as a Spirit.

Paul tried to turn the Greeks from their belief that there are many gods to worship to the truth that there is only one all-powerful, loving God.

The Acropolis in Athens

Painting by Raphael

²²Then Paul stood before the meeting of the Areopagus. He said, "Men of Athens, I can see that you are very religious in all things. ²³I was going through your city, and I saw the things you worship. I found an altar that had these words written on it: "TO A GOD WHO IS NOT KNOWN." You worship a god that you don't know. This is the God I am telling you about! ²⁴He is the God who made the whole world and everything in it. He is the Lord of the land and the sky. He does not live in temples that men build! ²⁵This God is the One who gives life, breath, and everything else to people. He does not need any help from them. He has everything he needs. ²⁶God began by making one man. From him came all the different people who live everywhere in the world. He decided exactly when and where they must live. ²⁷God wanted them to look for him and perhaps search all around for him and find him. But he is not far from any of us: ²⁸'By his power we live and move and exist.' Some of your own poets have said: 'For we are his children.' ²⁹We are God's children. So, you must not think that God is like something that people imagine or make. He is not like gold, silver, or rock. ³⁰In the past, people did not understand God, but God ignored this. But now, God tells everyone in the world to change his heart and life. ³¹God has decided on a day that he will judge all the world. He will be fair. He will use a man to do this. God chose that man long ago. And God has proved this to everyone by raising that man from death!"

³²When the people heard about Jesus being raised from death, some of them laughed. They said, "We will hear more about this from you later." ³³So Paul went away from them. ³⁴But some of the people believed Paul and joined him. One of those who believed was Dionysius, a member of the Areopagus. Also a woman named Damaris and some others believed.

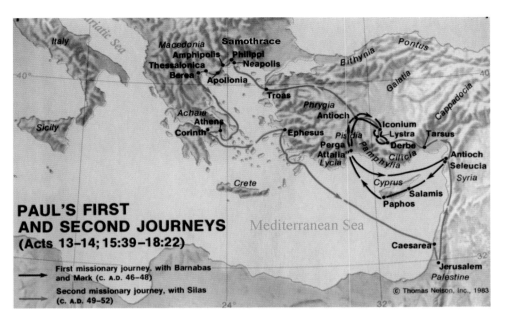

PAUL'S FIRST AND SECOND JOURNEYS
(Acts 13–14; 15:39–18:22)

→ First missionary journey, with Barnabas and Mark (c. A.D. 46–48)

→ Second missionary journey, with Silas (c. A.D. 49–52)

© Thomas Nelson, Inc., 1983

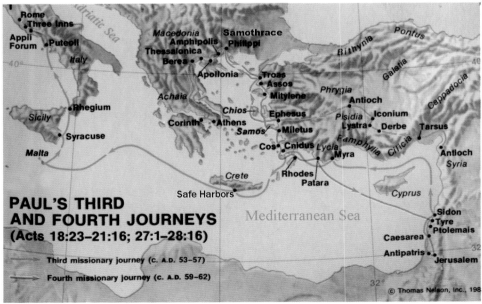

PAUL'S THIRD AND FOURTH JOURNEYS
(Acts 18:23–21:16; 27:1–28:16)

→ Third missionary journey (c. A.D. 53–57)

→ Fourth missionary journey (c. A.D. 59–62)

© Thomas Nelson, Inc., 198

About the Maps

Paul and his traveling partners planted new churches throughout the Roman Empire over a timespan of about 11 years. Afterward he wrote letters of encouragement and instruction to those churches. Thirteen of those letters became books of the New Testament.

The maps show that Paul traveled hundreds of miles by land and sea. The same passion he had once put into stopping the spread of Christianity was channeled into telling people about Christ and helping them understand. He was passionate and powerful in presenting the Good News.

300

MATTHEW MARK LUKE JOHN **ACTS** ROMANS 1 CORINTHIANS 2 CORINTHIANS GALATIANS EPHESIANS PHILIPPIANS COLOSSIANS 1 THESSALONIANS

ACTS

Shipwreck

Acts 27:1-44; 28:1-6

Paul was arrested and tried by Felix, Festus and King Herod Agrippa. He asked to be tried by Caesar because he was a Roman citizen. Agrippa said Paul could have been set free if he hadn't asked that. Instead he was put on a ship bound for Rome.

Behind the Story

As a Roman citizen, Paul had more rights than a Jewish person did. He had a right to a fair trial, and he was not supposed to be flogged. Flogging was done with a whip that had metal or bone pieces tied into it. The Romans used it on the people who were their slaves or worst enemies. It was cruel and brutal punishment.

If Paul had not insisted on being tried by Caesar, he could have been released from prison. But, by insisting, he was able to preach in Rome.

The type of ship Paul sailed on was sometimes as long as 300 feet and could carry as many as 600 passengers. There were 276 people on the ship with Paul (Acts 27:37).

The officer in charge of Paul was kind to him and allowed him to visit with friends in Sidon (27:3).

This story shows the difficulty of attempting to sail from east to west in the Mediterranean Sea. The winds blew from the west, so it was difficult to make progress.

Paul Sails for Rome

27 It was decided that we would sail for Italy. An officer named Julius, who served in the Emperor's army, guarded Paul and some other prisoners. ²We got on a ship and left. The ship was from the city of Adramyttium and was about to sail to different ports in Asia. Aristarchus, a man from the city of Thessalonica in Macedonia, went with us. ³The next day we came to Sidon. Julius was very good to Paul. He gave Paul freedom to go visit his friends, who took care of his needs. ⁴We left Sidon and sailed close to the island of Cyprus because the wind was blowing against us. ⁵We went across the sea by Cilicia and Pamphylia. Then we came to the city of Myra, in Lycia. ⁶There the officer found a ship from Alexandria that was going to Italy. So he put us on it.

The Coast of Cyprus

⁷We sailed slowly for many days. We had a hard time reaching Cnidus because the wind was blowing against us. We could not go any farther that way. So we sailed by the south side of the island of Crete near Salmone. ⁸We sailed along the coast, but the sailing was hard. Then we came to a place called Safe Harbors, near the city of Lasea.

⁹But we had lost much time. It was now dangerous to sail, because it was already after the Day of Cleansing. So Paul warned them, ¹⁰"Men, I can see there will be a lot of trouble on this trip. The ship and the things in the ship will be lost. Even our lives may be lost!" ¹¹But the captain and the owner of the ship did not agree with Paul. So the officer did not believe Paul. Instead, the officer believed what the captain

and owner of the ship said. [12]And that harbor was not a good place for the ship to stay for the winter. So most of the men decided that the ship should leave. The men hoped we could go to Phoenix. The ship could stay there for the winter. (Phoenix was a city on the island of Crete. It had a harbor which faced southwest and northwest.)

The Storm

[13]Then a good wind began to blow from the south. The men on the ship thought, "This is the wind we wanted, and now we have it!" So they pulled up the anchor. We sailed very close to the island of Crete. [14]But then a very strong wind named the "Northeaster" came from the island. [15]This wind took the ship and carried it away. The ship could not sail against it. So we stopped trying and let the wind blow us. [16]We went below a small island named Cauda. Then we were able to bring in the lifeboat, but it was very hard to do. [17]After the men took the lifeboat in, they tied ropes around the ship to hold it together. The men were afraid that the ship would hit the sandbanks of Syrtis. So they lowered the sail and let the wind carry the ship. [18]The next day the storm was blowing us so hard that the men threw out some of the cargo. [19]A day later they threw out the ship's equipment. [20]For many days we could not see the sun or the stars. The storm was very bad. We lost all hope of staying alive—we thought we would die.

[21]The men had gone without food for a long time. Then one day Paul stood up before them and said, "Men, I told you not to leave Crete. You should have listened to me. Then you would not have all this trouble and loss. [22]But now I tell you to cheer up. None of you will die! But the ship will be lost. [23]Last night an angel from God came to me. This is the God I worship. I am his. [24]God's angel said, 'Paul, do not be afraid! You must stand before Caesar. And God has given you this promise: He will save the lives of all those men sailing with you.' [25]So men, be cheerful! I trust in God. Everything will happen as his angel told me. [26]But we will crash on an island."

[27]On the fourteenth night we were floating around in the Adriatic Sea. The sailors thought we were close to land.

Think About This

Paul had sailed many times as he made his missionary journeys. He had even been shipwrecked two times before (see 2 Corinthians 11:25). He advised the sailors to stay in the port at Fair Haven until the stormy winter months had passed.

The storm that suddenly blew up had hurricane force winds.

God gave Paul the assurance of safety before the storm even started. God's protection of all who were on the ship was a miracle. Paul received the assurance from God because he was close to God and could, therefore, know that the angel who spoke to him was God's messenger.

Paul told the sailors that they should have listened to him, but he gave the credit to God for saving them. He gave them details, as God gave him, that they would crash, but no one would die. So when the ship wrecked, the men could know that God's plan was still unfolding.

302

MATTHEW MARK LUKE JOHN **ACTS** ROMANS 1 CORINTHIANS 2 CORINTHIANS GALATIANS EPHESIANS PHILIPPIANS COLOSSIANS 1 THESSALONIANS

ACTS

Trust in God

An important principle of the Bible is that God can be trusted all the time. When the storm was blowing and the ship was breaking up, Paul still trusted God's word that the passengers would all (every one of them) be saved. Trusting when things are hard is important. Read Proverbs 3:5-6 and 1 Peter 1:8 to learn more about trusting.

Some of the sailors wanted to leave the ship in a lifeboat. They tried to trick the others into thinking they were just lowering more anchors into the water. Paul stopped them because, if the sailors escaped, the Roman soldiers would be killed. God had said that no lives would be lost. The soldiers stopped the sailors from escaping.

When the ship broke up the soldiers decided to kill the prisoners because, if even one of them escaped, the soldiers themselves would be killed by their superiors. The officer who had been kind to Paul stopped this plan. He wanted Paul to get safely to Rome.

²⁸They threw a rope into the water with a weight on the end of it. They found that the water was 120 feet deep. They went a little farther and threw the rope in again. It was 90 feet deep. ²⁹The sailors were afraid that we would hit the rocks, so they threw four anchors into the water. Then they prayed for daylight to come. ³⁰Some of the sailors wanted to leave the ship, and they lowered the lifeboat. These sailors wanted the other men to think that they were throwing more anchors from the front of the ship. ³¹But Paul told the officer and the other soldiers, "If these men do not stay in the ship, your lives cannot be saved!" ³²So the soldiers cut the ropes and let the lifeboat fall into the water.

³³Just before dawn Paul began persuading all the people to eat something. He said, "For the past 14 days you have been waiting and watching. You have not eaten. ³⁴Now I beg you to eat something. You need it to stay alive. None of you will lose even one hair off your heads." ³⁵After he said this, Paul took some bread and thanked God for it before all of them. He broke off a piece and began eating. ³⁶All the men felt better. They all started eating too. ³⁷(There were 276 people on the ship.) ³⁸We ate all we wanted. Then we began making the ship lighter by throwing the grain into the sea.

The Coast of Malta

The Ship Is Destroyed

³⁹When daylight came, the sailors saw land. They did not know what land it was, but they saw a bay with a beach. They wanted to sail the ship to the beach, if they could. ⁴⁰So they cut the ropes to the anchors and left the anchors in the sea. At the same time, they untied the ropes that were holding the rudders. Then they raised the front sail into the wind and sailed toward the beach. ⁴¹But the ship hit a sandbank. The front of the ship stuck there and could not move. Then the big waves began to break the back of the ship to pieces.

⁴²The soldiers decided to kill the prisoners so that none of them could swim away and escape. ⁴³But Julius, the officer, wanted to let Paul live. He did not allow the soldiers to kill the prisoners. Instead he ordered everyone who could swim to jump into the water and swim to land. ⁴⁴The rest used wooden boards or pieces of the ship. And this is how all the people made it safely to land.

Paul on the Island of Malta

28 When we were safe on land, we learned that the island was called Malta. ²It was raining and very cold. But the people who lived there were very good to us. They made us a fire and welcomed all of us. ³Paul gathered a pile of sticks for the fire. He was putting them on the fire when a poisonous snake came out because of the heat and bit him on the hand. ⁴The people living on the island saw the snake hanging from Paul's hand. They said to each other, "This man must be a murderer! He did not die in the sea, but Justice does not want him to live." ⁵But Paul shook the snake off into the fire. He was not hurt. ⁶The people thought that Paul would swell up or fall down dead. The people waited and watched him for a long time, but nothing bad happened to him. So they changed their minds about Paul. Now they said, "He is a god!"

Paul in Rome

Acts 28:16-20

28 ¹⁶Then we arrived at Rome. There, Paul was allowed to live alone. But a soldier stayed with him to guard him.

The Colosseum in Rome

¹⁷Three days later Paul sent for the Jewish leaders there. When they came together, he said, "Brothers, I have done nothing against our people. I have done nothing against the customs of our fathers. But I was arrested in Jerusalem and given to the Romans. ¹⁸The Romans asked me many questions. But they could find no reason why I should be killed. They wanted to let me go free, ¹⁹but the Jews there did not want that. So I had to ask to come to Rome to have my trial before Caesar. But I have no charge to bring against my own people. ²⁰That is why I wanted to see you and talk with you. I am bound with this chain because I believe in the hope of Israel."

Think About This

The people who saw Paul bitten by the snake thought that he must be a murderer and the god named Justice was condemning him to death. But Paul didn't die or even get sick from the snakebite. God miraculously protected him once again. God has power over storms, seas, snakes—over all creation.

Once he arrived in Rome, Paul was allowed to live by himself with just a guard because he was a trusted prisoner.

Paul called the Jewish leaders to meet with him. He stated that he had done nothing against the Jews, but he had been arrested anyway. The Roman authorities in Judea believed he was innocent of any crime. Paul wanted to be cleared of any charges.

Paul was under house arrest in Rome for two years, during which time he preached to anyone who would listen. After he was freed, he took more missionary journeys and was eventually arrested and executed as a martyr of the faith.

More Stories from Acts

The book of Acts is filled with stories that record the birth of the church and the spread of Christianity.

Check these out:

A crippled man was healed by Peter and John when he asked them for money. "We don't have money," Peter told him, "but we can give you something better in the name of Jesus Christ." Then the Holy Spirit helped Peter heal the man (3:1-26).

Stephen preached about Jesus, and he did wonderful things in his name. But the religious leaders hated him. They had him arrested and tried for blasphemy. At his trial, Stephen preached a sermon that told the history of God's work with his people. When Stephen was stoned to death, he became the first Christian martyr. When Stephen was killed, a young man held the coats of those who were stoning him. His name was Saul . . . who became Paul (6:8—7:60).

The cost of lying to the Holy Spirit became apparent when Ananias and Sapphira sold some land. They claimed that they gave all the money to the church, but in fact they only gave part of it. Find out what happened to them by reading Acts 5:1-11.

Read Acts 20:7-12 to learn about Eutychus, a young man who fell asleep while Paul was preaching. He had an experience he would never forget!

THE EPISTLES

| 10 BC | 0 | 5 AD | 10 AD | 15 AD | 20 AD | 25 AD | 30 AD | 35 AD | 40 AD | 50 AD | 60 AD | 70 AD | 80 AD | 90 AD |

The next section of the New Testament contains the Epistles.

These are letters which were written by Jesus' followers. Some of the letters were written to churches, and some were written to individual people.

There are 21 Epistles in the New Testament. They were written to give instruction and encouragement to the churches and the believers. Through the Epistles, God gives instruction on how believers should live together and how they can serve him.

There are two kinds of Epistles:

- **The Pauline Epistles** which were written by Paul.

- **The General Epistles** which were written by Peter, John, Jude, James and the unknown writer of Hebrews.

Paul Writing in Prison
by Rembrandt

306

MATTHEW MARK LUKE JOHN ACTS ROMANS 1 CORINTHIANS 2 CORINTHIANS GALATIANS **EPHESIANS** PHILIPPIANS COLOSSIANS 1 THESSALONIANS

EPHESIANS

Instructions for Living

Ephesians 5:21–6:4

Paul wrote this letter to the church in Ephesus. He instructed the believers how God's presence in their lives should affect the way they treat each other and how they are to live together as husband and wife.

Wives and Husbands

5

²¹Be willing to obey each other. Do this because you respect Christ. ²²Wives, be under the authority of your husbands, as of the Lord. ²³The husband is the head of the wife, as Christ is the head of the church. The church is Christ's body—Christ is the Savior of the body. ²⁴The church is under the authority of Christ. So it is the same with you wives. You should be under the authority of your husbands in everything.

²⁵Husbands, love your wives as Christ loved the church. Christ died for the church ²⁶to make it belong to God. Christ used the word to make the church clean by washing it with water. ²⁷Christ died so that he could give the church to himself like a bride in all her beauty. He died so that the church could be pure and without fault, with no evil or sin or any other wrong thing in it. ²⁸And husbands should love their wives in the same way. They should love their wives as they love their own bodies. The man who loves his wife loves himself. ²⁹No person ever hates his own body, but feeds and takes care of it. And that is what Christ does for the church, ³⁰because

Behind the Story

This passage begins with the explanation of how a person lives when the Holy Spirit is working in his or her life.

Paul says that the Christian family should live in submission to one another. The Greek word for submission does not mean that one person is under the total control of another; instead, it means placing oneself under the authority of another. Christ is the model for this. He is not inferior to God the Father, but is equal to him.

Husbands are to love their wives just as Christ loved the church. He loved the church sacrificially and gave his life for it.

The love and respect that a husband and wife have for each other should reflect Christ's love for the church.

we are parts of his body. [31]The Scripture says, "So a man will leave his father and mother and be united with his wife. And the two people will become one body." [32]That secret truth is very important—I am talking about Christ and the church. [33]But each one of you must love his wife as he loves himself. And a wife must respect her husband.

Children and Parents

6 Children, obey your parents the way the Lord wants. This is the right thing to do. [2]The command says, "Honor your father and mother." This is the first command that has a promise with it. [3]The promise is: "Then everything will be well with you, and you will have a long life on the earth."

[4]Fathers, do not make your children angry, but raise them with the training and teaching of the Lord.

TAKING IT TO HEART

OBEDIENCE

Did you know that everyone has someone to obey? You should obey parents and teachers. Your parents must obey the law, their bosses and most of all God. Don't get discouraged about obeying. If you need help, talk to someone you trust.

EPHESIANS

The Armor of God

Ephesians 6:10-20

This passage is one of the most famous in the Bible. Paul compares the protection available to believers to armor such as the Roman guards wore.

Behind the Story

Being strong in the Lord is not something a person can do alone. The strength comes from God.

The fact that the believer needs armor means that there is evil all around, always waiting to attack. Satan is never quiet. First Peter 5:8 tells us he is like a lion who is always prowling around looking for someone to eat. The whole armor of God is the believer's protection against Satan.

There are six pieces of armor the believer needs to wear. Paul mentions them in the same order that the Roman guard would have put them on.

The belt protects the lower body. Paul says this belt is truth because a dishonest Christian will never be able to stand up against Satan's lies.

Wear the Full Armor of God

6 ¹⁰Finally, be strong in the Lord and in his great power. ¹¹Wear the full armor of God. Wear God's armor so that you can fight against the devil's evil tricks. ¹²Our fight is not against people on earth. We are fighting against the rulers and authorities and the powers of this world's darkness. We are fighting against the spiritual powers of evil in the heavenly world. ¹³That is why you need to get God's full armor. Then on

the day of evil you will be able to stand strong. And when you have finished the whole fight, you will still be standing. ¹⁴So stand strong, with the belt of truth tied around your waist. And on your chest wear the protection of right living. ¹⁵And on your feet wear the Good News of peace to help you stand strong. ¹⁶And also use the shield of faith. With that you can stop all the burning arrows of the Evil One. ¹⁷Accept God's salvation to be your helmet. And take the sword of the Spirit—that sword is the teaching of God. ¹⁸Pray in the Spirit at all times. Pray with all kinds of prayers, and ask for everything you need. To do this you must always be ready. Never give up. Always pray for all God's people.

¹⁹Also pray for me. Pray that when I speak, God will give me words so that I can tell the secret truth of the Good News without fear. ²⁰I have the work of speaking that Good News. I am doing that now, here in prison. Pray that when I preach the Good News I will speak without fear, as I should.

Think About This

The chest protector went all the way around the body so there was protection in front and back. Paul called this right living, which is good character, honesty and good deeds.

The guard wore boots with reinforced toes. For a believer this is the Good News of peace, the foundation of everything a Christian believes and the message to take to the world.

The guard's shield was held in front of him. It deflected arrows and spears. The shield of faith is the Christian's protection against all the fiery darts of Satan.

The helmet protects the head and the mind of the believer.

The sword is the only weapon the Christian has to fight with; that sword is the Word of God. Read it and memorize it.

TAKING IT TO HEART

DOING BATTLE

The best way to fight Satan is to know Scripture. Psalm 119:105 says "Your word is like a lamp for my feet and a light for my way." It must be very important to know Scripture because that is how Jesus fought off Satan when Satan was tempting him (see Matthew 4:1-11).

310

MATTHEW MARK LUKE JOHN ACTS ROMANS 1 CORINTHIANS 2 CORINTHIANS GALATIANS EPHESIANS **PHILIPPIANS** COLOSSIANS 1 THESSALONIANS

PHILIPPIANS

Be like Christ

Philippians 2:1-16; 4:4-9

Philippians is the letter Paul wrote to the church in Philippi. The major theme of Philippians is joy. There was some jealousy and competition among the believers in Philippi, and Paul wanted them to concentrate on the joy available to them in the Christian life.

Behind the Story

Philippians 2 actually begins with 1:27 and continues through 2:11. This is called the kenosis or self-emptying passage. The message is for the believer to empty his or her heart of selfish and personal desires and to be filled with the attitude of Christ. The answers to the four questions that begin Philippians 2 are what make joy possible:

1) Strength from life in Christ

2) Comfort from his love

3) Sharing with his Spirit

4) Mercy and kindness

The Christian's biggest battle for joy in serving Jesus often does not come from outside—persecution—but from inside, due to attitudes and anger. Paul was addressing this inner battle.

2 Does your life in Christ give you strength? Does his love comfort you? Do we share together in the Spirit? Do you have mercy and kindness? ²If so, make me very happy by having the same thoughts, sharing the same love, and having one mind and purpose. ³When you do things, do not let selfishness or pride be your guide. Be humble and give more honor to others than to yourselves. ⁴Do not be interested only in your own life, but be interested in the lives of others.

Be Unselfish like Christ

⁵In your lives you must think and act like Christ Jesus.
　⁶Christ himself was like God in everything.
　　He was equal with God.
　　But he did not think that being equal with God
　　　was something to be held on to.
　⁷He gave up his place with God and made himself
　　　nothing.
　　He was born as a man
　　　and became like a servant.
　⁸And when he was living as a man,
　　he humbled himself and was fully obedient to God.
　　He obeyed even when that caused his death—death
　　　on a cross.
　⁹So God raised Christ to the highest place.
　　God made the name of Christ greater than every
　　　other name.
　¹⁰God wants every knee to bow to Jesus—
　　everyone in heaven, on earth, and under the earth.
　¹¹Everyone will say, "Jesus Christ is Lord"
　　and bring glory to God the Father.

Be the People God Wants You to Be

¹²My dear friends, you have always obeyed. You obeyed God when I was with you. It is even more important that you obey now while I am not with you. Keep on working to complete your salvation, and do it with fear and trembling. ¹³Yes, God is working in you to help you want to do what pleases him. Then he gives you the power to do it.

¹⁴ Do everything without complaining or arguing. ¹⁵Then you will be innocent and without anything wrong in you. You will be God's children without fault. But you are living with crooked and mean people all around you. Among them you shine like stars in the dark world. ¹⁶You offer to them the teaching that gives life. So when Christ comes again, I can be happy because my work was not wasted. I ran in the race and won.

Be Thankful

4 ⁴Be full of joy in the Lord always. I will say again, be full of joy.

⁵Let all men see that you are gentle and kind. The Lord is coming soon. ⁶Do not worry about anything. But pray and ask God for everything you need. And when you pray, always give thanks. ⁷And God's peace will keep your hearts and minds in Christ Jesus. The peace that God gives is so great that we cannot understand it.

⁸Brothers, continue to think about the things that are good and worthy of praise. Think about the things that are true and honorable and right and pure and beautiful and respected. ⁹And do what you learned and received from me. Do what I told you and what you saw me do. And the God who gives peace will be with you.

Seeing Jesus

How can we be like Jesus?

We can imitate his ways in what we do, say and think. Paul gave the Philippians a lot of ideas:

• Show mercy

• Be kind

• Have unity with other believers

• Be humble; think highly of others

• Be serious about our faith

• Don't grumble or fight

• Be joyful and gentle

• Pray with thankfulness

• Try to only think about good things

• Keep on doing what we've learned

Think About This

Philippians 2:10-11 tells us that one day all people will bow to worship Jesus and confess that he is Lord. However, only those who have put their faith in him will have eternal life with him.

Paul's challenge to keep working "to complete your salvation" (2:12) means that the life of salvation is so deep it must be continually discovered and revealed in the believer's heart (see John 6:27, 29).

Philippians 2:14-16 encourages believers to be blameless in this world. The faith of Christians is like a light in a world filled with darkness. Paul is encouraging us not to grumble and fight with one another and give unbelievers something to criticize.

Christians are reminded to be full of joy even in hard situations because Christ is with us always (4:4). We can pray about everything that happens, and God will hear our prayers (4:6).

312

MATTHEW MARK LUKE JOHN ACTS ROMANS 1 CORINTHIANS 2 CORINTHIANS GALATIANS EPHESIANS PHILIPPIANS COLOSSIANS 1 THESSALONIANS

HEBREWS

The Hall of Faith

Hebrews 11:1-40

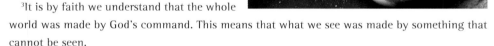

No one knows for certain who wrote the book of Hebrews. But it exalts Jesus Christ and makes the case that belief in him is the natural successor to Judaism.

Faith

11 Faith means being sure of the things we hope for. And faith means knowing that something is real even if we do not see it. ²People who lived in the past became famous because of faith.

³It is by faith we understand that the whole world was made by God's command. This means that what we see was made by something that cannot be seen.

⁴It was by faith that Abel offered God a better sacrifice than Cain did. God said he was pleased with the gifts Abel offered. So God called Abel a good man because of his faith. Abel died, but through his faith he is still speaking.

⁵It was by faith that Enoch was taken to heaven. He never died. He could not be found, because God had taken him away. Before he was taken, the Scripture says that he was a man who truly pleased God. ⁶Without faith no one can please God. Anyone who comes to God must believe that he is real and that he rewards those who truly want to find him.

⁷It was by faith Noah heard God's warnings about things that he could not yet see. He obeyed God and built a large boat to save his family. By his faith, Noah showed that the world was wrong. And he became one of those who are made right with God through faith.

⁸It was by faith Abraham obeyed God's call to go to another place that God promised to give him. He left his own country, not knowing where he was to go. ⁹It was by faith that he lived in the country God promised to give him. He lived there like a visitor who did not belong. He

Behind the Story

The Christians this letter was written to were discouraged and tired. The Christian life was difficult, and they were ready to return to life under Jewish Law where success could be measured by the rules they obeyed. The writer of Hebrews is encouraging them to stay true to Jesus and to see the benefits of a life of faith.

Hebrews 11 is like a hall of faith because the writer gives examples of biblical characters who lived their lives based on faith in God.

Hebrews 11:1 explains what faith does for the believer—it gives a confidence and assurance for life. We can't always see the result of our choices to live by faith; we don't know what the future holds.

But we do know that God is real, and he will triumph over evil.

313

2 THESSALONIANS 1 TIMOTHY 2 TIMOTHY TITUS PHILEMON **HEBREWS** JAMES 1 PETER 2 PETER 1 JOHN 2 JOHN 3 JOHN JUDE REVELATION

lived in tents with Isaac and Jacob, who had received that same promise from God. ¹⁰Abraham was waiting for the city that has real foundations—the city planned and built by God.

¹¹He was too old to have children, and Sarah was not able to have children. It was by faith that Abraham was made able to become a father. Abraham trusted God to do what he had promised. ¹²This man was so old that he was almost dead. But from him came as many descendants as there are stars in the sky. They are as many as the grains of sand on the seashore that cannot be counted.

¹³All these great men died in faith. They did not get the things that God promised his people. But they saw them coming far in the future and were glad. They said that they were like visitors and strangers on earth. ¹⁴When people say such things, then they show that they are looking for a country that will be their own country. ¹⁵If they had been thinking about that country they had left, they could have gone back. ¹⁶But those men were waiting for a better country—a heavenly country. So God is not ashamed to be called their God. For he has prepared a city for them.

¹⁷It was by faith that Abraham offered his son Isaac as a sacrifice. God made the promises to Abraham. But God tested him. And Abraham was ready to offer his own son as a sacrifice. ¹⁸God had said, "The descendants I promised you will be from Isaac." ¹⁹Abraham believed that God could raise the dead. And really, it was as if Abraham got Isaac back from death.

²⁰It was by faith that Isaac blessed the future of Jacob and Esau. ²¹It was by faith that Jacob blessed each one of Joseph's sons. He did this while he was dying. Then he worshiped as he leaned on the top of his walking stick.

²²It was by faith that Joseph spoke about the Israelites leaving Egypt while he was dying. He told them what to do with his body.

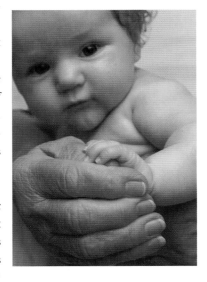

Think About This

The author does a quick overview of the faith actions of Old Testament believers. Then, in Hebrews 11:6, he explains that faith is absolutely necessary for those who want to come to God. He also reminds us that God rewards those who come to him.

The greatness of the people mentioned in this chapter is that they obeyed God—even when they didn't understand his direction. For example, Abraham packed up his family and moved, even without knowing where he was to go (11:8).

Living by faith is never easy. But the better the believer knows God, the easier it is to trust him when a doubtful, worrisome attitude attacks.

314

MATTHEW MARK LUKE JOHN ACTS ROMANS 1 CORINTHIANS 2 CORINTHIANS GALATIANS EPHESIANS PHILIPPIANS COLOSSIANS 1 THESSALONIANS

HEBREWS

The Life of Faith

The seven verses focused on Moses' life show the way a life of faith fights against opposition or evil. From the time of Moses' birth, there was an attempt to kill him. His mother's faith saved him, then his own faith took over as he grew to manhood. He could have been an Egyptian prince, but instead Moses chose to identify with the nation Israel—God's chosen people. Moses was not afraid of the king's anger when he led the Israelites out of Egypt. He obeyed God to protect the people from the angel of death at the Passover.

By recalling the victories over the Egyptians and at the city of Jericho (Hebrews 11:29-31), believers can look forward to victory over evil in their own lives as they live by faith.

²³It was by faith that Moses' parents hid him for three months after he was born. They saw that Moses was a beautiful baby. And they were not afraid to disobey the king's order.

²⁴It was by faith that Moses, when he grew up, refused to be called the son of the king of Egypt's daughter. ²⁵He chose to suffer with God's people instead of enjoying sin for a short time. ²⁶He thought that it was better to suffer for the Christ than to have all the treasures of Egypt. He was looking only for God's reward. ²⁷It was by faith that Moses left Egypt. He was not afraid of the king's anger. Moses

continued strong as if he could see the God that no one can see. ²⁸It was by faith that Moses prepared the Passover and spread the blood on the doors. It was spread so that the one who brings death would not kill the firstborn sons of Israel.

²⁹It was by faith that the people crossed the Red Sea as if it were dry land. The Egyptians also tried to do it, but they were drowned.

³⁰It was by faith that the walls of Jericho fell. They fell after the people had marched around the walls of Jericho for seven days.

³¹It was by faith that Rahab, the prostitute, welcomed the spies and was not killed with those who refused to obey God.

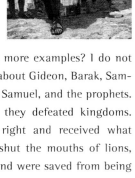

³²Do I need to give more examples? I do not have time to tell you about Gideon, Barak, Samson, Jephthah, David, Samuel, and the prophets. ³³Through their faith they defeated kingdoms. They did what was right and received what God promised. They shut the mouths of lions, ³⁴stopped great fires and were saved from being killed with swords. They were weak, and yet were made strong. They were powerful in battle and defeated other armies. ³⁵Women received their

315

2 THESSALONIANS 1 TIMOTHY 2 TIMOTHY TITUS PHILEMON **HEBREWS** JAMES 1 PETER 2 PETER 1 JOHN 2 JOHN 3 JOHN JUDE REVELATION

dead relatives raised back to life. Others were tortured and refused to accept their freedom. They did this so that they could be raised from death to a better life. ³⁶Some were laughed at and beaten. Others were tied and put into prison. ³⁷They were killed with stones and they were cut in half. They were killed with swords. Some wore the skins of sheep and goats. They were poor, abused, and treated badly. ³⁸The world was not good enough for them! They wandered in deserts and mountains, living in caves and holes in the earth.

³⁹All these people are known for their faith. But none of them received what God had promised. ⁴⁰God planned to give us something better. Then they would be made perfect, but only together with us.

Run the Race
Hebrews 12:1-3

Follow Jesus' Example

12 So we have many people of faith around us. Their lives tell us what faith means. So let us run the race that is before us and never give up. We should remove from our lives anything that would get in the way. And we should remove the sin that so easily catches us. ²Let us look only to Jesus. He is the one

who began our faith, and he makes our faith perfect. Jesus suffered death on the cross. But he accepted the shame of the cross as if it were nothing. He did this because of the joy that God put before him. And now he is sitting at the right side of God's throne. ³Think about Jesus. He held on patiently while sinful men were doing evil things against him. Look at Jesus' example so that you will not get tired and stop trying.

Strength from Trials

The second half of Hebrews 11:35-38 focuses on the torture and pain that some believers experienced. It may seem that evil triumphed. But, in reality, it did not. These people knew that the cause (Christianity) for which they were being persecuted was worthy. They had faith that a better future was ahead for them. Faith makes all the difference.

Cheering from the Stands

Hebrews 12 begins by once again recalling the witnesses around us. The author is referring to those heroes of the faith he just mentioned in chapter 11. It doesn't mean they are watching believers today, but that they are witnesses of a life lived by faith.

Believers are encouraged to keep focused on Jesus and the way he lived. All encouragement and strength comes from him.

316

MATTHEW MARK LUKE JOHN ACTS ROMANS 1 CORINTHIANS 2 CORINTHIANS GALATIANS EPHESIANS PHILIPPIANS COLOSSIANS 1 THESSALONIANS

JAMES

Faith That Works

James 1:2-8, 19-27; 3:1-12

Behind the Story

No one enjoys problems, but James encourages believers to trust God through their problems, instead of turning away from him. This will help faith grow stronger. He encourages them to look at problems as tests which their faith will help them pass (see Romans 5:3-5).

The wisdom promised in James 1:5 does not necessarily mean God will tell you how to get out of a problem. However, he will guide you through it and help you learn from it. When you ask God for wisdom, you must believe completely in him. God is not pleased with those who choose to trust him sometimes and at other times don't trust him at all.

James gives practical instruction on living the Christian life. It covers everything from judging others to speaking kindly to all. It describes the problems that occur when God is left out of the believer's life.

Faith and Wisdom

1 ²My brothers, you will have many kinds of troubles. But when these things happen, you should be very happy. ³You know that these things are testing your faith. And this will give you patience. ⁴Let your patience show itself perfectly in what you do. Then you will be perfect and complete. You will have everything you need. ⁵But if any of you needs wisdom, you should ask God for it. God is generous. He enjoys giving to all people, so God will give you wisdom. ⁶But when you ask God, you must believe. Do not doubt God. Anyone who doubts is like a wave in the sea. The wind blows the wave up and down. ⁷⁻⁸He who doubts is thinking two different things at the same time. He cannot decide about anything he does. A person like that should not think that he will receive anything from the Lord.

Listening and Obeying

¹⁹My dear brothers, always be willing to listen and slow to speak. Do not become angry easily. ²⁰Anger will not help you live a good life as God wants. ²¹So put out of your life every

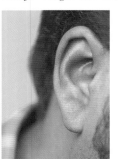

evil thing and every kind of wrong you do. Don't be proud but accept God's teaching that is planted in your hearts. This teaching can save your souls.

²²Do what God's teaching says; do not just listen and do nothing. When you only sit and listen, you are fooling yourselves. ²³A person who hears God's teaching and does nothing is like a man looking in a mirror. ²⁴He sees his face, then goes away and quickly forgets what he looked like. ²⁵But the truly happy person is the one who carefully studies God's perfect law that makes people free. He continues to study

317

2 THESSALONIANS 1 TIMOTHY 2 TIMOTHY TITUS PHILEMON HEBREWS **JAMES** 1 PETER 2 PETER 1 JOHN 2 JOHN 3 JOHN JUDE REVELATION

it. He listens to God's teaching and does not forget what he heard. Then he obeys what God's teaching says. When he does this, it makes him happy.

The True Way to Worship God

²⁶A person might think he is religious. But if he says things he should not say, then he is just fooling himself. His "religion" is worth nothing. ²⁷Religion that God accepts is this: caring for orphans or widows who need help; and keeping yourself free from the world's evil influence. This is the kind of religion that God accepts as pure and good.

Controlling the Things We Say

3 My brothers, not many of you should become teachers. You know that we who teach will be judged more strictly than others. ²We all make many mistakes. If there were a person who never said anything wrong, he would be perfect. He would be able to control his whole body, too. ³We put bits into the mouths of horses to make them obey us. We can control their whole bodies. ⁴It is the same with ships. A ship is very big, and it is pushed

by strong winds. But a very small rudder controls that big ship. The man who controls the rudder decides where the ship will go. The ship goes where the man wants. ⁵It is the same with the tongue. It is a small part of the body, but it brags about doing great things.

A big forest fire can be started with only a little flame. ⁶And the tongue is like a fire. It is a whole world of evil among the parts of our bodies. The tongue spreads its evil through the whole body. It starts a fire that influences all of life. The tongue gets this fire from hell. ⁷People can tame every kind of wild animal, bird, reptile, and fish, and they have tamed them. ⁸But no one can tame the tongue. It is wild and evil. It is full of poison that can kill. ⁹We use our tongues to praise our Lord and Father, but then we curse people. And God made them like himself. ¹⁰Praises and curses come from the same mouth! My brothers, this should not happen. ¹¹Do good and bad water flow from the same spring? ¹²My brothers, can a fig tree make olives? Can a grapevine make figs? No! And a well full of salty water cannot give good water.

Think About This

James 1:19-24 emphasizes the importance of listening and controlling anger. This kind of response to problems will let the presence of God shine through in the believer's life.

Putting evil out of one's life (1:21) encourages the believer to not let bad thoughts or habits settle in. Push them out of your life by focusing your thoughts on God's Word and the lessons taught in it.

Real happiness comes from knowing God's Word and letting it take control of how you live (1:25).

One important evidence of God controlling a life is the way a person speaks (3:5-6).

Using the tongue to praise God but curse people (3:9) may fool others, but does not fool God. It shows that God is not in control of that person's heart.

318

MATTHEW   MARK   LUKE   JOHN   ACTS   ROMANS   1 CORINTHIANS   2 CORINTHIANS   GALATIANS   EPHESIANS   PHILIPPIANS   COLOSSIANS   1 THESSALONIANS

1 JOHN

Live like God's Children

1 John 3:1-24

John reminds believers that the Christian life shows itself through a life of love. Any other kind of living is not true to God's Word.

We Are God's Children

3 The Father has loved us so much! He loved us so much that we are called children of God. And we really are his children. But the people in the world do not understand that we are God's children, because they have not known him. ²Dear friends, now we are children of God. We have not yet been shown what we will be in the future. But we know that when Christ comes again, we will be like him. We will see him as he really is. ³Christ is pure. And every person who has this hope in Christ keeps himself pure like Christ.

⁴When a person sins, he breaks God's law. Yes, sinning is the same as living against God's law. ⁵You know that Christ came to take away sins. There is no sin in Christ. ⁶So the person who lives in Christ does not go on sinning. If he goes on sinning, he has never really understood Christ and has never known him.

⁷Dear children, do not let any person lead you the wrong way. Christ is righteous. To be like Christ, a person must do what is right. ⁸The devil has been sinning since the beginning. Anyone who continues to sin belongs to the devil. The Son of God came for this purpose: to destroy the devil's work.

⁹When God makes someone his child, that person does not go on sinning. The new life God gave

Behind the Story

In this short book, John uses different concepts or types of the word "love" over 40 times.

First John 3 begins with the writer's complete amazement at how very much God loves us—so much that he considers all believers his children.

Verses 4-6 do not mean that believers never sin. Until we are in heaven, we will all struggle against sin. However, continued sinning with no effort to repent and draw close to Christ is unacceptable to God. Believers should not let Satan convince them that any "little" sin is okay.

Loving others is absolutely basic to living for Jesus and sharing him with others.

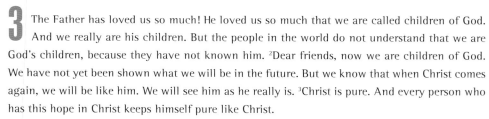

A Cup of Cold Water

TAKING IT TO HEART

Loving and helping others is a necessary part of living the Christian life. Read the words of Jesus in Matthew 25:35-45.

When others are hungry and thirsty and we have food and water, we should share it with them.

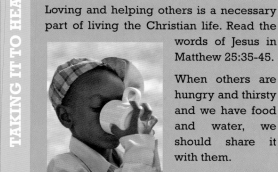

319

2 THESSALONIANS 1 TIMOTHY 2 TIMOTHY TITUS PHILEMON HEBREWS JAMES 1 PETER 2 PETER 1 JOHN 2 JOHN 3 JOHN JUDE REVELATION

that person stays in him. So he is not able to go on sinning, because he has become a child of God. ¹⁰ So we can see who God's children are and who the devil's children are. Those who do not do what is right are not children of God. And anyone who does not love his brother is not a child of God.

We Must Love Each Other

¹¹This is the teaching you have heard from the beginning: We must love each other. ¹²Do not be like Cain who belonged to the Evil One. Cain killed his brother. He killed his brother because the things Cain did were evil, and the things his brother did were good.

¹³Brothers, do not be surprised when the people of this world hate you. ¹⁴We know that we have left death and have come into life. We know this because we love our brothers in Christ. Whoever does not love is still in death. ¹⁵Everyone who hates his brother is a murderer. And you know that no murderer has eternal life in him. ¹⁶This is how we know what real love is: Jesus gave his life for us. So we should give our lives for our brothers. ¹⁷Suppose a believer is rich enough to have all that he needs. He sees his brother in Christ who is poor and does not have what he needs. What if the believer does not help the poor brother? Then the believer does not have God's love in his heart. ¹⁸My children, our love should not be only words and talk. Our love must be true love. And we should show that love by what we do.

¹⁹⁻²⁰This is the way we know that we belong to the way of truth. When our hearts make us feel guilty, we can still have peace before God. God is greater than our hearts, and he knows everything.

²¹My dear friends, if we do not feel that we are doing wrong, we can be without fear when we come to God. ²²And God gives us the things we ask for. We receive these things because we obey God's commands, and we do what pleases him. ²³This is what God commands: that we believe in his Son, Jesus Christ, and that we love each other, just as he commanded. ²⁴The person who obeys God's commands lives in God. And God lives in him. How do we know that God lives in us? We know because of the Spirit whom God gave us.

Think About This

John joined love and right actions together in 1 John 3:10. Loving others is an outgrowth of God's righteousness in the believer's heart.

The true Christian will show love by doing things to help others (3:18). Loving words spoken without loving deeds to back them up are empty words (see 1 Corinthians 13:1).

Real love was shown by Jesus' giving his life for others. Christians should be prepared to make sacrifices for others, by giving time, money, food, shelter or anything that another person needs.

This message by John gives explanation to what Jesus taught as the second greatest command-ment: "Love your neighbor as you love yourself" (Mark 12:31).

The Other Pauline Epistles

ROMANS 1 CORINTHIANS 2 CORINTHIANS

ROMANS

The apostle Paul wrote Romans to the Christians in Rome. He wrote it to carefully explain the Good News. Paul had heard of the tension between the Jewish Christians and the Gentile Christians. He wanted them to live together in peace. The message of Romans focuses on faith. Salvation does not come by works . . . what we do . . . but by whom we put our faith in . . . Jesus Christ.

The Roman Colosseum

1 & 2 CORINTHIANS

Paul wrote to the church in Corinth to address specific problems the church was having. The believers were getting confused by false teachers. They were compromising their Christian lives by letting the way the sinful people of Corinth lived creep into their lives. Paul challenged them to remember that their lives should be guided by their love for God.

Corinthian Ruins

Second Corinthians is a letter Paul wrote defending his own ministry, which had come under attack. In this letter Paul reveals some of the difficulties and problems of his ministry, but reminds the readers that his authority to minister came from Jesus Christ.

GALATIANS

Paul wrote this letter to the church in Galatia specifically to answer the false teaching that was infiltrating that church. False teachers were teaching that there were other ways to be saved than through faith in Jesus. Paul wrote that salvation comes through faith in Jesus alone. Nothing else will save us.

COLOSSIANS

As in many of his other books, Paul wrote here to a church that was struggling. This one was in Colosse and, once again, Paul was writing to correct false teaching that was creeping in. Some teachers were saying that Jesus was not God, but only a good teacher. Paul encouraged the believers to focus on Jesus. He proclaimed the deity of Christ and encouraged the believers to grow more mature in their faith.

The Ruins of the Acropolis at Colossae

1 & 2 THESSALONIANS

Paul planted the church in Thessalonica, then had to leave quickly. He wrote to this church like a father who wanted to teach his children. He hadn't been able to teach the new believers the foundational truths of their faith, so he wrote that information in a letter to them. Both letters to this church were filled with encouragement and affirmed that Christ would return one day, so they should be ready.

The Other Pauline Epistles, cont.

1 TIMOTHY 2 TIMOTHY TITUS PHILEMON

1 & 2 TIMOTHY

These two books were written to Paul's coworker, Timothy, who was working at the church in Ephesus. Timothy had traveled with Paul many times. The first letter encouraged him to stay strong in his faith. Paul instructed him on how a Christian leader behaves in the church and how Christians should relate to one another.

Second Timothy was written during Paul's final imprisonment. He was near death, but wanted to give Timothy more encouragement and instruction. He cautioned Timothy to treat God's Word with respect and to faithfully teach others about the faith.

TITUS

This little book, which Paul wrote to Titus, gives key information for elders, pastors and other believers. Paul makes very clear statements about God's grace and the Holy Spirit's work in our salvation. Paul points out that God desires for his people to devote themselves to doing good deeds and serving one another in love.

PHILEMON

This was a personal letter from Paul to a slave owner named Philemon about a runaway slave. In asking Philemon to forgive the slave for running away, Paul covers salvation, substitution and redemption—Christ's gifts to us. In pleading a slave's case, Paul says that salvation is available for all people. Anyone can become a child of God.

The Other General Epistles

HEBREWS   JAMES   1 PETER   2 PETER   1 JOHN   2 JOHN   3 JOHN   JUDE

1 & 2 PETER

Peter is the author of these two books. The first letter Peter wrote was to encourage Christians who were suffering. It was not written to one specific church or person, but was to be passed around among believers. Peter said that suffering is to be expected, but Christians should hold on to Christ during the hard times. They should never return evil for evil done to them. He told them that they didn't deserve the suffering they were experiencing; it came because they were serving God. He reminded them that Christ would one day return, so they should stay strong as they waited for that.

Peter's second letter picked up that same theme. He reminded them that they knew how to live and serve God, so they should get busy and do it. They should not accept false teaching, but should stay true to God's Word. That kind of living would set them apart from the world.

2 & 3 JOHN

These two letters were written by the apostle John. As the other Epistle writers have done, John addressed the messages of false teachers who were infiltrating the church. The false teachers were questioning who Jesus was. John wrote to affirm that Jesus is God's Son, and he did indeed come to earth and live as a man. He encouraged the believers to study the truth and let it become their armor.

JUDE

Jude was the half brother of Jesus. This letter was written to the church, which was growing in faith and numbers. Jude encouraged the believers to stay strong in their faith and reject the false teachings of those who were abusing their positions of authority. Jude encouraged believers to be holy, that is, to live differently from people who are not believers.

lp from Scripture

WHEN YOU FEEL . . .

Discouraged:

Psalm 138:7

John 14:1

John 14:27

1 Peter 5:6-9

Lonely:

Psalm 46:1

Isaiah 41:10

John 14:18

Romans 8:35-39

Scared:

Isaiah 40:31

Isaiah 43:2

Habakkuk 3:19

Philippians 4:13

Hebrews 13:6

THE REVELATION OF JESUS CHRIST

The final book of the New Testament is a book of prophecy—a picture of what is to come.

Revelation was written at a time when persecution against believers was at an all-time high, and problems within the church were worse than ever.

The first few chapters may be a review of things that have already happened, but most of the book focuses on what is in the future when Christ comes back to take believers to heaven and to judge those who have not chosen to know him.

■ The author of this book is the apostle John.

■ It was a vision given to him by God.

326

MATTHEW MARK LUKE JOHN ACTS ROMANS 1 CORINTHIANS 2 CORINTHIANS GALATIANS EPHESIANS PHILIPPIANS COLOSSIANS 1 THESSALONIANS

REVELATION

Heaven

Revelation 21:1-27

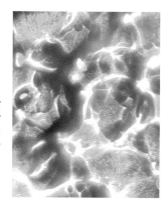

Jesus will return to take believers to heaven with him for eternity. Those who have not accepted Jesus as Savior will not be allowed into heaven. Satan will be cast into the "lake of fire" forever. Jesus is preparing the new heaven for believers right now.

The New Jerusalem

Behind the Story

It is important to see how John's vision relates to Old Testament prophecy about heaven. Read Isaiah 65:17; 66:22 for prophecies about heaven.

The new heaven and earth John saw were just that—new. The earth as it is now known was burned up in the great judgment described in Revelation 20.

The new Jerusalem is where Christ's bride—believers—will live with God forever.

Revelation 21:4-5 promises no more death and no more pain. This refers to the promise in Isaiah 25:8: God will wipe away the tears of his children. Heaven will be filled with the joy of being in God's presence.

21 Then I saw a new heaven and a new earth. The first heaven and the first earth had disappeared. Now there was no sea. ²And I saw the holy city coming down out of heaven from God. This holy city is the new Jerusalem. It was prepared like a bride dressed for her husband. ³I heard a loud voice from the throne. The voice said, "Now God's home is with men. He will live with them, and they will be his people. God himself will be with them and will be their God. ⁴He will wipe away every tear from their eyes. There will be no more death, sadness, crying, or pain. All the old ways are gone."

⁵The One who was sitting on the throne said, "Look! I am making everything new!" Then he said, "Write this, because these words are true and can be trusted."

⁶The One on the throne said to me: "It is finished! I am the Alpha and the Omega, the Beginning and the End. I will give free water from the spring of the water of life to anyone who is thirsty. ⁷Anyone who wins the victory will receive this. And I will be his God, and he will be my son. ⁸But those who are cowards, who refuse to believe, who do evil things, who kill, who sin sexually, who do evil magic, who worship idols, and who tell lies—all these will have a place in the lake of burning sulfur. This is the second death."

⁹One of the seven angels came to me. This was one of the angels who had the seven bowls full of the seven last troubles. He said, "Come with me. I will show you the bride, the wife of the Lamb." ¹⁰The angel carried me away by the Spirit to a very large and high mountain. He showed me the holy city, Jerusalem. It was coming down out of heaven from God. ¹¹It was shining with the glory of God. It was shining bright like a very expensive jewel, like a jasper. It was clear as crystal. ¹²The city had a great high wall with 12 gates. There were 12 angels at the gates. On each gate was written the name of 1 of the 12 tribes of Israel. ¹³There were three gates on the east, three on the north, three on the south, and three on the west. ¹⁴The walls of the city were built

327

2 THESSALONIANS 1 TIMOTHY 2 TIMOTHY TITUS PHILEMON HEBREWS JAMES 1 PETER 2 PETER 1 JOHN 2 JOHN 3 JOHN JUDE **REVELATION**

on 12 foundation stones. On the stones were written the names of the 12 apostles of the Lamb.

¹⁵The angel who talked with me had a measuring rod made of gold. He had this rod to measure the city, its gates, and its wall. ¹⁶The city was built in a square. Its length was equal to its width. The angel measured the city with the rod. The city was 1,500 miles long, 1,500 miles wide, and 1,500 miles high. ¹⁷The angel also measured the wall. It was 216 feet high, by man's measurement. That was the measurement the angel was using. ¹⁸The wall was made of jasper. The city was made of pure gold, as pure as glass. ¹⁹The foundation stones of the city walls had every kind of jewel in them. The first cornerstone was jasper, the second was sapphire, the third was chalcedony, the fourth was emerald, ²⁰the fifth was onyx, the sixth was carnelian, the seventh was chrysolite, the eighth was beryl, the ninth was topaz, the tenth was chrysoprase, the eleventh was jacinth, and the twelfth was amethyst. ²¹The 12 gates were 12 pearls. Each gate was made

Think About This

Alpha and Omega (Revelation 21:6) are the first and last letters of the Greek alphabet. This title shows God's completeness. He is the source of all things and controls all things.

The most wonderful promise is that believers will be God's children forever. But 21:8 gives a description of those who have not accepted Christ. Remember that God judges by looking at the heart; he cannot be fooled by outwardly good actions or words.

Revelation 21:11 describes the new city which is filled with God's glory to the point of shining like a precious jewel.

The 12 gates mentioned in 21:12 echo the prophecy of Ezekiel 48:30-35.

328

MATTHEW MARK LUKE JOHN ACTS ROMANS 1 CORINTHIANS 2 CORINTHIANS GALATIANS EPHESIANS PHILIPPIANS COLOSSIANS 1 THESSALONIANS

REVELATION

The City of God

The new Jerusalem is shaped like a cube, which was an ancient symbol of perfection (Revelation 21:15-17).

The foundation stones are named for the 12 apostles. Jesus had promised them a place of honor in his new kingdom (see Matthew 19:28).

The city is surrounded by walls that are 200 feet high. The walls are transparent. The streets are as clear as glass, though they are made of pure gold (Revelation 21:21).

Each of the 12 gates are named for one of the 12 tribes of Israel. Each gate is a giant pearl.

There is no need for the sun or moon because God's glory is so bright, it lights the entire city (21:23).

from a single pearl. The street of the city was made of pure gold. The gold was clear as glass.

²²I did not see a temple in the city. The Lord God All-Powerful and the Lamb are the city's temple. ²³The city does not need the sun or the moon to shine on it. The glory of God is its light, and the Lamb is the city's lamp. ²⁴By its light the people of the world will walk. The kings of the earth will bring their glory into it. ²⁵The city's gates will never be shut on any day, because there is no night there. ²⁶The greatness and the honor of the nations will be brought into it. ²⁷Nothing unclean will ever enter the city. No one who does shameful things or tells lies will ever go into it. Only those whose names are written in the Lamb's book of life will enter the city.

Worship In Heaven

Then the 24 elders and the four living things bowed down. They worshiped God, who sits on the throne. They said:

"Amen, Hallelujah!"

Then a voice came from the throne:

"Praise our God, all you who serve him!

Praise our God, all you who honor him, both small and great!"

Then I heard what sounded like a great many people. It sounded like the noise of flooding water and like loud thunder. The people were saying:

"Hallelujah!

Our Lord God rules. He is the All-Powerful.

Let us rejoice and be happy

and give God glory!

Give God glory, because the wedding of the Lamb has come."

—Revelation 19:4-7

329

2 THESSALONIANS 1 TIMOTHY 2 TIMOTHY TITUS PHILEMON HEBREWS JAMES 1 PETER 2 PETER 1 JOHN 2 JOHN 3 JOHN JUDE **REVELATION**

The Glory of God

The glory of heaven is beyond anything the human mind can imagine. As magnificent as it will be, our ultimate joy will come from being in God's presence. The response of the believer's heart will be constant, unending praise to God.

God, who began his work in Genesis 1:1 with creation, has faithfully guided his people throughout history. He has given his Son for our salvation, forgiven our failures, provided for our needs, written his Word for our instruction and one day will take us to be with him . . . forever. Praise God!

The Writing of Revelation

John was a prisoner who had been banished to live on the Island of Patmos. The Christian church at this time was experiencing terrible persecution—from outside and from within there were disagreements and tension.

While John was on Patmos, God gave him a vision of what the future held. He told John to write down what he was allowed to see. It would be encouraging for the church to know that God would prevail over evil.

John was allowed to see the resurrected Jesus in all of his glory and power. Jesus actually dictated letters to seven churches which represented the spiritual conditions of churches and believers throughout history.

The last part of Revelation describes what will happen when Jesus returns and judges mankind. Those who do not know Jesus will not get another chance to believe. However, believers will be taken to heaven to live with him forever.

The Island of Patmos

A Church on Patmos

International
Children's Bible

CREDITS

The following graphics are copyrighted by the individuals or organizations listed below. They are used by permission and all rights are reserved by the original copyright holder.

www.abcgallery.com

119, Samson; 140, David; 143, beheading; 152, painting by Fouquet; 156, the judgment; 195, painting; 209, Jeremiah; 249, depiction by Theophanes; 251, painting by Semiradsky; 275, painting by Caravaggio; 284, painting by Caravaggio; 292, large fresco; 298, painting by Raphael; 305, painting by Rembrandt; 330, painting

Diane Bay

2, smoke; 32, rocks; 61, script; 72, pillar of cloud; 86, pillar of fire; 102, rocks; 213, collage; 248, walking on water; 280, dove on fire; 289, animals; 312, creation; 328-329, valley

www.biblepicturegallery.com

vi, Elijah; 39, the pit; 40, painting by Overbeck; 42, Joseph in prison; 50, Joseph; 52, Semites; 67, Passover; 84, tabernacle; 84, box of agreement; 84, lampstand; 84, altar; 85, altar of burnt offerings; 85, breastplate; 98, Joshua; 100, box; 101, crossing Jordan; 122, Ruth and Naomi; 124, Boaz's field; 125, gleaners; 127, farming; 131, Samuel and Eli; 132, God calling Samuel; 134, Saul anointed; 135, Saul denounced; 150, Abigail; 151, yarn; 151, woman with pot; 151, cooking; 160, Temple Mount; 165, kingdom; 166, ruins; 167, Mt. Carmel; 167, oxen; 168, rock pile; 168, lightning; 169, Moses; 169, Elijah; 170, sword; 171, caves; 173, Elijah; 181, Esther; 182, well; 183, David; 194, fountain of Job; 203, Belshazzar; 205, painting; 209, Ezekiel; 210, Joel; 211, Micah; 211, Nahum; 211, Habakkuk; 212, Haggai; 218, shepherds; 235, painting by Hole; 238, painting by Tissot; 238, painting by Hole; 239, painting by Hole; 244, painting by Raphael; 246, painting by Vos; 247, painting by Tissot; 249, transfiguration (left and right); 250, Good Samaritan; 251, painting by Tissot; 253, painting by Murillo; 254, painting by Hole; 256, painting by Tissot; 266, painting by Hunt; 266, temple; 274, painting by Hole; 279, Damascus road; 279, crowd; 283, painting by Vos; 289, tablet; 291, washing; 292, deliverance of Peter; 293, prison; 304, crippled man; 314, crossing Jordan; 330, church

www.bigstockphoto.com

i, animals; vi, tablet; 3, surf; 3, sky; 3, planets; 4, dolphin; 4, bird; 4, lion; 4, dog; 4, bee; 4, iguana; 4, lamb; 9, animals; 9, boards; 10, river; 11, sunrise; 12, dove; 13, mountains; 38, sun, moon, and stars; 214, earth and sun; 224, sand dune; 226, water to wine; 240, Sea of Galilee; 242, yellow flower

www.cc-art.com

53, Goshen; 59, Hebrews

www.dreamstime.com

285, man; 287, holding hands; 288, angel; 300, coast of Cyprus; 302, Malta; 303, snake; 327, coast

Liita Forsyth

5, painting of Eden

www.freestockphotos.com

23, ram; 48, papyrus; 54, statue; 54, tower; 72, leaving Egypt; 147, Judean desert; 236, Sea of Galilee; 247, fish

www.ibiblio.com

120, Samson

www.istockphoto.com

iii, world; v, world; vi, dove; vi, map; vii, boat; vii, palms; 1, tablet; 2, earth; 2, water drop; 3, sprout; 6, snake; 7, baby; 7, angel; 8, ark; 10, clouds; 12, mountain; 13, olive branch; 14, rainbows; 15, tower of Babel; 19, tents; 19, desert man; 20, trees; 20, shepherd; 21, Sarah; 21, baby; 22, road; 24, Rebekah; 27, camels; 28, face; 28, arrows; 31, desert; 31, ancient writing; 34, bucket; 34, wildlife; 34, kissing; 35, home; 36, desert child; 37, donkeys; 40, caravan; 48, ring; 49, seed bags; 50, grain in hand; 51, brothers; 51, map of Egypt; 53, pyramids; 56, baby; 56, Nile; 57, column; 58, desert walk; 58, map; 59, shepherd; 60, footprints;

63, hands; 65, fly; 65, bull; 66, hail; 69, matza; 69, seder; 75, quail; 75, manna; 76, manna; 77, worship; 78, men; 80, 10 Commandments; 80, worship; 81, girl at rest; 81, tent; 82, jewelry; 87, Torah; 87, reading Bible; 90, flowers; 95, mountain range; 95, dove; 96, mountains; 96, Torah; 99, rope; 99, shaking hands; 104, gates; 104, Jewish man; 105, wall; 106, fire; 110, oak tree; 112, hands; 113, broken pot; 113, bugle; 116, baby; 117, angel; 118, man; 118, tied hands; 119, bald man; 120, Samson's temple; 122, woman; 126, tools; 130, praying; 131, woman; 133, menorah; 139, boy; 139, pouring; 142, sling; 145, rock field; 146, bow and arrow; 148, shearing sheep; 154, hand with cane; 160, dome; 162, jewelry; 163, cup; 164, pottery; 165, boy; 172, clouds; 173, hand; 175, Galilee; 176, boy sleeping; 178, holding hands; 179, hands; 180, woman; 184, stars; 184, sunrise; 185, praying; 185, Bible; 187, reading Bible; 192, toddler; 192, building; 193, throwing stone; 193, soldier; 193, flag; 197, lamb; 204, praying; 217, sign language; 221, camels; 222, shepherd; 224, stained glass; 228, sunset; 228, dove; 232, girl; 233, Galilee; 233, boat; 235, coins; 237, Torah; 240, bird; 240, weeds; 240, field; 240, rock; 241, stained glass; 242, field; 243, bread; 244, fishing net; 245, sea and sky; 252, coin; 252, sheep; 253, pigs; 255, boy in tree; 257, palm branches; 259, hands; 261, vine; 262, Last Supper; 263, Mount of Olives; 264, stained glass; 265, garden; 270, cross; 277, earth; 277, key; 281, person raising hands; 282, reading Bible; 284, rocky field; 286, basket; 290, stained glass; 291, churches; 293, handcuffs; 294, jail; 296, road; 296, ruins; 297, Torah; 298, Athens; 301, boat; 303, fire; 304, building; 306, hands; 308, armor; 309, armor; 311, sky; 312, construction; 313, forest; 313, baby; 314, desert; 314, blowing horn; 316, reading Bible; 318, praying; 318, drinking; 319, friends; 320, Colosseum; 322, Bible; 324, girl; 324, boy; 327, gemstones

The Life of Our Lord and Saviour Jesus Christ
The London Printing and Publishing Company, Limited
Circa 1850

219, John the Baptist; 225, fishers of men; 227, Persian temple; 231, woman at the well; 245, Christ in storm; 257, entry; 260, washing of feet; 265, kiss; 267, Christ before Pilate; 276, ascension; 281, Peter

www.lorentonh.nsw.edu.au

230, Jacob's well; 239, Roman Empire; 286, synagogue

www.nypl.org

55, construction; 68, exodus; 79, Moses; 86, tabernacle

www.photos.com

vi, grapes; vii, baby; vii, Jesus; vii, Roman road; 6, stained glass; 7, thistle; 13, rock formation; 16, path; 17, wheat; 17, cattle; 18, silver; 18, Jordan Valley; 18, sheep; 22, knife; 22, wood; 23, mountains; 24, well; 25, camels; 25, rings; 26, hands; 29, food; 29, wheat; 30, old man; 30, young man; 33, angels; 36, wildlife; 37, camels; 37, sheep; 37, goats; 39, landscape; 41, pot; 42, chains; 43, jogger; 43, jail; 45, grapes; 45, bread; 46, cows; 46, wheat; 47, grain; 48, chariot; 49, drought; 52, statue; 53, sheep; 53, statue; 56, basket; 58, whip; 59, trees; 60, burning bush; 61, gold; 62, snake; 62, walking stick; 63, tomb; 64, water; 64, frog; 66, locusts; 67, sun; 68, crowd; 70, the king; 70, Egypt; 71, map; 71, palms; 71, sand; 73, waves; 74, bread; 75, worms; 76, beehive; 80, statue; 81, gavel; 83, water; 88, Mount of Olives; 88, stained glass; 89, man; 91, waterfall; 91, snake;

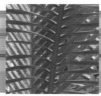

92, river; 93, donkey; 94, donkey; 94, angel; 97, field; 100, Jordan River; 101, dry river bed; 106, ruins; 107, compass; 107, chopsticks; 107, Trojan Horse; 108, sun; 109, caves #1; 109, caves #2; 110, angel; 111, cooking; 111, flaming rock; 113, bread; 113, torch; 114, swords; 121, Stonehenge; 123, barley; 124, people in field; 127, hands with food; 128, shoe; 129, wedding; 130, baby; 137, death; 138, oil; 140, breastplate; 140, leg guard; 140, spear; 141, bread and cheese; 142, stones; 145, arrows; 145, spear; 149, sheep; 149, bread; 149, grain; 149, wineskins; 150, woman; 151, wool; 151, potter; 151, kneading; 152, David; 155, farming; 158, western wall; 161, carving; 164, valley; 172, water; 174, pot; 174, pots; 175, coin; 179, washing; 180, crown; 181, noose; 186, stained glass; 187, waves; 192, newborn; 192, dancing; 192, old woman; 192, bowl; 193, plant; 193, couple; 193, three girls; 193, boy; 193, father and son; 193, apples; 193, yarn and buttons; 194, wedding hands; 196, cross; 196, hand; 198, woman; 199, cup; 199, food; 199, water; 199, broccoli; 200, statue; 200, praying; 201, fire; 204, ring; 205, lion; 206, ship; 206, hands; 207, whale; 208, beach; 208, wool; 216, stained glass; 217, stained glass; 218, birth of Jesus; 219, shepherds; 220, baby; 222, desert; 223, stained glass; 226, cup; 229, crucifixion; 232, plains; 233, synagogue; 236, Jesus; 237, Jerusalem; 239, Roman road; 243, pearl; 244, girl; 245, waves; 254, cave; 258, coins; 263, bread; 268, stained glass; 269, stained glass; 270, stained glass; 271, passion; 272, stained glass; 273, stained glass; 275, Jesus; 278, stained glass; 286, window; 292, ball and chain; 294, handcuffs; 295, stained glass; 300, ship; 301, beach; 306, family; 306, wedding; 307, families; 309, swords; 310, stained glass; 315, stained glass; 315, running; 316, ear; 317, feet and hands; 317, ship wheel; 320, ruins; 326, gold

Thomas Nelson, Inc.

115, map of the judges; 299, first and second missionary journeys; 299, third and fourth missionary journeys

www.wells.net

120, engraving of Samson

www.wikimedia.org

16, map; 41, copper; 41, bronze; 55, Egyptian writing; 82, 10 Commandments; 159, Solomon's temple; 214, mosaic; 221, gold; 221, myrrh; 221, frankincense; 227, whip; 285, map; 303, ruins; 321, road; 325, St. John; 330, island

Elena Zapassk

234, pilgrim